Business Management and Systems Analysis

GW00726879

INFORMATION SYSTEMS SERIES

Consulting Editors

D. E. AVISON
BA, MSc, PhD, FBCS
Professor of Information Systems,
Department of Accounting
and Management Science,
Southampton University, UK

G. FITZGERALD
BA, MSc, MBCS
Department of Computer Science
Birkbeck College, University of London, UK

This series of student texts covers a wide variety of topics relating to information systems. It is designed to fulfil the needs of the growing number of courses on, and interest in, computing and information systems which do not focus on the purely technological aspects, but seek to relate these to business and organisational context.

INFORMATION SYSTEMS SERIES

BUSINESS MANAGEMENT AND SYSTEMS ANALYSIS

EDDIE MOYNIHAN
MBCS, APMI, ACIS

ALFRED WALLER LIMITED
HENLEY-ON-THAMES

© 1993 Eddie Moynihan

First published in 1993 by
Alfred Waller Limited, Publishers
Orchards
Fawley
Henley-on-Thames
Oxfordshire RG9 6JF

Reprinted 1994

British Library Cataloguing in Publication Data.
A catalogue record for this book is available from the British Library.

ISBN: 1−872474−05−5

Produced for the publishers by
John Taylor Book Ventures
Hatfield, Herts

Typeset by Setrite Typesetters Limited

Printed and bound in Great Britain
by Hollen Street Press, Berwick-upon-Tweed

Contents

Foreword

This Series on Information Systems contains student texts covering a wide variety of topics relating to information systems. It is designed to fulfil the needs of a growing number of courses on, and interest in, computing and information systems which do not focus on the purely technical aspects, but seek to relate these to the organisational context. There are also titles which deal with topics in greater depth and are more research oriented.

Information systems has been defined as the effective design, delivery, use and impact of information technology in organisations and society. Utilising this fairly wide definition, it is clear that the subject is somewhat interdisciplinary. Thus the series seeks to integrate technological disciplines with management and other disciplines, for example, psychology and sociology. It is felt that these areas do not have a natural home, they are rarely represented by single departments in polytechnics and universities, and to put such books in a purely computer science or management series restricts potential readership and the benefits that such texts can provide. This series on information systems now provides such a home.

The books will be mainly student texts, although certain topics may be dealt with at a deeper, more research-oriented level.

The series is expected to include the following areas, although this is not an exhaustive list: information systems development methodologies, office information systems, management information systems, decision support systems, information modelling and databases, systems theory, human aspects and the human-computer interface, application systems, technology strategy, planning and control, and expert systems, knowledge acquisition and its representation.

A mention of the books so far published in the series gives a 'flavour' of the richness of the information systems world. *Information Systems Development: Methodologies, Techniques and Tools* (D. E. Avison and G. Fitzgerald), looks at many of the areas discussed above in overview form; *Information and Data Modelling* (David Benyon), concerns itself with one very important aspect, the world of data, in some depth; *Structured Systems Analysis and Design Methodology* (G. Cutts) looks at one particular information systems development methodology in detail; *Multiview: An Exploration in Information Systems Development* (D. E. Avison and A. T. Wood-Harper) looks at an approach to information systems development which combines human and technical considerations; *Software Engineering for Information Systems* (D. McDermid) discusses software engineering in the context of information systems; *Information Systems Research: Issues, Techniques and Practical Guidelines* (R. Galliers (ed)) provides a collection of papers on key information systems issues; and *Relational Database Design* (P. Beynon-Davies) looks at relational database design in detail. New titles include *Decision Support Systems* by Paul Rhodes; *Why Systems Fail* by Chris Sauer; and *Systems Analysis, Systems Design* by David Mason and Leslie Willcocks.

This latest addition to the series is entitled *Business Management and Systems Analysis* by Eddie Moynihan. It is a book with an approach that has been required for some time and it is surprising that until now no such book has existed. It addresses the important area where business and information systems meet. It sets information systems and systems analysis in a business context, it draws upon the author's extensive practical experience, and it approaches the topics from a UK perspective. It is an introductory book, to what is a very broad subject area, that provides both a framework and a solid foundation that should prove sufficient for most typical early information systems and business courses. Where more depth is required the book provides guidance that enables the reader to progress to more detailed texts and readings with confidence. It is a welcome addition to the Information Systems Series.

David Avison and Guy Fitzgerald

Preface

Outline

This book provides a basic foundation in both management and computing which these days is an important part of any business or technical career. Its approach to business administration and information technology is that of the practising computer systems analyst.

The book concentrates on explaining common business functions such as finance and marketing, and shows how computing can be organised to support them. Because practical business automation is about successfully combining people, technology, and administrative practice, the management aspects are also explained. In addition it outlines subjects like law and quality management which are of great practical importance in business and IT generally. The Information Systems Series and its rivals already cover the more technical aspects of systems analysis in detail, so topics such as development methodologies are merely outlined with an appropriate reference to other books.

Objectives

Four main categories of reader are intended: the IT practitioner, the business executive, the student in higher education, and the student taking professional examinations.

The practical objectives of the book are:

- To provide a framework and background for more specialised studies in IT.
- To complement other books in the Information Systems Series.
- To give an introduction to business management.
- To explain the link between management, administration, and computing.

- To provide some introductory advice on solving business computing problems.
- To prepare students for examinations and more advanced training in business and computing.
- To explain both IT and management using commonplace examples and a UK perspective.

When studying for a specialist examination the subject often seems to have no connection with the real world. For instance the theory of double-entry book-keeping, or a lecture on computer telecommunications, can seem remote from a clerk keying the details of a purchase invoice into a computer accounts system. However this book should help the reader supply the connection between business and technology for themselves and study specialist texts with more confidence.

Prerequisites

To benefit from this book the following are desirable:

- A basic knowledge of computing, e.g. an understanding of how a magnetic disk drive works.
- Some practical experience of computing, e.g. keyboard use of simple software such as a word processor or spreadsheet.
- An everyday appreciation of business, e.g. the clerical activities in a bank.
- Having continual exposure to IT or business administration either through work experience or by studying on an advanced course.
- An incentive to master what many people consider rather dry business and technical subjects.

Typical incentives are college examinations that must be passed, or the need for a computer programmer to understand business and management before transferring to systems analysis. Of course a minority of people are motivated by a genuine interest in business and IT, and they welcome anything which increases their understanding and skills.

Contents and use

The book is split into six parts:

I *Introduction*
Part I provides a survey of the role of systems analysis in business.
Some common administrative computer applications like a sales ledger
system are explained, and there is a brief survey of current information
technology. This part is meant as a refresher, or a survey for people
who have a limited technical background in computing. Anyone with
good experience and training is recommended to skim through this
material.

II *Business Administration and Management*
The essential business knowledge of a systems analyst is outlined in
Part II. The organisation of a typical business is explained and an
overview given of topics like law, finance, and human resource management from an IT viewpoint. This part is particularly aimed at the
student of IT and the technical computer practitioner. Payroll administration is considered in some depth as it occurs in every business. It is a
surprisingly complex subject which can be used to illustrate very clearly
many aspects of management, administration, and computing.

III *Systems Development*
This part outlines how computer systems are analysed and designed.
There is a brief introduction to systems development methodologies
and the theory of business and IT systems.

IV *Systems Analysis*
The main tasks and techniques of the systems analyst are explained in
this part. It covers topics such as specification, investigation, design,
maintenance, implementation, and quality control. The aim is to provide
a more detailed explanation of the techniques of systems analysis.

V *IT Management*
Part V describes the IT 'industry' and the various ways of organising
an IT function. The management of IT projects is discussed, and the
problems illustrated with some well-known technical projects which

failed dramatically. The final chapter discusses the management of systems development.

VI *Appendices*

The main Appendices are primarily intended for students and contain details on questions from professional examinations. Even the general reader may find the examination questions interesting, and a means of checking their business and computer knowledge.

The book has been designed so that the chapters are in a rational sequence. However most people do not work through a book from beginning to end, but read a particular chapter according to the needs of the moment. Some duplication and cross-referencing has been included to make this easier. Technical terms and abbreviations are always a difficult area for an author, and a frustrating reality of business and technological life. It is also an unfortunate fact that much of the terminology is not standardised. To overcome this, abbreviations and jargon are explained and their use is limited. A brief list of common abbreviations has been included in the Appendix. Also common examples from business and technology are frequently used to explain abstract concepts.

Student courses

Though introductory, this book is not aimed at any particular level in higher education or at any particular professional examinations. It should be useful on the following courses:

- Degrees and HNCs/HNDs in technical and business computing.
- Degrees and HNCs/HNDs in business.
- Business professional examinations such those for CIMA, the Chartered Institute of Management Accountants, or ICSA the Institute of Chartered Company Secretaries and Administrators.
- Computing professional examinations for the BCS (British Computer Society) and the IDPM (Institute of Data Processing Management).

People often start studying for professional examinations and degrees in specialist business subjects without an explanation of how the various topics fit together. The business part of the book is intended to do this, and should prove a useful survey for those who are starting a career in business administration. To help students with examinations the Appendix contains examination hints and sample questions. There are also comments on a few of the examination questions suggesting solutions. In addition students should find the summary of key points at the end of each chapter useful for revision.

Limitations

When reading the book most of the assertions should be treated as usually or commonly true. Constant reminders about exceptions become tedious and are therefore used occasionally. Also in business IT there is a gap between theory and practice. The book tends to focus on current practice rather than theoretical ideals, i.e. it is descriptive rather than prescriptive. Many topics, examples, and diagrams are simplified for brevity. It should also be borne in mind that most chapters are an outline of topics which have an extensive literature. Further details on IT systems development can usually be found in other books in the Information Systems Series.

Acknowledgements

All the government forms in this are book subject to Crown copyright and are published with the permission of the Controller of Her Majesty's Stationery Office. The author wishes to thank Peterborough Software and Sapphire Business Systems for their assistance.

The business and IT examination questions in Appendix III are published with the permission of the British Computer Society (BCS), the Chartered Institute of Management Accountants (CIMA), and the Institute of Chartered Secretaries and Administrators (ICSA).

Thanks are also due to the following individuals who read and commented on drafts of the book:

Paul Vickers,   lecturer in the School of Computing and Mathematical Sciences at Liverpool John Moores University.

Ken McKelvie,   lecturer in the School of Computing and Mathematical Sciences at Liverpool John Moores University.

Albert Mearns,   lecturer in the Business School at Liverpool John Moores University.

Steve Piggott,   computer consultant of Altcross Computer Consultants.

This book would not have been possible without the assistance of numerous students of computing, and public and private sector organisations in Merseyside.

Part 1
Introduction

Chapters 1 to 4 provide an introduction to systems development and a survey of information technology.

Chapter 1
Background to Business Systems

1.1 Introduction

This chapter outlines the application of IT (Information Technology) and the process of systems development in business administration. It provides an introduction to the more specialist chapters which describe the work and techniques of systems analysts when automating business functions such as payroll and accounting. The role of management is also discussed, as is the importance of business knowledge in IT systems development.

In practice systems analysts are not often concerned with automating clerical paperwork systems. In many cases such manual systems were automated over 50 years ago. This means that the main concern of systems analysts is the continual updating and revision of existing office computer systems. Less frequently systems analysts design and install entirely new IT systems.

1.2 Business systems

In the context of this book a business 'system' means everything, not just a set of computer programs. Taking banking as an example the system includes the paperwork like cheques, people like bank clerks, clerical procedures, and the computer hardware and software which prints bank statements. The whole combination provides a money transfer system. The planning, design, and adjustment of such systems are the primary concern of systems analysis. A more correct term which is sometimes used instead of 'business system' is 'administrative system'. This term is more accurate because such systems are used by public services and charities as well as businesses. Strictly speaking a 'business' is a profit-making organisation.

1.3 Business systems and technology

Business systems have always been a vital part of industry, commerce, and government. The reality of these systems has always been complicated. They involve, for instance, the procedures and paperwork necessary to export and import goods, transfer company shares via the stock exchange, or collect income tax. The automation of these activities using IT can significantly reduce the costs of administration and raise its quality. IT has such a useful and essential role that even a tiny part-time business can benefit from the use of computer software for word processing and accounting.

Although it is common to regard IT as a recent innovation, it has been making a growing contribution to business administration for over a 100 years. Familiar examples of 19th century IT are the telegraph, the typewriter, and the mechanical calculator. The following quotation from a business book published in 1918 demonstrates that the role of the systems analyst is not new:

> 'In a large organisation someone must be a supervisor of systems...
> These men must always have time to investigate any new time-,
> labour- or money-saving machinery or contrivance. If a new typewriter
> or adding machine is offered it must be looked at, and accepted or
> declined according to the judgement of the manager of systems.'

As discussed later, modern administrative IT is really the result of continuous technical development over many decades. As a consequence systems analysis is often concerned with converting systems from old forms of business automation to take advantage of technical progress. For instance in the 1950s and 1960s many financial systems were often based on accounting machines, which were a combination of a calculator and a typewriter. During this period financial systems, such as sales invoicing, were transferred from accounting machines to mainframe computers which used magnetic tapes for data storage. The author was last involved in a project to computerise an accounting machine system in 1980! Similarly today many financial systems are frequently taken off mainframe computers and put onto networks of personal computers, a process called down-sizing. Personal computers offer convenience and economy for small-scale office applications.

In a large company or government department the IT systems (hardware and software) are valued at tens of millions of pounds. As the number of IT staff employed can reach hundreds their annual wage bill is also measured in millions of pounds.

1.4   Terminology

IT is notorious for its jargon and confusing terminology. Several general terms describe the use of 'information technology' in business, for instance 'data processing' and 'management services'. These terms are sometimes used interchangeably. However they usually have different but over-lapping meanings. As it is sometimes important to appreciate the exact meaning, some of the more common terms are explained in Appendix II.

1.5   Systems analysis

The application of business automation requires 'systems analysis'. This is described in more detail below, but briefly it is the investigation or analysis of business administration followed by the identification, design, and implementation of improvements in its automation. So the administrative systems seen in, say, banking and insurance are the result of decades of systems analysis. Again the terminology is rather confused and several related words and phrases are in frequent use. Some common terms which are similar to systems analysis such as business analysis and O&M (Organisation and Methods) are also explained in Appendix II.

1.6   Systems development and maintenance

The process of producing or amending computer systems is called systems 'development', although the word development is often restricted to imply producing new systems only. The process of changing and adjusting existing IT systems is an important activity and called systems 'maintenance'. Systems development, including maintenance, is basically the combination of systems analysis and computer programming.

One way of looking at systems analysis is to say that it involves everything in IT systems development except computer programming. From another point of view the systems analyst is merely a 'middleman' between the users of administrative IT and the suppliers of the various components of an IT system such as hardware companies, programmers, and the vendors of standard software packages. The use of hybrid analyst-programmers is quite common, and they do both analysis and programming work.

In more detail a computer systems analyst would traditionally carry out the following main functions:

- *Feasibility studies*

The basic intention is to identify whether changes are economically and technically feasible, e.g. is it worthwhile introducing a new IT stock control system in a warehouse? Feasibility studies are meant to be fairly brief and determine whether a systems development project is worth continuing, and if it is, what is the best approach.

- *Analysis*

The analyst conducts a detailed examination of existing computer and manual systems, and any future requirements. An example of analysis (or investigation) is studying the current procedures in a sales office by interviewing the clerks.

- *Design*

This involves the analyst in producing a design of a new or amended IT system. It could involve selecting ready-made packaged software, or preparing specifications for computer programmers to write new software or amend existing software.

- *User documentation*

An important task is writing user guides for the clerical and administrative staff who are to operate the new or amended business system.

- *Quality*

The analyst must ensure that new or amended systems operate correctly. Many 'computer errors' are due to faulty work by systems development staff. Eliminating errors from analysis, design, and programming activities means careful meticulous work at all stages of systems development. For example there must be detailed checking of documentation, computer hardware and software. In particular, software must be extensively tested before it is used. User staff must also be actively involved in work like checking the specifications of new systems and testing software.

- *Implementation*

New or amended systems must be implemented by the analyst, for instance by installing new hardware and software for a system to control warehouse stock.

- *Maintenance*

As already mentioned any faults in computer systems must be corrected, or the system changed to meet new business requirements. Typically this so-called maintenance work on old systems occupies 80% of the time of analysts and programmers. Only the remaining 20% of their time is spent on new systems.

Chapter 2 gives some examples of the work of a systems analyst. Developing new IT systems or maintaining old systems is often done according to a 'methodology'. A methodology is basically a set of standard rules for computer analysis and programming work which lay down exactly how systems are to be developed. For instance, with regard to documentation a methodology would normally specify the symbols to be used on software design diagrams. A common analysis example is SSADM (Structured Systems Analysis and Design Method). By using an analysis or programming methodology all systems are developed and documented in a proven way, and different people produce work in the same standardised style. This improves both the quality and consistency of the work. Producing systems development documentation is an important part of professional systems analysis and programming. This documentation should include specifications of new software systems, user manuals, notes on how software has been programmed, project plans, system test plans, and so on. However there are many IT departments which skimp the production of documentation.

Traditionally, in the 1960s and 1970s, business computer systems were developed on mainframes with the software written using computer programming languages like COBOL. This approach is still important, particularly in big organisations. Analysis work is more varied than programming as the list above shows, but in a traditional development environment there might be two programmers for every systems analyst. In other words the amount of programming work considerably exceeds the amount of analysis work. The time-consuming and expensive nature of programming work in the traditional environment was one stimulus in the search for cheaper and more effective methods. For instance it is rare today for an ordinary business to design and write the software for a computer payroll system. The majority of organisations prefer instead to install a ready-written payroll software package from a reputable supplier. Another way of reducing programming work is to use fourth generation programming languages which are easier to apply than traditional programming languages like COBOL. The extensive use of these modern approaches to business systems development tends to favour the use of analysts rather than programmers.

1.7   User systems analysis

It has always been necessary for the users of administrative systems to have an elementary understanding of IT. It has also always been necessary for them to participate in the development and maintenance of IT systems. More fundamentally the management of an organisation have to control systems development and maintenance to ensure that the IT systems promised by the analyst are correct and meet cost, quality, and delivery-date targets.

Most office jobs now involve some IT with a VDU (Visual Display Unit) or PC (Personal Computer) on every second desk. A typical example would be a clerk entering details on employee educational qualifications into a PC so that the computer system can update personnel records. In the past, of course, the clerk would have written the details on a record card which was stored in a filing cabinet. As business IT is both vital and extensive, all grades of administrative and clerical staff are forced to take IT seriously.

In some cases the more technically-minded IT users can partially usurp the role of both the systems analyst and programmer. Particularly with small business systems on personal computers, administrative users can develop their own systems. The process of systems development is often simplified by using standard packaged software. Sometimes the users write their own software, i.e. they tackle the programmer's job as well as that of the systems analyst. Usually they receive some help from computer staff who work for a software house or an internal computer department. User staff are also increasingly being trained and educated in computer technology so it is easier for them to develop small systems on their own, or take a major role in the development of large computer systems.

1.8 Types of business and systems analysis

One of the key determinants of the analyst's work is the size of the employing organisation. In a small company a systems analyst is expected to turn his or her hand to many different jobs. The analyst could work on several different types of system in the course of a week such as amending accounting software, preparing a feasibility study for a new manufacturing system, and perhaps substituting for a computer programmer who is off sick. By way of contrast in a large organisation, like a government department, analysts might work for years in specialist teams on one application area like taxation.

Systems analysts are also employed by computer companies, particularly software houses or systems houses. Systems houses are companies that provide both computer hardware and software. In this case the analyst's responsibility is to develop and install IT systems for customer organisations. This involves much more of a sales support role.

1.9 Management

In an ideal world the systems analyst serves three groups of managers:

- *The general management*
The directors or general management of a business set the general framework for systems development such as the amount of money available for a computer project and the priority and timing of the project.

- *The user management*
People such as a marketing manager or accountant determine what they want from computer systems with the help of an analyst. Typically

the user management are regarded as 'clients' or 'customers'. Where the analyst represents a software house this would be both the actual and legal situation. In practice user managers delegate a lot of the detailed specification of requirements to their staff.

- *IT management*

The IT management determine such matters as the systems development methodologies used and the favoured computer hardware supplier. Also of course they exercise direct authority over an analyst, e.g. analysts would agree the timing of their holidays with their immediate superior, say, a systems development manager.

In theory these three groups of management should be compatible in their demands on the analyst, and any disagreements are in principle resolved by the general management.

From another viewpoint a systems analyst is often concerned with the management of a computer project such as installing a new raw materials stock control system in a factory. It is his or her responsibility to ensure that a computer system, which may cost anything from thousands to hundreds of thousands of pounds, is developed and installed 'on-time, on-budget, and on-quality'. Typically such a project takes several months if not years and requires some basic management skills to ensure that all the other parties such as the user staff, computer programmers, and hardware suppliers all do their job. In a nutshell systems analysts often act as project managers.

1.10   The importance of business knowledge to IT specialists

It appears reasonable that if the job of the systems analyst is to automate business systems then he or she should understand something of business. However this is too glib because 'business' in its entirety is beyond the grasp of any one person. Most executives themselves only understand a limited part of business and administration such as local government, banking, retailing, or personnel management. So from a practical point of view a systems analyst needs a knowledge of those aspects of business theory and practice which are common to most administrative computer systems, such as project management. Furthermore a good knowledge of the IT application area is also extremely useful, e.g. a sound appreciation of accounting helps considerably when computerising financial systems.

Executives often criticise computer people for being over technical and not able to understand 'business' or the users' needs. This argument is often used by managers who wish to organise their own computing. To counter these arguments there is currently some interest in developing computer-business hybrids, i.e. people who are trained in both IT and business. Some businesses, particularly software houses, also train business practitioners such as pensions administrators to act as systems analysts, the so-called 'dual' professional approach. However these theories have their opponents and there are unlikely to be enough hybrids or duals over the next decade. So most analysts will still tend to pick up their business knowledge on the job, supplemented by a few days formal training.

Although book learning, training, and education have their place, most computer managers and business executives emphasise the 'school of hard knocks', i.e. lengthy practical experience. Probably this view applies even more to the business aspects of systems analysis than the technical aspects. One consequence is that systems analysts are only considered reliable, competent, and experienced if they have personally supervised a major business system successfully through all the stages from inception to implementation.

1.11 Organising the development and maintenance of computer systems

There are a multitude of views as to how business computer systems should be developed, operated, and maintained. Expanding the discussion in Section 1.10 above the two extremes are:

- *The business-dominant view*

Business system users should do as much systems development as possible. This will ensure that the system meets their needs. They have the business understanding which systems analysts and their like do not. Furthermore involving systems analysts is a communications overhead and just a source of confusion. The development of systems is easy with modern IT and well within the scope of senior administrative and business staff. User staff are perfectly capable of operating modern IT systems.

In other words the use of computer staff should be minimised.

- *The IT-dominant view*

Systems development needs specialist training and considerable practice to do a professional job. User staff have insufficient skill and insufficient time away from their main duties to act as systems analysts and programmers. Furthermore systems analysts are in a better position to serve the business as a whole. Users in an ordinary administrative department tend to think only of their own needs and not those of the business generally. Systems analysts are trained to identify both the requirements of individual departments and the business generally. They are also best placed to organise the delivery of high-quality systems to meet these requirements.

Some large systems, or systems shared between various user departments, need to run on large computers. These can only be controlled by trained computer operations staff. Also although small modern computer systems are easy to use, considerations such as security require that the equipment and systems have some supervision from professional computer staff.

In short computer staff are essential. Only they know how best to serve the interests of both the business as a whole and departmental users.

Both of the above views are met, although in practice it is more common to find in-between positions.

1.12 The future

Technical progress is continuing, possibly at an even faster rate than the past. This means that a modern colour-graphics personal computer with its laser printer will soon look as antique as a 1920's candlestick telephone. Today's technical curiosity like computerised voice recognition tends to become tomorrow's commonplace item. This technical progress offers considerable business advantages like faster cheaper administration. However the new technology has to be organised into workable business systems, so there is unlikely to be a shortage of work for systems analysts. Furthermore systems analysts themselves can expect to use computers much more as tools for developing IT systems. This will go far beyond the current limited use of software by systems analysts for purposes such as drawing diagrams of office procedures. More controversial is the relationship between the business user, the systems analyst, the programmer, and the computer operator. As the technology changes so will the boundaries between jobs. New jobs will also emerge just as that of the computer programmer did in the early 1950s.

A confident prediction is that by the year 2000 most business users will be even more IT-literate. IT-literacy will probably be regarded as even more essential than today. As a result most users will certainly be able to manage many small-scale computer jobs themselves. But even small-scale office computing requires technical support from an analyst-programmer. Large-scale business IT projects involving, say, government social security administration, will always require a systems analyst or equivalent to provide both coordination and technical skills. Of course large scale IT projects represent a considerable use of time and money, and business executives and their staff will demand greater participation both to maximise the benefits and minimise the risks.

All this suggests that there will be numerous ways of allocating systems development work amongst both technical and business staff, according to preference and circumstances. Undoubtedly however, the basic knowledge and skills of systems analysis will develop, but they are likely to be more widespread in the business of the future.

1.13 Summary

- IT has had a growing role in human organisations for perhaps a 100 years, and administrative systems are now totally dependent on it.
- The role of the systems analyst is managing IT projects, identifying system requirements, designing new or amended systems, and implementing these systems with office users. Alternatively the systems analyst is responsible for most systems development work except computer programming.
- Careful quality control is required at all stages of a computer project. User involvement is essential to ensure a quality system.

- Changing or adapting old systems is called maintenance. This forms about 80% of the work of the analysts and programmers. The remaining 20% is the development of new or replacement systems.
- In some cases administrative staff can develop their own IT systems.
- Systems analysts can benefit from a general knowledge of business and administration. A specialist knowledge of the business areas to which they are applying computers, such as life insurance, is even more useful.
- Good practical experience is considered of vital importance for systems development staff.
- Systems analysis has a promising future, and will develop in line with the technical progress of IT. However, in the future the skills and knowledge embodied in systems analysis will be wide-spread amongst white-collar staff generally.

Chapter 2
Examples of Computer Systems and The Analyst's Work

2.1 Introduction

This chapter gives the essential background to the book as a whole. It outlines the main features of common computer systems, and then provides some examples of how systems analysts work. It is meant as an introductory chapter for those who are relatively new to business IT.

A knowledge of common business and IT systems is useful. For instance personnel systems provide a familiar example of a typical computer terminal display. This is simply because the data for an employee details screen is found on most job application forms. A payroll system uses similar data and provides another example of a common screen display as shown in Fig. 16.7. A stock of such every-day illustrations is particularly important for students entered for academic and professional examinations. They often face questions like this:

> With reference to a business computer system known to you discuss two possible methods of collecting and inputing data. Also discuss the data validation techniques used.

This sort of question is only straightforward if a candidate has modest practical experience and some textbook knowledge. So an answer might be based on a stock control system mentioning input devices like hand-held data entry terminals which are used during stock-taking.

Practising systems analysts and computer salesmen also need a knowledge of common systems during discussions with colleagues or customers. Of course professional analysts also need a deeper knowledge of the core systems unique to their own industry and specialist work such as MRP (Manufacturing Resource Planning) in a factory environment.

2.2   An outline of common business IT systems

Many systems are unique to particular types of organisation. For
instance, a computerised register of citizens is used by a local authority
to administer national and local government elections. By way of
contrast the following IT systems are very common:

- *Personnel*

Computerised personnel information systems (CPISs) hold all the
personal details of employees, e.g. name, job title, and pay rate. These
are entered into the computer from documents such as application
forms. The details are stored on magnetic disk and the data is accessed
to produce a whole series of reports, e.g. the number of staff in various
age bands. The reports are used to improve administration in areas
like recruitment, attendance, pay and employee benefits (such as free
medical insurance), employee performance appraisals, and industrial
relations. For instance personnel computer systems can print various
standard letters concerned with recruitment, an example being an
invitation to an interview.

- *Payroll*

This is discussed separately in Section 2.3 below.

- *Accounting*

Chapters 11 and 12 discuss the theory of accounting and book-keeping
which provide a major computer application area in most organisations.
There are several accounting systems that are important, all of which
are commonly computerised. Most involve a 'ledger', which in a traditional manual system is a large book, hence the term book-keeping.
Ledgers contain a set of accounts, e.g. for customers. Each account
contains a record of all the transactions which affect it. An ordinary
bank statement is a copy of a ledger account. The word ledger is also
frequently used to describe the electronic equivalent of a large accounts
book, i.e. the main magnetic disk file in a computerised accounting
system. The main accounting systems and ledgers used in a trading
company are summarised below:

(1)   A sales invoicing system, as the name implies, prepares and prints
      invoices.

(2) A sales ledger system stores records of sales debts, hence the American term 'accounts receivable'. An example of a sales ledger screen display is shown in Fig. 12.4. Sales ledger systems also print customer statements.

(3) A purchase ledger system records the amounts of money owed to suppliers for the purchase of goods and services. The American term is 'accounts payable'.

(4) A nominal (or general ledger) contains all the miscellaneous expense and revenue accounts of a business together with summaries of other ledgers. Using these details a nominal ledger system can print the 'final accounts' of the business, i.e. the profit and loss account and balance sheet. Figure 11.1 shows an example.

(5) A budgetary control system monitors the expenditure of a business department or project. For example the budgeted wages of the staff of an IT department are compared with the actual wages paid to detect excess expenditure. See Fig. 11.2.

- *Stock control*

An IT stock system records the stock level of items in warehouses and stores. The system can automatically print replenishment orders for items when their stock is low.

- *Sales order processing*

Sales order processing is important where there is a regular call for goods on credit. The usual example is a wholesaler supplying retailers with consumer goods. Typically there are hundreds of orders per day for goods to be despatched from a warehouse to customers. The sales orders may be received directly from customers by telephone or letter and the details are then entered into a VDU. Alternatively a direct salesforce may collect the orders, perhaps using laptop computers to enter and store the data. The laptop data is then transmitted directly to the computer system using the public telephone network. The computer system can print the 'picking' list and despatch documents for the warehouse. These are used to select the appropriate goods and transport them to the customer.

Personnel, payroll, and accounting systems are used in virtually all organisations, for instance the Civil Service, local authorities, hospitals, and manufacturing companies.

The development and maintenance of computer systems such as those above is the prime duty of the systems analyst. In practice these duties become highly specific tasks such as designing a new payslip, or testing an amended program which prints sales statistics. The discussion which follows concentrates on the computer system (hardware and software). However it should always be borne in mind that hardware and software are just part of the wider business system which includes people and office procedures.

2.3 Payroll systems

Payroll with accounting is perhaps the most common business function. It is also very important as staff wages and salaries can exceed 50% of total costs in some businesses. From the viewpoint of the systems analyst it is also one of the most rigorous and demanding applications in business computing. Payroll systems are very sensitive to mistakes, and any failure may mean employees receive the wrong pay, or no pay at all.

Payroll administration is much more complicated than most people imagine. Much of it is however ideal for automation. This is because, although complicated, it operates according to strict rules such as those of PAYE (Pay As You Earn) income tax. There is often a large volume of work to be done and it must be done on time. Automation offers the advantages of labour-saving, quality, and speed. Most of the automation involves the application of normal business computing, but there is some use of paper-handling machines, e.g. for trimming the sprocket holes off payslips.

An outline configuration chart of a computer system is shown in Fig. 2.1. This diagram shows the hardware components of a typical computer system and it could also represent a payroll system. A very brief summary of the use of the hardware for payroll purposes is given below:

- Data is input via a terminal keyboard and display. So the input might be an employee's payroll number and the number of hours worked. See Fig. 16.5 for an example of a typical input form and Fig. 16.7 for an example of a typical input display.
- The employee details such as name and pay are stored on a magnetic disk file.

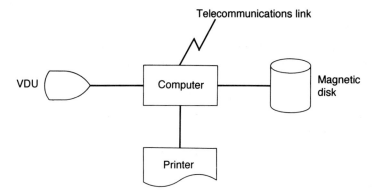

Fig. 2.1 The basic configuration chart of many business computer systems, large and small. Taking a purchase ledger system as an example the input could be details of money owed to suppliers. The magnetic disk would contain details like the names and addresses of suppliers, and the output could be printed statements of the amount owed. Such a system would pay suppliers either by printing cheques or by crediting their bank accounts via a telecommunications link using a service called BACSTEL. A more complicated configuration chart is shown in Fig. 16.6.

Often there are several input screens (terminals or workstations). With some systems other input and output devices are used, for instance an optical scanner. These days virtually all readily-accessible permanent data is stored on magnetic or optical disks. Magnetic tapes are mainly used for security copies of data.

- The computer software processes the stored data performing income tax calculations and the like.
- The results of the processing are printed out as payslips and cheques. Electronic payment methods can also be used. Various reports are printed by the system, for instance a total of all the tax deducted from pay. See Fig. 16.9 for a simple example of output.

Chapter 16 discusses payroll administration in some detail as an example of a typical business IT application. Figure 2.1 shows a computer configuration which is broadly similar for many business systems whether running on a mainframe, mini-, or micro-computer. The size of the computer merely influences factors like the number of VDU terminals that access the system and the maximum size of the magnetic disk files. So a personal computer might be used for paying the 60 employees of a small company and a mainframe for paying the 50 000 employees of a large central government department. Of course the whole operation of the computer is controlled by payroll software, and this software is often, but not always, the main area of interest for systems analysts.

2.4   No standard systems

There is no truly standardised version of any of the business computer systems discussed so far. For instance one version of a payroll system may be very basic and require all the elements of gross pay such as bonus payments and Statutory Sick Pay (SSP) to be calculated elsewhere and entered into the system manually by the user. This basic system might then work out standard deductions such as income tax and then the net pay. A basic payroll system would finally print a few outputs such as payslips and a summary of the payroll financial totals.

A more comprehensive system might calculate gross pay elements such as bonus payments and SSP and pass these details on automatically to the next stage which is calculating deductions and net pay. Furthermore it would support all the other administrative requirements of SSP such as keeping sickness records. This means that users ordering new software must be careful to examine the specification of any proposed system in detail. This is true whether considering a software package or a bespoke system. For instance SSP facilities might be provided as part of a separate software package which can be linked to the main payroll system. Needless to say such an SSP package is usually available as a chargeable extra.

2.5   Systems integration

Accounting systems in particular form part of a whole. For instance a sales ledger system needs to pass the sales debts outstanding over to the nominal ledger system so that it can produce a balance sheet. This can be done manually by taking the required total from a sales ledger print-out and entering it into the nominal ledger through a VDU. However it is far better that this is done automatically to avoid the possibility of a transcription error. Integrated accounting software provides this automatic transfer of data between ledgers as a standard facility. The automatic transfer is normally done using magnetic disk files to link systems. Furthermore systems are designed so that the VDU screens and print-outs have a consistent format making them easy to use. Integrated software packages are sometimes sold as a set, e.g. for the sales, nominal and purchase ledgers, or available separately if required. Commercially available examples in the UK include the Tetra and Pegasus accounting software packages.

A further stage of integration comes with database systems. According to one simple view a database is one large file containing an extensive collection of data. For instance a human resources database system contains a common database which serves the needs of payroll and personnel administration. This has several advantages such as consistency. So a payroll system accessing a human resources database uses the same employee surname data as the personnel system, avoiding the possibility of different spellings, and the waste of magnetic disk space caused by duplicating an employee's name for different applications.

2.6 Scenarios for systems development and maintenance

The detailed work pattern work of systems analysts is mainly conditioned by the environment in which they work. Some typical systems analysis environments are:

- A major central government department, e.g. the Ministry of Defence.
- A large PLC (Public Limited Company), e.g. a large insurance company.
- A medium-sized business, e.g. a subsidiary company (physically one factory plus a warehouse) which is part of a large group of manufacturing companies.
- A small business, perhaps employing 100 staff.
- A software or systems house.

A large business employs tens of thousands of staff with hundreds of people devoted to IT systems. Such organisations tend to have very formal procedures, even a bureaucracy, for developing and operating IT systems. Small companies can be very informal. Software or systems houses need to sell IT products and services, and this does to some extent alter the way systems analysis is conducted. Chapters 27 and 28 discuss how the type and organisation of a business can effect the work of systems analysts.

2.7 Typical work patterns for systems analysts

The following scenarios give some idea of the mainstream work of a systems analyst.

- *Feasibility*

A team of systems analysts in the Civil Service are studying the feasibility of an IT project to develop a new government financial system. They are using SSADM (Structured Systems Analysis and Design Method) Version 4 which lays down standard procedures for analysis and design work. The basic idea is to collect the facts on current administrative and IT activities. The new IT requirements for financial information must also be identified and various options for meeting these requirements investigated and outlined. For example one option might be to down-load mainframe data to a personal computer system.

One major purpose of the feasibility study is to establish whether it is economically and technically viable to develop new or amended systems. If this is so the study has collected the main facts and identified the IT approach to be followed when developing a full system using the remaining stages of SSADM.

SSADM is the official government approved methodology for developing computer systems. SSADM Version 4 has just been introduced, and is starting to replace Version 3. One part of the SSADM Version 4 manual gives a detailed description of all the steps to be followed in producing a feasibility study which is called Stage 0. This consists of four steps: Step 010 Prepare for the Feasibility Study, Step 020 Define the Problem, Step 030 Select Feasibility Options, and Step 040 Assemble Feasibility Report. The Version 4 manuals define all these steps in detail (see also Sections 18.12 to 18.15 for further information).

- *Analysis*

A computer consultant specialising in pensions has to advise a client about the possible use of new computer systems for pensions administration. As a first stage she must carry out a fairly detailed investigation into the client's existing office procedures for pensions administration. As this is a large pension scheme there are about 50 administrative and clerical staff to interview and dozens of forms and office procedures in use. As a result of her investigations the consultant prepares a specification containing an analysis of the client's existing paperwork and computer systems, as well as any future IT requirements.

- *Design*

A company distributes car components to garages and retailers. It requires a new sub-system which is effectively a major extension to its current sales analysis system. The new system is to show the sales of car components in various categories based on invoiced sales. The systems analyst must formally design all the print-outs and VDU screen layouts in detail. The necessary software system must also be designed as a set of interlinked computer programs. Specifications must be produced for the company marketing department stating exactly what it is to receive. Once these have been approved the analyst must produce specifications for COBOL programmers to produce the software.

● *System quality control*
A systems analyst tests a new purchase ledger system. The system is to control the payment of suppliers and handle all the necessary accounting. Initially the testing requires taking a small quantity of simple representative data from the old computer system and running it through the new system to check that the results are as expected. Assuming this is satisfactory the analyst does more extensive tests on each part of the system, for example checking that supplier statements are printed correctly under all circumstances. The users, who are accounts staff, also participate in later tests. These 'user acceptance tests' are conducted once the analyst thinks the package is working satisfactorily.

If errors are discovered at any stage the system is immediately corrected. Errors can occur in the purchase ledger software itself, or the way the analyst has installed it on the computer, or in the documentation describing the operating procedures.

● *Implementation*
A new stock control system involving several VDUs and small printers is to be installed in a factory store which contains thousands of different engineering components. For instance the store-keeper can key a product number into a VDU to receive a display showing the location of the product in which he is interested. The systems analyst must supervise the installation of the computer equipment and then test it. He must then train the store-keepers in the use of the new system.

● *Maintenance*
A system for processing sales orders has been installed by a software house. The customer reports by telephone that the computer-printed total of daily orders received appears to contain an error. An analyst-programmer must determine the exact nature of the fault. It is possible

for instance that the customer is mistaken. Assuming the fault is genuine, the analyst collects all the evidence and then traces the fault to a particular program and asks a programmer to correct it.

Once corrected the system needs full testing to ensure that the original error is cleared and that further errors have not been inadvertently introduced. The analyst and programmer have a telecommunications link to the customer's computer. This together with mail and telephone means that collecting the evidence and the correction of the software can hopefully be done without visiting the customer's premises.

2.8   Other types of analysis work

Systems analysts can be involved in other types of work, of which prototyping is the most common.

● *Prototyping*

An analyst-programmer from a software house works together with a financial consultant. They discuss a new accounting system that is to be developed as a software package. The analyst-programmer uses a 4GL (Fourth Generation Language) to program a rough system quickly. A 4GL provides a quick and easy way of writing computer programs. The rough system displays a set of screens on a terminal. These should match the ideas of the financial specialist. The analyst-programmer runs this rough prototype system on the computer and lets the consultant revise his ideas and then the analyst-programmer changes the screens accordingly. By working interactively in this fashion the financial consultant and the analyst-programmer soon agree on how the accounting system is to appear to a clerk. However the analyst-programmer has faked the appearance of the screens. For instance most of the logic for updating the accounts ledger is omitted. This sort of detail must now be added either in the original fourth generation language, or by rewriting the system properly in a third generation language such as C or COBOL. The primary purpose of the prototype is merely to develop the ideas in an interactive way.

● *OR (Operational Research)*

A systems analyst is working on a production control system in a factory making plastic goods. One requirement is producing production schedules which is time-consuming and difficult with the current system which is partly manual. The schedules tell the factory which items to produce, on which machine, and when. Good production schedules must be based on reliable forecasts of future demand and they aim to minimise the costs of holding stock and minimise the time spent in changing the dies on injection moulding machines. This problem has many mathematical aspects.

The company calls in an operational research consultant (basically a business mathematician). Together with the systems analyst the OR consultant investigates the business, mathematical, and technological requirements. They go on to consider increased computer support for the production control function. Ultimately they recommend a design based on standard software packages and bespoke software.

- *O&M (Organisation and Methods)*

A company is too small to employ professional O&M officers so systems analysts have to fulfil this function as well. One job is to consider typing and word processing throughout the company. Currently this is done on an ad hoc basis by each department on different equipment. A systems analyst must examine the current position and make recommendations. The investigation can extend to other office equipment such as the use of fax machines where appropriate.

The O&M recommendations by the systems analyst could include using a pool of typists (the traditional approach), formalising the current arrangements with standardised word processing machines in each department, or introducing an office automation system throughout the company where the ordinary office staff would all have their own terminals and do their own typing.

- *Miscellaneous work*

The finance director and internal audit department of a wholesale distributor are concerned about inaccuracies in warehouse stock figures. They believe that the deficiencies lie not in the computer software, but more probably in the clerical and warehouse procedures. Theft of stock and fraud are also strong possibilities. A systems analyst is asked to help them investigate the problem and make recommendations for improvement. As part of the investigation the systems analyst interviews warehouse, accounts, and sales administration staff, observes all the procedures concerned with handling goods in and out of the warehouse, checks samples of the paperwork, and studies the operational use of the computer system.

2.9 Summary

- Payroll, personnel, and accounts computer systems are used in most large organisations. Stock control systems are also very common. Sales order processing is a popular computer application in the private sector.
- The main accounting computer applications besides payroll include systems for sales invoicing, sales ledger, purchase ledger, and the nominal (or general) ledger.
- Systems analysts are involved in the development of computer systems at most stages, usually with the exception of programming.
- Systems analysts occasionally work on O&M and OR projects. They can also be asked to help on special projects outside IT.

Chapter 3
Types of Business System

3.1 Introduction

There are always useful lessons to be learned from the past so this chapter provides a brief history of IT. Also traces of old IT systems survive for decades so an appreciation of history has a some practical value. This chapter also outlines the main categories of IT system that are met in business administration. For instance it describes Management Information Systems (MISs) and Expert Systems (ESs). The next chapter considers the hardware and software used to implement these systems.

3.2 A brief history of business information technology

There is a tendency to regard IT as new. However some IT companies like ATT (American Telegraph and Telephone) and NCR (National Cash Register) originated in the last century, as their names imply. The ancestors of ICL (International Computers Limited) and IBM (International Business Machines) were also operating in the early 20th century. By way of contrast one of the largest modern computer companies, DEC (Digital Equipment Corporation), was started in 1957, and other companies such as the personal computer manufacturers Apple and Compaq have originated within the last fifteen years.

The telegraph, typewriter, telephone, and mechanical calculator were all introduced commercially in the 19th century. Punched card machines were also developed at the end of this era, and were first used on a large scale to compile statistics for the United States population census in 1890.

By the 1920s punched card systems were processing data for large financial systems in many major companies. These machines read data recorded as holes punched into cards and were used for applications like life assurance or local authority taxes. They worked by sorting the punched cards, performing calculations on the data, and printing the results. However, small-scale office systems in the 1920s used accounting machines which were a combination of a typewriter and calculator.

In the mid-1940s primitive computers were developed primarily for military and scientific appiications. Examples are the Harvard Mark 1 and ENIAC (Electronic Numerical Integrator and Computer). Commercial computers were produced a few years later, and one of the first was developed in the early 1950s by Lyons, the catering firm. Their computer, LEO (Lyons Electronic Office), was used for sales administration and payroll. From the 1950s onwards the computer gradually replaced punched card machines and other primitive forms of data processing equipment. High level programming languages were also developed, notably FORTRAN in the 1950s for scientific work, and COBOL in the 1960s for business computing.

A major development in 1964 was the introduction of the 360 series. This was an immensely successful series of mainframe computers produced by IBM. The series is still being developed and extended, for instance the IBM 3090 Model 1200 mainframe announced in 1990. Companies like DEC (Digital Equipment Corporation) also developed successful ranges of mini-computers such as the PDP11 and VAX in the 1970s. In 1981 IBM entered the new micro-computer market with its personal computer, the IBM PC. This was followed by the new PS/2 series of personal computers in 1987. The 1980s also saw the large-scale introduction of fourth generation programming languages, the use of artificial intelligence techniques, and structured systems analysis and design. Of course all these innovations had been conceived earlier. There is no halt in the rate of technical progress and new hardware and software systems are continually coming onto the market, e.g. optical computer technology.

Whether discussing large water-cooled mainframes, mini-computers, or desk-top personal computers the dramatic improvements in price and performance are mainly due to progress in electronics. It is often observed that systems analysis and programming have progressed little by comparison. Take one ordinary computer memory chip as an example. It uses a piece of silicon smaller than a human finger nail, and yet it contains the equivalent of several million electronic valves. Valves were bulky, unreliable, and power-hungry devices, but a few thousand of them were essential in the computers of the 1940s. Improved telecommunications, for instance using fibre optics and satellites, has also had a major effect on modern information technology. The continuous progress of technology means that a modern IBM PC is roughly equivalent, in processor and memory terms, to a 1970s mainframe. Of course since then the mainframes themselves have also been developed enormously, exploiting the same progress in electronics.

The discussion so far has concentrated on hardware, but there has been a less dramatic development of software over the last few decades. In the 1950s, for example, programs were written directly in binary notation, whereas in the 1990s the computer instructions used in fourth generation programming languages resemble English. In the early days of computing hardware was extremely expensive. Today hardware is relatively cheap, and software can be the most expensive part of a business system.

One interesting aspect of technical progress is the recognition of the problems of systems development. O&M (Organisation and Methods) was developed in the 1940s as a formal approach to developing and maintaining large clerical systems which used primitive office machinery. O&M can be regarded as a early form of systems analysis. When computers were first applied to business administration in the 1950s both the systems analysis and programming aspects were found to be surprisingly time-consuming and difficult. Business computer systems were discovered to take months or years to develop, and in many ways this has not changed.

3.3 Upgrading

As the history of IT implies, administrative systems in established businesses have been regularly amended and converted to use the latest technology. This 'upgrading' will continue as long as IT progresses at a startling rate.

When equipment has reached the end of its life the original supplier has the advantage over others in providing replacement machines, usually on compatibility grounds alone. In the simplest case the old software is just run on the new hardware with a minimum of change, and hopefully it should run more efficiently. The hardware and software suppliers have a vested interest in making the transition from old generation technology to new generation technology as easy as possible. This is simply because it is far cheaper to keep an old customer than find a new one.

There is a natural tendency to upgrade conservatively, and to run business systems on the new or improved machines in much the same way as on the old. This approach relies on exploiting factors in the new hardware like greater reliability, and superior performance. However new technology sometimes offers more radical opportunities. This can be either newer concepts like expert systems which are discussed below, or exploiting new technology to change fundamentally the way a business operates. This radical approach is perhaps more apparent in manufacturing with CAD (Computer Aided Design) and CAM (Computer Aided Manufacture). It is even more obvious with the dramatic manifestations of new technology such as computer-controlled machine tools and robots. However there are examples in business administration. For instance a supplier can accept sales orders directly from retailers. The orders can be transmitted from the retailer's personal computer by telephone line straight into the supplier's mainframe system. This speeds up the whole process of ordering and despatching goods, and reduces dependence on manual sales administration. As discussed later the benefits of new technology may further be enhanced by a major reorganisation of the departments and workflow in a business as well as changing the jobs of employees. Whichever way IT is used its on-going development offers systems analysts continuous employment in revising business systems to take advantage of technical progress.

3.4 Types of system

There are several ways of classifying the various types of computer-based information systems (CBISs). One common classification of the systems used in administration is given below. It is not intended to imply any kind of hierarchy or sequence of systems.

● *Transaction processing systems (TPSs)*
In this context a TPS refers to a system which processes business transactions in any way. An invoicing system is a good example as its prime purpose is to process transactions such as details of despatched goods, and then create sales invoices which are themselves another kind of transaction. Transaction processing in this general sense is probably the most fundamental and important area of business administration and applied IT. It covers all the basic business systems such as payroll, stock control, and accounting.

(The term transaction processing systems also refers to any large multi-terminal systems with a central computer, e.g. airline booking systems. In this case the 'transaction' is any electronic message from the terminals to the central computer.)

- *Management information systems (MISs)*

An MIS provides summarised data for management. An aged-debt print-out is a simple example. This summarises the debts stored on a sales ledger according to how overdue they are, e.g. the total of debts which are one month old, two months old, three months old and so on. From a managerial viewpoint MISs are an essential aspect of computer use. This is because the computer can provide quickly and reliably the quantitative information necessary to control a business function like sales accounting. Needless to say the details summarised are collected and processed by transaction processing systems.

- *Information retrieval systems (IRSs)*

IRSs are often known loosely as viewdata systems or on-line databases. The idea is to make available to a remote terminal on request a library of text (or pictorial) data. IRSs are used for disseminating volatile data like insurance company policy rates, or more permanent data like details of official publications. The systems may be available commercially, e.g. the Datastream service which provides financial information such as share prices and foreign exchange rates. Alternatively businesses may provide their own internal information service, for instance giving access to up-to-date internal company news and price-lists.

- *Office automation (OA)*

In the modern sense OA includes systems for word processing, electronic mail, and facsimile (fax) transmission. Other modern forms of electronic communication are often included such as voice-mail where voice messages are stored in a 'mailbox' for later retrieval by telephone.

- *Decision support systems (DSSs)*

A DSS is an interactive system which aids decision-making. An example of a DSS is planning the marketing-mix of a product. The marketing-mix is the set of factors such as the price of a product, advertising, the use of a sales force, special offers, and so on. Clearly all these factors individually and together affect sales volume and profits, and a marketing manager is keen to find the optimum mix. A DSS for the marketing-mix is a software system that allows the manager to explore the consequences of any changes thought feasible as he seeks to find the optimum. For instance 'what if' he increases the price of the product, or decreases the size of the salesforce, both of which affect the annual sales and profit. The underlying software uses a mathematical model of the marketing mix situation to predict the consequences of the manager's decisions. A DSS can also analyse data to aid decisions, e.g. by producing *ad hoc* sales reports for a marketing manager. Rather than design and program such a system from first principles it is often cheaper and more effective to buy DSS software packages which can adapted for particular problems.

- *Executive information systems (EISs)*

These present business information in a convenient fashion, often graphical, for senior managers. Alternatively they are sometimes known as executive support systems (ESSs). The information is from other internal computer systems such as the accounting systems. However external business data can also be included, e.g. government statistics.

- *Expert systems (ESs)*

Expert systems simulate a human expert using artificial intelligence techniques. They basically incorporate a set of rules and knowledge on a specific subject such as personnel recruitment. The details of a particular case, say from an individual's job application form, are fed into the computer which applies its rules and knowledge to reach a decision such as whether to interview the candidate or not. Expert 'systems are useful for situations like recruitment where the selection rules are a mixture of company policies, rules of thumb based on experience, some legal requirements, and the details of a particular candidate. Though the term is wider, intelligent knowledge-based systems (IKBSs) are often equated with ESs. IKBSs rely on a mixture of artificial intelligence and electronically-stored knowledge.

The above classification is not completely adequate even in a business context. EDI (Electronic Data Interchange), for instance, is an important part of modern business computing. However according to the above scheme it is merely an automatic method of transferring transactions like purchase orders between the computers in different organisations. Another example is 'groupware' which is software that allows people to work together more effectively using electronic communication, i.e. it is a kind of extended office automation. Ordinary business systems frequently combine two or more of the above features. For instance a sales ledger system is essentially a TPS recording unpaid sales invoices. However as mentioned above it can include some MIS features such as a list of aged debts. Other types of system are found outside business administration, for example process control systems which continuously monitor and control chemical plant. Systems analysts can also meet other non-administrative IT such as CBT (Computer Based Training).

The types of CBIS above frequently use similar hardware technology, and the primary difference is conceptual. The concepts are often implemented via special software such as a 'shell' which can be used to develop a wide-range of expert system applications. In some cases hardware is an important component of the concept, e.g. good graphics displays are a key part of EIS. From a systems development point of view the types of system discussed above require different approaches to analysis, design, IT quality control, implementation, and maintenance. The emphasis of this book is on the development of TPSs and MISs.

3.5 Summary

- IT has a history stretching back over 100 years. Data processing was well-established by the 1920s with administrative systems using punched card equipment. Computers were first developed for military applications in the 1940s, and applied to administration in the 1950s.
- The continuing advance of IT means that business systems must be revised frequently to take advantage of new developments.
- A business IT system may be categorised as a TPS, MIS, IRS, OA, DSS, EIS (alternatively ESS), or an ES (sometimes an IKBS). Actual systems may combine these categories.

Chapter 4
A Survey of Systems Technology

4.1 Introduction

This chapter provides a brief review of the current technology which systems analysts use to design or amend business systems. Readers are recommended to supplement this review with a more detailed study of the latest literature on computer and telecommunications technology.

In some cases the primary purpose of the analyst's project is to exploit new technology, and to convert existing administrative systems to use it. A simple example is upgrading a payments system from one which prints cheques to one which also allows computerised credit transfers directly into the payee's bank account. This can be done by using BACS (Bankers Automated Clearing Services) which provides telecommunication links as one method of paying business suppliers. It should be remembered however that the issue of new technology is frequently irrelevant. For example when an accounting system is modified to produce new management information the hardware is often the same before and after the amendments which only affect software.

4.2 The role of IT strategy

It is relatively rare to have a completely free hand in selecting new technology, as the choice is usually made within the IT strategy of the business. This is basically a long-term overall plan for developing IT systems. One key aspect of an IT strategy is the policy rules it stipulates for buying new hardware and software. The policy may, for instance, stipulate that equipment can be purchased only if it is compatible with that of a particular supplier such as IBM or ICL. It is usually even more restrictive about software. So the policy rules in an IT strategy may be to develop systems using ICL equipment with INGRES providing the programming environment and database management software. Such rules help to ensure compatible systems, limit the skills required, and offer the prospect of price discounts from suppliers. Without an IT strategy there is a tendency to create a series of isolated and incompatible 'islands of information' throughout an organisation.

There is a bewildering choice of hardware and software products, as well as ancillary equipment such as small telephone exchanges. The catalogues from major IT companies like ICL or DEC can contain hundreds of different products. These include various models of computer processor, printers, and disk drives. The catalogues also include different software products, e.g. database management systems and programming languages. Frequently similar products are available from other sources such as 'plug-compatible' manufacturers. These manufacturers deliberately set out to produce equipment like disk drives which can operate as part of the computer hardware systems provided by major suppliers such as IBM or DEC. Usually their equipment is intended to be more cost-effective. Software houses are another major source of IT products, particularly for software packages in application areas such as stock control.

Given the wide choice it is hardly surprising that major businesses have different types of hardware and software. However each business tends to have a similar general technology to its competitors, and it is usually the fine detail that is different. So one business might use the INGRES database system for its ICL equipment and another might use the DB2 database system for its IBM mainframe. Where a business has standardised as part of its computer strategy, say on ICL-compatible products, then this automatically simplifies the choices that must be made from the large range of hardware and software products available. As discussed below 'open systems' which are compatible with the products of a wide-range of suppliers offer considerable promise.

4.3 Typical hardware

When discussing electronic hardware in particular the advance of technology is very rapid. Equipment can become out-of-date within three years. However because hardware is not replaced immediately there can be a gap of up to ten years between the first machine sold and the last one withdrawn from service. Also old equipment is often upgraded to extend its life, e.g. by adding extra memory boards to a computer. Then of course there is a second-hand market in refurbished machines.

A typical equipment configuration used for payroll processing is shown in Fig. 16.6. When systems analysts are designing systems they can have several main options within the IT procurement policies. In price terms the hardware options embrace a mainframe configuration costing millions of pounds, a mini-computer configuration costing tens or hundreds of thousands of pounds, and an entry-level personal computer which costs about one thousand pounds. The scope of modern hardware is best illustrated by taking a sample of products in use in 1990. All the types and ranges of computer mentioned below are being continuously improved. (In the following descriptions one megabyte is one million characters. One gigabyte is one thousand million characters.)

- *A typical mainframe*

(Based on the ICL Series 39 mainframe.)

Central processor − Memory 256 to 1024 megabytes (Model SX 580−20)

Magnetic disk units − 5000 megabytes per unit (FDS5000)

Impact printer − 2000 lines per minute (FP2000)

Mainframe configurations constructed from such equipment often consist of two or more processors with total disk capacities measured in tens of gigabytes and they can support hundreds of VDUs. Large mainframe configurations require special computer rooms with air-conditioning. Mainframe sales in the UK might be measured in hundreds for a popular range of machines.

- *A typical mid-range computer or mini-computer*

One example of a mid-range computer is the IBM AS/400. A representative model (the B35) would have a maximum memory of 40 megabytes, a disk capacity up to 13.7 gigabytes, and supports up to 160 VDUs. Minicomputers can often run in an ordinary office environment. A top of the range mini-computer would compete with a small mainframe, whilst a small mini-computer would compete against a multi-user micro-computer system. The AS/400 series is exceptionally popular with sales of 150 000 computers world-wide by 1990.

- *A typical personal computer*

A typical office example would be an IBM-compatible personal computer from a supplier like Compaq or Amstrad. It could have a colour screen, four megabytes of memory, and 110 megabytes of fixed disk. There would be a small printer capable of operating at 300 characters per second or a laser printer capable of printing several pages per minute. Sales volumes can reach millions of machines world-wide.

- *Telecommunications*

One key feature of modern computing on both a small and large scale is the importance of telecommunications for transmitting data. These may be LANs (Local Area Networks) or WANs (Wide Area Networks). LANs cover one business site such as an office block. WANs generally use the public telephone system, on a regional, national, or international basis. A chain of retail shops scattered across the country provides an example, as each shop can transmit their sales details to a central computer. Even in a small office the personal computers are frequently linked together in a local area network.

Telecommunications involves special hardware such as multiplexors which allow several devices to share one communications link. Special software is needed to control the transmission of data. Special services are also required such as those provided by a telephone company. Telecommunication links can have speeds of millions of characters per second, e.g. by using optical fibres. However slower links are common where speeds are measured in hundreds of characters per second. As a VDU screen can contain up to two thousand characters this means that when using slower lines it can take a few seconds to transmit enough data to fill a screen.

- *Input output devices*

Most business computer systems rely on VDUs and small printers as input and output peripherals. However there is plenty of scope for the analyst to use more specialist peripherals in the system design. Many devices such as light pens and mice are commonly found on technical systems including systems development workbenches (see Section 4.6 below). Mice have also become popular on business systems. Some examples of special input methods relevant to business systems are listed below.

(1) Bar-codes are one of the most commonly met forms of computer input. For instance in retailing bar-code readers can be part of a POS (Point of Sale) system which records sales.

(2)   OCR (Optical Character Recognition) allows text readable by a human being to be scanned directly into a computer.

(3)   MICR (Magnetic Ink Character Recognition) is used with cheques. These contain magnetic ink characters which can be read both by humans and machines.

(4)   Magnetic stripes on plastic cards contain data readable by a variety of terminals including retail point-of-sale payment systems.

(5)   Voice output has been available for many years but it is not widely-used in business systems. Practical voice input systems are in their infancy.

● *Further examples of special devices*

(1)   Time-and-attendance terminals are an example of special terminals that can employ several input technologies. These terminals are used to record the arrival or departure of employees who place their computer-readable identity card into a terminal. The cards can use barcodes, or a pattern of holes, or magnetic stripes to contain the identifying information. (See Fig. 16.6 for an illustration of how these terminals are linked to a payroll computer system.)

(2)   One way of protecting confidentiality is by encrypting data transmitted over a communications link. Encryption hardware inserted into the link can translate the electronic messages into secret codes to safeguard the transmitted data. If the line is 'tapped' the message is undecipherable. A decryption device turns the message back into the original form.

(3)   Portable and laptop computers have become popular and can be used to collect sales order data. For instance salesmen can take orders for goods from shop-keepers, and transmit the details by telephone line back to head office. Another example is their use in life assurance where the salesman or saleswoman can enter the details of a potential client. The laptop can then produce financial planning projections, to help sell life assurance and pension policies.

(4)   A PDET (Programmable Data Entry Terminal) is a hand-held portable device which allows the user to enter data into the terminal where it is stored for later automatic transfer to the main computer system. PDETs can be used for stock-taking or stock-checking where the current number of items in stock is counted

by the user and entered into the hand-held terminal rather than written onto stock sheets.

(5) Optical disk drives have been introduced slowly over the last few years and could compete with magnetic disks in the future. Currently one single optical disk unit from Kodak can store 75 gigabytes.

(6) A more expensive and exotic device is an RCS (Robotic Cartridge System) from ICL. This can contain thousands of magnetic tape cartridges within a 'library module'. The cartridges are bar-coded and accessed by a robotic arm under the control of a Series 39 computer. The arm places the cartridges in a drive unit to transfer data to or from the computer. The maximum capacity of an RCS is about one terabyte (1000 gigabytes or a million million bytes).

4.4 Standard software

Systems development staff have a series of design choices to make in connection with computer equipment. As regards software, some major elements in a typical computer system are described below.

● *The operating system*

Perhaps the most fundamental decision is choosing the operating system which controls the hardware and provides the environment for other software. To some extent the decision is made when the hardware range is selected. So ICL Series 39 mainframe computers use VME (Virtual Machine Environment) as the operating system. As another example, IBM-compatible personal computers use PC-DOS (Personal Computer Disk Operating System) or the more recent OS/2 (Operating System/2). In modern PCs the GUI (Graphical User Interface) handles the screen, mouse, and keyboard to produce elegant and easy-to-use displays for controlling the computer. Some GUIs like Microsoft Windows can be seen as a partner of the operating system. The Unix operating system is popular as a means of achieving compatibility on smaller computers. Unix is supported by many computer manufacturers, including companies like ICL and IBM who also have their own proprietary operating systems.

- *Language software*

Business software is commonly programmed in 3GLs (Third Generation Languages) like COBOL (Common Business Oriented Language). A 3GL uses statements that resemble English or mathematics, but it may take over a hundred carefully written statements (instructions or 'code') to write even a simple program, say, for printing a list of supplier details from a purchase ledger file. Many programs are much larger, and programs over 1000 instructions in length are common. The time taken to write and test software written in 3GLs makes them relatively expensive to use. A carefully produced commercial third generation program could easily take an experienced person over a month. However one main advantage of 3GL software is that it runs on many different types of computer.

4GLs (Fourth Generation Languages) such as FOCUS and INGRES make it easier to write software compared to using 3GLs. They usually require far fewer instructions to do a particular job — say about ten instructions to print off the list of supplier details mentioned above. This makes it significantly cheaper and quicker to develop software than using a 3GL. However they tend to use more computer resources such as memory and processor time, and each one is confined to a limited range of computers.

- *Software packages*

The word 'package' is computer and business slang for any collection of items, particularly a standardised one. An example would be an employee's remuneration package, i.e. the pay rates and benefits like sick pay, holidays, and a company car. In computing the term package sometimes refers to a collection of standardised hardware, software, and support services. It frequently applies to a collection of standardised software alone.

Software packages are popular in business application areas like payroll and accounting. Here there are many major similarities in administrative procedures and computer requirements between various businesses. This makes it worthwhile to provide standard software. Some well-known examples of application packages are the UNIPAY payroll package from Peterborough Software which is available on a wide range of mainframe and other computers. Another example is the Sage accounting packages which are popular with micro-computer users. The users can accept the package as it comes, and even though it may not meet their requirements perfectly it is much cheaper than writing 'bespoke' software to meet their needs more exactly. Many packages are designed to be flexible so that they can be 'tailored' (adjusted) to meet the users requirements. This is the case with UNIPAY. It should be noted that operating systems, programming language software, and database systems are really standardised software packages, although they are not often described in this way.

- *Databases*

A database may be viewed as a complex computer file holding fields of data on several subjects simultaneously. One example is a human resources database which holds all the data for payroll, personnel, and pensions purposes. Using a database means that duplicated data is avoided or reduced, and that it is easy to access data from several different business areas simultaneously. The software which organises the accessing and use of this common data is called a DBMS (Database Management System). So with a human resources database a DBMS would easily allow a computer report to be produced combining personnel and payroll data. Examples of database management software are INGRES, ORACLE, IDMS, and DB2. A DBMS is often combined with a 4GL as is the case, for instance, with INGRES and ORACLE.

- *Communication software*

There is a vast variety of standard software for managing computer networks. At the small end an example is micro-computer software such as Datatalk which allows a PC to communicate over a telephone line with another computer. At the large-end there is mainframe 'transaction processing' software, e.g. CICS (IBM's Customer Information Control System). This can manage a large number of VDUs linked simultaneously to different software modules or programs running on a mainframe for applications like order processing or insurance administration.

There are of course many standard software elements in a major business computer system. For instance a sort utility is a program which allows the records on a disk file to be sorted into any sequence, e.g. sorting a list of customer records by name into alphabetic order.

4.5   Other types of business automation

Systems analysts can employ other forms of business automation. Some examples are listed below.

- Communications devices such as portable telephones and fax.
- Office equipment such as paper-shredders, or sealing machines which fold and seal computer-printed output to form a letter ready for posting.
- Microfilm for storing images of ordinary documents. COM (Computer Output on Microfilm) involves automatically putting computer print-outs onto microfilm.

Systems analysts may also be interested in business services such as on-line database services or EDI (Electronic Data Interchange). With EDI a telecommunications network service is used to link the computers of two different organisations, e.g. to convey invoices between them.

4.6   Systems development automation

Systems analysts and programmers can employ the power of modern computing to help them produce and maintain business systems. The software products which help with systems development are often called 'software tools'. The more comprehensive and advanced sets of software tools are usually called CASE (Computer Aided Software Engineering). 'Front-end' CASE is used by analysts and managers. 'Back-end' CASE is designed for programmers. Basically software tools improve productivity and quality. Just some of the software tools that are available to systems analysts include:

- Word processors − much of a systems analyst's work consists of preparing documentation so a good word processor with a spelling checker is indispensable.
- Diagramming software − enables analysts to produce and edit diagrams of office procedures and system designs.
- Desktop publishing (DTP) − this is useful for writing manuals and preparing computer sales literature in a software house.
- Presentation graphics software − systems for producing elegant

graphical illustrations such as pie charts. These are useful when preparing IT training courses.

- Spreadsheets − for instance products such as Lotus 1−2−3 can be used to prepare the costing of a proposed new IT system.
- Project management software − these packages are, for instance, useful for planning and controlling the development of a new large business system.
- Testing tools − a whole series of software tools exists to help systems analysts and programmers test their software. For instance a coverage analysis could be produced showing how much of a program had actually been executed during a test. See Section 26.13 for further details.
- Performance tools − these are used by both systems analysts and computer operations staff to analyse the performance of existing operational systems or predict the performance of future systems. For example monitoring software could reveal that critical programs involved too many disk accesses. The software could then be redesigned to eliminate the unnecessary accesses and speed up the processing.
- Analyst's workbenches − workbenches incorporate an integrated set of software tools to support a particular role like analysis and programming. An example of an analyst's workbench is Excelerator from INTERSOLV. These workbenches streamline the development of specifications allowing the production of all the analysis and design diagrams plus other documentation. Analyst workbenches are often linked to a particular systems development methodology such as SSADM.

Programmers also use a wide range of software tools to write software. The simplest and most basic tool is an editor which allows them to write their program code, for instance COBOL instructions, directly into the computer. Much more sophisticated are programmer's workbenches which can for instance automatically generate most of the required COBOL instructions from program design diagrams. Furthermore such workbenches can allow programs can be viewed whilst they are actually running in order to identify faults.

An elementary software tool like a personal computer word processing package can cost a few hundred pounds. By way of contrast the more extensive and sophisticated CASE tools running on mainframes can cost over £100 000 (for the software alone). The above list of software tools concentrates on those used by analysts and programmers. Software tools are abundantly available for related occupations such as business planning and industrial engineering.

4.7 Systems integration

One of the jobs of the systems analyst is 'systems integration', i.e. selecting the most appropriate technological components and fitting them harmoniously together to create a new or amended business IT system. However hardware and software from different sources are often incompatible and frequently cannot operate together. As the incompatibility is not always apparent, systems integration demands considerable care. One purpose of an IT strategy is to minimise compatibility problems. Computer manufacturers are progressing towards 'open systems', i.e. mutually compatible hardware and software. However there is some scepticism about suppliers producing truly open systems and making it possible to mix products from different suppliers in an easy fashion. There is also a tendency towards introducing new technology on a piece-meal basis, creating 'points of automation' or 'islands of automation'. The disadvantage of this is that the benefits of integration can be lost.

4.8 Technical progress

As discussed in Chapter 3, information technology has been continuously evolving for over 100 years. The process shows no signs of stopping and the technology discussed in this chapter is already out-of-date in terms of what is emerging from research and development laboratories as commercial products. However advertising and articles in the technical press tend to create a false impression of current technology as they mostly represent the latest concepts and products. As already implied, hardware can, in practice, remain in use from five to seven years. Software, with amendments, can remain in use for well over a decade. This leads to a mixture of old and new technology co-existing in one business organisation. As an extreme illustration the author visited one local authority in the late 1980s and was amazed to see punched cards in use, as well as a fourth generation language and personal computers. In most organisations punched cards disappeared over a decade before!

As the outline of IT history in Section 3.2 implies, administrative systems in established businesses have been continually amended and upgraded to use the latest technology. This process shows every sign of continuing indefinitely. In general technical progress requires an orderly planned transition from the old to the new for both IT suppliers and their customers. Basically they must both continually update to meet the threats and opportunities, and to remain competitive. A recent example of the effect of new technology is found in life assurance where image processing can be used for paperwork such as pension policies. These can be scanned, and the image stored and retrieved electronically. This reduces the need for the storage of paper documents, and provides staff with immediate access via a terminal instead of having to hunt for a paper file. One result is considerably improved customer service when dealing with queries.

When a machine has reached the end of its life the original supplier has the advantage over others in providing new equipment. See Section 3.3 on upgrading.

4.9   Other application areas

This book concentrates on administrative IT. However, similar technology is employed in other application areas such as medicine, the police, the armed forces, and science. Typical applications include databases of criminal records, battlefield computers to control artillery, and weather forecasting with fast supercomputers.

4.10   Summary

- An IT strategy is a long-term plan for the computer systems to be used by an organisation. Policies which are part of the IT strategy lay down the type of software and hardware to be employed as well as plans establishing the priority and timetable for future systems development work. This framework eases the problem of selecting from a plethora of hardware, software, and services.

- Systems analysts need a good working knowledge of a wide variety of standard hardware and software components.
- Systems developers need to use software tools such as spreadsheet systems or an analyst's workbench to boost their personal and collective productivity.
- One major responsibility of the systems analyst is integrating hardware, software, and services from different sources to operate successfully together.
- Open systems considerably ease the problems of integration. They are an important development which should allow organisations to choose their IT suppliers more freely.
- Technological progress forces a continual revision of business systems. Ease of transition from the use of old technology to new is an important consideration.

Part 2
Business Administration and Management

Chapters 5 to 16 give the principles of business administration and management concentrating on those aspects that are of particular interest to the IT practitioner. Chapter 16 illustrates the application of business and computer concepts through a study of payroll administration.

Chapter 5
Business Background

5.1 Introduction

This chapter concentrates on describing the economic and legal background to business. This is an important subject as ultimately everything of interest to systems analysts is determined by the business environment in which they operate. Amongst many other things the business environment determines the nature of the technology employed, the projects undertaken, and the salaries received by IT staff. As a simple example at the time of writing (mid 1992) the UK is in the midst of a serious economic recession. Most businesses, including IT companies, are suffering in terms of reduced sales and profits. This has led to cutbacks on major projects and unemployment for some IT staff.

5.2 Business environment

An organisation sets out to achieve certain objectives and must of necessity interact with its environment whilst doing this. In the case of a trading concern the objective is making a profit in a particular market like dairy produce or aerospace. For local and national government the objectives are the provision of public services such as policing. Figure 5.1 illustrates the interaction of a manufacturing company with its environment. Many of the computer systems in use in such a manufacturing company are concerned with its business environment. For instance suppliers send invoices for goods delivered. The customer must then record what is owed on a purchase ledger system until the supplier is paid, perhaps by a computer-printed cheque.

5.3 Types of organisation

Systems analysts may meet several different types of organisation during their work. This is particularly true of analysts working for software

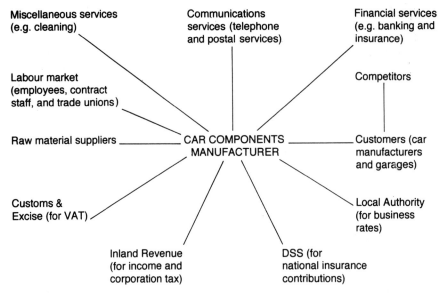

Miscellaneous services
(e.g. cleaning)

Communications
services (telephone
and postal services)

Financial services
(e.g. banking and
insurance)

Labour market
(employees, contract
staff, and trade unions)

Competitors

Raw material suppliers

CAR COMPONENTS
MANUFACTURER

Customers (car
manufacturers
and garages)

Customs &
Excise (for VAT)

Local Authority
(for business
rates)

Inland Revenue
(for income and
corporation tax)

DSS (for
national insurance
contributions)

Fig. 5.1 A simplified view of the business environment of a manufacturing company. Information, as well as money, goods, and services, flows along most links. Systems analysts are particularly interested in the information flows such as sales orders from customers.

houses. There are several ways of classifying businesses and some general categories are listed below. Needless to say these classifications are fairly rough and ready.

5.4 Classification by purpose and ownership

One of the most important distinctions is between profit making and non-profit-making organisations. The word 'business' traditionally implies an organisation trading for a profit, although there is an unfortunate tendency to extend the word to imply any kind of organisation. The most common profit-making organisations are ordinary trading companies in activities like retailing or manufacturing. Non-profit-making organisations include local authorities, the civil service, trade unions, and charities.

Another distinction is between private and public sector organisations. Whilst there is no doubt that the armed forces belong to the public sector, and the corner shop to the private sector, there is a grey area between the two sectors. This depends on the enthusiasm of politicians for nationalisation or privatisation. So for instance the UK steel industry has been transferred from private to public ownership and back again.

For the UK economy in 1990 the workforce of about 28.5 million was divided as follows:

- Unemployed   1.6 million
- Public sector   6.0 million
  (Armed forces,
  central government,
  local government,
  public corporations)
- Private sector (Includes   20.9 million
  about 3 million self-
  employed)

There is also a 'third sector'. This consists of non-profit making organisations such as the Girl Guides and Red Cross with a high proportion of unpaid volunteers.

5.5 Economic classification

The traditional classification of economic activities is:

- Primary   – the extraction of natural resources, e.g. by mining and farming.
- Secondary – the conversion of natural resources into useful products, for example manufacturing, food processing, and construction.
- Tertiary   – the provision of services, e.g. insurance and health care.

The following figures for 1990 give an analysis of the UK employees by economic sector:

- Primary sector   4%
- Secondary sector   33%
- Tertiary sector   63%

As can be seen in terms of employment the UK economy is primarily a service economy. The figures show the result of one of the key trends over the last couple of decades — the decline of UK manufacturing and the rise of service industries.

5.6 Some IT industry statistics

IT companies are amongst the largest and most important companies in the world. The world's top 50 industrial companies each had sales over £15 billion per annum in 1990. They include Sumitomo, General Motors, Mitsubishi, Exxon, British Petroleum, and Unilever, as well as the IT companies IBM and ATT (American Telephone and Telegraph). The largest British company in terms of employment in 1990 was an IT business, namely British Telecom with 247 000 employees. ICL is the largest computer manufacturer in the UK with about 20 000 employees.

Many major computer companies are American and some statistics published in 1991 are:

Company	Annual Sales Billions $	Employees
IBM	63.4	383 000
DEC	12.9	126 000
Hewlett Packard	11.9	95 000
Apple	5.3	12 000
Compaq	2.9	9 700

Some companies like Hitachi (Japanese) and Siemens (German) are comparable with IBM in terms of sales and employment, but a significant proportion of their activities lies outside computing.

There were believed to be over 150 000 systems analysts and programmers in the UK in the late 1980s. There was a comparable number of other IT staff such as managers and computer operators.

Some forecasts were then suggesting a total UK staff shortage of over 50 000 analysts, programmers, and IT managers in the 1990s. However as already indicated, the recession of 1991/1992 has led to unemployment in computing.

5.7 Legal classification of organisations

Organisations can adopt a multitude of different legal forms depending on their objectives. Some major types of business which IT staff might meet are as follows:

- *Sole traders*

The term sole trader refers to the ownership, and not the number of participants in a business. Thus a sole trader often has employees. Operating as a sole trader is suitable for small businesses such as shopkeepers or self-employed plumbers. There are some income tax advantages attached to self-employment and there is no need to reach agreement with anyone else on the management of the business. Also there are fewer formalities, e.g. there is no legal requirement to prepare audited accounts. The main disadvantages with sole trading are the unlimited liability of the owner of the business for its debts, the difficulty of sharing management responsibilities, and the problem of raising extra capital. Unlimited liability means that the owner must not only pay any business debts from the assets of his or her business, but where these are inadequate the sole trader must use personal assets. For example a sole trader might have to sell his house to meet the debts of his insolvent business. IT staff may meet sole traders in the form of small businesses tendering for work like installing power and signal cabling for office equipment.

- *Partnerships*

Basically partnerships occur where sole traders agree to pool resources and act together. Partners still have unlimited liability for the debts of the business. However they at least partially overcome the problems of people working alone in business. Also as each partner can contribute it is easier to raise capital. Inevitably the degree of formality is increased, e.g. there has to be an agreement on how the profits are to be shared. Partnerships are most commonly met amongst solicitors and accountants in private practice. As partners are self-employed any tax advantages are similar to those of sole traders.

- *Companies*

The company is a very popular form of organisation – there are about one million registered companies in the UK. Basically a company is the most suitable legal form where the trading activities are carried out on a significant scale. The nature of companies is discussed in Section 5.9 below.

The legal form of a business such as partnership is obviously important with regard to issues like income tax and personal liability. However in many situations the economic reality is that of owner-managers whatever the legal form.

5.8   Other types of organisation

There are many types of organisation recognised by English law. Important examples are the Crown and local authorities. The Crown in this context is a euphemism for the British state. For IT staff it is usually met in the form of the civil service, i.e. as government departments like the Inland Revenue or Customs and Excise. The civil service has been a major employer of IT staff.

The other reason for the importance of national or local government is of course their legal powers and the seemingly endless regulations which they impose on ordinary businesses. A common example is PAYE legislation which is administered by the Inland Revenue. All these regulations significantly affect the design and operation of administrative computer systems.

Other types of organisation include: chartered bodies such as the British Computer Society; co-operatives; trade unions; building societies; and friendly societies (a misleading name as they are a kind of life insurance company).

All these types of organisation have their own unique legal framework, for instance local authorities are controlled by the Local Government Act 1972 and various other Acts of Parliament. Some types of business may be subject to special regulation in addition to general business law. Insurance companies are an example.

5.9 Companies

Companies are probably the most important type of business organisation. The main advantages of a company compared to most other forms of organisation are:

- *Limited liability*

The owners of a company are the shareholders (often called the 'members'). In the case of the company becoming insolvent the members can only lose the value of their shares. Their personal assets are secure from any creditors.

- *Transferability*

Shares can be issued by a company, and transferred from one person to another with relative ease.

- *Ease of raising finance*

Shares can be sold by a company to provide capital.

- *Incorporation*

A company is a corporation, i.e. something akin to a natural person in terms of legal rights like owning property. A company is a legally distinct entity from its owners and for all intents and purposes potentially immortal, i.e. it can continue to exist forever despite changes in ownership when shares change hands. The process of creating an organisation with an independent legal existence is called 'incorporation', hence the American abbreviation 'inc' (incorporated).

Collectively the shareholders ultimately control a company. An example of a very large company is British Telecom PLC which had 1 200 000 shareholders in 1989. By way of contrast a small private company might be controlled by a handful of people (one is now the legal minimum). In theory, and often in practice, a company operates by the shareholders electing directors to manage the company. Shareholders may, of course, elect themselves as directors, and often do in small companies. The shareholders (or members) can control a company by appointing directors to act in their interests. Holding a majority of shares is usually sufficient to guarantee control of a company. The directors are effectively employees of the company, even if they own its shares. The profits of a company are paid out on the recommendation of the directors as a dividend for each share issued. Typically some of the profits are not distributed to shareholders but retained in a company for business expansion.

The company has proved to be a good legal form for business activities, hence its popularity, and most IT businesses are companies. The two main types of company are private limited companies (usually just described as limited companies), and a public limited companies (PLCs or just public companies). The distinction is primarily that an ordinary limited company can only sell its shares privately, whereas a PLC can openly advertise and sell its shares to the public. The shares of a PLC are often traded on the stock exchange.

Another type of company which is often met is the 'guarantee' company. This is a legal form adopted by non-profit-making organisations such as professional associations like the IMS (Institute of Management Services). Guarantee status offers similar legal advantages to an ordinary limited company such as a legal existence independent of its members. The word 'guarantee' is often a slight misnomer and refers to the fact that the member's liability to any creditors of the company is limited to a financial guarantee which is often nominal, for instance one pound.

All types of companies must be registered and provide fairly detailed information about their activities, both whenever there is a significant change and annually. These details are sent to the Registrar of Companies and the information on each company is available for public inspection. For instance these details usually include the accounts and the names of directors and shareholders. This administrative chore and loss of secrecy is not a requirement for sole traders and partnerships. Another disadvantage is that owner directors of small companies are taxed as if they are employees, and not as if they were self-employed which is the case with a sole trader or partner. As already implied taxation of the self-employed can be more favourable than that for the employed. Company law imposes many standard rules on the administration of a company, such as the need for an annual general meeting (AGM) of the shareholders. Though complicated these rules are familiar and designed to protect the rights of the shareholder in particular. The net effect of company law and related legislation is to make the legal form of a company attractive for larger business operations.

It is difficult for self-employed people to act as a computer contractor and sell their personal skills, as for instance a programmer. The Inland Revenue tend to insist that so-called self-employed contractors are legally the employees of their clients. To avoid such tax and legal problems analysts and programmers usually form their own private limited companies. The contractor is then employed by his or her own company, and legally it is the company that sells the skills to a client business. This can impose a tax and administrative disadvantage on contractors, and is a clear case of the legal form (a company) being at variance with the economic reality (self-employment).

5.10 Importance of legal form to the systems analyst

The legal classification of businesses is important to IT staff. Most legal entities are subject to statutory controls and this has a significant effect on the administration and computerisation. For instance the Companies Act 1985, as amended, defines such matters as the format of accounts and auditing. Section 723 of the Companies Act also allows company share registers, which contain details of the shareholders, to be kept on a computer system. This is an important legal provision for PLCs with tens of thousands of shareholders.

5.11 Organisational objectives

Organisations are formed to pursue particular objectives. Local authorities for instance have to meet a whole series of responsibilities which can include maintaining roads and the provision of police and fire services. In the case of a company the objectives are legally published in a document known as the memorandum of association. However the memorandum is merely a general statement of the kind of business in which the company is involved. Some companies provide a 'mission statement' which declares what they see as fundamental to their activities. Thus J. Sainsbury PLC, the retail chain, stated its goals in its published accounts. These include being the leaders in its trade, providing unrivalled value to its customers, achieving the highest standards of hygiene and customer service, and offering staff outstanding opportunities. Clearly these statements provide IT staff (and all employees) with a framework of business values.

The word 'vision' is sometimes used to indicate a generalised and invariably optimistic future towards which an organisation or department can move. Of more direct relevance are the strategies and long-term business plans of an organisation. These can dictate what systems are needed to serve the interests of the business. Take for example a business which has long-term plans to reduce manufacturing, and develop the wholesaling of products from other companies. A business with these plans is unlikely to be interested in new factory production control systems. However it is likely to be interested in new software for controlling purchase orders. Business planning should mean that changing a few lines of COBOL in a computer program is a small but integral part of some long-term strategy. The strategy could be increasing sales through improved computer-based information. In some cases IT is so fundamental to the business that it becomes a major part of the business plan.

5.12   Business regulation: the importance of administrative law

One prime area of interest for systems analysts is the influence of the state, usually through business law and its effect on administration. Some examples can make the point:

● *Pensions*
The pension funds of UK employers and insurance companies can be large (some are worth billions of pounds). These pension funds must eventually pay people a retirement income maybe 50 years after they started work. Pension schemes are encouraged by tax and national insurance privileges. They must also be strictly controlled to prevent abuse and ensure that they meet their obligations. As a result pensions law is notoriously complex. The Social Security Act 1986 included several major changes to pensions legislation, amongst which was a major extension of personal pensions. The new types of personal pension meant that employees as well as the self-employed could have their own private pension scheme with an insurance company. This offered insurance companies and other financial institutions a superb opportunity to sell new pension policies. It also meant introducing new or changed computer systems to handle the administration which was covered by complex regulations, e.g. from the DSS (Department of Social Security).

● *Company secretarial systems*

A large group of companies might have 200 or more subsidiary companies. As already mentioned each one of these companies must make returns to the Registrar of Companies who is a government official. Figure 5.2 gives an example of the form that must be completed each time a company changes its directors. The volume of administrative work associated with these returns in a large group is such that it is worth computerising. There are personal computer packages which produce all the necessary forms which must comply with regulations made under the Companies Acts of 1985 and 1989. The computer system must also hold all the necessary records such as registers of directors for each subsidiary. Major producers of these systems responded to the Companies Act 1985 and to the arrival of powerful personal computers by the mid-1980s. By exploiting their professional expertise in company legislation they were able to design software packages and sell them in hundreds by 1990.

5.13   General business trends

There are several major factors and trends that affect the UK economy, and usually affect most businesses in some way. Just a few are mentioned in the following paragraphs.

5.14   International business

UK business has had a significant international component for centuries. However, over the last few decades, improved communications exploiting air transport and electronics has meant that business is far more international than in the past. As one simple example, and there are many, a well-known American database service called Dialog is sold in the UK. This links UK customers to a large database in America for an acceptable cost. For instance an on-line session interrogating the database for details about publications on food additives might cost 20 dollars. Such services would of course be impossible without efficient and relatively cheap telecommunications. A further example is producing software in Third World countries and exporting it to developed countries like the UK. In Third World countries, such as India, programming labour is cheap and plentiful.

BLUEPRINT Company Secretary
CHA 101

This form should be completed in black

288

Change of director or secretary or change of particulars.

Company number	**CN** _____ ☐
Company name	_____

Appointment

(Turn to following page for resignation and change of particulars).

		Day Month Year
Date of appointment	**DA**	┆ ┆ ┆ ┆
Appointment of director	**CD** ☐	Please mark the appropriate box
Appointment of secretary	**CS** ☐	If appointment is as a director and secretary mark both boxes.

Name * Style/ Title _____

Forenames _____

Surname _____

* Honours etc _____

Previous forenames _____

Previous surname _____

Usual residential address **AD** _____

_____

Post town _____

County/ Region _____

Postcode _____ Country _____

Date of birth † **DO** ┆ ┆ ┆ ┆ ┆   Nationality † **NA** _____

Business occupation † **OC** _____

Other directorships † _____

_____

_____

I consent to act as director/ secretary of the above named company

Consent signature   Signed _____   Date _____

* Voluntary details   † Directors only   **A serving director etc must also sign the form following.**

Fig. 5.2 An example of one the returns that must be made to the Registrar of Companies. This form, number 288, is used whenever one of the directors of a company changes. The form can be printed automatically by a company secretarial system such as Blueprint from Sapphire Business Systems. Paper forms are still an important means of transferring and storing business information. However they are progressively being replaced by their electronic equivalents.

International trade is limited, as in the past, where individual countries, or groups of countries like the European Community, impose import tariffs and other restrictions.

Another important aspect of international business is the role of multi-national companies operating in the UK. Examples are ICI, IBM, Nissan and Ford. These companies use subsidiaries in the UK and other countries, both for manufacturing and selling.

5.15 The European Community (EC)

The terms EC (European Communities or European Community), EEC (European Economic Community), or Common Market tend to mean roughly the same thing. The EC is an economic and political federation, currently of twelve western European countries, which includes for example Germany, France, Italy, Holland, Spain, and the UK. In 1987 the combined population of the EEC was 320 million, and for comparison the USA has a population of 234 million. Because the EC is both a political and trading association European legislation can have legal effect in the UK.

From 1992 the EEC hopes to achieve a 'single market'. Within the EEC this refers to:

- The removal of technical barriers — the harmonisation or standard-isation of different product regulations, technical regulations, business laws, and public sector procurement.
- The removal of physical barriers — effectively the removal of customs controls and internal immigration controls.
- The removal of fiscal barriers — this refers to the rules covering matters like banking, insurance, and VAT.

The purpose of the single European market is to remove trade barriers. A corollary of this is increased competition from continental organisations in the UK and at the same time it offers opportunities for British businesses in Europe. For software suppliers for instance this may mean providing systems and documentation in several languages. An interesting example of the effect of the EEC is the attempt to establish a standard European framework for systems development methodologies called 'Euromethod' which could incorporate SSADM (see Section 18.12). Another illustration is the EEC health and safety directive on computer screen displays.

5.16 An emphasis on free enterprise

In the 1980s there was a marked political distaste for direct involvement by the government in the economy. This has been summarised saying that the business of government is not the government of business! It was felt that both British and foreign experience demonstrated that state control and state intervention in the economy were a failure. There was a corresponding belief in the virtues of free-enterprise. According to this view direct government control of business is inefficient because of the inevitable bureaucracy. Also business decisions are made on political rather than economic grounds. Though outside the scope of this book there is a more general belief that governments are severely limited in their ability to tackle not only economic issues, but also social problems such as poverty and crime. In the economic sphere in the UK this belief has led to the privatisation of state-owned businesses throughout the 1980s, e.g. steel and telecommunications. It has also led to efforts to weaken the control of the state on its own organisations in order to promote economic performance. This is usually attempted by, at least partially, simulating free enterprise. This can be done in several ways. For instance central government has established a series of semi-autonomous executive agencies in place of ordinary civil service departments. An example is the Benefits Agency which makes social security payments for the DSS (Department of Social Security). In local government there is competitive tendering where local authority departments must compete against private-sector businesses for work such as refuse collection.

In large-scale private-sector business there has long been a similar emphasis. This is revealed as a preference for decentralisation where local divisions or subsidiaries have considerable autonomy, for instance in matters such as setting employee pay and conditions. There is also a greater willingness to sub-contract peripheral work rather than use employees. So for instance factory security guards can be provided by an external security company.

As far as IT staff are concerned this view, in both the private and public sector, can lead to decisions that minimise the use of employees for computer work. Computer employees can be minimised by the use of packages, software houses, contract staff, consultants, and facilities management (where an outside specialist company does the computing work for an organisation). In theory the decision to use outsiders rather than employees is subject to straight-forward cost-benefit analysis.

IT has always offered both individuals and companies many opportunities for enterprise. Lyons, a catering company, built the first administrative computer in the 1950s for its own use. It then sold computers commercially. There is every reason to believe that IT offers even greater scope for enterprise in the future. See also Section 29.5.

5.17 Human resources

There are many trends which affect the use of human resources, and some of these are discussed in Chapter 13. One key trend is the 'demographic crisis' where a falling birth rate is leading to a shortage of young recruits and an ageing workforce. Another is the increase in the flexibility of labour. This is discussed in Sections 6.11 and 13.6 and includes the use of temporary staff, ordinary staff being willing to do different jobs, and people working a variable number of hours per week according to business need. The decline in traditional manual and industrial work is often seen as associated with increasing employment of 'knowledge workers' such as lawyers or computer programmers. Clearly this changes the emphasis of human resources management.

5.18 Other trends

There are several major trends apparent, some of which have been developing over the last few decades. One is the decline of British (and American) industry with a concomitant rise in German and Far Eastern industry. Along with the decline in manufacturing jobs in the UK and America there has been a rise in the number of service jobs. It is usually assumed that there is a growing long-term demand for IT products and services. The recent changes in Eastern Europe with the collapse of communism must also lead to significant political and economic developments which will affect both government and business.

In addition to major economic and political developments there are general fashions which can be influential for a few years. One example that is particularly important to systems analysts is the increasing emphasis on quality management which is discussed in Chapters 15 and 26.

5.19 Summary

- There are three main sectors of economic activity: primary, secondary, and tertiary. In the UK, primary sector employment, e.g. in agriculture and mining is small, secondary sector employment such as that in manufacturing is still significant, but the tertiary sector (services) is of greater importance than either.
- IT companies such as IBM are amongst the largest businesses in the world. Large IT companies can employ over 100 000 people with an annual sales turnover exceeding $10 billion.
- The legal form of a business has important administrative implications. Aside from the public sector the most important business entities are sole traders, partnerships, and companies. Special types of organisation include the Crown (the state), local authorities, trade unions, and co-operatives.
- Business law has a significant affect on the work of the systems analyst as it leads to administrative requirements for IT systems like handling PAYE.
- Several business trends are important to systems analysts. These include the importance of international business and the European single market; a preference for more autonomy and competition in the running of business operations; flexible working; a growing IT market; and quality management.

Chapter 6
Business Organisation

6.1 Introduction

This chapter describes the formal principles of human organisations. It concentrates on ordinary businesses, although the same principles apply with other types of organisation such as a government department.

IT systems are designed to serve organisations, and the design of IT systems is significantly influenced by factors such as the division of an organisation into departments, sections, and jobs. Furthermore systems analysts have to make alterations to an organisation when they change peoples' jobs as part of amending or replacing an administrative IT system. Sometimes they are asked to help during a fundamental reorganisation of a business. Indeed the sister discipline of O&M (Organisation and Methods) includes the organisation of business activities as a major objective.

6.2 What is an organisation?

What is a 'business' and what is an 'organisation'? The issues can be demonstrated by taking the important example of companies quoted on the stock exchange which own and manage a group of businesses from their head office. Though the terminology is often confusing, the individual businesses in a group may be called subsidiaries, divisions, plants, factories, and business units. An example is British Aerospace which in 1990 consisted of over 50 subsidiary and associated companies at home and abroad. A subsidiary is a legally separate company where a majority of the shares are owned by the parent company. An associated company is one where the company concerned owns a significant minority of the shares. British Aerospace is an engineering group with subsidiaries whose activities include manufacturing aircraft, ammunition, and motor vehicles. Another UK example is the GEC group, which employs 120 000 in the UK. As the name General Electric

Company implies, the group has subsidiaries in electrical power equipment, telecommunications, and defence electronics. A 'conglomerate' is a company with diverse interests which have little in common. Hanson Trust is a contemporary example which owns subsidiaries such as Imperial Tobacco, London Brick, and Berec (which makes electric batteries). In the case of a conglomerate the objective is mainly financial and subsidiaries exist purely to make a profit, and not because they complement other activities within the group. The pattern of control and ownership within a group is illustrated in Fig. 6.1. A multinational company has major business operations in several countries, usually as subsidiaries of the parent company. In the case of the Ford Motor Company, which is based in Dearborn in the USA, there are 15 subsidiaries in Europe alone, one of which is in the UK.

The upshot of all this is that the question 'what is an organisation' is determined by the purpose of the discussion. To a systems analyst working on a stock control system the 'organisation' might be one factory of a subsidiary company as well as its stock depots scattered across the country. To another analyst in the same group of companies, working on a system for the group employee pension scheme, all subsidiary companies might be part of the same 'organisation'. The analysts in both cases are only interested in the parts of the organisation which are relevant to their system. However they need some awareness of the rest of the organisation so they can deal with inter-connected

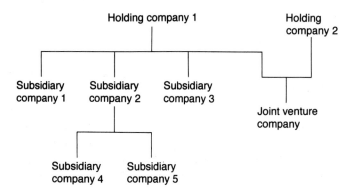

Fig. 6.1 The diagram shows the pattern of ownership and control in a group of companies. A holding company often wholly-owns a subsidiary. However holding enough shares to control the appointment of the directors is sufficient. Note that a subsidiary can also have subsidiaries and that some companies are jointly owned as shown.

systems. Thus the systems analyst working on stock control needs some awareness of the production and transport systems used to maintain stocks across the country.

Clearly an organisation like British Aerospace which in 1990 had a sales turnover exceeding £10 billion and 128 000 employees needs some way of organising them for effective management, and the usual way is to subdivide them into groups like divisions, subsidiaries, units, departments, and sections. These terms have variable meanings depending on the business. There are also other considerations. For instance the use of subsidiaries has several advantages, one being that it is easier to buy or sell legally separate businesses than untangle part of an existing business for sale. Companies often find it sensible to establish subsidiaries abroad. An obvious example is IBM United Kingdom Limited which is the UK subsidiary of the American International Business Machines Corporation. However it should not be forgotten that a subsidiary is primarily a legal concept, i.e. legally it is a separate company from the parent. This legal separation may or may not be significant in terms of day-to-day management.

6.3 The relationship with head office

The practical relationship between a subsidiary, division, or business unit, and the head office is very variable. Frequently a subsidiary company is left very much to its own devices with relatively few constraints. The financial controls are obviously important and there is usually a profit target that must be achieved. Other constraints could include avoiding competition with other members of the group, and the requirement to use certain common services such as a group pension scheme. Sometimes the constraints are strict and a factory in a group may have matters like its production and expenditure on new equipment rigidly controlled. The rules governing subordinate organisations are often available in writing, usually in a series of semi-confidential documents. Important examples are the policies on issues like local or national pay bargaining, and the plans detailing such matters as profit or sales targets.

As far as computer and management services staff are concerned the role of the head office of an organisation can be very important. Head office may determine the IT strategy of the whole organisation.

This could mean that the equipment of a particular computer supplier like DEC is imposed on all units within the organisation. Head office may provide special services to subsidiary businesses. For instance operations research (business mathematics) requires specialist skills which subsidiary companies may only require for a few weeks a year, and these can be provided by head office on a consultancy basis. The internal audit function is also often provided by head office. Another key aspect of the relationship with head office is when it asks for 'returns' or 'reports', i.e. summaries of business activities and particularly financial statistics. These are usually produced from the main computer systems of the subsidiary.

6.4   Centralisation and decentralisation

Where there is a set of subordinate units like factories or subsidiaries, the question of the degree of autonomy arises. A centralised arrangement can be adopted where the subordinate organisations are too small, or too specialised to be independent, or where they are to be strictly controlled. So in a centralised organisation many decisions are referred to the remote head office (the 'centre'). Some important functions, e.g. sales invoicing, may also be performed there. By way of contrast in a decentralised organisation many important decisions are taken by the local management, and they can operate their own services like payroll computing, or they can choose to contract out such work. Centralisation and decentralisation are basically a question of degree.

6.5   Business functions

The most important way of organising people in business is by the type of work they do, and by their authority. Figure 6.2 outlines the organisation of a classical manufacturing business, employing say 1000 people. Basically the shareholders appoint directors who manage the business functions of finance, personnel, production, and marketing. The nature of these business functions is explained in greater detail in Chapter 7. Other more minor functions such as purchasing or IT are managed as part of one of the main functions. For instance IT is often the responsibility of the finance director. Figure 6.3 shows the organisation of a

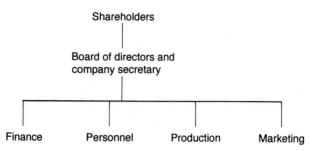

Fig. 6.2 The outline organisation chart of a medium-sized manufacturing company with about 1000 employees. There is usually a director in charge of each function. Figures 7.1 and 7.2 illustrate the possible organisation of the marketing and finance functions. In the common case of a subsidiary company where the parent company effectively owns all the shares the directors are often managers of the subsidiary or parent company. The company secretary's department of the parent company can provide all the company secretarial administration.

Fig. 6.3 An outline organisation chart for a software house employing about 70 people. The majority of staff would come under systems development which would include maintenance and customer support. The marketing director would be responsible for a few sales staff and marketing matters such as advertising. The company secretary would be responsible for the administration. This would mainly be accounts, routine personnel matters, and miscellaneous matters such as managing the premises.

smaller company of about 50 employees. It is a software house where the finance, personnel, and office administration are merged under a company secretary.

In an ordinary small business the IT function may be treated as simple office automation without any specialists. In this case any technical support for IT is provided by software houses and equipment suppliers. However because IT can be so vital it is not uncommon for companies of, say, 100 employees to have computer departments of two or three staff.

6.6 Other types of business

The previous chapter mentions that manufacturing employment has declined significantly in the UK since the 1950s. The same phenomenon has occurred in the USA. As a result, employment has shifted into service businesses such as banking and insurance. Figure 6.4 outlines the organisation of a large insurance company. Local and national government are also major providers of services and major employers in the UK.

6.7 Classical organisation theory

There are many theories on how to organise business. However one set of principles is still particularly influential and was enunciated by a series of management thinkers in the early part of the 20th century. The essence of these ideas was summarised by Scott as the 'pillars of classical organisation theory' which are:

- *The division of labour*

Work is divided into tasks, and a small number of related tasks makes up a job which can be performed by an individual. Specialisation of occupations, like those of the clerk or electrician, is an essential part of the division of labour. This allows people to become good at a small manageable set of related tasks rather trying to learn many tasks inefficiently.

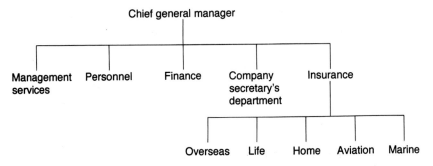

Fig. 6.4 The organisation of a large composite insurance company selling both life and general insurance.

- *The chain of command (the hierarchy)*

This provides a line of authority moving down an organisation from the most senior to the most junior positions. Unity of command, where each employee has only one boss, is usually an important part of this.

- *Span of control*

There is a limit to the number of subordinates that one person can control. The actual number of people per superior varies considerably, although six is often considered the optimum.

- *Structure*

Employees and the tasks they perform have to be grouped into rational units such as departments, sections, and teams, which carry out a set of related business functions such as accounting.

The principles enunciated above are clearly ancient, even though first expressly formulated in this century. They have for example been intuitively followed in the past, particularly by armies and navies. The application of these principles leads to the familiar organisation chart. The example in Fig. 7.1 gives some idea of the complexity of medium-sized businesses in terms of the chain of command and specialists that come under just one main function like marketing.

Organisation charts illustrate hierarchies. 'Flat' organisations have few levels in their hierarchy as opposed to 'tall' organisations which have many levels, e.g. Fig. 7.1. Flat organisations are often considered desirable, one reason being that the communication routes from senior to junior staff are short. However a flat organisation can mean wide spans of control, i.e. each boss has many subordinates, and there is a limit to this. One modern approach is to 'delayer' tall organisations by reducing the number of middle management levels. New technology and alternative approaches to management can help overcome the problems of flat organisations.

To the systems analyst an organisation chart is particularly useful when operating in a new business area. It can illustrate to some degree:

- The functions and jobs performed.
- The number of people in various categories.
- The names of individuals (not always shown).
- The demarcation of responsibility.

- The lines of authority.
- The formal channels of communication.
- The relationship between departments and employees.

An examination of Fig. 7.1 should demonstrate these points. The principles of classical organisation theory are clearly useful for designing a set of jobs under a supervisor or manager. Though there are exceptions, a systems analyst's role in restructuring a department is often limited and advisory. The management make most of the decisions, sometimes constrained by trade unions. It is a common complaint that O&M (Organisation & Methods) is in practice only a little O with a lot of M!

6.8   Other aspects of classical organisation theory

- *Bureaucracy*

In a neutral sense a bureaucracy is a formal hierarchical organisation with well-defined jobs, i.e. it conforms with Scott's pillars. Bureaucracies are traditionally associated with 'paper-work' organisations, e.g. the civil service and insurance companies. Though often criticised, bureaucracy can be effective for large organisations in stable environments.

- *Authority, responsibility, and delegation*

Authority is the legal power to do something. So for instance a computer systems development manager usually has the authority to instruct systems analysts or programmers to work paid overtime.

Responsibility is a natural consequence of organisational structure, and is the obligation to complete, or supervise the completion of certain activities. Examples are a systems programmer responsible for implementing a new version of a mainframe operating system, or a personnel officer responsible for supervising a recruitment campaign. If you are responsible for something, then you are accountable for the results, e.g. the systems programmer can legitimately be blamed for failing to install the latest version of the operating system satisfactorily, or is entitled to recognition if he is successful.

Delegation is where part of a superior's authority is transferred to a subordinate. Thus a systems development manager may delegate to a project leader the job of establishing the holiday roster amongst systems analysts and programmers.

● *The organisational pyramid*

It is usual to represent a business as a pyramid similar to that shown in Fig. 6.5. This is supposed to summarise the functions of the various levels in a hierarchical organisation and stress the fact that there are fewer people in the top levels. Decisions taken higher up the hierarchy tend to have consequences on a wider scale, e.g. a production director plans next year's factory output and a clerk plans to process a batch of forms over the next quarter of an hour. As each level in the organisational pyramid has different information requirements this view influences the design of computer systems. So a production director is likely to require an EIS (Executive Information System) with graphical displays of the production statistics for a whole factory. At a junior level an accounts clerk might need a VDU screen display showing payments made so as to answer a telephone query from a supplier.

● *Line and staff*

Classical theory emphasises the distinction between line and staff jobs. Line personnel are those who contribute directly to the business, e.g. those in production and sales. Staff personnel are those with an advisory or service role, e.g. management accountants and systems analysts advise and assist production managers. This distinction is less popular today, but still heard.

● *Functional organisation*

Much of what has been said so far implies that organisations are divided into functions like accounting, production, and selling. In its

Fig. 6.5 The traditional organisational pyramid showing the functions of the various levels in an organisation in general terms. Strategic activities imply long-term and large-scale outcomes, for example planning a new factory. Tactical activities imply the medium-term and medium-scale outcomes, for instance starting a new sales campaign. Operational activities imply the basic jobs done in an organisation, e.g. moving goods with a fork lift truck. The vertical direction is meant to imply status, and the width of each layer suggests the number of people involved.

extreme form this can mean for instance that a local finance manager takes his instructions directly from the group finance department at head office and not from anyone locally. Alternatively as implied in Section 6.4 the local organisation may be functional and reasonably autonomous, e.g. with large subsidiaries the local marketing director may have considerable discretion. As discussed below under divisionalisation, there are several ways of splitting up a large business into manageable units.

● *Divisionalisation*

Divisionalisation works on the assumption that the primary basis for dividing up an organisation is some factor like geographical area, products, or type of customer. Functions like personnel are regarded as secondary. Figure 6.6 illustrates a chemical business which has been divisionalised by the type of chemical produced.

6.9 Non-classical views of organisation

The classical view as discussed in Sections 6.7 and 6.8 is seen as outdated by some people. It can be regarded as belonging to a past with different business requirements and limited IT. For instance the primitive IT of the past made necessary an army of clerks processing information on paper, and the ˙classical bureaucracy was the only practical way to organise them. As a result a radical rethink of both business organisation and administration may be necessary to get the best out of new tech-

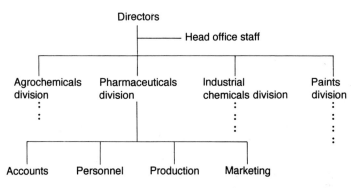

Fig. 6.6 The divisionalisation of a chemical company by the type of product where each division includes the functions of accounting, personnel, production and marketing.

nology. There can also be situations where significant business benefits, such as quick processing of insurance quotations and proposals, can come from a fundamental reorganisation (or 're-engineering') of office work. In these cases the IT helps, but sometimes the reorganisation itself can be the major factor in the improvement.

Modern and future business may be established on different organisational principles. For instance most forms of new technology will generally allow much smaller more responsive workforces with a greater economic output. Smaller workforces can be organised more flexibly and informally. They can be geographically scattered and linked together via modern telecommunications and IT. Also new innovative methods of business organisation may emerge. Some of the alternative ideas and refinements in organisational thinking are presented in the following sections. An opposing conservative view is that new technology and the classical principles of organisation merely need adapting to new circumstances.

6.10   Other views on organisation

The principles of classical organisation theory have been challenged for a long time, and particularly by more recent thinking. Just a few other ideas about business organisation are:

● *The value chain*
This is the set of activities that create a service or product for customers, e.g. buy goods, sell them, and provide after-sales support. Computer systems can partially automate or support value chain activities.

● *Functional management*
Not to be confused with functional organisation, this term is used for the old idea that a person may have a different boss for each aspect (function) of their work. This breaches the classical principle of unity of command. Thus a safety officer has authority over a factory worker in all safety matters rather than a foreman. In computing a standards officer, or a quality assurance analyst, may be able to tell systems analysts and programmers that their work needs adjusting to meet standards and quality requirements. However, their direct supervisor may be a project leader.

● *Matrix management*

This is a development of functional management which is influential in computing circles and discussed in Chapter 28. An example of matrix management is where an engineering project manager can call on the services of a draftsman, laboratory scientist, and purchasing officer, each contributing to the project but responsible to the boss of their own function. This means that to some extent people like the draftsman have two bosses − their ordinary manager and the project manager.

● *Multi-skilled teams and autonomous work groups*

The basic idea is that teams contain all the necessary skills and decide amongst themselves how to divide up the work, i.e. the allocation of duties is not fixed, but varies according to circumstances. Computer project teams often operate this way as the team members have all the analysis and programming skills needed. Some analyst-programmers may be able to do either job according to need.

● *Adhocracy*

This is almost the opposite of a bureaucracy. In an adhocracy work groups are continually being formed and dissolved according to business needs. There is no permanent organisational structure because of the continually changing nature of the work. Adhocracy is associated with industries like film-making and advertising. Some software houses are also adhocracies because of the continually changing customers and projects.

● *Informal organisation*

There is an unofficial social network in most organisations which is an important part of the way the business actually works. Section 14.4 discusses this further.

● *The systems approach*

The classical organisational view can be rather static. The systems view treats an organisation as a dynamic system composed of subsystems which interact with the environment. A business is viewed almost like a biological organism which seeks essentials like food from the environment and needs sub-systems for respiration and the circulation of blood. Thus a factory needs raw materials like sheet steel to survive and has sub-systems like raw materials purchasing and raw materials stores which operate to serve this need. One part of the systems approach concentrates on information flows such as the paper forms and electronic messages between the departments in a business. Obviously this approach is relevant to systems analysts. The systems approach is discussed further in Chapter 19.

6.11   The flexi-business and contracting-out

The classical organisation implies a relatively fixed hierarchical structure of permanent employees. An alternative supposedly modern idea is the flexi-business where the number and types of staff vary according to changing circumstances. With this model there is a small core workforce who are permanent full-time employees, and a large peripheral workforce. The peripheral workforce is composed of temporary staff, part-timers, and the self-employed (see Fig. 6.7). Further flexibility is gained by sub-contracting work to other businesses.

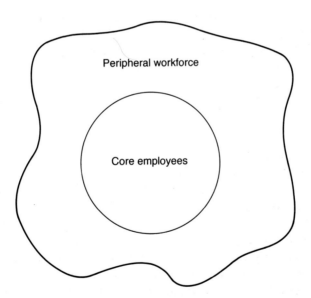

Fig. 6.7 The flexible organisation with a permanent core workforce surrounded by peripheral employees and contractors. The peripheral employees are temporary staff and part-timers. The contractors may be self-employed individuals or businesses. The use of peripheral workers and contractors may be changed according to circumstances. Even core staff may have to work flexibly, e.g. by changing jobs as required.

Flexibility is achieved by varying the peripheral workforce and contractors according to business needs. Flexibility also applies to
permanent employees as well, and they need to be multi-skilled and
work variable hours. This flexi-business approach is not particularly
new. Publishers for instance have always used one form of it by
contracting out work to authors, artists, photographers, and printers.
Also historically, the taking-on and laying-off of labour according to
business conditions was one of the causes of social discontent.

However, the flexible approach has undoubtedly become more
popular, e.g. there is a marked preference to contract out the fringe
activities of an ordinary business like catering or cleaning. A term
often used for contracting out computing work to other organisations is
'outsourcing'. An example is an ordinary business contracting out the
maintenance of its mainframe operating system software to a specialist
company.

Contracting work out has clear implications in computing. So the
selling of IT products is often done through intermediaries rather than
selling directly to customers. This reduces the need for a salesforce and
is done where a hardware supplier sells through a software house (an
agent). Another consequence is that ordinary systems analysts must be
prepared to manage outside suppliers like contract programmers rather
than deal with fellow employees.

6.12 Further details

This chapter has taken a rather legal and structural view of business
organisation. Using the word in a neutral sense, it has presented many
businesses as bureaucracies. Organisation theory often takes a more
sociological approach and the human factors in business are considered
in Chapter 14. The management aspects of organisations are considered
in Chapter 8, and the way IT is organised to serve a business is
considered in some detail in Chapter 28. The systems aspects of organisations are discussed in Chapter 19.

6.13 Summary

- Systems analysts need to understand the principles of organisation theory. This helps with tasks like IT systems design, job design, and organising departments.

- Groups of companies consist of subsidiaries which may be fairly autonomous or strictly controlled by head office depending on the degree of centralisation.
- The division into functions like personnel or accounting is an important feature of traditional business organisations.
- Classical organisation theory stresses the division of labour, chain of command, span of control, and structure.
- Other aspects of business organisation include matrix management, the informal organisation, and multi-skilled teams.
- New technology and changing business environments may encourage new and sometimes radical methods of organisation. One example is the flexi-business.
- There is currently, in both the public and private sector, an emphasis on contracting out all types of work to specialist individuals and organisations. Computing is significantly affected by this trend.

Chapter 7
Business Functions

7.1 Introduction

This chapter outlines the major business functions in a manufacturing company. The personnel and financial functions are broadly similar in most types of organisation, e.g. in a retail company or local authority as well as a factory. However functions like 'sales and marketing' or 'production' have no obvious analogue in other types of organisation such as a civil service department.

The major role of IT staff is to provide the computer systems and services which support the administrative and managerial functions in an organisation. Many computer systems do this by serving primarily one function, e.g. a sales ledger system serves the accounts department by partially automating the management of sales debts. However computer systems often require links between various functions. So a computerised pension system requires pension contributions data from the payroll system. A company pensions system may also need basic employee details from the personnel department. Where a database system is used, the same data can in principle be shared between functions like accounts and production. For example a production department could have access to figures of finished stock for planning production, and the accounts department could have access to the same data so that the value of stock could be included in the accounts.

The common business functions, such as marketing, outlined below, are also whole subjects and professions in their own right. Some systems analysts specialise in certain business functions, accounting for instance, as one way of producing and maintaining better IT systems. However the links between business systems mean that a general understanding of the main business functions is useful.

As already discussed organisation charts are important to systems analysts. For instance as Fig. 7.2 shows, they help the analyst understand the managerial relationship between functions like payroll and costing and allow analysts to identify whom to interview when investigating a system.

7.2 Business organisation

There is no one way of organising a company, and even similar-sized businesses in the same trade can be different in this respect. Figure 6.2 outlines the organisation of a traditional manufacturing business, employing, say, 1000 people. Basically the shareholders appoint directors who manage the main business functions of finance, personnel, production, and marketing.

By way of contrast the insurance company of Fig. 6.4 has a significantly different set of functions. Minor functions such as purchasing or IT are usually managed as part of one of the main functions. For instance, IT in a manufacturing business is often the responsibility of the finance director. Sometimes where a more specialist function is of considerable importance to a business, it has its own director, e.g. a research and development director. Where a company is part of a group some functions, and pensions administration is an example, may be handled by the head office of the parent company or by another subsidiary. Figure 7.1 gives some idea of the complexity of a large business in terms of the chain of command and specialist sub-functions that come under just one main function like marketing.

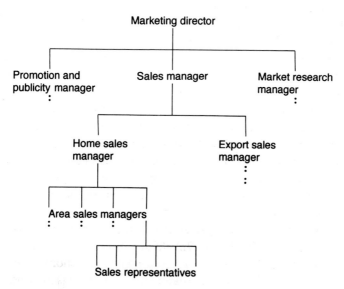

Fig. 7.1 The structure of a large marketing department.

7.3   The board of directors

In theory and sometimes in practice the ultimate authority for running a company lies with the shareholders. They establish the purpose of the company and appoint directors to carry out their wishes. However the board of directors, when acting as a formally constituted meeting, is the practical source of authority for most of the decisions in operating a company. This authority is often delegated to committees of directors, individual directors, and managers for specific purposes.

Some directors are executive, i.e. participate in the management of the company. So a finance director manages accounting administration. Other directors may be non-executive and they have no management responsibilities. They are usually part-time and there for various reasons such as representing the interests of major shareholders or providing business advice. The role of directors and the rules for conducting board meetings are contained in the 'articles of association' which are established when the company is founded.

7.4   The company secretary's office

It is a legal requirement for a company to have a secretary. Company law lays down many requirements for the administration of companies, and it is the secretary's job to ensure compliance. In a large group of companies the secretary of the parent company is responsible for legal obligations such as convening meetings of shareholders, organising the paperwork behind board meetings, maintaining the share register, new share issues, paying dividends, and dealing with the stock exchange. Other administrative responsibilities could include risk management, the company pension scheme, executive pay, and benefits such as company cars. Risk management is basically the control of the security and insurance arrangements for a company.

It is an enormous amount of work to maintain a share register and pay dividends for a quoted company with tens or hundreds of thousands of shareholders. In the past a company registrar was employed under the company secretary and managed a department handling the administration for this. Today the work is often given to a 'service registrar', frequently the subsidiary of a bank, which performs the registrar's function as a commercial service. The combination of complexity and volume makes share registration ideal for computerisation.

With a subsidiary company much of the paperwork associated with the company secretary's job is done by the group company secretary's department at head office. In a small company the company secretary may also be responsible for most office administration. In a very small company the company secretarial work together with other financial administration may be contracted out to an accountant in private practice. The 'one man' companies used by contract programmers and systems analysts tend to do this.

7.5   Finance

This function implies more than just accounting, and many important computer applications are financial. Chapters 11 and 12 discuss the theory of accounting and finance. Figure 7.2 illustrates the possible organisation of the various financial sub-functions. Typically the work is broken down as follows, with each activity often being the responsibility of a department or section ultimately controlled by the finance director.

- *The cashier's work*

The cashier's section is concerned with remittances (i.e. payments) in and out of the organisation. This involves controlling cash, cheques, bank accounts, and the like. Some businesses, like retailing, involve large amounts of cash. Where employees are paid in cash the cashiers

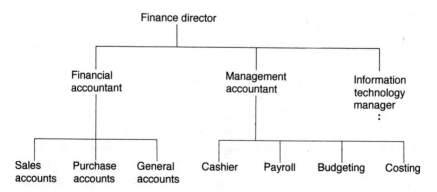

Fig. 7.2 The structure of a medium sized finance department. It is common in this situation to find the IT function under the finance director.

may make up the wage packets according to the instructions of a separate payroll department and actually hand out the wage packets.

● *Sales accounting*

This involves raising sales invoices and recording customer debts in the sales ledger. Credit control is an important part of the sales accounting work, and involves trying to ensure that debts are paid on time, ideally within a month of the customer receiving the goods. Unfortunately many commercial customers pay several months in arrears which means that the supplier is effectively giving the customer an interest-free loan. Other important parts of the credit control function include checking that new customers are credit worthy, and stopping delivery to 'delinquent' customers, i.e. those who do not pay within a reasonable time. A computerised sales invoicing and sales ledger system can help with all these jobs.

● *Purchase accounting*

This involves recording the debts owing to suppliers in the purchase ledger and paying them when due.

● *General accounting*

Depending on the organisation this can involve all the miscellaneous functions, e.g. accounting for expenses and the financial recording of fixed assets like plant and machinery. The prime responsibility however is the preparation of the final accounts − mainly the balance sheet and the profit and loss account.

● *Management accounting*

This section is concerned with setting budgets and costing.

● *Payroll*

The payroll staff are concerned with calculating wages and salaries and ensuring that the payment details are passed over to the cashiers. Besides employees there are other payees who receive the various deductions from pay. Some examples are the Inland Revenue for income tax and national insurance contributions, building societies for employee savings, and charities to which employees donate via the payroll. Payroll is discussed in depth in Chapter 16 as a function common to all organisations.

● *Internal audit*

In a large organisation there is often an internal audit department which is concerned with matters like security procedures and maintaining the quality and efficiency of the financial systems.

7.6 Personnel

The work involves matters like recruitment, industrial relations (dealing with trade unions), employee performance and appraisal, training, and welfare work. Chapter 13 discusses human resources management, which is another term for personnel work.

7.7 Production

The main job is to ensure that the factory produces goods. Much of the work is concerned with the supervision of the workforce and machinery in the main production areas. Subsidiary functions include store-keeping, factory maintenance, and production planning and control. Production planning involves determining future production and matters such as raw material requirements. Typically this is based on customer orders for bespoke (made to order) items, and forecast demand for standard items. Some businesses survive entirely on bespoke products. The nature of the planning process depends on the type of product and the production technology − clearly ships and plate glass are entirely different in this respect. Production needs to be controlled in the sense that production plans are not always met and corrective action must be taken to prevent shortfalls or surpluses compared to the plan.

7.8 Sales and marketing

In theory marketing is seen as the whole process of identifying and profitably satisfying the needs of the customer. The marketing function, which often includes the sales function, could include market research, advertising, salesforce management, and sales administration. Figure 7.1 shows the organisation of a large sales and marketing department. The marketing director may also be in charge of other areas such as distribution.

Marketing is often seen as the most fundamental business function. If the marketing is wrong then sales are poor and hence profits and employment are threatened. Basically if there are no happy customers then there is no business. Conversely good marketing will generate plenty of sales, good profits, employment, and general expansion. There are, of course, underlying assumptions here. One is that marketing is not only fundamental, but by implication difficult, and in competitive fields such as selling software packages this is often true. Also this view tends to assume that once the marketing is correct then other business functions such as personnel and production can, with relative ease, make their contribution to meeting customer needs profitably.

7.9   Distribution

This is a rather loose term which in a manufacturing company covers warehousing and transport (see below). The term also refers to wholesaling and retailing.

7.10   Warehousing

This may be taken to include both the warehousing of finished goods and their transport to the customer. The main job of the finished goods warehouse is to receive goods from the factory and other suppliers. Finished goods are of course often bought ready for resale even by manufacturers. The goods are stored and when the customer's order arrives the relevant goods are picked for delivery. Controlling the stock of finished goods can be a key requirement which requires computer assistance.

7.11   Transport

The management of transport services, usually via trucks, is a major operation for any organisation handling goods in volume whether they be pharmaceutical products or engineering components. The main function is to ensure that the goods are delivered to the customer who may be manufacturers, wholesalers, or retailers. In many cases transport work is contracted out to hauliers.

7.12 Purchasing

This department may come under production. In a large manufacturing company it assumes considerable importance as bought-in supplies are usually a large part of finished goods costs. Other issues like delivery and quality are also essential for smooth production. The purchasing department negotiate long-term contracts with suppliers of essential raw materials and components. They also buy in most other supplies such as computer stationery.

7.13 Importing and exporting

Importing and exporting are complex administrative processes, involving greater risks than home trade. Complications include foreign languages, currency, licences, and documentation. Further complications are technical standards, e.g. electrical equipment may operate at 120 volts rather than the 240 volts of the UK. The law and regulations applicable can be those of several different countries including the UK. Companies in the UK may arrange to export from one foreign country and import the same goods directly into another. Taking exports, the main jobs are:

- To ensure the product conforms with any technical requirements or other requirements of the country of destination.
- To arrange adequate documentation, e.g. consignment notes, shipping instructions, and customs forms.
- To communicate with overseas agents and branches.
- To arrange insurance, packing, and despatch by ship, truck, or air.
- To arrange payment via UK and foreign banks.

Export functions may be partly or fully contracted out to specialist businesses. For example one role of an 'export house' is to act as an agent of a manufacturer and handle matters like transport for overseas sales.

7.14 Design

The design of new or bespoke products is a common manufacturing function. Designs are produced in a drawing office and the details passed over to the planning office to arrange production. More modern practice is to design both products and their manufacturing processes together. This ensures that products are easy to manufacture. If a product is innovative, and not merely an improved or modified version of previous products, then it may be designed by the research and development department. The drawing office and production planning office usually originate much of the data concerned with manufacturing such as the part numbers of components, and the quantities of components and raw materials associated with each finished item. This data is used by computerised production planning systems.

7.15 Research and development (R&D)

Research and development for entirely new products tends to be a large company function, requiring special laboratories and workshops. Computer manufacturers have a good R&D record − indeed it is essential for their survival. Companies like ICL and IBM have been producing revolutionary new IT products for 50 to a 100 years. There has been a continual series of improved products from the punched card machine of 1920 to the mainframe of 1990 with its gigabytes of disk storage. The hardware technology has changed from being mechanical, to being based on electronic valves, then transistors, and now integrated circuits on silicon chips. One possible future for information technology is the greater use of optical devices. The research and development required to maintain this progress is expensive, but it is the price of staying in business.

However ultimately every business has to be prepared to innovate or go out of business, and this does not just apply to 'high tech' businesses such as aerospace and electronics. Part-time research and development work is often undertaken in smaller more traditional companies as part of another function like production.

7.16 Summary

- Systems analysts need a wide understanding of the functions in a business so that they can understand the data flow between departments and systems.
- Organisation charts are useful for purposes such as understanding the relationship between business functions.
- In a company the shareholders and the board of directors are the ultimate authority.
- It is a legal requirement for a company to have a secretary. The company secretary's function includes the administration of the legal responsibilities associated with running a company such as convening share-holders' meetings and maintaining the share register. Other functions such as pensions are often controlled by the company secretary.
- The functions that are common to all businesses are personnel and accounting (including payroll). Sales and marketing is a function common to most trading businesses.
- In manufacturing the production function involves managing the factory operatives and machinery plus the supporting functions such as store-keeping.
- Importing and exporting are complex administrative functions.
- Other functions such as purchasing, warehousing, and transport are often of major importance depending on the type of business.
- Some functions, e.g. transport may be contracted out.
- Continual research and development is the only way that a trading business can keep its products or services up-to-date.

Chapter 8
Principles of Management

8.1 Introduction

This chapter outlines the common core of business and technical management. However other chapters also contain material on management which is a very mixed subject. The most important of these chapters with management-related material are those on organisation, finance, human resources, quality, and the theory of systems. The last three chapters of this book concentrate on IT and project management.

In terms of formal theory there was little written on management before the 20th century, and most of that was of a political or military nature. From the beginning of the 20th century there was a rapid development of management studies particularly in America. However there were similar developments in Europe and the French management thinker Henri Fayol gave the following definition in 1916:

'To manage is to forecast and plan, to organise, to command, to coordinate and to control.'

An updated version of this definition is discussed in detail below. However a couple of simple examples act as reminders of the reality of management. A trivial but regular management decision is letting a member of staff have a holiday the following week. By way of contrast, controlling the construction of a petro-chemical plant is a major management activity.

As far as systems analysts are concerned management is important for several reasons:

- It is the fundamental process that ensures that an organisation continues to operate and develop.
- User and IT managers are the analyst's source of authority for developing and implementing new systems.
- Analysts themselves often manage IT projects.

Most of this chapter concentrates on the planning and control role of management in general, though there are references to IT.

8.2 Management schools of thought

There are various academic views on management. However there are three broad schools of thought amongst practising managers:

- Management is an applied science.
- Management is a practical craft skill.
- Management is basically about people.

These schools of thought may or may not be compatible depending on how they are interpreted. To some extent these three views coexist uneasily in any one organisation or individual manager. Particular managers, or even whole organisations, may stress one view at the expense of another.

The view that management is the 'appliance of science' stresses techniques such as formal planning and budgetary control. This approach is often based on administrative, financial, engineering, and mathematical views as to how an organisation should operate. However it also includes management practices based on social sciences, e.g. the use of psychometric tests when selecting new staff.

The other perspective is that management is a practical activity. This theory sees controlling a whole organisation, or a business function such as marketing, as a skilled craft combined with a little rudimentary general business knowledge and individual talent. As any craft it also requires the right personal attributes such as strength of character. It sees management as a mixture of factors like leadership, organisational politics, and sound administration. A combination of aptitude and good experience are seen as the essential prerequisites for being a good manager. There are two contradictory versions of this theory. According to one version the management skills needed to run a marmalade factory can be transferred to running a computer department. The rival version says that management is a specific practical skill based on in-depth experience of a function like factory production, usually in a particular industry such as textiles. According to this view management is not a particularly transferable skill, and the manager of a marmalade factory would find it difficult to run a computer department. The theory that management is personal attributes combined with a set of practical skills plus in-depth knowledge of a particular trade or profession is common. It is frequently found, for instance, amongst middle managers and professionals such as accountants, insurance administrators, engineers, and IT managers.

The people theory of management stresses the prime importance of people in making an organisation work. This view can take many forms such as the manager being a democratic leader of his staff. Another approach sees the manager as facilitating his or her staff to achieve business objectives. On a practical level this management view implies spending significant amounts of time on the human side of the business. This could involve activities like motivating staff, resolving personality conflicts, counselling individuals about work difficulties, and attending committee meetings.

8.3   Related concepts

There are some important words related to the word 'manager'. These are:

- *Entrepreneur*

An entrepreneur is a person who creates new and innovative profitable business projects. Clearly some managers are entrepreneurial, but others with more humdrum roles are not.

- *Director*

In the public sector the term director usually indicates the head of a function, i.e. a senior manager such as the director of social services in a local authority.

The term director when applied to a company has legal implications contained in company law. In this case directors are responsible to the share-holders for the direction and control of a company. A company director is often a manager with specific executive responsibilities for normal business activities, e.g. a sales director. A non-executive director does not have these management responsibilities, but does act as a member of the board of directors which controls the company for the share-holders.

- *Executive*

Almost a synonym for a manager, but perhaps more literally any person with a responsible role in executing (carrying out) a business function, plan, or policy.

- *Supervisor*

A person who controls the routine work of other people, e.g. a factory foreman.

- *Administrator*

Administration is a word that overlaps significantly with management. In the private-sector it implies the general function concerned with the technicalities and procedures involved in running an organisation such as complying with company or employment law. It is often associated with the management of clerical activities and large volumes of paper-work or their electronic equivalent, e.g. payroll or sales administration. Some businesses such as banking or insurance are primarily based on administration. Because the title describes a general function rather than a job the word 'administrator' may apply to anyone with a responsible position from a senior clerk to a senior manager.

- *Hybrid management*

A term that refers to managers who combine IT and business skills. It is discussed in Section 28.17.

8.4 Management defined

A convenient summary of management was published in 1937 by Luther Gulick, an American research worker in public administration. Gulick's view, slightly revised, is summarised by the acronym POSDCIR. The letters in POSDCIR represent the following:

- *Planning*

All managers need to plan future work both on a day-to-day basis and for the long-term.

- *Organising*

This means deciding on how the overall work of a department, section, or team is to be divided into jobs in order to meet business objectives.

- *Staffing*

This involves factors such as the recruitment and motivation of staff.

- *Directing*

Managers have to explain to staff what is required and what their contribution is expected to be.

- *Controlling*

This means monitoring work to ensure that progress is satisfactory, and taking corrective action where necessary. It also involves controlling people personally, e.g. disciplinary action or counselling.

- *Innovating*

We live in an era of continual change where it is essential for businesses and individuals to adapt. Part of this adaptation requires a willingness to innovate. Innovation in this context need not be particularly grand, e.g. no more than updating office technology or introducing new methods of working.

- *Representing*

Managers must represent their organisation, their department, and sometimes their staff. For instance, a shop manageress has to represent her company when customers complain.

The control aspect of management can also be considered under cybernetics which is the science of control. Its concepts can be applied to both management and business systems design. Cybernetics and its main ideas like feedback and feedforward are discussed in Chapter 19.

8.5   Objectives and policies

The fundamental objectives of a business are an essential starting point for all planning. This was discussed in Section 5.11, for example with reference to Sainsbury's, the retailing company. Clearly the fundamental objectives of the armed forces, a state hospital, a local authority, and a manufacturing company are all different. A state hospital exists to provide medical services to the public within its budget. A manufacturing company exists to make profits for its shareholders through a

specialism like the making and selling of rubber gaskets. These fundamental objectives are sometimes known as goals, aims, or more pre-
tentiously as the mission of a business. Some writers try to define such
terms more specifically, but they are used casually in ordinary speech.

The idea of a hierarchy of objectives occurs in several management
contexts, particularly planning. The basic idea is to take an overall
objective like profit and convert it to a series of lower-level objectives,
e.g. a cost reduction objective for a manufacturing department. One
scheme called MBO (Management by Objectives) tries to set personal
objectives for individuals. The idea is to motivate individuals with
personal objectives which contribute to departmental and corporate
objectives.

One key aspect of planning is policies. Policies are rules which can
guide and explain actions at all levels. Examples of policies are:

- A retailer buys from British suppliers wherever possible.
- A manufacturer only produces high-quality expensive items even
  when there is a profitable market for lower-quality cheap goods.
- A software house specialises in software for IBM mid-range
  computers.

As an example of the rationale behind policies take the manufacturer
producing only expensive high-quality items. One justification for this
is that if both were produced then the image of low-quality items
would destroy credibility in the market for high-quality goods. Policies
are particularly important in computing. Thus a company might decide
that its policy was to use only SSADM as a development methodology
and only COBOL as a programming language. Policies like this provide
consistency.

8.6 Organisational levels

Diagrams such as Figs. 7.1 and 7.2 show typical organisation charts.
Figure 6.5 shows a common schematic of the organisational pyramid,
which illustrates the main type of employee associated with each level
in the main functions such as human resources or production. The
pyramid shape is partly to suggest the level of authority and partly to
suggest the number of people at each level. Each level in Fig. 6.5 also

implies the time-span and importance of the decisions made. Thus the strategic level is concerned with activities which have long-term implications, e.g. developing entirely new markets. The tactical level is concerned with medium term issues, e.g. planning the replacement of old office equipment. The operational level is concerned with day-to-day activities such as dealing with customer sales queries. Some modern thinking challenges the traditional organisational pyramid (see Section 6.10).

8.7   Planning

Planning is one of the key features of management. It varies enormously in scale. For instance on a small-scale a warehouse manager might plan for a few people to check stock over a week-end. A plan might be no more than list of tasks to be done. More sophisticated plans indicate the time of each activity and the person carrying out the task. Charts and diagrams may also be used. Figures 30.1 and 30.2 contain illustrations of simple systems analysis plans. At the other end of the scale there are corporate or strategic plans which cover the future of a large business over the next decade. A plan for checking warehouse stock might be summarised on one piece of paper. A long-term strategic plan covering a multinational business might fill a heavy volume if not several volumes. Obviously many plans lie in between these two extremes. Some examples of common business plans include:

- A plan to build a new branch office.
- A plan to install new machine tools in a factory.
- A plan to move some administrative staff from one office to another in a different town.
- A monthly sales plan in terms of targets that sales personnel must achieve.
- A production plan in terms of the items that must be produced during the coming week.
- A recruitment plan for university graduates.

8.8   Levels of planning

In line with Fig. 6.5 planning is often divided into three categories:

- Strategic plans – fundamental and long-term, e.g. plans governing the development of the whole business.
- Tactical plans – medium term plans, e.g. the sources and timing of the finance needed for a business over the coming year.
- Operational plans – covering day-to-day work, e.g. planning the next day's truck deliveries to customers.

Each level of planning should be consistent with the other.

8.9 Business and strategic planning

Long term or strategic plans were mentioned above. These provide the general direction of the future of a business, and are a major responsibility for senior management. Other terms are used such as corporate plan, business plan, or management plan. In outline the stages of corporate planning are:

- *Agree the mission*
What overall purpose is the business to serve?

- *Appraise past performance and future possibilities*
This can be done by collecting information to survey past performance and the current business and technical environment. SWOT analysis is often used. SWOT stands for strengths, weaknesses, opportunities, and threats. These form a set of headings for examining the present and future of a business. For example legal controls on pollution may represent a future threat for a chemical company, and multimedia systems may represent a new opportunity for a publisher.

- *Agree high level policies and strategic objectives*
Strategic objectives for a car maker could include, for instance, targets of market share and sales volume over the next few years. Another strategic objective could be the development of a new environmentally friendly car, e.g. one powered by electric batteries.

- *Prepare and evaluate alternative strategies*

- *Evaluate alternative strategies and agree on one strategic master plan*
The master plan is broken down into a series of strategic sub-plans for each function, e.g. for sales, finance, and IT.

- *Ensure consistency*

The strategic plans for each function like personnel and IT must be consistent with the master plan and each other. The more detailed tactical and operational plans should also be consistent with the strategic plans.

- *Monitor results against the plan*

- *Review and revise the strategic plan*

Note that the strategic plan might stretch five or more years ahead but the revision is usually yearly. Where a plan is revised regularly like this it is known as a 'rolling' plan.

The purpose of each business function in a strategic plan should be designed to support the overall master plan and to cater for matters unique to that function. So a car maker's strategic marketing plan may call for complex electronic systems to be designed into new car designs for the coming decade. In this case the derivative personnel strategy could be concerned with the recruitment and training of electronic design engineers. Similarly the IT function needs a strategy just as much as other functions such as marketing and personnel. As discussed in Section 28.19 IT systems development must be aligned with the overall business plan, support the strategic plans of functions like marketing, and cater for the threats and opportunities unique to IT. Alignment is one aspect of consistency. It means that future IT development must match other business plans. For example if retail selling is planned to be more responsive to customer needs then IT systems should provide rapid information on the changing popularity of products. An IT systems plan lays down a timetable for several years ahead covering the development of new systems and the extension of old ones.

An IT strategy is a mixture of policies and long-term plans and of major interest to systems analysts. It is also a key responsibility of IT managers. For example EDI (Electronic Data Interchange) offers significant potential for manufacturing businesses. Using EDI, businesses can automatically exchange data like sales and purchase orders, as well as technical information such as engineering drawings. EDI operates rapidly and accurately via telecommunications networks for both customers and suppliers. Thus developing EDI can be an important part of a IT strategy in manufacturing. So amongst many other things an IT strategy could lay down the communication standards to be employed and the future implementation dates of new EDI systems.

8.10 Computer systems and planning

Planning is a key management activity in which computers can make a significant contribution. A plan itself is useless unless it is used as a guide for action. The actual performance needs to be monitored regularly against the plan, e.g. using feedback of actual supplier deliveries each month against the planned amounts. Where the actual or predicted performance deviates from the plan attempts are made to correct the situation. Being over or under planned levels can cause problems. So in the previous example deliveries which are incomplete or late could lead to stock-outs, and when deliveries are early they may lead to excessive stocks, both of which are undesirable. The importance of the computer is that it can automatically produce control reports as print-outs or graphical displays showing progress against plans. Used in this way the computer forms part of an MIS (Management Information System) or an EIS (Executive Information System) as described in Section 3.4. Computers can also be used to help prepare plans, for instance by performing 'what if' analyses. An example is 'what if' factory production were raised by 20%, what would the overtime pay be, and would the extra production be worth the extra cost? Used in this way computers can provide DSSs (Decision Support Systems) and can be a great help to managers who are producing plans. They can remove a substantial amount of the guess-work from planning.

8.11 Summary

- There are three common views of management. It can be seen as an applied science, or as a set of practical skills developed by those with aptitude through long experience, or as being primarily concerned with people.
- A convenient summary of the activities of any manager is given by POSDCIR (Planning, Organising, Staffing, Directing, Controlling, Innovating, and Representing).

- There are often considered to be three levels in an organisation, viz strategic, tactical, and operational.
- IT can not only support business operations such as routine accounting, but it can also provide support for business planning and management decisions. This can be done via an MIS (Management Information System), an EIS (Executive Information System), and a DSS (Decision Support System).
- Business objectives and policies are the starting point for business planning.
- One important part of management is business planning. Long-term strategic plans for a whole business should be based on all major aspects of a business such as marketing, finance, production and human resources. IT strategic plans need to be aligned to business plans.

Chapter 9
Business Services

9.1 Introduction

This chapter outlines some common business services that are of interest to IT staff. Some important examples of these services are:

- Risk management (basically security services)
- Auditing
- Banking
- Contracting and consultancy

Organisations need such services if they are to operate satisfactorily. As suggested by Fig. 5.1 there are a host of services which are used in business, the most important being the postal and telephone services. Other important examples are insurance broking and all the services associated with transporting goods.

Services can often be provided either by internal staff, or by external organisations. There is a trend to subcontract services rather than provide them internally. So for instance a business can use a catering company to provide canteen facilities rather than employ its own staff. See Section 5.16 for a further discussion on contracting-out.

Services such as money transmission via banks are an important part of IT systems design. In this case the internal systems of a company must interface (link) with those of the service providers. For instance the cheques printed by a purchase ledger system to pay suppliers must be formatted to meet the specification of the banks.

9.2 Risk management

Perhaps one of the most important areas for the systems analyst is risk management. Here the concern is to protect computer systems from the risks of damage and fraud. Risk management is the process of identifying, measuring, and controlling 'pure' risks in business. Examples of 'pure' risks are theft, fraud, vandalism, fire damage, and the accidental loss of computer data. Pure risks only involve the prospect of harmful results. By way of contrast 'speculative' risks can have either good or bad outcomes. An example of speculative risk is making a financial loss on trading, but there is of course the probability of profit. Needless to say the usual confusion of terminology means that sometimes the term 'risk management' is confined to speculative risks such as managing fluctuating exchange rates when buying foreign currency.

Risk management is a fairly broad term, but in computing the narrower term 'security management' is often used. Risk management should be an integrated, systematic, and organisation-wide approach to minimising the pure risks like sabotage and industrial accidents to which a business is exposed. Thus IT risk management is only part of the overall management of the risk in an organisation. For instance an IT department automatically benefits along with all other departments from the fence surrounding a factory and the patrolling security guards with their dogs. Risk management is also concerned with insurance to ensure that if the worst happens, like a burst water pipe damaging computer equipment, then there are adequate funds to finance repairs or replacement machines.

The process of risk management has three main elements and is illustrated visually in Fig. 9.1 and explained below:

● *Risk identification*
Hazards need to be systematically identified. For instance software viruses can stop or interfere with computers.

● *Risk measurement*
The frequency and consequences of a hazard must be estimated. For

Fig. 9.1 The main elements of risk management.

example, how probable is the loss of a database or master file, and what are the financial and other consequences of the loss?

- *Risk control*

The adverse effects of a hazard can often be cost-effectively minimised. For instance taking simple security copies of data files on a small computer may only cost a few minutes every day. If the current copy of a file is lost then only a few hours work need be re-entered to restore the file from its security copy.

Risk controls include obvious precautions like fire extinguishers. They also include health and safety training for employees and insurance which provides the funds for recovery should there be adverse incidents such as the sabotage or theft of equipment.

Risk controls have a price and part of the risk management process is to determine whether precautions are economic. That is the cost of risk controls should not exceed their benefits. The purpose of risk measurement is to use estimates to determine what level of control is economic.

9.3 Main IT risk areas

Risks are usually easier to control if the computer systems concerned are restricted to one location and a few users. Conversely wide-spread systems such as a network of ATMs (Automated Teller Machines) used by members of the public present far greater security problems. These of course, are solved by techniques such as the customer entering a magnetic identity card and a PIN (Personal Identity Number) into the ATM.

Usually the responsibility for developing and operating most risk control measures lies with IT staff and the immediate users of their systems. As already implied, the responsibility for some control measures can lie elsewhere, e.g. the company secretary could arrange the insurance cover for IT systems. A few of the common IT risks and control measures are described below.

- *The environment*

Typical environmental threats include fire and water damage. Water damage occurs because of burst pipes or where computer facilities are low lying in a wet area. Loss of electrical power and communication links are other possibilities. These threats are all frequent in the sense that they occur in many organisations in a small way every few years. The effect is usually small precisely because the precautions are taken and are effective. Fire is the biggest risk and controlled by the usual precautions such as extinguishers, limiting the amount of inflammable material including paper, regular fire drills, and halon flooding. With the latter nozzles in the ceiling of large computer rooms spray halon on the fire. Halon is a non-poisonous gas, which does not damage equipment, and it is more effective than carbon dioxide at extinguishing fires. Power problems are solved by using standby generators with mainframes or UPSs (Uninterruptable Power Supplies based on batteries) for small computers.

- *Hardware*

The possibility of problems with hardware is overcome in several ways. The most obvious way is to have a good maintenance contract which should keep the equipment operational in most circumstances. Even then some interruption to the computing service must be expected, even if it is just for preventive maintenance. With critical applications like 'on-line ATMs, 'non-stop' or fault tolerant computers are used. These are designed to keep operating even if there is a partial failure and they achieve this through special systems software and duplicate hardware components. Another arrangement is the use of a duplicate computer or a duplicate computer site. These are employed where the system is critical. Even with the simplest business system based on a personal computer alternative equipment should be available in case of a disaster like a large-scale fire.

- *Software*

Software can suffer from ordinary bugs (faults), and accidental or deliberate interference. The most dramatic and common form of threat is the software virus which is malignant or mischievous program code which can replicate itself and spread from one computer system to another. It can be inadvertently introduced to computer networks on magnetic disks containing genuine software. The virus may merely cause a few irritating special effects like displaying messages containing childish humour. Some viruses may corrupt data or render the whole system inoperative. Less common is financial software which is modified to perpetrate a fraud. The main defence against these problems is sound security procedures, for instance checking all incoming software disks for viruses.

- *Data*

One major advantage of computer systems compared to old-fashioned manual systems is the ease of duplicating data. A large old-fashioned accounts ledger, or thousands of record cards, could not easily be copied. At least three regular backup copies of computer data (and software) are essential.

- *Access*

Simple electronic key systems are often used to restrict physically the access of personnel to sensitive areas of an office such as computer operations or systems development.

Hackers are intruders who access IT systems and who are often intent on vandalism. They can maliciously use computer telecommunications to try to view or amend remote computer data. Defences include the use of passwords which are changed regularly.

- *Miscware*

The miscellaneous items like microfiche are often important parts of a system. Microfiche or microfilm records need careful protection from damage, and must often be kept secure and confidential. Some stationery like preprinted cheques is obviously attractive to fraudsters. However even blank forms for common stationery like invoices and payslips must be protected from damage.

- *Procedures*

Risk management procedures should document such matters as introducing new software. This is to minimise the chance of releasing the wrong software and minimise the chance of inadvertently introducing a software virus into a system.

Documented contingency plans should specify how normal services are to be restored for all the major possibilities like power cuts, fire damage, and virus attacks.

- *People*

Obviously the first line of defence is careful selection of staff. For instance criminals have been appointed to positions of responsibility and have taken advantage of the situation to defraud their new employer. In addition of course all employees can be trained to be security-minded.

Naturally all the above problem areas should be covered by insurance as this provides the funds to make good any damage. Regular audits are necessary to ensure that procedures and precautions are adequate and that procedures are actually followed. As IT has increased in importance and complexity over the years IT risk management has become correspondingly more elaborate both from a technical and business point of view. Businesses which are large IT users employ specialists and consultants in computer security. When developing computer systems the analyst has to include many technical security features in the design. One example is 'mirroring' where the data is kept in duplicate on separate magnetic disks. If there is a hardware failure with one disk the data is still available on the other. Of course all security features have a price. As already mentioned the extra costs of precautions like mirroring need to be balanced against the cost of lost data due to disk failure and the probability of this happening.

9.4 Auditing

In general an audit is a fundamental examination of any area in an organisation, usually with a view to ensuring that things are satisfactory, or to identify improvements. Thus there are energy audits, security audits, quality audits, and computer audits. In the case of a computer audit the emphasis is on proper management of systems development and computer operations. An audit is often conducted by an independent person. More usually audits are concerned with financial systems, both manual and computer. Financial auditing is related to risk management in that its functions also include checking the security of systems and the prevention of fraud. As financial audits are usually a legal necessity systems analysts have to expect systems that have financial implications to be regularly examined by an auditor. It is worth remembering that a sales order processing system, say, has financial implications in that despatches of goods affect stock and result in invoices. Auditors look for weaknesses in the design of a system and weaknesses in its use, as well as for errors and possible fraud. For this reason analysts are wise to have their proposed systems, where relevant, checked by a financial auditor before the final design is approved. Auditing is also discussed in Section 11.12.

9.5 Banking services

Banking services are of great interest to analysts who are often concerned with the best methods of handling computerised payments. However banking is sometimes of wider interest, particularly where the analysts work in a smaller business, e.g. a bank or finance house may be used to borrow the money to buy IT equipment.

Banks offer a wide range of services to businesses and individuals and they are of course major and very professional users of IT themselves. Other forms of financial institution, particularly the Post Office, building societies, finance houses, and insurance companies, partially compete with banks. Thus the Post Office offers a money transmission service in the form of postal orders, and building societies are very effective at offering deposit accounts to individuals.

As far as the systems analyst is concerned the banking services which are of major interest are current accounts and money transfer. Some important areas of money transfer include:

- *Night safes*
These allow the cash takings of small businesses to be accepted through a safe in the wall of the bank after normal closing hours.

- *Cheques*
Many cheques are printed by computer systems and must comply with both general banking law and the practical regulations of the banks regarding such matters as format and size. For instance crossings such as 'Account Payee Only' can be pre-printed to make cheques more secure — in this case they can only be paid into a bank account and not cashed.

- *Bank drafts*
These are effectively cheques made out by a bank. The bank makes out the draft in its own name, and it is made payable for an agreed

amount to whomever the bank's customer wishes. As the draft is backed by the bank the payment is guaranteed. The bank charges the customer accordingly for this service.

● *Bank giro credits*
These are forms which transfer funds from one bank account to another.

● *Standing orders*
A person or a business orders their bank to make regular payments from their current account, e.g. for hire purchase payments.

● *Direct debits*
An account holder authorises a bank to make payments (direct debits) to another organisation at the request of that organisation, e.g. when paying premiums to an insurance company.

● *Cards*
There are several types of card used for payment. They are also issued by organisations outside banking, e.g. retail groups. The credit card is perhaps the most familiar. As the name implies the cards allow spending on credit, i.e. via loans. With paper-based systems a retailer prepares a voucher for the amount of goods purchased on the authority of the credit card. The voucher is then signed by the customer, and the retailer uses the voucher to reclaim the money from the credit card company who then charge the card-holder's account.

● *EFT and BACS*
EFT (Electronic Funds Transfer) is any method making payments electronically. BACS (Bankers Automated Clearing Services) is explained in Section 16.10 and is one form of EFT. It is used where a business sends payment details to the banks on magnetic tape or by telecommunications. BACS can be used for direct debits where money is transferred out of other peoples' accounts e.g. to collect life insurance premiums. Alternatively it can be used for credit transfers into bank accounts of payees e.g. for paying suppliers.

EFTPOS (Electronic Funds Transfer at Point of Sale) is where a customer in a shop buys goods and pays for them using a card which is placed in a terminal at the till. The purchase amount is entered by the shop assistant and the customer can authenticate the transaction by entering the PIN (Personal Identity Number), or by signing a sales slip. The customer's account is automatically debited and the retailer's account credited.

● *Overseas transfers*
Banks offer facilities to receive money from abroad, or send money abroad e.g. by electronic IMTs (International Money Transfers) via SWIFT (Society for Worldwide Interbank Financial Tele-communication).

● *Cash management systems*
These are used by the multinational companies which are the customers of a bank. Using an office terminal the treasurer of a company is able to control accounts in different currencies in different branches of the bank throughout the world. Funds can be transferred from one account to another by the treasurer via the VDU.

Banks are also important sources of business loans. Overdrafts are the simplest form, but medium-term loans for, say, one to seven years are a common form of finance. Another vital set of business services offered by banks are concerned with importing and exporting. As discussed in Section 7.13 foreign trade involves complicated documentation and obviously payment and communications are much more difficult than with home trade. The services of banks include information on foreign countries, foreign exchange, travel services, and payment methods. Other examples of the way banks can help business include factoring (discussed below), insurance, payroll processing on a bureau basis, and advisory services.

9.6 Other financial services

Other financial services may be important in IT. For instance the leasing of computer equipment is common. Very crudely leasing may be seen as a kind of long-term renting of equipment which is legally owned by the lessor (usually a finance house).

Factoring is a service banks offer through subsidiary companies. This takes several forms such as the purchase of sales debts from businesses, and the 'factor' then collects the debt for itself. Another variety of factoring is where the factoring company operates a sales ledger on behalf of its client. A related service is 'invoice discounting' where, say, 75% of the value of a set of invoices is advanced as a loan which is repaid as the sales invoice payments are collected by the original seller.

Ordinary IT staff rarely have much involvement with insurance. These matters are handled by the finance office or company secretary's department. Occasionally an IT practitioner has to arrange special insurance, for instance for new equipment. In this case he or she collects the details like the cost of any new equipment to be insured and gives the details to the specialist staff concerned. These staff then make the arrangements, usually through an insurance broker. If an IT practitioner is concerned with founding a software house or a small computer contracting business, then arranging insurance is an import-ant part of the business formation work. Typically policies are taken out for employer's liability, public liability, vehicles, PHI (Permanent Health Insurance which basically provides an income during any long-term sickness or disablement), and pensions and life assurance. One key form of insurance is a PI (Professional Indemnity) policy which insures a business or individual against claims for professional negli-gence by customers. It should be remembered, for example, that one error made by an analyst or programmer could result in hundreds of computerised payments being wrong with the possibility of a large claim for damages. The total insurance bill for a one man contracting business could exceed £2000 per annum, excluding pension policies.

9.7 Consultancies and contractors

Contract staff, whether they be consultants, systems analysts, or prog-rammers, are common in computing work. Such staff are useful for purposes such as providing skills which are only required for a short time, or for helping out when the workload peaks. Consultancy services are used by most functions in business. Thus a personnel department may use an occupational psychologist as a consultant to help them devise selection criteria for recruitment. IT departments may use a specialist to advise on the design of a new on-line system, or the introduction of a new systems development methodology.

The reasons for using a consultant include:

- *Expertise*

Many consultants are specialists who can offer skill and knowledge which a business only needs occasionally and so it is not worthwhile employing specialist staff permanently.

- *Independence*

Some problems, particularly of a management nature, may require an independent mind. The ordinary employees and managers are sometimes too close to a problem to solve it rationally in an unbiased way. An example of where an outside opinion is helpful is reorganising a business in which the managers have vested interests and prejudices in favour of the old ways or particular changes.

- *Workload problems*

Some consultants are just employed to work with permanent employees during a peak in the workload or because of staff sickness.

- *Unpleasant work*

There are some jobs which ordinary employees are loathe to do, or which taint their relationships with colleagues afterwards. An example is advising staff who have been made redundant. In a large company this work is often done by a redundancy or 'outplacement' consultant.

Consultants are expensive – as a rule of thumb a consultancy firm will charge three or four times the salary of an equivalent employee. So a database specialist employed for a few weeks might cost the equivalent of £110 000 per annum (£500 per day for 220 working days). This compares to wages and related costs of, say, £30 000 per annum for an employee. Of course some fees are partly necessary to cover the period when the consultant is not on fee earning work as well as the associated marketing and administration overheads.

The selection of consultants needs care, particularly as they are often used for important and sensitive work. In many businesses there is a tendency to accept the reputation and word of the consultancy firm rather than carefully select the individual consultant. However some businesses first carefully select the firm of consultants and then select the individual consultant as if he or she were an employee. For example the consultant must provide a detailed curriculum vitae and then be rigorously interviewed.

Besides cost and availability the basic criteria for selecting consultants are sometimes called the four C's:

● *Capability*
Has the consultant the necessary skills, knowledge and experience to do the work? This can be assessed in the usual way from the curriculum vitae in terms of relevant qualifications, relevant experience, and references from previous satisfied clients.

● *Capacity*
Is the consultant able to put enough time and effort into the assignment? It should be remembered that consultants often work on several assignments simultaneously and often work away from home.

● *Continuity*
Has the consultant an established track record in the field, preferably with his or her present firm. If they leave their present employer or are sick are there adequate replacements?

● *Character*
This is the more undefinable part of the selection process where the personal and social attributes of the consultant are assessed.

Assuming all the other qualities such as technical competence are satisfactory one of the more controversial areas is 'independence'. An independent consultant has no special links with hardware and software suppliers. At the other extreme a consultant may work for a particular supplier and can only advise on the application of their products. Thus a consultant may be independent or linked with suppliers. However as long as this is clear then circumstances dictate which is best. However it is not unknown for a so-called independent consultant to receive secret commissions by recommending the products of one supplier.

To impose ethical and professional standards there are codes of conduct and practice, such as those of the British Computer Society. The BCS code of practice specifically refers to computer consultancy. There are other examples such as the Management Consultants Association which also has a code of professional conduct. (See also Section 9.9 below on professional services.)

9.8 Contractors

The distinction between contract staff and consultants is sometimes rather fine. Basically however contractors are there to do a specific job like COBOL programming rather than advise. Sometimes of course contract work is given to a company rather than an individual. Contractors are taken on for similar reasons to consultants, e.g. to meet a short-term demand for their type of work, or help during a temporary shortage of staff. As the term implies, contractors work to a special short-term contract. Contract programmers are quite common, and contract analyst-programmers are also found. Contract analysts are met less frequently. The reason for this is presumably that most organisations like to keep their business and applications knowledge within the organisation. Also analysis depends a lot on local knowledge which takes months to acquire. Contract programmers can be effective within hours of starting a new assignment. Some contract analysts make a living by specialising in particular IT applications, or by being experts in a particular development methodology. However in these cases they tend to class themselves as consultants and probably with some justification.

Selecting contractors can be similar to selecting full-time employees. The 4Cs above can also be adapted for contractors. The usual difference between an employee and a contractor is that contractors may only be doing a job for weeks. This means they must be working effectively within a day and often time and money limit familiarisation and training. So, for example, a programmer must have IBM COBOL expertise, or an analyst must have SSADM experience in a financial environment. This is the only way they can be productive quickly.

9.9 Professional services

A professional person can be regarded as superior type of consultant, invariably formally qualified in their field, and often operating in a traditional occupation like law. Professional staff in private practice provide many of the advisory and support services required by both small and large organisations. It is just not possible to employ permanent staff with all the necessary expertise. Private practice implies professionals operating via sole trading, a partnership, or a company.

Perhaps the most commonly used professionals are accountants and solicitors. When setting up a small IT business the services of an accountant in private practice are usually indispensable for advice on financial management. Accountants in private practice also offer other services such as auditing and book-keeping.

Other types of specialist professional may be of interest, for instance pension consultants and actuaries advise on the design, administration, and computerisation of large company pension schemes. Such schemes are akin to life insurance companies in their financing and administration. A pensions department may use a consulting actuary (financial mathematician) to determine what the correct level of pension scheme contributions should be. It could also use a pensions consultant to revise its pension scheme booklets, change its administration, and introduce new computer systems. Another example of professional advice is using the help of a chartered surveyor when seeking business premises.

9.10   Summary

- The use of services to support IT activities can be an important part of systems analysis.
- Risk or security management is an important subject for all IT staff.
- Analysts must design systems to meet the requirements of financial auditors.
- Banking services, particularly money transfer, are important for some business systems.
- Consultants, contractors, and professional advisors represent an important source of temporary labour and expertise. They must be selected as carefully as full-time employees.

Chapter 10
Law and Information Technology

10.1 Introduction

This chapter discusses the significant impact of law on business administration and IT. Systems analysts often need a working knowledge
of relevant legislation when analysing and designing administrative
systems. IT operations staff may also need an appreciation of relevant
law, e.g. in the data protection area. A common example is tax law
and its effect on payroll software. Furthermore business automation
demands buying and selling hardware, software, and services, and
so an appreciation of contract law is useful. Stories in the computer
and business press frequently report legal situations such as copyright
infringement, the difficulties caused by new legislation, or cases where
an IT system has failed disastrously.

Business law is also known under other names such as mercantile
law or commercial law. It is an agglomeration of various specialist
branches of law and includes such topics as company law, contract law,
and the law of property. There are also important branches of business
law covering specific types of business such as banking and insurance,
as well as business functions such as personnel management. The
discussion on law below can only be regarded as an elementary survey
of a large and complex field.

10.2 IT law

Information technology has started to develop its own special legislation
such as the Data Protection Act 1984. Furthermore some aspects of
business law, such as those covering copyright and patents, are particularly relevant to IT. As IT is a new subject, old statutes and legal
precedents based on 'horse-and-cart' technology may, or may not
apply. Because the development of British law has lagged behind the
development of technology some legal aspects of IT are uncertain or

115

unsatisfactory. European and American legal precedents may provide indicators as to how the situation will evolve in the UK.

10.3   Practical implications of business law

Needless to say a business must comply with statutory regulations, and any legally-binding agreements. It is a matter of judgement when to seek the services of a lawyer, or other legal specialists such as a taxation consultant or a patent agent. If specialists are not used at the appropriate time then the consequences can be costly. For instance it would be advisable to take the advice of a surveyor on both the technical and legal aspects of altering commercial buildings, otherwise planning regulations could be infringed. By the same token it is not sensible to seek advice on the legalities of every small error on a sales invoice, so a pragmatic approach must be adopted. Litigation, or taking legal action, is usually considered a last resort, and it is desirable to settle most matters outside the court room, avoiding both expense and publicity.

In England and Wales a 'lawyer' means a solicitor or barrister. However as already implied other specialists are used for many aspects of law. So the State employs policemen, Inland Revenue officers, and health and safety inspectors. The private sector employs company secretaries. Personnel officers and accountants are employed by both sectors. All these people are trained in those aspects of law that are relevant to their job. So accountants and company secretaries often have a good working knowledge of company and contract law, but usually know little of family law or the procedures in a court of law. Of course major matters do require a lawyer, and usually one who is a specialist in a particular field. For example as discussed in Section 10.9 below, a software house might use a solicitor to draft a standard contract for the sale of its IT systems.

Successful compliance with the law in areas like payroll or personnel administration requires a sound working knowledge of the regulations combined with good administrative practice. For instance a good pay-roll administrator knows that a person over state pension age is not legally entitled to SSP (Statutory Sick Pay). However their records and procedures must be good enough to detect this where a female employee agrees to continue working after the age of 60.

10.4 Automating legal requirements

Many IT systems are concerned with complex business administration, much of which has a significant legal basis. A simple financial services example is the abolition of tax relief on life assurance policies taken out after 13 March 1984. Policies originating prior to that date, but still in force, retain tax relief. Life insurance administration systems must allow for this. The current relevant legislation is the Income and Corporation Taxes Act 1988.

The most common example however of the effect of law is shown by the payroll system found in virtually every business. A sample of the legislation relevant to payroll includes:

- The Social Security Act 1975 for National Insurance Contributions.
- The Income and Corporation Tax 1988, e.g. for PAYE regulations.
- The Employment Protection (Consolidation) Act 1978, for example with redundancy payments.
- The Social Security and Housing Benefits Act 1982 for SSP (Statutory Sick Pay).
- The Wages Act 1986, e.g. for deductions from wages.
- The Social Security Act 1986, for instance the membership of an employer's pension scheme must be voluntary.
- The Local Government Finance Act 1988 for deductions from wages where an employee has not paid community charge (a local authority tax).

Legislation such as that above is continually amended, e.g. by annual Finance Acts. The details are often contained in regulations made under an Act of Parliament. For instance PAYE records, such as computer print-outs, need to be retained for at least three years according to regulation 32 of the Income Tax (Employment) Regulations (SI 1973 No 334).

In practice many payroll practitioners and systems analysts rely on practical descriptions of the legal requirements contained in government booklets or private publications which are discussed below. Package designers may use the original legislation and any associated regulations because of the speed with which software changes must be applied in a business area like payroll – sometimes within a few months. So in this context systems development staff regard the law as basically a set of principles and complex rules which are part of the requirements of the IT system. Many aspects of business law are clearly amenable to IT automation, e.g. word processing sales contracts, mainframe company share registration systems, and expert systems which incorporate tax law.

10.5 Legal aspects of the British Constitution

The theory of the British Constitution makes Parliament the supreme law-making authority, and it is the duty of judges to interpret and apply the law. A modification to this results from the UK membership of the European Community (EC) which means that in some cases EC decisions can be the supreme source of legal authority. A typical example is the Barber Case whereby the European Court of Justice decided in 1990 that sex discrimination against men in pension schemes was illegal, something which was not true under UK law prior to the decision. This case seriously affected the administration and financing of pension schemes because of the necessity to change the retirement age so that it was the same for both men and women.

Business law is primarily civil law rather than criminal law. Nevertheless criminal law cases can occur in business, for instance, fraud. There is a broad distinction between the two. In a criminal case, e.g. murder, the State regards society as a whole as being attacked or damaged, as well as any individuals involved. Whereas in a civil case, for instance breach of contract, any dispute is basically a private matter, in which the courts may be asked to adjudicate. The main practical distinctions are that civil cases involve virtually no government assistance (such as police investigation), and a lower standard of proof. Also the penalties imposed as a result of losing a civil case are usually less severe. Examples of the 'penalties' in a civil case are an unfavourable interpretation of a business contract by a court and injunctions (legal prohibitions from a particular activity). Another primary purpose of a civil legal action is to obtain some form of redress, e.g. compensation for negligence or breach of contract. Sometimes, of course, a matter is both civil and criminal, for example infringing copyright by selling 'pirated' software.

Statutes are Acts of Parliament. As illustrated above with payroll administration the government can, under powers given by an Act, make detailed regulations, usually called Statutory Instruments or Orders. The common law is law based on centuries of custom and precedent as interpreted by judges. It supplements, and is inferior to, any statutory provisions.

Foreign and international legal considerations havé always been important in business even in classical Roman times and the Middle Ages. This is simply because trade has always crossed national boundaries. However it is a matter of growing interest primarily because Britain is now part of the EC (European Community). One of the EC aims is a 'single market' with similar legislation on business matters. An important developing and contentious area of European and international law is intellectual property rights which are discussed in Sections 10.10 to 10.13 below. The international or foreign aspects of business law, e.g. international patents or foreign company law, are very much a matter for specialist advice. Normally a contract specifies that the law of England applies to ensure that its interpretation is governed by English courts. This can be important in the UK, because Scotland for one, has a different system of law.

10.6 Legal and quasi-legal controls

Some legislation is permissive, i.e. it gives organisations rights which they may or may not exercise. The Wages Act 1986 provides an example as it allows employers to pay wages by cashless methods such as cheques and computerised credit transfers if they wish. However statutes often compel organisations to comply with certain requirements with the threat of penalties if they do not. For instance, employers must provide safe working conditions under the Health and Safety at Work Act 1974. Health and safety is an important moral, legal, and common-sense consideration when installing and operating IT equipment. Fortunately it is relatively easy to provide healthy and safe IT systems.

Section 27.5 explains that members of trade and professional associations have to abide by the relevant codes of conduct and practice such as those of the British Computer Society. Associations have disciplinary committees to enforce such codes.

10.7   Data protection and computer misuse

An important example of legal control over IT systems is the Data
Protection Act 1984. IT systems processing *personal* data must be
registered with the Data Protection Registrar. Personal data is data
about 'natural persons', i.e. human beings. Data about companies or
animals for instance is not covered by the Act. IT systems using
personal data must comply with the principles of data protection contained in the Act. For example people must be allowed access to any
computer data held about them. Also the personal data must be
accurate, secure, and used only for the registered purposes.

The Computer Misuse Act 1990 is aimed at stopping hackers and
viruses. It makes a crime any intentional unauthorised access to a
computer system, or any unauthorised modification of a computer
system. As an example, deliberately 'hacking' into a remote computer
system with a terminal is now illegal, even if no damage is done. A
programmer would be modifying software in an unauthorised manner
if he put a 'logic bomb' in the program code. Logic bombs are pieces
of program code which may just display rude messages, or destroy
data. They can be triggered for instance when the computer reaches
a particular calendar date, or when it detects that the originating
programmer has left and his records are no longer on the computer
payroll system.

10.8   Buying and selling

Buying and selling between businesses is mainly a matter of contract,
and within broad limits the parties to a contract can agree anything.
The law is not usually concerned with the fairness or otherwise of
the bargain, and the role of the courts is primarily to clarify and
enforce contracts, or to grant other remedies such as compensation.
Consumers, i.e. ordinary people who buy goods and services for personal use, do enjoy some additional statutory rights which are not
available to businesses. The law of contract is extensive and complicated. The main statutory provisions are. provided by the Sale of
Goods Act 1979, and the Supply of Goods and Services Act 1982, both
of which effectively codify the previous common law position. Besides
these general provisions there is special legislation covering such mat-

ters as property or insurance. Many of the numerous contract cases in business law concern the clarification or interpretation of the terms of a contract.

Legally a contract is a purely abstract thing, merely a legally-enforceable agreement. What is usually called a 'contract', i.e. the written record of an agreement is often incomplete. Taking an example, a software house and its customer may refer to a 'contract', by which they mean a standard list of pre-printed terms together with a few extra details like the price and delivery date of the bespoke software to be produced. However, in law the specification of the software, which is usually in a separate document, is also part of the contract, as is any other relevant documentation such as an implementation plan.

Contracts do not usually have to be in writing. However, written agreements are highly desirable to avoid confusion, and provide legal evidence. It is an old joke that a verbal contract is not worth the paper on which it is written. Common practice is for businesses to use standard pre-printed contracts or terms of trade. Standard terms or standard contracts do not have to be accepted and terms can be struck out or amended by mutual agreement. Besides the express terms that are specifically agreed, there may be implied terms which are understood to apply even if not explicitly mentioned. As an example, in the absence of an agreement to the contrary, the Sale of Goods Act 1979, Section 14 implies that, goods should be of merchantable quality, as a standard term in all consumer and business contracts, e.g. a new personal computer should operate successfully without a power pack failure.

Just to give a flavour of contract law it is worth citing a few well-known cases which can warn IT staff of the dangers of buying and selling.

- *Tarling* v. *Baxter (1827)*

A haystack was sold, but before the buyer took it away, it burned down. It was held that the buyer was still liable to pay for it because he became the owner of the haystack when the contract was made. It was immaterial that he had not yet taken delivery of the goods.

(Note that the point at which the ownership of a supplier's computer equipment passes to a customer is important. The customer may not accept the equipment for several days after delivery until all the necessary tests have been performed.)

- *Hadley* v. *Baxendale (1854)*

Hadley was a miller and the crankshaft of his mill broke. Baxendale was a carrier who was much slower than agreed in delivering the crankshaft to London for a replica to be made. Hadley unsuccessfully sued Baxendale for the loss of profits resulting from the delay. If however Hadley had made it clear that any delay would have damaged his business he might have been successful.

(This case brings home the necessity of a customer to make the consequences of failure clear to a computer supplier. However computer suppliers expressly try to exclude or reduce liability for consequential loss as part of the standard terms of a contract.)

- *L'Estrange* v. *Graucob Ltd (1934)*

The plaintiff, Miss L'Estrange, ordered, for her café, an automatic slot machine, which did not work satisfactorily. The form she signed for the machine stated in small print that 'any express or implied condition, statement, or warranty . . . is hereby excluded'. She still had to pay for the machine because having signed the contract she had accepted the terms, bad though they were. In this case the terms allowed the supplier to evade responsibility.

(As an aside most computer contracts contain similar clauses excluding or reducing liability for failure. Since 1934 the position has since been partly modified by the Unfair Contract Terms Act 1977 for business contracts on standard terms, as in the L'Estrange case above. In essence this only allows such exclusion clauses if they are reasonable.)

10.9   The terms of a typical computer contract

The Institute of Purchasing and Supply (IPS) has introduced standard written computer contracts, which however are not often used. Many standard contracts from computer suppliers and software houses are notoriously unfair to the customer, but as already mentioned, changes in the terms can be negotiated. The contracts can cover such matters as licences for standard packages, the purchase of equipment, and consultancy services. Take as an example a typical agreement between a software house and a client business to deliver a bespoke computer system. Some of the main headings of the written contract might be as follows.

- *Introductory section*

This gives such matters as the names and addresses of the parties to the contract and a list of supplementary documents which are part of the agreement, e.g. a system requirements specification. There is usually a clause to the effect that only listed documents are part of the agreement, and that everything else is excluded. This avoids confusion at a later date as to what was included or excluded from an agreement. So for instance correspondence and statements from the salesman are excluded by such a clause, unless specifically itemised as belonging to the agreement.

- *The obligations of the software house*

This paragraph usually refers to some other document such as a 'systems specification' which describes the work to be done.

- *The client's obligations*

For instance, this could include the provision of working space and terminals by the customer for the software house programmers.

- *Acceptance*

These are the procedures that the client must adopt to accept the software and any hardware involved. Under this heading the corrective action of the software house must be defined where the client finds faults. The client often has a period of say a month in which to test any software after which it is deemed to be accepted.

- *Charges*

The method of calculating charges and their payment is specified.

- *Confidentiality*

All sensitive information about the client or supplier is to be kept secret.

- *Restrictions on employing each other's staff*

The client and the supplier agree not to try to recruit each other's staff for a period of, say, six months after the completion of the contract.

- *Exclusions and liabilities*

Client and supplier are usually not liable to each other for delays where there are dramatic intervening factors such as a major fire or strikes (this is called 'force majeure'). The maximum liability of the software house would be defined, particularly for consequential loss.

- *Ownership and intellectual property rights*

Typically the ownership of the software and documentation would be clearly stated. Often in a standard contract the client who is paying for a software system does not own the copyright, but only acquires a non-exclusive licence to use the software. This means that the software house can use the bespoke software for its own benefit elsewhere.

- *Miscellaneous*

There are a multitude of points, each one of which might be important in some circumstances. Examples are: the transfer of the contract rights and obligations to third parties; the status or identity of employees who have the right to vary the contractual terms (often specific directors or managers); and the procedure for resolving disputes.

As can be seen from the above list of terms the drafting (wording) of a contract is very much the province of a lawyer. The usual way of proceeding is for the software house to draft its own ideas loosely in line with general practice and its own special requirements. This is then discussed with a solicitor specialising in business law and preferably IT. The solicitor offers advice and then prepares the detailed legal wording.

10.10   Intellectual property rights (IPR)

IPR includes such matters as copyright, patents, and registered designs. Basically all these involve a creation of the human mind such as an invention. With an invention the law effectively grants a limited monopoly in the form of a patent for a novel device, e.g. for integrated circuits which were invented in America.

In business IT the most important form of IPR is probably copyright. With software, copyright means that the use or copying of software is forbidden without the owner's permission. In the UK there is no need for any formal legal process to register copyright. It is acquired automatically when something like a piece of music, a book, or software is first produced. The copyright monopoly is limited because it expires 50 years after the death of the 'author' (who could be a programmer). Normally the employer of an 'author' acquires the copyright where the work is produced in the course of employment. Unlike patent law there is no requirement that the work produced, say a program or computer manual, be innovative. It is enough that it is original, in the sense that it is not a copy of another work. So there are several hundred payroll software packages in the UK, but each has its own copyright, despite the fact that they are trying to achieve very similar ends with similar means. There are some differences between the legal treatment of software copyright and the copyright in music, films, literature, and radio broadcasts. For example authors of literature have 'moral rights' to prevent distortion of their 'creative' works. Normally breach of copyright is a civil law matter. However in some commercial circumstances it is a criminal offence to infringe copyright, e.g. by selling software without the owner's permission.

Related to IPR are other valuable intangible assets like business names, trade marks, customer lists, and trade secrets. The intangible property owned by a business such as patents or customer lists can be commercially very valuable. Patents and copyright can for instance be bought and sold. These assets are also vulnerable to abuse. For example 'counterfeiting' involves deceiving customers by selling low quality products under the reputable trade name of another business. The protective law for intangible assets differs according to the circumstances, e.g. the law of confidentiality is used with trade secrets. In practice a software product may involve several forms of intangible asset simultaneously − a trade mark, designs on the packaging, software, literature (manuals), and even music. IPR can of course have multiple sources, e.g. different authors and software writers (employees or freelance), or software combining the products of several suppliers under licencing agreements.

10.11 Protecting intangible property

Protecting intangible assets from theft or abuse by others involves both legal and practical precautions. Feasible precautions may be not always be adequate. For example when trying to protect books and articles from illicit photocopying can the 'pirates' be caught? Protective methods include:

- *Copyright*

Use of the work and copies are only legal with the owner's permission. Techniques to protect copyright include controlled circulation of software, or dongles (electronic or software devices to prevent the copying of software).

- *Patents*

Legal protection is by registration.

- *Designs*

Legal protection is by registration, e.g. wallpaper patterns

- *Business names and trade marks*

Company names like 'ICL' are registered. Trade marks are usually registered too. Legal protection against others using similar names is also possible by a 'passing off' court action (see Section 10.12 below). The term 'trade mark' refers to something used to identify and distinguish a product, e.g. invented names like Coca Cola, Hovis, and dBASE. Distinctive designs may also be used as part of a trade mark.

- *Service marks*

Similar to trade marks except that they apply to services rather than products.

- *Certification*

.A certification trade mark signifies that a product or service has reached the approved standard of the mark owner. An example is the BSI kitemark. The mark is registered and the owner controls the certification process and the use of the mark.

- *Trade secrets*

Protection is under the law of confidentiality or contract. This is used considerably in computing, e.g. a customer evaluating a supplier's hardware and software signs a 'confidentiality agreement' agreeing not to pass on information to the supplier's competitors.

- *Trade and professional associations*

Examples are the CSA (Computer Services Association) and FAST (The Federation Against Software Theft). These can press for new laws and stronger enforcement, and give practical help on IPR.

In practice contracts provide the strongest protection for software copyright where circulation is restricted to a few customers paying high prices. With mass circulation of low-cost software, e.g. domestic computer games, it is difficult to prevent infringement, especially by private individuals.

Two areas of the law can potentially conflict, i.e. the right for a business to protect its intangible assets, and the right for the public to benefit from free trade. So clearly patents or copyright grant a monopoly for a limited period, and deliberately restrict free trade. Some contractual agreements may be in 'restraint of trade' which are unenforceable, or even worse 'restrictive trade practices' which can be prohibited. Restraint of trade also affects employees who cannot be *unreasonably* restricted by their contracts of employment from using knowledge gained in their employment − see the *Faccenda Chicken* case below. These considerations also apply in matters other than intangible assets. For example restraint of trade may apply when employees try to set up in competition to a previous employer, and restrictive trade practices might be held to exist when businesses agree to 'fix' market prices.

10.12 Legal provisions

The main statutory and common law provisions covering intangible assets include the following:

- Copyright, Designs and Patents Act 1988.
- Companies Act 1985 (for registering company names).
- Patents Act 1977.
- Trade Marks Act 1938.
- Trade Marks (Amendment) Act 1984.
- Contract law.
- Confidentiality.
- Passing off (selling goods under a similar name to that of another business or its product).
- Slander of goods (making false statements about products).

Some relevant court cases include:

- *Bollinger* v. *Costa Brava Wine Ltd (1959)*

French champagne producers successfully objected to the name 'Spanish Champagne' (a passing off action).

- *Robb* v. *Green (1895)*

A manager used his employer's customer list to found his own business in live gamebirds and eggs (confidentiality is part of an employee's duty of fidelity).

- *Faccenda Chicken Ltd* v. *Fowler and Others (1986)*

An ex-sales manager recruited several employees from his previous employer. They were all in competition with their ex-employer selling chickens using their experience of the ex-employer's customers. Unlike the previous case the action failed because the court did not regard this as a breach of confidentiality. A carefully drafted clause in the contract of employment restricting competition after leaving employment might have been effective. Such clauses are common in software house employment contracts.

- *Oxford* v. *Moss (1978)*

An undergraduate read the examination paper before an examination − he was acquitted of theft (information is not property).

10.13 Some American examples

The following examples refer mainly to the American legal and business environment. However they provide an indication of the commercial importance of IPR.

- *The formulation of Coca Cola*

It has been a trade secret since 1886.

- *Shredded Wheat*

The patent was granted in 1895 and transferred to Nabisco, but exploited by Kellogg's in the 1920s after the patent had expired.

- *Patent No 174,465*

This is the number of the American patent for the telephone taken out in 1876 by Alexander Graham Bell. He fought hundreds of legal cases against competitors.

● *Teddy Ruxpin*

A 1986 American 'look-and-feel' case where Worlds of Wonder Inc successfully contended that Vector Intercontinental Inc had infringed their audio-visual copyright in an animated toy bear (Teddy Ruxpin). The defendants had produced cassettes containing stories and control software which were similar to those of Worlds of Wonder.

10.14 Sources of legal information

Systems analysts are concerned about legal requirements which are sometimes a major part of their logical and physical systems design. The precise meaning of logical and physical design is explained in Section 18.6. Examples of legal requirements are SSP (Statutory Sick Pay) regulations and the format of magnetic tapes for transmitting year-end tax data to the Inland Revenue. Analysts need to follow the development of any new legislation or changes to old legislation. Figure 10.1 illustrates the development of legislation in the UK, a process which can take several years.

New or changed regulations can take effect very quickly – sometimes within weeks of being issued. Government booklets are practical renditions of the regulations. An example is 'P7, The Employer's Guide to PAYE'. This booklet summarises the Income Tax (Employments) Regulations made under the Income and Corporation Taxes Act 1988, s 203. The lead-time between legal rules being available and the law taking effect is often inadequate for planning and implementing detailed changes in business administration and computer systems. Thus the systems analyst and business executives must extract as much information as possible from the precursors of any regulations such as a White Paper and an Act. They must also use any other sources such as articles in the business press which discuss the practical consequences of impending legislation. Note that these statutory changes sometimes require policy decisions, e.g. whether to switch to cashless pay under the Wages Act 1986. They almost invariably involve maintenance of existing business systems as a whole (procedures, forms, and so on, as well as software). An example is Statutory Maternity Pay (SMP) in

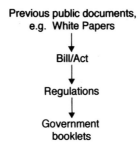

Fig. 10.1 The diagram indicates how UK legislation can be introduced through Parliament. Both business staff and systems analysts need to follow the documentation produced to ensure that administrative systems are maintained or developed in time to meet legal deadlines. White Papers are a type of government report.

1987 which involved amending payroll and related software plus new forms plus new payroll and personnel procedures. Entirely new systems can occasionally result from legislation, e.g. community charge was a revolutionary new local authority tax introduced by the Local Government Finance Act 1988 (it was replaced by council tax in 1993).

10.15 Summary

IT staff need to have a general appreciation of law in the following areas:

- Common business activities, e.g. health and safety.
- The law governing particular business applications, e.g. tax and social security law for payroll systems.
- Contract law for IT sales and purchases.
- Data protection and computer misuse.
- IPR and other intangible assets.

Chapter 11
Finance

11.1 Introduction

This chapter outlines the business role of finance and its supporting administrative systems. The implications for IT are also discussed. The details of book-keeping are considered in the next chapter. Good financial administration is essential for activities such as paying suppliers. Without adequate financial administration even a non-profit making organisation would soon cease to operate. Computer systems can automate and improve financial administration. As they are very common, most IT staff are almost certain to meet financial systems at some stage during their career.

The term financial systems refers not only to basic accounting but also supporting systems such as invoicing and payroll. In addition it includes the main administrative systems in banking and investment management. Basic financial systems such as payroll are a necessary function in all industries. However whole sections of the economy such as the stock exchange and insurance have the provision of 'financial services' as their primary purpose. Though not usually considered as such, state organisations such as the Department of Social Security and Inland Revenue (often through agencies), also exist to provide financial services.

Many business computer systems are primarily financial, such as the system for processing cheques in a bank. Other business systems can provide financial data as a by-product. For instance a stock system recording the number of goods in a warehouse is the origin of the financial value of stocks entered in the balance sheet of a business.

The financial transactions of a part-time business may be hundreds per year. In a manufacturing business of, say, 2000 employees, financial transactions could easily number hundreds of thousands per year. The number of sales transactions alone could be hundreds or thousands per week. All this data needs to be correctly processed and summarised. Also financial systems usually require greater rigour than other administrative systems.

Needless to say computer activities themselves make and cost money, e.g. IT systems produced and delivered by a software house. They therefore require accounting procedures just like any other business activity.

11.2   Financial terminology

In this context 'financial' merely implies something where money or monetary values are important. As usual a 'system' may be human activities, computer processes, or both. Needless to say all the terminology is used fairly loosely, and terms have several variants. So a 'purchase ledger' and 'creditor ledger' are almost the same thing — both are records of the amounts a business owes to its creditors, usually as a result of purchases from suppliers.

Book-keeping is the clerical and computer routines for maintaining the financial records of activities like buying and selling. It also involves preparing the final accounts of a business from these records. The term final accounts refers to the balance sheet and the profit-and-loss account of an organisation. Simple examples of these are shown in Fig. 11.1.

Financial accounting includes raising funds and controlling book-keeping. The financial information produced applies to a whole organisation. Management accounting includes such topics as budgeting and costing, i.e. it is mainly concerned with financial information at departmental or product level.

11.3   Purpose of accounting

Financial systems can involve more than just book-keeping and accounting. For instance a sales invoicing system provides basic marketing data. However ultimately the financial implications of all business and technical activities must be included in the accounts of an organisation. So a production engineer may be concerned to install a large press tool to cut and squeeze steel into car body panels. But this is valuable machinery which must be included in the accounts of the company. So the relevant records must be summarised in the balance sheet. This summarises the value of assets like press tools and manufacturing robots as well as liabilities such as the money owed to creditors.

```
KANGAROO ELECTRONICS LTD

ACCOUNTS 1993


PROFIT AND LOSS                    BALANCE SHEET
  ACCOUNT £K                            £K

Sales income      280        Use of funds
(Turnover)                   (Assets)

Less:                          Premises          100
Expenditure       235          Equipment          30
                               Stock              35
Profit             45          Debtors            50
                  ===          Money in bank      35
                                                 ___
                                                 250
                                                 ===

                             Source of funds
                             (Liabilities)

                               Capital (Shares)  155
                               Profit             45
                               Loans              35
                               Creditors          15
                                                 ___
                                                 250
                                                 ===
```

Fig. 11.1 A simple example of final accounts showing both the profit and loss account and balance sheet. Real examples have more detail, a more complex layout, and extensive notes. Capital and profit are treated as liabilities because they are owed to the shareholders. With a balance sheet, as the name implies, the totals of assets and liabilities must be equal.
(£K = thousands of pounds)

The financial performance of a trading business is shown in its profit-and-loss account.

This leads onto the basic purpose of book-keeping and financial accounting which is traditionally defined as stewardship and management control. Part of stewardship requires reporting to the owners of an organisation. In particular it means producing final accounts which give a 'true and fair' view of how the financial affairs of the organisation have been conducted. The 'owners' could be the shareholders of a company, the members of a club, or the citizens of a county administered by a local authority. Even in a non-profit-making organisation, the management must husband financial resources carefully and the accounts provide much of the control information for this. Also, of course, the final accounts are used for determining the tax liability on profits.

Potential investors are interested in the final accounts of a company. These are scrutinised to determine its financial health. In particular investors look at the value of assets and the profits generated. The prospects for producing future dividends (distributions of profits to share-holders) are also very important. Potential creditors, e.g. banks or suppliers, also use final accounts as an indicator of the financial state of a business. In this case they wish to be confident that a business can repay any loans or credit. A potential customer, for example an organisation buying IT products and services, often wishes to ensure that their suppliers are viable. Nobody wants to buy a mainframe computer and find the supplier goes into liquidation a month later. This could leave the customer with an expensive large computer which has no future and no maintenance! Again the final accounts provide an indication of a supplier's financial stability.

Figure 11.1 shows an example of how the financial affairs of a trading company, Kangaroo Electronics in this case, can be reported to its share-holders. These accounts show a healthy business with good profits (compared to capital invested) and reasonable liquidity (cash). From the point of view of the book-keeper and computer staff the reported final accounts are an important objective of the financial systems. Another objective is the financial control of the business, and the book-keeping systems support this. Figure 12.1 shows part of the 'books' (financial records) of Kangaroo Electronics. Figure 12.1 is part of the sales ledger, and by adding together the balances for all the accounts in this ledger the total sales debt, or debtors entry, is obtained for the balance sheet of Fig. 11.1. The sales ledger also provides the information to chase customers for payment of overdue debts.

11.4   Cash and profits

One elementary but vital aspect of finance is the distinction between profits and cash. Profit is the total trading surplus accumulated over a period, usually a year. This may be physically represented partly by cash, partly by unsold goods, and partly by unpaid sales debts. The balance sheet of Figure 11.1 shows this in the case of Kangaroo

Electronics. The Kangaroo final accounts show that the profit is greater than the cash at the bank. So some of the profit is represented by other assets. It is of course possible to convert the non-cash assets into cash given time, often by simply selling them. However a minimum amount of cash is essential for trading, e.g. employees and suppliers want to be paid in cash not goods. Businesses which were fundamentally profitable have gone into liquidation simply because they had inadequate cash to continue operating in the short-term, and no one was prepared to lend them any more. This means that immediate cash can be more important than profits, hence the emphasis by accountants on cash-flow analyses like that of Fig. 25.2.

One common cause of lack of cash is the delay in customers paying their debts. This leads to a demand for IT sales ledger systems to print out detailed analyses of sales ledger debts and letters requesting payment. In the long-run of course a business must generate both sufficient cash and profits if it is to survive. A business which made regular losses, but still generated enough cash to continue trading, would find its assets shrinking until it could continue no longer, i.e. it would slowly lose capital until it ceased to be viable.

11.5 Control theory

Financial information is often produced for business control purposes. For example, in terms of the control theory explained in Section 19.9, accounts provide feedback on a company's financial performance like the profits earned. Financial systems are themselves maintained by extensive corrective feedback to maintain the quality of the information, e.g. office control procedures such as input checking, or auditing (see Sections 11.11 and 11.12 below).

Some financial systems exist to communicate information, usually for action, e.g. sales invoices are produced for payment. Like all communication channels, such systems are vulnerable to 'noise' (errors).

11.6 Basic financial systems

The main financial systems for a trading business are as follows:

- Sales invoicing.
- Sales or debtors ledger.
- Purchase or creditors ledger.
- Cash book.
- Nominal (or general) ledger.
- Payroll.
- Costing.
- Budgeting.
- Financial planning.

Most of the above systems are described in Section 2.2. The cash book records cash and bank transactions like receiving a cheque. Costing systems are used for monitoring the costs of products and services in terms of factors like labour and raw materials. An example of financial planning is given by the cash flow analysis of Fig. 25.2. Many other financial systems exist depending on the business. Some may just have different names for the above systems, e.g. a 'fees ledger' for a firm of accountants is really a sales ledger. Some systems may be unique to a particular organisation. For example CODA (Computerisation of Schedule D Assessment) is a system used by the Inland Revenue for handling the taxation of the self-employed. Special organisations like pension trusts do not trade for profit and their accounts are organised to reflect this. As a separate example the term 'surplus' is used rather than 'profit' in the accounts of a private club or charitable organisation.

11.7   Organisation

In a small business all the financial and general administration including data processing may be controlled by a company secretary or an office manager and a few clerks. Other titles may be used for the chief financial administrator, e.g. the bursar in a private school. In a group of companies as well as a group finance director there may be a local finance director for each subsidiary. The local finance director may be in charge of financial and management accountants who themselves control sections covering functions like sales ledgering, payroll, and budgeting. Figure 7.2 shows a typical organisation chart. In a large organisation there would also be internal auditors on the staff. However other financial functions could come under a different heading than finance. So the local personnel manager may be partly responsible for sickness and holiday pay schemes, and a group company secretary may be responsible for the company share register, employee share scheme, pensions, and company insurance arrangements.

Most financial systems are managed by qualified specialists, e.g. bankers, insurance administrators, accountants, company secretaries, and pension managers. Also the managers of these businesses, large and small, seek various types of financial advice from people like external auditors, insurance brokers, and actuaries.

11.8   Law

Most financial systems are regulated by common and statute law, e.g. The Insurance Companies Act 1982. The Companies Act 1985 as amended contains many provisions which relate to accounting for companies. For instance the format and layout of company accounts is described in Schedule 4 of this Act. Financial and legal requirements are extensive and have a major effect on system design. For instance the Value Added Tax Act 1983 and regulations made under it affect sales invoicing.

Frequent changes in the law create major systems maintenance problems and opportunities. For example a change in NIC (National Insurance Contribution) regulations is usually a problem for the employer. It could imply increased NIC charges, and almost certainly implies changing payroll software and office procedures. A current example is the introduction in 1991 of NIC charges on the value of an employee's company car. Sometimes legislation provides opportunities rather than problems. As mentioned in Section 5.12 the Social Security Act 1986 led to a business bonanza for life insurance companies. This Act introduced a complicated but very favourable tax and NIC regime for personal pensions. It created a whole new area of business administration which demanded supporting computer systems.

11.9   Double-entry book-keeping

The method used to maintain the financial records of a business and produce the final accounts is called double-entry book-keeping. This was invented by the Italians in the Middle Ages and has always daunted beginners to financial systems because of its apparently confusing complexity. There is no doubt that a mastery of double-entry requires considerable practice, and this is part of normal financial training. However, because computerised book-keeping systems are so common, systems analysts often need an appreciation of the principles of double-entry. If they ever run their own small IT business then a working knowledge of book-keeping is even more desirable. Chapter 12 discusses the operation of double-entry book-keeping in more detail.

Traditional book-keeping does not provide much guidance on topics like the depreciation of equipment, foreign exchange, inflation, and long-term liabilities like pensions. These issues are addressed in the UK, at least partly, by documents like SSAPs (Statements of Standard Accounting Practice) which provide a further set of rules for correct accounting.

11.10   Management accounting and budgeting

The distinction between financial and management accounting is sometimes rather artificial. However financial accounting tends to be concerned with conventional book-keeping and the broad financial control of a business in terms of its overall profit or sales turnover. Management accounting is more concerned with the fine details of financial performance such as the cost of running the computer department or personnel department. It is often concerned with the costs of producing a product or running a project.

One key area of management accounting is budgetary control. This is straightforward in principle but often complicated in practice. In budgetary control each part of a business such as a department or project has a set of financial targets to meet over a period. For instance, an IT manager may have a salaries budget of £2 520 000 for 140 staff over a year. Part way through the year he may see that he is likely to exceed his annual budget due to unexpected overtime pay and an over-generous pay award. As a result the manager may delay recruitment or cut overtime so as to achieve the overall yearly pay target. To do this the manager needs regular budget reports, usually from a computer system every month. A simplified example is shown in Fig. 11.2. The reports show, for each cost heading like salaries, the

KOALA INSURANCE COMPANY						
Budgetary Control Report						
Computer Department Pay						
	January 1994			1993/94 Year-to-Date		
	Budgeted	Actual	Variance	Budgeted	Actual	Variance
* Basic Pay	200 000	213 000	(13 000)	2 000 000	2 030 000	(30 000)
* Overtime	10 000	5 000	5 000	60 000	70 000	(10 000)
* Total	210 000	218 000	(8 000)	2 060 000	2 100 000	(40 000)

Fig. 11.2 A simple example of a computerised budgetary control report. The use of brackets () is an accounting method of showing a negative value.

current actual expenditure against that expected together with the variance or deviation from the target value. Budgetary control provides another example of how overall objectives, in this case the financial targets of a business, can be broken down into departmental sub-objectives. So if each department meets its budgeted targets then the whole company makes its predicted profit.

11.11 Quality control

More than most systems financial systems need careful control to avoid errors and fraud, and this is achieved by means of a fairly strict set of office procedures. Though not usually described as such, these are essentially security and quality control activities. The usual term for them is just (clerical or data) 'control procedures', and they include the following:

- *Batch controls on input documents*
For example if 20 supplier invoices are received in a batch and worth £5000, then the computer system should request the batch total in advance. It should then check that the total of the input values matches the batch total in case there are input entry errors.

- *File or database checks*
On a payroll file for instance the number of employees after processing

should equal the number before, allowing for any new employees or leavers. If the before and after figures cannot be reconciled this could indicate, for instance, illicit interference with the file without the knowledge of the payroll users. Thus bogus employee details could have been put on the payroll file fraudulently by a computer programmer, or a clerk, hoping to collect the pay of fictitious employees.

- *Segregation of duties*

Where possible no one person should operate a financial system and the work should be spread amongst several people. With this arrangement people automatically check each other's work and errors are more unlikely. Fraud is also more difficult as it often requires the collusion of two or more staff.

The academic theory of control is explained in Section 19.9. Quality is discussed in Chapters 15 and 26.

11.12   Auditing

The job of an external auditor is defined partly by legislation, and partly by professional accountancy rules. So in the case of a company an auditor is appointed by the shareholders under the Companies Act 1985 as amended. The job of the external auditor is to certify to the shareholder that the accounts of a company are a 'true and fair' record. In practice, this requires a thorough investigation of the accounting systems of a business. The external auditor cannot be an employee of the client company and usually comes from a firm of accountants.

The internal auditor is employed by the managers of a organisation. The role of the internal auditor is partly to ensure that the external auditor finds nothing wrong, and partly to carry out reviews to improve the security and efficiency of internal systems. Besides fraud, auditors are also concerned with the quality and reliability of the financial systems rather than individual errors. Auditors look for weaknesses in areas like security, controls, error handling, and office procedures. One key requirement with all financial systems is an audit trail. This is a record of all the intermediate steps showing how a transaction like a purchase requisition ultimately becomes a payment to a supplier. Computer systems produce audit trail printouts to prove correct processing.

Auditors apply the argument that good financial systems and good administration considerably reduce the possibility of errors and fraud. Because auditors have a keen interest in computer systems wise computer staff ensure that they have advice on the audit implications of any new or changed systems.

11.13 Mathematics

Most financial systems only involve basic arithmetic and algebra. Sometimes a much more mathematical approach is required. For instance in life assurance the probability of policy holders dying must enter into the calculations which are used to determine premiums. As another example, investment analysts can use mathematics to try to predict the movement of share prices. Some financial algorithms can be complex, e.g. SERPS (State Earnings Related Pensions) calculations.

Mathematical models are frequently used in finance and though simple in concept they can be quite elaborate in detail, for example cash flow predictions like those shown in Fig. 25.2.

11.14 Systems analysis and design implications

Financial systems are vital and must therefore be of high quality, reliable, and secure from fraud or damage. This applies both to the development and operation of systems. Systems quality is discussed in Chapters 15 and 26. IT security is discussed under risk management in Section 9.2.

Financial systems are frequently subject to revision and therefore there can be a considerable amount of systems and software maintenance. For example payroll systems and state social security systems are exposed to continual legislative change. Systems maintenance is discussed in Sections 23.7 and 23.8.

There are frequently interfaces between financial and other systems, e.g. an invoicing system usually provides the raw data for a sales analysis system. Inter-organisational data flows are common, for instance EFT (Electronic Funds Transfer) in all its forms.

11.15   Sources of finance

Computer staff can be concerned with sources of finance for several reasons. For instance they may control their own IT business and need funds to develop the business. Also even in a large company projects may not be approved unless there is adequate finance available. Of course the details of raising the finance in a large company are normally left to accountants. IT managers and systems analysts are primarily concerned with capital, e.g. finding the money to invest in an IT project for its longer-term financial and intangible benefits. However as mentioned above the finance of short-term operational activities is often of more pressing importance in a business, e.g. a small retailer needs to buy goods today for sale at a profit next week.

It is part of the fundamental nature of projects that money is spent for months and years on wages and equipment. The return in terms of cash and more intangible benefits lags the investment and may take years to materialise. Obviously no one provides finance for a business or technical project unless it is fundamentally sound, i.e. unless there is a good chance of the benefits justifying the costs within a reasonable time frame. Cost-benefit analysis is briefly discussed in Section 19.3. However the source of finance affects the costs of a project and hence its viability, e.g. if interest rates are high, borrowing money may make a project too expensive. Questions of finance are particularly important in a software house, for instance when developing new products and services, or when trading is poor.

In the private sector some common sources of finance are:

- *Selling shares*
New shares, often called 'equity', can be sold to investors. Of course this option is only open to a company.

- *Loans*
There are various types of loan and they can come from individuals or financial institutions, particularly high-street banks. For example overdrafts are temporary and expensive bank loans, and debentures are long-term loans made to a company.

- *Grants*
These can come from the government or semi-charitable organisations.

- *Second-tier finance*

Examples are hire-purchase, leasing, and factoring. Factoring involves selling sales debts to a specialist organisation which then collects them (see Section 9.6).

- *Internal sources*

For instance sales revenue and profits can be used to provide finance for new projects. A less common approach is to sell assets.

- *Customers and suppliers*

As an example a software house may ask a customer to buy any equipment needed to develop software; or a supplier may provide equipment on attractive credit terms.

- *Paying suppliers late and making customers pay early*

This may be ethically dubious and can be difficult to achieve, but it is often attempted.

Each of the above methods of raising finance has its own pros and cons. However raising finance can be difficult for small private businesses. For instance private companies cannot advertise shares for sale like a public limited company. Also their money requirements are often not big enough to justify the interest of institutions which specialise in providing venture capital, typically in amounts in excess of £100 000. Overdrafts and bank loans are expensive, but are a major source of business finance in practice.

11.16 Summary

- Financial systems are very common both in business generally and systems analysis. In fact it is difficult for computer staff to avoid systems with financial implications.
- Whole organisations like banks and the DSS are devoted to financial services and IT is an essential part of their infra-structure.
- All professional accounting is based on double-entry book-keeping. One main objective of this is the preparation of final accounts.
- The distinction between cash and profits is elementary but vital.
- The most common financial IT systems are: sales invoicing, sales

ledger, purchase ledger, nominal or general ledger, and payroll. Costing and budgeting are also important IT application areas.

- An auditor's job is basically to ensure that financial systems are correctly designed and used. Audit considerations are a major part of the design of new or amended systems.
- The various sources of finance such as leasing can sometimes be important in practical IT work.

Chapter 12
Book-keeping

12.1 Introduction

This chapter outlines the operation of double-entry book-keeping. The 'books' concerned are of course the financial records of an organisation. As explained below, true book-keeping involves 'double-entry'. This is a method of entering the details of each financial transaction, like a payment for computer maintenance, into the financial records twice. The book-keeping system can of course be either a computerised or manual system, or a combination of the two.

Chapter 11 explains the financial background to book-keeping. The prime purpose of a book-keeping system is to maintain the financial records of an organisation. From these records reports such as the balance sheet are prepared to give a 'true and fair' view of the financial state of the organisation. The book-keeping system also allows financial control, e.g. keeping track of the cash and bank account position. Book-keeping is commonly seen as an arcane subject which is primarily of interest to accountants. However it is relevant to IT staff because book-keeping is usually computerised and an important computer application area.

12.2 Alternatives to double-entry book-keeping

Double-entry book-keeping is explained below. To beginners it may at first seem artificial and complicated. So it is reasonable to ask is it necessary? The strict accounting answer is almost certainly yes! In practice small businesses often use simplified manual book-keeping arrangements which are adequate on a practical rather than theoretical level. One alternative, which is frequently met in small businesses, is receipts and payments accounting. This basically means listing all the receipts of money, and all the payments out and the difference is supposed to be the profit or loss. This approach is not really acceptable as the problems are fairly obvious. For instance this system does not distinguish between the purchase of an asset like a personal computer or an expenditure item like business travelling expenses. The personal computer, as an asset, continues to benefit the business for several years. The money spent on a train ticket is lost forever once the business journey is completed. Also this system does not record debts, i.e. the money owed from customers which is an asset. Similarly this system does not reveal the money which is owed to suppliers which is a liability. Needless to say, both the money owed by customers and the money owed to suppliers are frequently substantial.

The receipts and payments approach to book-keeping is crude, and its only virtue is simplicity at the expense of accuracy. It can be used for very simple businesses where transactions are primarily by cash or cheque with virtually no credit, and where the assets are insignificant. Other simplified manual accounting systems also exist and special stationery is sold for these. A common practice is for a small business to keep simple records and then give these to an accountant in private practice to prepare accounts in the proper form for taxation and other purposes.

12.3   The rules of double-entry

The whole double-entry process is illustrated in Fig. 12.3 for a fictitious company called Emu Contract Programmers. Double-entry book-keeping is perhaps best explained first as a series of abstract rules and then by illustrating how these rules apply with simplified examples. The rules of double-entry are normally discussed in terms of traditional manual methods, but the principles apply equally to computer systems. The double-entry procedures in a simplified form are as follows:

● *Transactions*

Book-keeping is based on a series of transactions like sales invoices, sales credit notes, purchase invoices, and cheque payments. In previous times these transactions were often entered into an intermediate record called a journal or day-book which formed a log of the transactions. The details were then transferred from the day-books or journals to the main accounts (see below). It is of practical clerical value to log transactions with both manual and computer systems. However it is not theoretically necessary and this practice is not included in the examples below.

- *A set of accounts*

The double-entry system requires a set of accounts for recording financial transactions. These accounts are ultimately summarised in the 'final accounts' (basically the profit and loss account and balance sheet). Simple final accounts are illustrated for the Kangaroo Electronics company in Fig. 11.1. Even in a small business there can be tens of different accounts summarised by the final accounts. In a large public company there can be millions of accounts. For instance in a bank or an electricity company millions of customers each have an account.

- *Account lay-out*

Each account groups together related transactions, say those for wage payments. The basic accounts are traditionally laid out as pages in a ruled book called a ledger. The left-hand side of each page is for recording the debit aspect of transactions and the right-hand side for recording the credit aspects. Ledger accounts are usually represented in text-books as T-accounts which are a simplified version of the real arrangement. Figure 12.1 illustrates one account in the records of a supplier, Kangaroo Electronics. The transactions with customers, Dingo Navigation Ltd in the example, are recorded in a 'T' shape.

- *Ledgers*

When the number of accounts is significant then sets of similar accounts are grouped together for convenience in separate ledgers. In the large manual systems of the past this allowed several clerks to access the accounts simultaneously. So all sales accounts are in the sales ledger. All purchase accounts are grouped together in the purchase ledger, and miscellaneous accounts are held in the general or nominal ledger. Other terms are used, for instance 'accounts receivable' is the American term for a sales ledger.

- *The perspective of the business*

The ledgers and accounts always represent the view of a business as a separate entity. The accounts do *not*, for instance, represent the view of the owners of the business, its customers, or its bank. Each of these usually has their own accounting systems of course.

SALES LEDGER OF KANGAROO ELECTRONICS LTD

DEBTOR'S ACCOUNT 1/10/93

DINGO NAVIGATION LTD

Dr	£s	Cr	
Balance 1/9/93	0		
(1) Sale of Electronic Components 9/9/93	100	(3) Payment for Electronic Components 18/9/93	100
(2) Sale of Electrical Wire 12/9/93	50		
Balance 1/10/93	50		

Fig. 12.1 A simplified traditional presentation of a sales ledger account showing a record of sales transactions. This arrangement simulates the pages of an old-fashioned ledger, and is sometimes called a T-account. The Dr (debit) and Cr (credit) signs are usually not shown, and the convention is always to put debits on the left and credits on the right. The reason for Dr being an abbreviation for debit is that both Dr and Cr have an Italian origin. In this example the transaction number is shown in brackets. Note that the balance is the net effect of the debits and credits.

The perspective of the accounts can cause confusion to beginners without careful thinking or clear wording. For instance a supplier's sales ledger represents those customers who are debtors and who have not yet paid for goods received. From the opposite perspective these customers include the supplier as a creditor in their own purchase ledger records.

● *Debits and credits*

A little thought reveals that transactions should affect two accounts. So a cheque payment must reduce a customer's outstanding debt and must increase the amount in the supplier's bank account. So when any transaction enters the system the same amount is recorded twice in two different accounts. By convention this is once as a debit and once as a credit, hence the term double-entry. A debit and credit can be regarded as having opposing arithmetical signs. Figure 12.2 shows in a simplified form how the accounts of a supplier, Kangaroo Electronics, are posted (updated) with a transaction. A cheque payment of £50, transaction number (4), has been received from the customer and credited to the customer's account. The other equal but opposite side of the double-entry is shown in the bank account in the Kangaroo records.

Which account is debited, and which is credited? The ancient rule is:

> '*Debit the account which receives, and credit the account which gives.*'

Thus Fig. 12.2 shows part of the 'books' of the supplier Kangaroo Electronics. Here payment of £50 is shown as transaction number 4 and dated 18/10/93. It is 'received' by the Kangaroo Electronics bank account and hence is a debit. The Dingo Navigation sales account in the same books 'gives' the value and hence this is a credit.

Debiting a bank account when cash or a cheque is placed in it can puzzle some people. They remember that their own personal bank statement is credited in similar circumstances. The reason for this credit is that the bank statement is a copy of the bank's own accounting records. A bank statement reflects the bank's view that a company or individual who deposits money or cheques in a bank account is to be credited. This is because the amount concerned is owed to the depositor. In a company's accounting system a bank account would record a debit for a deposit. This records the fact that the bank would then be a debtor and owe the company this money. Of course the effect of other transactions is ignored in this example. After making some allowances, e.g. for delays in processing transactions, a company's bank account in its own records should agree with the bank statement, except that the debits and credits are reversed due to the differing perspective. In fact this 'bank reconciliation' is an important book-keeping check for errors or missing transactions.

● *The trial balance*

Regularly, say every month, the *net* figure or balance on each account is calculated. This is called 'balancing-off', and the balance is the result of several transactions which could have opposing signs, i.e. the balance is often the sum of several debit and credit transactions. This is shown in Figs 12.1, 12.2, and 12.3. Balancing-off is not necessary with computer systems as they can calculate a new balance after every transaction. The balances on the accounts can then be used to prepare the profit-and-loss account and balance sheet.

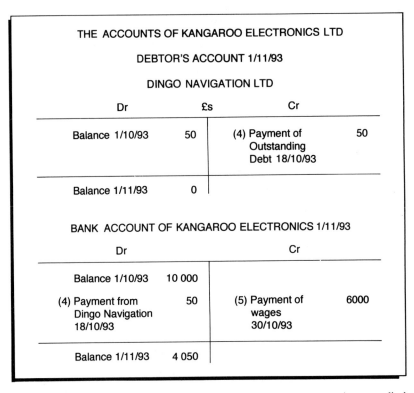

THE ACCOUNTS OF KANGAROO ELECTRONICS LTD

DEBTOR'S ACCOUNT 1/11/93

DINGO NAVIGATION LTD

Dr	£s	Cr	
Balance 1/10/93	50	(4) Payment of Outstanding Debt 18/10/93	50
Balance 1/11/93	0		

BANK ACCOUNT OF KANGAROO ELECTRONICS 1/11/93

Dr		Cr	
Balance 1/10/93	10 000		
(4) Payment from Dingo Navigation 18/10/93	50	(5) Payment of wages 30/10/93	6000
Balance 1/11/93	4 050		

Fig. 12.2 Illustration of the double-entry of *one* customer's payment in a supplier's accounts. Dingo Navigation have paid Kangaroo Electronics £50 which is shown as transaction (4). As a result there is a credit entry in the Kangaroo sales ledger account clearing the debt, and a matching debit entry in the Kangaroo bank account. The sales ledger account gives value and hence is credited. The bank account in the Kangaroo books receives value and hence is debited. Remember that in all cases the balance shown is the net result of the debits and credits.
The payment of £6000 in wages (5) to the Kangaroo employees is a bank account credit. This would also have a corresponding £6000 debit entry in the Kangaroo Wages Account which is not included in the diagram.

First the resulting balances on the various accounts are transferred to a 'trial balance' which is merely a list of the balances on the various accounts. If the total debits and total credits in the trial balance do not agree then there has been an error in the book-keeping. The total debts and total credits must agree because of the matching individual debits and credits which have made up these totals under double-entry. Of course, even if the total debits and credits do agree, the trial

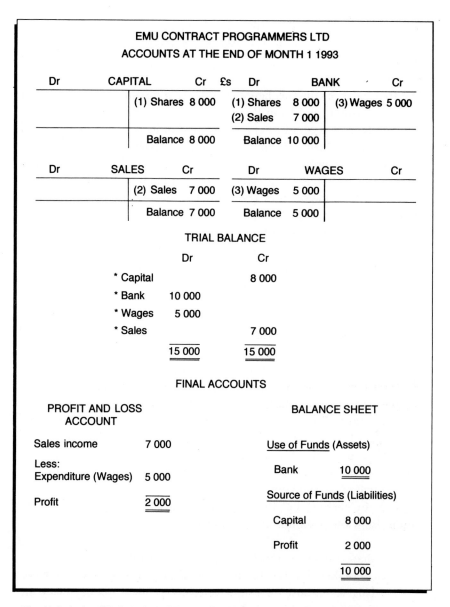

Fig. 12.3 A simplified version of the ledger accounts, trial balance, and final accounts of a trading company. This shows the whole history of the double-entry process as described in Section 12.4 for Emu Contract Programmers Ltd. Corresponding parts of a double-entry have the same transaction number.

balance is not necessarily correct. For instance the matching debits and credits could have gone to the wrong accounts.

● *Final accounts*

The trial balance contains figures which are a mixture of two different types of account, and from these the final accounts can be prepared. The first type of account refers to any kind of income and expenditure account such as sales revenue (income) or office rent (an expense). From these the profit-and-loss account can be prepared. The second kind of account refers to any kind of asset or liability such as total sales debts and the value of stock (both assets), or purchase debts (owed to suppliers and therefore a liability). From these asset and liability accounts together, with any profit or loss, the balance sheet can be prepared. The simple example of Fig. 11.1 uses the terms 'use of funds' for an asset, and 'source of funds' for a liability. There are several different layouts used for final accounts.

12.4   Example of the derivation of final accounts

The Kangaroo Electronics examples of Figs 12.1, 12.2, and 11.1 *partly* illustrate how the double process operates in the common and often complicated situation where there are sales debtors. A very simple but complete illustration of the double-entry process is shown in Fig. 12.3. This gives the theoretical minimum in terms of book-keeping for a company called Emu Programmer Recruitment. Emu finds computer programmers for other businesses for which it receives a fee. Emu is in the fortunate (and unlikely) situation of being able to ask for immediate payment by cheque, i.e. there are no sales debtors. The transactions during Emu's first month are as follows:

(1)   Share capital of £8000 received from investors.
(Book-keeping regards investors as a special kind of creditor. This is because investors can receive their money back in circumstances like winding up a company.)
(2)   Sales income of £7000.
(3)   Wage payments of £5000.

All transactions go through the Emu bank account. The results of the trading during the first month are shown in the profit-and-loss account and balance sheet in Fig. 12.3. Though the double-entry procedure looks ponderous for a trivial case like this, the procedure is essential when there are hundreds, thousands, or millions of transactions.

12.5 Book-keeping and the computer

The simplified treatment of double-entry book-keeping given here provides an introduction to the traditional presentation in accounting textbooks. However that presentation basically simulates old-fashioned book-keeping where the ledgers were large books in the Victorian 'counting house', now known as the accounts office. The traditional form of double-entry was disappearing from major businesses in the early part of the 20th century, long before computers as such. The office systems then being introduced were based on loose-leaf record cards and electro-mechanical accounting machines. From the 1950s these primitive automated systems were themselves replaced by computerised accounting. Whilst the fundamental principles of double-entry are preserved it is sometimes difficult to see the connection between an automated system and the T-account presentation given in the previous sections.

**** SALES LEDGER ENQUIRY ****							
Account Number A1123							
Customer: Dingo Navigation Ltd							
Date	Reference Number	Transaction	Value	Transaction	Value	Balance	
01/09/93	—	—	—	—	—	0.00	
09/09/93	S123	Invoice	100.00	—	—	100.00	
12/09/93	S356	Invoice	50.00	—	—	150.00	
18/09/93	P234	—	—	Payment	100.00	50.00	

Fig. 12.4 A VDU or print-out version of the T-account of Fig. 12.1. This shows some of the extra detail which any practical manual or computer system needs, particularly document cross-reference numbers. This arrangement is often called a three-column layout with the left-hand value column showing debits, the middle value column showing credits, and the third right-hand column showing a running balance. With manual systems the burden of calculation is such that the balance is only calculated occasionally, say every month.

The simple sales ledger VDU display of Fig. 12.4 reconciles the computer display with the T-account format. The screen display is actually a formatted copy of what is stored on the magnetic disk file, which is still often called a 'ledger' rather than a file or database. The accounts transactions are posted (updated) onto the magnetic disk ledger via data entry using other screens, or sometimes the transactions come directly from other computer systems. For instance when sales invoices are printed by an invoicing system the details are automatically posted onto a magnetic disk sales ledger. A computer system can of course check incoming VDU transactions for simple keying errors and any inadvertent attempt to infringe the rules of double-entry. This reduces but does not eliminate errors, and so raises the quality of computerised book-keeping when compared to a manual system.

12.6 Summary

- The purpose of a book-keeping system is the maintenance of accounting records for financial control and the preparation of final accounts.
- All professional accounting is based on double-entry book-keeping.
- Double-entry requires matching debit and credit entries for each transaction that is posted to the accounts.
- The double-entry rule for updating ledgers is to debit the account which receives and credit the account which gives.
- The balances on each account in a double-entry system are transferred to a trial balance in readiness for preparing the final accounts. This is used as a check on the double-entry process.
- Broadly the final accounts of a business consist of the profit-and-loss account and balance sheet.

Chapter 13
Human Resource Management

13.1 Introduction

This chapter discusses personnel management and its relationship with business IT. It concentrates on the more administrative, formal, and organisation-wide aspects of personnel work. The next chapter discusses the small-scale human issues such as ergonomics, the motivation of employees, and individual job design.

Today personnel management is often renamed HRM (Human Resource Management), though in the past it went under titles like labour management or employment management. Modern management theory stresses the idea that people are the key factor in business, and emphasises this by using the term 'human resources', in preference to older terms like 'staff' or 'employees'. Human resource management is a particularly important area for systems analysts working in large organisations such as insurance companies, local authorities, and government departments. New or amended IT systems change the way employees work, hence their jobs. This leads to personnel department considerations like job grading and pay.

Trade unions can also be an important factor in large organisations. For instance computer systems have been implicated in industrial unrest such as strikes. Furthermore from the point of view of the personnel officer, computer staff are themselves people who are subject to normal HRM processes such as recruitment, performance appraisal, and training.

13.2 Role of personnel management

The personnel or human resource manager is responsible for most aspects of employment other than directly supervising people at work. Some major personnel areas are:

- *Staffing*

An organisation must be kept adequately staffed despite the normal losses of staff through processes like resignation or retirement. Typically the annual turnover of white-collar staff might be 10% though it is often higher in IT departments. The role of the personnel department is to find new recruits to replace losses and to support any business expansion. Besides the recruitment and selection of staff, personnel departments regulate promotions and staff transfers from one department to another. Other matters are handled more occasionally such as dismissals, redundancies, and retirements.

- *Performance management*

In particular, performance management covers the operation of formal appraisal schemes where the work of each employee is regularly assessed. It also covers matters which can improve performance such as counselling.

- *Reward management*

Examples of reward management are the determination of pay rises, and the allocation of employee benefits such as pensions and company cars.

- *Welfare*

This can involve matters like canteen and medical services.

- *Organisational planning and development*

This includes such matters as job analysis and job design. As discussed below this personnel role overlaps with the traditional activities of O&M officers and systems analysts.

- *Training*

For example, new recruits may need training to work on current computer systems, and existing staff may need training for new systems.

- *Industrial relations*

This basically means dealing with trade unions.

- *Health and safety*

Health and safety considerations affect all areas of a business and not just exotic situations involving nuclear engineering or dangerous chemicals. A more mundane example relevant to the systems analyst is the safe installation of IT equipment.

- *Employment regulation*

This includes several areas such as disciplinary procedures, time-keeping, and equal opportunities.

13.3 Personnel departments and IT

Personnel departments need computer systems to support the functions listed in 13.2 above. A minimal system would be a computerised personnel records system containing information on all employees and producing reports, e.g. a listing giving basic details on all the staff in the computer department. For further details see Section 2.2.

Personnel departments are also useful sources of information for systems analysts. For instance they should be able to provide organisation charts and job descriptions for all employees. Figure 16.2 gives an example of the organisation chart of a payroll department and Fig. 22.2 shows an example of a job description for a works manager. This kind of background information can save an analyst a lot of time when he or she is investigating the requirements for new or amended business systems.

Many personnel functions also impinge on the systems analyst. For instance the systems analyst, personnel officer, and user manager are all interested in job design. The work of the systems analyst can mean significant job changes for clerical, administrative, and executive staff as new technology and new systems are introduced. So when computer systems are introduced into a library, the staff must abandon the use of paper-based systems. The jobs change and involve using VDUs and barcode readers to control the borrowings and stock of books.

One 'knock-on' effect of IT system changes is on job evaluation. This is an important personnel technique in large organisations with consequences for reward management, i.e. the employees' pay. In one form of job evaluation the basic idea is to examine each job in a business and rate the jobs on a points scheme for factors like the skill required and the amount of responsibility. Crudely the more points a job receives the higher its grade, and of course this ultimately determines the pay. As analysts often change the jobs of employees by introducing new or amended systems this means that the modified jobs must be re-evaluated.

In practice with office systems health and safety is elementary, but it needs careful attention. Typically it means considering simple but important matters, e.g. installing fire extinguishers, avoiding trailing cables, and giving reasonable breaks for VDU operators to reduce eye and wrist strain. Occasionally an experienced health and safety officer must be consulted.

Industrial relations is another important consideration for analysts in a large organisation. For instance even today new technology can result in strike action. The 1986 industrial dispute at News International in Wapping is a dramatic example which involved violent mass picketing. Despite this the printworkers failed to prevent the loss of thousands of their jobs which was mainly due to the new information technology for producing newspapers. Significant labour savings are perhaps less common now with office systems, but can still occur. To cover this trade unions often have an agreement with the management of an organisation concerning new technology of any kind. Clearly new or amended IT systems can affect or involve these agreements. The systems analyst must ensure that any proposals are compatible with union agreements and the industrial relations environment generally. See Section 13.5 below for further details.

The personnel function also affects an IT department significantly in the same way that it affects any other department. So for instance health and safety rules must be followed by IT departments. More fundamentally personnel departments can control activities like the recruitment of systems analysts and the job evaluation of programmers.

13.4   Role of law

As in other countries, such as the USA, employment in the UK is extensively regulated by law. The following list of Acts of Parliament contains a *sample* of legislation covering employment and related matters:

- Factories Act 1961.
- Equal Pay Act 1970.
- Health and Safety at Work Act 1974.

- Trade Union and Labour Relations Act 1974.
- Sex Discrimination Acts 1975 and 1986.
- Race Relations Act 1976.
- Employment Protection (Consolidation) Act 1978.
- Employment Acts 1980, 1982, 1988, and 1990.
- Trade Union Act 1984.

Finance and Social Security Acts can also be important, e.g. with regard to tax relief on employee benefit schemes.

13.5 Trade unions

Trade unions are an important factor in certain types of business, and systems analysts receive short shrift if they inadvertently antagonise a union or its members. In practice trade unions tend to represent the staff of large employers like local authorities, banks, and major manufacturing businesses. Trade unions exist to help their members, and many take a pragmatic approach to industrial relations. As mentioned above by the time the systems analyst appears on the scene, unions and management have often established a series of formal and informal agreements which the analyst must respect. Union agreements with management which are relevant to the analyst could cover job evaluation, redundancy, productivity, and new technology. This is in addition to matters that are directly included in the employee's contract of employment such as the hours of work. Clearly some of the systems analyst's work relates to these areas. So changes in jobs to meet the demands of new systems may mean a change in working hours. As the systems analyst represents management it is his or her job to respect these agreements and identify any problem areas.

One example of an agreement between the management of a large business and trade unions is a new technology agreement. Some of the main terms in such agreements are outlined below:

- All changes in systems and technology are to be agreed between the unions and management, and until an agreement is reached no changes should be introduced.
- Collaboration between different unions is to be defined.
- Information on proposed changes is to be provided to the unions.

- Information technology should be used to improve output and quality and not cut manning.
- Schemes for retraining the staff affected by new technology should be established.
- The aim should be to use new technology to reduce normal hours of work, reduce systematic overtime, and increase holidays.
- The benefits of the new system in terms of pay increases should be spread amongst the employees.
- Computer gathered information should not be used for monitoring work performance.
- Health and safety standards must be applied.
- Joint management and union teams should monitor the progress of new technology.

Companies may also issue new technology policies or guidelines with a broadly similar content to the agreement above. The distinction between a new technology agreement and a new technology policy is that the latter is a statement of intentions issued by management alone.

13.6 Labour flexibility

In the UK the workforce and trade unions have supposedly had very rigid ideas on employment and adhered to regular well-defined jobs. The most extreme example of this is the 'demarcation' dispute where people in one job dispute with the people in another job as to whether a particular task is theirs or not.

A classic example is in shipbuilding where traditionally an electrician would not tackle simple jobs belonging to a boilermaker no matter how inconvenient this was. This rigid view of employment may make it difficult for managers to operate a business efficiently. For instance, it is common to find a surplus of people in one part of an organisation and a shortage in another. However moving people from the surplus area to the shortage area has often not been practical, at least in the short-term. This can partly be due to the objections of employees and their trade unions, and partly because the employees concerned do not have the skills to cope with two different jobs.

Over the last decade there has been a trend to adopt more flexible approaches to work. Flexible working may be an amalgam of several approaches. As already mentioned in Section 6.11 it can rely on a greater use of temporary staff like contract programmers, or sub-contracting work to other organisations like a computer bureau. It may include a reliance on flexible hours by ordinary employees. Flexible hours could include overtime on request, shift working, or an annual hours approach. With an annual hours contract, employees agree to a fixed number of hours per year, but the number of hours worked each week depends on the level of business activity. Another example of flexible working is multi-skilling where people have several skills and exercise whichever skill is required according to the needs of the moment.

The classic example of multi-skilling in computing is of course the analyst-programmer who shifts from analysis to programming and back again as required. The use of team work is another aspect of flexible working. The teams concerned have all the skills necessary to perform their work and organise the distribution of tasks amongst themselves. None of these ideas is particularly new, in the sense that most have always existed in one form or another in the past. However what is new is the attempt to escape from the rigidly defined job of the large government office, the large insurance company, or the large factory. There is a view that this is better for business, better for employees, and much more sensible with modern technology. Clearly this view of the importance of work flexibility affects the design of jobs based on IT systems.

13.7 Trends

There are several ongoing trends in current human resource management which are important for business systems design. These include:

- People are increasingly regarded as the key business asset − this is a major tenet of human resource management.
- Changes in the demographic structure of the workforce in the UK and elsewhere imply older employees, and possibly shortages of suitable staff.
- A reduction in the scale of formal hierarchies within organisations, as mentioned in Section 6.9.
- Smaller employment units − factors such as increasing automation,

greater decentralisation, and more sub-contracting can lead to smaller organisations in both the public and private sectors.
- Job redesign, particularly via modern IT, will embrace more novel ways of organising work such as tele-working (working from home or elsewhere via telecommunication links to the office).
- Work flexibility — new patterns of working and employment which imply a less rigid approach to employment. This is discussed in Section 13.6 above.
- Reward management — for instance fixed pay scales may decline in importance. Pay will be fixed more by the contribution of individual employees and their market value.
- Performance management — people are becoming more subject to the formal assessment of their work performance. Associated with this are programmes to improve performance in terms of factors like personal productivity, flexibility, and initiative.
- The extended use of IT in personnel management — this includes advanced administrative IT systems, with extras like DSSs (Decision Support Systems) for manpower planning, ESs (Expert Systems) for staff selection, and CBT (Computer Based Training).
- Industrial relations — the rise of 'mutuality' where trade unions and their members tend to see a mutual interest in cooperating with management to make a successful organisation. Another trend is declining trade union membership.
- Lack of stability — organisations and employee jobs are in a state of flux due to continuous changes in the business and technical world. Old ideas like a 'job for life' or 'career progression' are becoming less appropriate under modern conditions.

See also Sections 5.13 to 5.18 for general business trends which frequently have human resource implications.

13.8 Summary

- Human resources management covers functions like recruitment, reward management, performance management, health and safety, and industrial relations.
- The personnel function can have a significant effect on the work of

the systems analyst in user departments, and it can be a source of useful information.

- The personnel function can control or influence many staff matters in an IT department, e.g. training programmers.
- Employment is subject to extensive legal regulation.
- Trade unions can be an important consideration and systems analysts must respect arrangements between unions and management such as new technology agreements.
- There are several important trends in human resource management which affect business systems analysis, e.g. flexible working arrangements.

Chapter 14
Human Factors

14.1 Introduction

This chapter discusses human factors in business IT systems. It adopts the perspective of computer practitioners, the individual employee, and small groups of staff. Chapter 13 describes the related subject of general personnel management. Very few systems are totally automatic, and most systems are developed and operated by several people. Large scale systems such as those in high-street banking have a very large number of users. Design faults can make business systems difficult to operate and frustrate their users. Given the fact that people can 'make or break' a system it is obviously essential for the systems analyst to consider the human factors in the development, implementation, and operation of IT systems.

On a personal level some computerised jobs like that of a business planner can be interesting and financially rewarding. Others can be boring, repetitive, and low-paid like that of a data input clerk. Thus IT does not necessarily improve working conditions, and it is perfectly possible to envisage an electronic sweatshop.

Using rather dated American jargon a 'man-machine system' conveys the concept of a system which closely integrates people and machines to perform a particular function. According to this view a battleship, a factory, a business IT system, or just a VDU and its operator, may be regarded as a kind of composite machine. This perspective embraces a more bureaucratic and technical view of human factors. Opposing views consider the more human aspects like politics, social relationships, and employee aspirations.

Many people would probably agree that human resources and human factors are a key aspect, and often the key aspect, to success in business and technology. Basically the argument is: 'Get the people-side right, then everything else comes right'. However this is a counsel of perfection and it is difficult to even approximate to this in practice. Nearly everyone has an opinion on personnel issues which tend to be more controversial than other areas of business like finance. It is a paradox that differing, and even opposing views, on human factors can often be demonstrated to work adequately. So both authoritarian and democratic approaches to managing people can manifestly work. This leads to the 'contingency' approach which says that the right or wrong approach to human factors in business is determined very much by circumstances, rather than abstract general theories. Naturally human factors thinking can also be applied to systems development staff and their work.

14.2 Social sciences

The social sciences such as psychology and sociology have a role in the development of computer business systems. Social science has studied the workplace for about a century and the general conclusions are of use to systems analysts. Unfortunately most social science appears as either common sense expressed in technical language, or as an exaggerated and simplistic view of work, business, and human nature. Maslow's theory of human motivation is discussed later and is just one of many such theories. The conclusions from social sciences can also be controversial, but they are particularly influential in personnel departments, and many ordinary managers are introduced to these sciences as part of their training. An IT practitioner needs to know the more elementary concepts and terminology from these fields just to be able to conduct a conversation about people and job issues. There is also a need to counter the common slur that computer staff are 'techies' with no interest in people.

14.3 Ergonomics

This subject is about the relationship of people and their working environment. It usually implies the scientific design of machines and systems so that they match the needs of their human users. Ergonomics concerns itself with such factors as the effect of temperature and humidity on job performance. Perhaps one of the more extreme applications of ergonomics is the design of fighter aircraft where the pilot's life can literally depend on split second decisions under great physical and mental stress. This means that the aircraft instrument displays and controls must be designed so that they can be used at maximum speed without error. In business computing ergonomics is much more mundane. As far as the systems analyst is concerned this means a common-sense approach to matters such as the HCI (Human Computer Interface). For instance VDU screens should not be too densely packed with data and the use of colour should be restrained and not garish. Above all they should be easy and convenient to use, or 'user-friendly'. The analysis, design and programming are consequently more time-consuming and expensive. But this is justified on the basis that a few extra hours producing a good screen display can save minutes per day for each user and the extra expense is recovered within a few weeks.

A wider view of ergonomics considers the whole office and its work activities so as to optimise human performance. This means examining matters such as correct lighting, heating, ventilation, and seating, as well as proper layout of the workplace. Though all these issues are common-sense, they are important, and many businesses lose valuable productivity by ignoring elementary ergonomics.

An interesting ergonomic anomaly in computing is the standard QWERTY keyboard used on most VDUs, personal computers, and workstations. This was originally produced by Sholes in the 19th century and may be deliberately unergonomic! The inefficient keyboard layout slowed down typing and could prevent the jammimg of mechanical typewriters. Any need for the QWERTY layout has long since disappeared, and an ergonomic keyboard layout was designed by Dvorak in the 1930s. However it has never been successful in replacing the entrenched QWERTY design.

14.4   The informal organisation and politics

The informal organisation is the network of social contacts which exists in a business separately from the official channels of authority and communication. Thus the sales accountant may play golf with the production manager though their jobs rarely bring them into contact at work. Similarly the production manager may be friendly with a factory store-keeper simply because many years before the manager worked in the store as part of his engineering apprenticeship. The systems analyst needs to appreciate this informal network of social contacts as it may provide another means of communication and affect business decisions.

Occasionally the informal organisation is credited with being more influential than the formal organisation.

Systems analysts often meet 'politics' as part of their work. Politics in this sense are the internal politics of an organisation which are seen as being analogous to national and international politics. Internal politics involve policies, criteria, and actions which are not justified from a technical or business viewpoint. Such politics are usually unofficial but can still be very real. So one manager may try to expand his department ('empire-building'), sometimes at the expense of another. A personnel department, for instance, may try to acquire some payroll or pensions work which might normally go to a finance department.

Like real politics internal politics can consist of alliances and hostile uncooperative behaviour between various factions. Occasionally the hostility is severe enough to be called a 'war'. Internal politics is driven by motives like personal ambition, the search for organisational power and status, and a natural desire to defend one's 'territory'. Needless to say, the real motives are concealed behind seemingly respectable technical and business arguments. As regards IT, one example of political behaviour is where a manager uses a computer system as an excuse for an extensive reorganisation of staff jobs, far beyond what the new IT system requires.

Assuming the IT department is initially neutral, which is not always true, it can be asked to take sides in the arguments between groups of employees and departments. This is especially true when new IT systems require some redistribution of work between groups and departments. These political situations can be quite uncomfortable for systems analysts as the various protagonists try to recruit them to their cause. Alternatively the analysis staff may be opposed because the IT project is perceived as a threat. The usual advice is that systems analysts should remain detached and try to minimise all involvement in the internal politics of an organisation. This can however be a difficult position to maintain, particularly as analysts are usually sponsored by user and IT managers who may have political ambitions.

14.5 User response

A complete business system includes its human operators and to achieve high overall performance their role needs to be carefully considered. Clearly if the clerks in a sales office have a negative approach then the performance of the sales order processing system as a whole could easily be degraded.

Protocol and common sense mean that analysts should work with the consent, authorisation and encouragement of the management of a business. Given this, a prime duty of a systems analyst is not to demotivate staff, and preferably to enhance motivation wherever possible. This is easier said than done because the very presence of a systems analyst with the support of the management often implies impending changes in the pattern of office work. Needless to say this is unsettling for many clerical and administrative staff.

There is a wide range of responses from user staff to a proposed change in business systems. Just a few of the possible responses to systems analysts investigating new requirements and producing proposals for new or amended business systems are listed below:

- *Complete rejection*

In trade union terms the project is 'blacked', i.e. the user staff refuse to work with the analysts or new technology, and try to prevent anyone else's involvement.

- *Active opposition*

This is sometimes abusive or damaging, but at least there is some communication and the possibility of persuasion leading to progress. Opposition from managers and supervisors can be more destructive than that from staff and trade unions.

- *Passive opposition*

Usually this means reluctant and unenthusiastic cooperation with the analysts.

- *Neutrality*

The analyst is given the things requested, but everything is left as much as possible to him or her.

- *Active cooperation*

The analyst receives every assistance. There is a constructive attitude and the user staff actively participate with the analyst. Needless to say this is probably the most desirable situation from the analyst's viewpoint.

- *Enthusiastic adoption*

Where the users can take charge of the project and constantly push the IT staff for more rapid progress. The users are even willing to do some IT work themselves.

- *User take-over*

The users organise their own IT, either by developing their own systems or by using a software house working under their control. At best the analyst becomes a contractor or consultant working for, rather than with, the users.

Sometimes the extremes of reaction to IT are described flippantly as cyberphobia (fear or dislike of automation) or cyberphilia (love of automation). Similar responses to new technology have occurred in the past. The Luddites of early 19th century England were machine wreckers and rioters who smashed factory machines. Their assumption was that new technology destroyed the need for old craft skills and employment. Opponents of computer projects are still derided as Luddites. A counter-example occurred later in 19th century Britain when there was railway mania. This was an over-enthusiastic and unrealistic promotion of railways, followed by financial failures.

The responses of users and their managers to change exist on two levels. First there is a personal response based on the hopes and fears of the individual. Secondly there may be response, particularly from senior staff, based on their professional role in a particular business function such as purchasing or marketing.

14.6 Adoption

Part of the job of the systems analyst is to persuade managers and their staff to adopt new systems, new technology, and new ways of working. This persuasion can be viewed as selling. One way of persuading people to adopt something new is to respect the elementary psychology of the process. So assuming that a proposal is fundamentally sound and broadly in the interests of the prospective users how are they to be persuaded to adopt it?

One way is to accept a gradual staged process of persuasion. Take the example of convincing administrative managers to adopt an office automation system with word processing and electronic mail for all staff. Then the stages are as follows:

- *Awareness*

Prior to any successful persuasion there needs to be some awareness. If this does not exist it must be created. In this example, the managers and staff are already aware that office automation has some promise for them.

- *Interest*

Arousing the interest of the managers and staff is important. Only if they are interested are they going to devote time to investigating a new system. Good salesmen are adept at stimulating interest. One obvious method is to compare the hopefully significant benefits of the new system with the defects of the old systems based on internal mail and typing.

- *Evaluation*

A good salesman helps users perform a favourable evaluation. This means providing all the necessary information and helping people discover ways round possible obstacles. Visits to other businesses already using the new technology can also help the evaluation process.

- *Trial*

Evaluations based on verbal discussion, documentation, and sight-seeing are all very well, but trying something in practice can be very persuasive. In the case of the office automation system this could include hands-on use of a small trial system, preferably set up in the users' own office.

- *Adoption*

Assuming the users have satisfactorily progressed through the previous stages they can adopt the new technology. This means converting to the new system.

The above scheme can be used for individuals or businesses. Throughout the process of adoption the analyst can ease the job of the decision makers and their staff, for example by providing information and arranging practical demonstrations.

Some people and some businesses are more receptive to innovation than others, and this provides a basis for classifying them. The range from the enthusiastic to the reluctant is:

- Innovators
- Early adopters
- Early majority
- Late majority
- Laggards

As the names imply, most people and businesses lie in the majority groups above. A systems analyst would be well advised to introduce new adventurous projects with people who are known to be innovators rather than laggards!

14.7 Work performance

The work performance of an employee or group of employees is the result of many positive and negative factors. Clearly job requirements, like good experience of computer systems for a clerk, are important determinants of work performance. Similarly ergonomics affects performance − people cannot do mental work well if there is too much noise or disruption. The various considerations in job design are discussed in Section 14.10 below. On a more personal level some determinants of work performance are:

- *Selection*

When seeking capable and suitable people a variety of techniques are often used together. Well-known methods include recruiting according to educational qualifications, psychometric tests for ability and personality, interviews, and references. Selection is basically about identifying employees with the right innate attributes such as intelligence and good health, and the right acquired attributes such as computer programming skills in COBOL.

- *Motivation*

This is usually regarded as a key factor. There are many practical ways of increasing motivation, e.g. commission for computer sales staff. Motivation is discussed further in Section 14.8 below.

- *Leadership*

The style of leadership may be authoritarian (dictatorial), democratic (seeking consensus through meetings), and laissez-faire (where the manager or supervisor leaves their subordinates to continue their work without much interference or support). Whether a particular style is appropriate or not depends on circumstances.

- *Culture*

The culture of an organisation is all the collective assumptions and ways of working in an organisation. Thus the culture of some companies involves a collective approach to solving work problems whereas others encourage individual initiative and action. Computer companies like ICL and IBM (supposedly) have quite different cultures, i.e. different ways of viewing and handling similar situations. Many people who change employer for an ostensibly similar job immediately detect a change in culture. In the author's experience this is particularly true in computing.

- *Training*

Training is an important factor which allows staff to develop new skills rapidly. Formal training is a lot more efficient than trying to pick up knowledge and skills on the job.

- *Information*

People need feedback on whether they are performing well or not, and where their strengths and weaknesses lie.

14.8 Employee work motivation

Managers have an obvious interest in employee work motivation. As a general rule of thumb, a well-motivated person is 30% more productive than somebody who is unmotivated (or 'plodding'). A demotivated or hostile person may actually do more harm than good. Indeed there is the old military saying that one volunteer is worth ten pressed men. Because the issue of motivation is so important it has been studied intensively, and there are numerous theories. To most people these theories seem to be little more than a structuring of common sense, but they are taught to all management trainees and it is important for systems analysts to appreciate them.

The example of a motivational theory used here is Maslow's hierarchy of needs. It is popular and has its uses in several common IT situations. Maslow's theory develops the obvious fact that people's needs are prioritised, and his ideas are often shown as a triangle with the lowest needs at the bottom as shown in Fig. 14.1. According to Maslow the lower needs must be satisfied before higher needs can become a motivator. Thus people who are satisfied with the level of their pay (a basic need for most people) are not motivated by more pay, but may well want greater security of employment which then becomes a motivator. Once security is satisfied, people then seek social satisfaction and so on. In an employment context the levels in Maslow's theory may be interpreted as follows:

- *Basic needs*

These are interpreted as factors like food, clothing, and shelter. In a work environment basic needs are often satisfied by money which is used to purchase the necessities of life. However, providing satisfactory working conditions is clearly important. For instance clerks and programmers cannot operate VDUs properly if they are too cold, and constantly striving to keep warm.

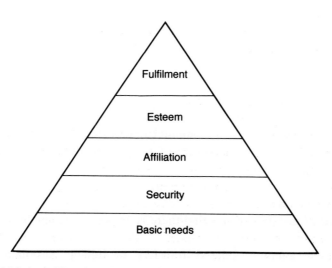

Fig. 14.1 Maslow's hierarchy of needs (with minor changes of terminology). The lower needs must first be satisfied before a particular need can become a motivator.

- *Security*

In an employment context these needs are usually satisfied by a safe working environment, and benefits such as sick pay and pensions.

- *Affiliation*

People need company and many prefer to work in a team with good relationships.

- *Esteem*

People need both respect from other people and self-respect.

- *Self-fulfilment*

This is the idea that people have personal ambitions and potential which need to be fulfilled. So a systems analyst could develop an interest in business management. One way he or she could be partially fulfilled in this direction is by studying for business qualifications.

Maslow's view can be criticised on many grounds. For example it seems an unduly selfish view and does not include charitable, political, or religious motivation. However it can still be useful. As an example of how Maslow's theory can be applied, assume that a company has decided to reduce its mainframe computer operations staff gradually. This is partly because of a transfer of work to smaller office-based computers, and partly because of more automatic methods of operating mainframes. In this situation it is important to maintain the motivation and cooperation of the operations staff during the transition period. Maslow's hierarchy can structure an ethical business solution:

- *Basic needs*

Some staff may fear losing their income, e.g. through redundancy or a loss of shift allowances for computer operators.

Possible solution: guarantees of future employment or generous redundancy payments.

- *Security needs*

Some staff may be anxious that there is no long term employment for them.

Possible solution: phased transfers to suitable alternative employment.

● *Affiliation needs*

The existing work group will be dissolved, yet it is quite sociable and works well together.

Possible argument: The changes will take place over several months and new work groups are likely to be just as sociable and work just as well together.

● *Esteem needs*

Staff will lose the respect of their colleagues which is based on competence in computer operations. It is unfortunate that these skills are less relevant to the business in the future.

Possible argument: with training and sympathetic support, transferred staff will soon achieve competence in their new jobs and then earn the respect of their new supervisors and colleagues.

● *Fulfilment*

Career aspiration in computer operations have been dashed.

Possible argument: the restructuring of the company's work offers opportunities for some operations staff to learn new skills like programming and acquire new careers.

As can be seen by looking at the possible hopes and fears of the staff under Maslow's headings it may be possible to devise strategies which retain and even develop staff motivation. Alternatively demotivation may be minimised. Naturally this sort of approach is not guaranteed to work perfectly, but at least it forces managers to consider the human factors when planning change.

14.9   Job design

The design of jobs, clerical jobs in particular, is implicit in computer systems design. So the boxes on the systems analyst's data flow diagrams for a new computer system mean new human or machine processes. For examples of these diagrams see Figs 16.3 to 16.4. Designing a VDU input screen implies that somebody is going to have the task of obtaining and entering data via the screen. Installing an office personal computer network implies that some one will have the task of making regular security copies of the essential data. The sum total of a series of apparently small changes like these can mean a significant change in the amount and type of work, as well as the skills required. Thus one consequence of the computerisation of accounting over the last 30 years has been a decline in the number of clerical staff with a good knowledge of manual book-keeping as much of the work is now done by computer. Conversely most accounts staff need and have acquired a good working knowledge of computers. Practical computer skills are an important requirement in many white-collar job advertisements.

A job is, of course, a set of regular and related tasks or duties. When the organisation of a business function or department is decided, this automatically implies a particular distribution of tasks. So as shown in Fig. 16.2 a large payroll department may have been set up with a wages section dealing with the weekly pay of manual workers, and a salaries section paying white-collar staff monthly. By setting up a department in this way there is the strong implication that the staff in both sections must apply general payroll practices such as PAYE procedures.

An alternative arrangement is to set up the payroll department with a computer input section, a computer processing section, and an output section, with all sections covering wages and salaries. By working this way the staff in each section only need a partial knowledge of payroll practice, e.g. those procedures concerned with collecting and inputing pay data. Only the manager and his or her deputy still need an overall knowledge of payroll, and they can handle any exceptions.

There are numerous approaches to job design which may be broadly classified as:

- *The technical and bureaucratic approach*

The aim is to find organisational and job designs which optimise 'hard' factors such as productivity, quality, service, and cost. This approach tends to be associated with dividing work into jobs which are specialised, repetitive, have little variety, and require minimum skill. The approach is often quantitative and supported with detailed calculations of work rates, job times, and written work instructions. The classic example of applying this in computing is data preparation. Here operators spend all day entering data from forms into a computer system. Data entry rates can be high — over 15 000 key depressions per hour with modern equipment. With this approach human factors are considered in a rather technical way, such as ensuring that physical considerations like workplace layout are correct.

- *The human-centred approach*

The aim is to optimise 'soft' factors, e.g. by producing work environments which are socially and personally satisfying to human beings on the assumption that this leads to good performance. This view tends to be associated with democratic management, and ideas like job enrichment and team work. It tends to downplay the technical aspects of job design.

Several theories of job design are mentioned in the academic literature. Usually they are discussed in terms of particular variants of each school of thought above, e.g. scientific management (one version of the technical and bureaucratic view), and the human relations school (as the name implies a version of the human-oriented approach). However, versions of each approach are rare in their pure form. These approaches are sometimes satirised by using extremes, e.g. an office using human robots or an office run like a social club!

Current trends sometimes seem to favour simultaneously both a more human approach and more strict control of work. For instance teamwork is developed in one organisation, whilst another introduces automatic work surveillance. This is where each individual's work with a computer system is automatically monitored for performance assessment, e.g. in terms of productivity. In practice systems analysts meet pragmatic mixed views that are biased towards one extreme or another. The mixed view seeks the optimum way of organising people, tasks, and technology with due regard for human nature. In academic circles this is called the 'socio-technical' approach. See also Section 19.16 for a further discussion of the technical and human perspectives on human work activities.

Designing a job involves several factors like selecting the regular tasks or duties that make up a job, for instance all those tasks associated with purchase ledger in an accounts department. As already implied, individual jobs need also to be designed in the context of the whole department and the whole organisation. In computer terminology jobs can be designed by top-down or bottom-up processes or a combination of the two. In the top-down process the various requirements and functions of an organisation are split between departments which are further split into jobs and tasks. In the bottom-up process the various tasks required are combined into jobs which are then combined into sections and departments. The reason why both are rare is simply that most organisations already exist and most job design is about modifying current jobs.

Even new businesses often start from small beginnings and evolve slowly. Working from first principles only tends to occur when an existing business is extensively reorganised, or an existing business builds a new factory, or establishes a new subsidiary. However, in the writer's experience, managers in this situation tend not to use a scientific systematic approach, but rely on precedents and personal judgement when planning both departments and jobs.

14.10   The factors in job design

Lack of job satisfaction is common and bad jobs can be discussed in terms related to Maslow's hierarchy of needs, e.g. low pay, insecurity, poor esteem, boredom, and lack of prospects. Good job design can also be discussed using Maslow's hierarchy. Another view is that besides good pay and conditions other factors in a worthwhile job include: the exercise of skills and discretion; meaningfulness; challenge; equitable treatment; and time for personal, family, and community activities. However there are many factors in job design besides motivation and personal satisfaction. In more detail some considerations with employee job design include:

- *Standardised procedures*
Many jobs have defined standard ways of dealing with most eventualities. The documentation containing these office procedures can be useful to analysts investigating administrative systems.

- *Work study*
This is the 'scientific' approach to job design that is often associated with timing manual work to set performance standards. It can also be applied in the office. It is normally split into two areas − methods study and work measurement. Methods study is about determining the best way to do a job, whilst work measurement is about establishing the amount of work in a task, and often about establishing the time to do a task.

- *Job demands*
Jobs can make demands on staff because of factors like attention to detail, work pressure (a fast pace), and unpleasant or hazardous conditions, e.g. in mining.

- *Ergonomics*

This is discussed in Section 14.3 above. Unergonomic jobs lead to employee frustration and wastefully reduce employee performance.

- *Feedback*

Both individual employees and their supervisors need feedback on the quantity and quality of their work. With computer systems this can be done using control totals and throughput statistics.

- *Communication*

Each job needs to be linked with other jobs either verbally, or by paperwork, or electronically.

- *Motivation*

This is an essential factor discussed in Section 14.8 above. Informally motivation can be improved by things like praise for doing a job well. Formally it can be improved by approaches like performance appraisal and bonus schemes.

- *Autonomy*

Many people value autonomy and discretion. This means giving freedom to employees so that they themselves can significantly control the way their work is done. A popular modern word, that roughly implies giving employees a measure of autonomy, is 'empowerment'. Of course, autonomy and discretion are given in the expectation of an improvement in work performance.

- *The use of abilities*

Jobs require abilities like manual dexterity and skills like typing or programming. Individuals usually like to use their training and skills. From the point of view of the organisation this often makes sense also. One danger however is designing jobs which are unique to individuals, and this makes it difficult to find replacements. Developing skills through training is another consideration.

- *Equity*

This is the subtle concept of fairness which is open to varying interpretations. However it is a matter of common experience that people react in an adverse way if they believe their treatment is unfair.

Though it is subjective, equity must be addressed as part of job design and reward management (see Section 13.2).

- *Supervision*

Being in charge of other people requires skills and experience, and it is often not an easy role.

- *Responsibility*

The amount of responsibility in a job is an important factor. Staff can for instance be responsible for managing the work of others, controlling an IT implementation project as a systems analyst, or responsible for money as a cashier.

- *Job rotation*

This involves moving people regularly to other work to reduce monotony.

- *Job enlargement*

Combining a large number of tasks into one job to increase the meaning and variety of the work.

- *Job enrichment*

The idea is to make work more challenging and more interesting by increasing the skills required and responsibility.

- *Autonomous work groups*

Self-regulating groups of employees who organise the work amongst themselves with little supervision.

There is a modern view that in many cases future work activities cannot be foreseen in detail because business changes frequently and unexpectedly. As mentioned in previous chapters this leads to the idea that people should work in a team and be multi-skilled, willingly doing whatever is necessary. This approach tends to de-emphasise the design and specification of jobs, particularly permanent jobs, and looks for flexibility instead.

In practice the issue of job design is often obscured by the user management, systems analysts, and clerical staff, particularly with small systems. The analyst's proposals tend to concentrate on the various tasks that must be done, and there is little direct mention of combining the tasks into jobs. Once the analyst's proposals are revised and adjusted everyone is satisfied. Then the management and staff often accommodate the new system by informally and amicably distributing the new pattern of tasks amongst themselves. This is less likely to happen with big systems in large organisations where there is more interest in formal job design.

14.11 Summary

- Human factors in systems design can be a mixture of the controversial and common-sense. However everyone agrees that businesses can benefit significantly by handling the human factors correctly, and that mistakes in this area have expensive repercussions.
- Ironically it is possible for opposing strategies about personnel issues and human factors to work reasonably well in different businesses. This leads to the 'contingency' approach, e.g. letting circumstances be a major determinant of human factors planning rather than abstract principles.
- Ergonomics is useful when designing the HCI and the workplace features of an IT system.
- The response of users to new systems varies from rejection and hostility to enthusiasm and IT take-over depending on circumstances.
- The introduction of new technology can be encouraged by taking people progressively through the stages of awareness, interest, evaluation, trial, and adoption.
- Social science theories such as Maslow's hierarchy of needs can be useful when considering the human aspects of business and computer activities.
- Job design can emphasise the technical factors or human issues or both.
- When designing jobs it is necessary to consider factors like standardised procedures, ergonomics, control, feedback, discretion, use of abilities, and job enrichment.

Chapter 15
Quality Management in Business

15.1 Introduction

This chapter discusses quality management in general. The IT aspects of quality are discussed in Chapter 26. Quality is a fashionable subject that business has rediscovered. There is a lot of hype about quality, but behind the propaganda is the basic idea that systematically producing and improving a good product not only benefits the customer and the organisation itself, but also all other parties. These other parties include suppliers, employees, and society at large.

Quality in business does not only apply to expensive manufactured items such as Rolls Royce motor cars; it also applies to more mundane products such as aspirins and pensions administration manuals. Furthermore it applies to service operations such as sales invoicing, fast food, and car repairs! To ensure the quality of the vast volume of goods and services it produces modern business has to apply some quite complicated procedures and careful management. Some organisations adopt TQM (Total Quality Management) to demonstrate their complete commitment to quality. TQM focuses on the customer and emphasises quality as a well-resourced pervasive organisation-wide activity involving all employees. It needs the enthusiastic support of top management. Furthermore TQM requires the continuous improvement of all aspects of an organisation, and particularly its products and services.

With regard to the public sector, in 1991 the UK government announced its Citizen's Charter programme. This is an attempt to introduce more concepts on quality (amongst other matters) into services such as health and education.

Many quality concepts and techniques originated in manufacturing, and these need to be modified or changed in other areas of business such as producing software or providing services.

The interest in quality often extends beyond a business to imposing high standards on suppliers in a constructive way. Modern quality programmes include an emphasis on customer care. However as well as defect elimination there should also be a drive for the continuous improvement of products, services, and business activities. This should lead to:

- Customer satisfaction
- Reduced costs
- Employee pride in achievement
- Competitive advantage

Quality can be a confusing subject in that there are several sources for the basic ideas. These include leading quality experts like Crosby, Deming, and Ishikawa, as well as organisations like the British Standards Institute. The subject can become almost philosophical and quasi-religious, and some individuals and organisations can become very fervent about quality management. Furthermore, each business appears to interpret mainstream quality ideas in its own way. This leads to a confusion of terminology, and though the concepts from different sources are similar they are not always identical, and sometimes they appear to conflict.

Because quality is pervasive, it overlaps considerably with other business and technical subjects. So it is impossible to consider, say, the quality of textiles without considering their design, manufacture, and raw materials. Thus quality in this case is very intimately mixed with weaving and spinning technology. Similarly software quality is closely associated with, say, programming techniques. Continuous improvement is a subject which is frequently associated with quality. However it not only includes quality, but also issues like improving productivity.

15.2 Quality and IT staff

Quality is important to IT staff from several points of view:

- *The work of IT staff*

This needs to be of good quality. For instance, simple errors and omissions by a systems analyst can be extremely expensive to correct later. A mistake in the design of a business form could mean scrapping ten thousand copies of the form after it has been printed.

- *Computer systems*

These are designed for users like management accountants. Any software and other system components must not only be of good quality in themselves, but they must also assist the users in providing a quality service. For instance good accounting software has extensive data checking facilities which are designed to trap VDU input errors.

- *Computer operations*

Computer operations staff are responsible for vital matters like maintaining the service on a telecommunications network and day-to-day IT security.

- *Quality commitment*

In a modern organisation where quality is a central concern everyone must demonstrate a practical commitment to quality.

15.3   Quality policies

Mission statements and policies are adopted by all organisations who are serious about quality. The following are summaries of real examples.

Xerox Corporation

- Quality is fundamental to a leadership company.
- Understand the customers' requirements.
- Meet the requirements of internal and external customers.
- Employee involvement.
- Error-free work.

Girobank

Customers are to receive the best possible service in terms of quality and value for money at a cost which ensures the continued success of the Bank.

Similar approaches are found in the public sector where 'charters' are issued laying down the principles on which a service is to operate. One example is the Tax Payers' Charter from the Inland Revenue.

15.4 The meaning of quality in business

The word quality has many connotations and associated concepts such as excellence, reliability, and lack of defects. Some business definitions of quality include:

- Fitness for use.
- Defect free.
- Conformance to specification.
- Conformance to requirements.
- Satisfaction in ownership.
- Meeting the customer's needs and expectations.
- The totality of all attributes specified, required, and expected by all interested parties such as the customer and government.

The broad distinction between quality assurance (QA) and quality control (QC) is:

- QA is the system for setting standards and procedures for quality control and ensuring that these are applied.
- QC is verifying conformance, e.g. the detailed inspecting or testing of computer programs or manufactured items to ensure that they meet their specifications.

Unfortunately the two are often treated as synonymous, particularly in ordinary speech. In computing, the term QA frequently implies any activity concerned with quality. For example a computer program is often said to 'in QA', i.e. in the process of being inspected and tested prior to release for live use. The process of managing all aspects of quality is sometimes called quality management, i.e. it includes both QA and QC. There is a British Standard for quality terminology, BS 4778, but as already implied there is only limited standardisation in practice. The situation as usual in computing is confused by the frequent use of American terminology and the terminology of particular companies.

A production process or service is designed as mixture of the five M's — **machines**, **materials**, **men** (people generally), **methods** (procedures), and **miscellaneous** items. Some would add a sixth M for a guaranteed success — **magic**! In practice the quality of a process like computer programming or a service like personnel administration is often managed by QA and QC of each of the constituent five Ms. For example in manufacturing processes maintenance standards are set for machine tools and specifications are prepared stipulating the quality of the materials used. The five Ms can also be used as a basis for improving quality, e.g. raising the quality of a payroll service by formally training new clerks (the 'men') in PAYE. Section 15.6 below discusses the quality of design.

15.5   The cost of quality

There is a view that quality is free, i.e. the savings in producing quality goods and services balance or outweigh the extra costs. The cost of quality may be defined in terms of:

- Appraisal (usually inspection and testing).
- Prevention, e.g. regular servicing of hardware to reduce the chance of failure.
- Failure, e.g. a major insurance computer system 'crashing' due to a software bug which then has to be corrected and re-run.

In addition there may be hidden costs such as customer or user dissatisfaction caused by an unreported product failure. Failure costs are often classified as internal or external. Internal failure costs arise from those failure effects which are entirely within the organisation like the cost of scrapping defective products before they are sold. External failure costs arise from those effects which are outside the organisation and can involve the customer, the user, or society in general. An extreme example is an aeroplane crash due to defective design or manufacture which affects the airline (customer), passengers (users), and possibly other parties like domestic residents near an airport.

Another way of looking at this is the PONC (Price of Non-Conformance), i.e. the price or cost as described above of failing to meet product or service requirements. The PONC is quoted as being 20% to 40% of sales value in traditional organisations.

15.6 Crosby's absolutes

Phil Crosby is an American quality expert and his four 'absolutes' of quality are a useful summary of quality ideas:

- Conformance to requirements.
- Prevention of defects.
- Zero defects (or 'right first time').
- Measurement of quality.

These are really slogans which need to be interpreted. They also illustrate some of the conceptual difficulties with quality.

- *Conformance to requirements*

Taking a narrow interpretation a programmer is expected to produce software that meets the systems analyst's specification. However this view that the requirements are what is specified is useful but incomplete. It is a production-oriented view which does not address the problem of how one determines whether the specification is correct in the first place. This is a major problem in systems analysis and business generally which leads onto the rather nebulous market-oriented concept of the 'quality of design'. This is how well the specified design of a product or service can meet all the various requirements, which may be both explicit and implicit. Note the design requirements are those of all parties such as the supplier, customer, user, and government. Requirements can include considerations like user satisfaction, price, profit, health and safety, pollution, and aesthetics.

Hence with a product both the quality of the design and the quality of production must be right. With services there is an analogous view. Not only must the design of a service be correct but also the quality of the operations which lead to its delivery must also be satisfactory.

- *Prevention of defects*

All modern quality concepts put the emphasis on preventing errors not merely detecting and correcting. Figure 15.1 shows the modern view that the costs of quality *should* fall as more effort is put into the prevention of defects.

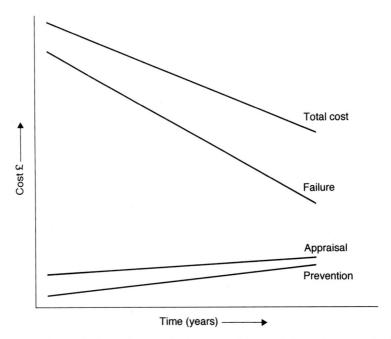

Fig. 15.1 The graph shows the contribution to total costs of the various aspects of quality. There is an *expectation* that increased preventive activity reduces failure costs in the long term.

- *Zero defects (or 'right first time')*

Zero defects, if interpreted literally, is an aim in many situations rather than a reality. It is often used to encapsulate the view that excuses for shoddy work should not be allowed, and also that continuous improvement in quality is a major aim. In the sense of no departures from a specification it can be achievable, particularly with an easy specification.

- *Measurement*

A prime measurement of quality is the PONC (price of non-conformance), i.e. the cost of producing goods and services which do not meet their requirements. The PONC was previously described and includes the financial costs of dealing with returned faulty goods, possible compensation to customers, correcting faulty goods, and so on. Again, in practice this kind of financial measurement is not available to the computer programmer or factory machinist. They must rely on other quality measurements, e.g. the size and strength of steel components.

15.7 Everyone is a customer and supplier

Many people think backwards from the customer and derive a series of stages for considering quality issues as shown in Fig. 15.2. This diagram is also applied within a business. In terms of a person in a factory or office the next department or employee down the chain of processes is an internal customer, and should be regarded as such. Similarly the next department or person up the chain of processes is an internal supplier. Providing quality for an internal or external customer demands not only careful responsive work from each employee but also good quality from all suppliers. This is not particularly new thinking to systems analysts who have always tended to regard the IT user as a customer and the programmer as a supplier.

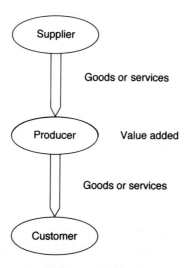

Fig. 15.2 The chain of supply provides one way of looking for areas of quality improvement. The diagram can refer not only to whole organisations but to departments and individual employees within an organisation. According to this view most employees in business have 'customers' and 'suppliers'. For example an office supervisor completes an overtime form for her clerical staff. The recipient of the form, the payroll clerk in this example, is a 'customer' of the supervisor. Errors on the form just cause needless problems, queries, and extra work for all parties.

15.8   Standards

Part of the process of delivering quality goods and services requires meeting standards. A standard is effectively a kind of general specification which applies to a wide range of goods and activities. There are a whole series of standards relevant to computing and some examples include:

● *Local standards*
For example the conventions for numbering computer programs or engineering components in a business. So a prefix PY could be used to signify a payroll program, with PY01 the first program, PY02 the second, and so on.

● *Methodologies*
SSADM (Structured Systems Analysis and Design Methodology) Version 4 is documented in four thick manuals.

● *Products*
For example, it is usual to standardise within a business on the use of a software product like the Lotus 1−2−3 spreadsheet package. With personal computers, hardware standards are important for buying components like disk drives, telecommunication boards, and graphics cards, e.g. an important standard for memory boards is LIM 4.0 (LIM = Lotus Intel and Microsoft).

● *Services*
An illustration is the data transmission standards which are necessary when designing systems that use public telecommunication services.

● *National standards*
The national standards issued by the British Standards Institute (BSI) provide an excellent example, e.g. BS 6498 which concerns the preparation of microfilm for use as legal evidence.

● *Foreign standards*
These are issued by the foreign equivalent of the BSI such as the American National Standards Institute (ANSI).

● *International standards*

An example is the Open Systems Interconnection (OSI) telecommunications standard. This is issued by the International Standards Organisation (ISO).

Several British Standards and other standards such the NATO AQAP 13 are directly relevant to systems development. As discussed below, a general standard such as BS 5750, even though designed for manufacturing, can be applied to systems development and computer operations.

15.9   The organisation of quality

Quality assurance and control is often the responsibility of special sections of a business. Typical names for these business sections or departments include. Quality Assurance, Quality Control, Inspection, Standards, Quality Auditing, and Testing. Ordinary functional sections such as a production department in a factory often have some responsibility for their own quality as well. Semi-formal or transient arrangements are also frequently found. For instance, quality circles are small groups of staff, often from the same department, who voluntarily get together to improve quality. Quality project teams exist for a specific short-term purpose and cross departmental boundaries, e.g. a project to improve product quality could involve design engineers, production management, and purchasing officers.

Within a commercial computing context, software quality management is fundamentally a function of size measured in terms of the number of staff involved, the number of lines of software code produced, and so on. Thus in a large organisation separate teams for standards and QA/QC can be established. In a small organisation the development staff can do their own QA/QC, though as separately defined tasks. Project management and systems development methodologies all require specific forms of QA/QC.

Quality should also be a continuous consideration built into business and technical activities at all stages. This is in addition to any formally separate QA or QC work. Modern thinking also stresses the importance of imbuing all staff with an interest in the quality of their own work. This is just as true for computing staff as for those in other functions such as manufacturing.

15.10 BS 5750

BS 5750 is a general civilian standard for quality systems and is similar
to military defence standards. It is identical with the international ISO
9000 series of standards. Though often used for quality systems in
manufacturing it is increasingly used for software production. Interest-
ingly enough BS 5750 can also be applied to services such as legal
advice and banking.

BS 5750 concerns quality systems and their management rather than
the quality of goods and services themselves. A quality system involves
such matters as management responsibility for quality, quality auditing,
documentation, e.g. work instructions, and records like test results. A
quality system also involves procedures. Examples are those procedures
for the control of product designs, quality control in production such as
inspecting raw materials, checking test equipment, handling defective
items, and dealing with customer complaints.

BS 5750 consists of several parts and covers quality procedures for
design, manufacture, installation, and servicing. The application of BS
5750 to software production is covered by the TickIT manual published
by the Department of Trade and Industry. BS 5750 certification involves
regular inspections to ensure that quality systems are kept up-to-date
and applied.

It is seen as important to be certified under BS 5750, both in
business generally and in the IT industry. Certification provides a
marketing advantage as well as the benefits of improved quality. However BS 5750 is sometimes seen as bureaucratic and expensive. It was
estimated in 1988 to cost over £100 000 to introduce BS 5750 into a
typical software house with 50 to 100 employees and a sales turnover
of £3 million. It could involve operating costs of £200 000 per annum.
The main assumption is that improved quality makes this worthwhile.
It should be noted that these costs refer to the quality management
system and not just BS 5750 compliance.

15.11 Activities and documentation

Quality activities can be routine, for instance regular inspection of
samples of machined metal components on a factory floor. Some are
more occasional, e.g. appraising a supplier of raw materials in terms of

failings in the material or late deliveries. Whatever the activity there is an emphasis on documentation, e.g. specifications of the physical and chemical properties of raw materials such as steel bars, engineering drawings to check dimensions of machined components, and contracts to check delivery dates. Information technology is of course no different and again relies extensively on documentation such as EDI (Electronic Data Interchange) specifications. Service operations can be specified in a similar way to production processes, e.g. the procedures for welcoming customers into a restaurant.

15.12   Techniques

There is an extensive range of quality control techniques used in business which depend to some extent on the nature of the product or service. Some familiar and important techniques include:

- *Process monitoring*
For instance ensuring that the right temperature is maintained for storing milk or operating mainframe computers.

- *Inspection*
Checking output is correct, e.g. examining paintwork for blemishes.

- *Destructive testing*
An example is testing the maximum tension that a fabric can bear before tearing. Destructive testing does not usually apply in business computing.

- *Non-destructive testing*
Cars, for instance, are test driven after they have been assembled. Adjustments are made, faults corrected, and efforts are made to prevent a re-occurrence of any problems. Electronic components are often non-destructively tested before delivery to the customer. Needless to say non-destructive testing is a major method of QC with software.

- *Statistical Process Control (SPC)*
This involves controlling quality by continually plotting quality measurements on charts and using statistical rules. SPC can be employed,

for example, to ensure that the dimensions of volume-produced pressed steel components are maintained within tolerances.

● *Special investigations*
For example investigating the source of packing faults in cartons of footwear, or the errors in a computer stock recording system, with a view to minimising them.

15.13 Measurement and data

A common example of a quality measurement is the hardness of steel. One way of measuring this is by the size of the hole made in the steel by a small diamond under a standard load. Other examples of quality measurements are the interior diameter of a cylinder, the number of bugs per 1000 lines of program code, the time to fix a software bug, or the number of faults per 1000 invoices. In computer jargon such measurements or estimates are called 'metrics'. Once defined, data needs to be collected both for analysing history, predicting trends, and quality monitoring. SPC mentioned above is one important version of this. Data is often collected continually in manufacturing and graphed so that trends can be identified. For instance as the tools in a manufacturing process wear, the components manufactured may gradually become too large. Such trends can be identified by sampling the production and plotting graphs. A computer company maintaining hardware can similarly identify quality trends by examining the reports of service engineers. In practice this requires a modicum of administrative discipline, i.e. measurements, faults, and corrective action must be properly recorded and not just handled on an informal basis.

15.14 Variables and attributes

In the quality context a variable is a numeric measure that is continuous, but must be confined to a specified range, e.g. the temperature for pasteurising milk, or the diameter of an axle. By way of contrast, an attribute is discrete and can only be counted e.g. program bugs or faults in woven cloth.

15.15 Mathematics and statistics

Quality, via metrics, is amenable to mathematical and statistical treatment. Both elementary and advanced techniques can have a pay-off. Elementary techniques such as pie charts may be useful when communicating with relatively innumerate personnel. Every technique should be chosen in terms of fitness for purpose and the costs and benefits. Though the theory of, say, SPC (Statistical Process Control) is advanced by most people's standards it can be reduced to a few practical procedures for use by ordinary personnel. The role of mathematics and statistics is discussed in Chapter 25.

15.16 Service quality

Section 5.5 mentions that the UK is primarily a service economy. This means that the quality of service is an important issue. As already discussed, quality principles apply to services as well as products, i.e. basically specification, conformance, and measurement.

A service can fall into the following broad categories:

- Personal, e.g. a legal advisor or barber.
- Anonymous, e.g. a postal service.
- Automated, e.g. a telephone system or vending machine.

All these can be combined as in a hotel. Some of the problems associated with service quality are discussed in 15.17 below.

15.17 Problem areas

Some products and some services, e.g. business legal advice, can present difficulties with defining 'quality'. Basically this means that the users of the service may have differing expectations, or no clear expectations.

Measurement is more than defining appropriate metrics. It also involves the systems and discipline for collecting the necessary data during business processes such as mainframe computer operations.

There are often 'soft' aspects to the quality of service. Examples include a tasteful approach, politeness, and customer-care. How are these to be specified and measured? Questionnaires are often used to assess the soft aspects of quality. For example questionnaires can be issued after a training course to assess whether the course was of good quality in terms of attributes like relevance, interest, presentation, and support services like administration.

The quality of any service or product must include health and safety considerations. With some services, particularly business systems, security in its widest sense is an important aspect of quality. Security means everything from hacker-proofing a networked IT system to regular backup copies of essential data.

The appropriate quality control techniques depend on circumstances. So SPC (Statistical Process Control) may not always be relevant in software production, but it is relevant to volume manufacturing.

15.18   Summary

- Quality is a major factor in modern business covering both products and services. It is also important in public services.
- Modern quality management is also concerned with issues like customer care and the continuous improvement of products, services, and business activities.
- Quality has several definitions which are broadly compatible. Two of use to the systems analyst are 'fitness for purpose' and 'conformance to requirements'.
- The cost of quality is the costs of appraisal, prevention, and failure. The benefits of good quality management should outweigh any costs involved.
- Crosby's absolutes are: conformance to requirements, prevention, zero defects, and measurement.
- Formal standards are important, e.g. SSADM and OSI.
- BS 5750 is a quality systems standard which is important in business generally. It is also important for IT products and services.
- The main techniques for controlling quality include inspection and testing.
- Some quality techniques involve mathematics and statistics.
- Both soft and hard factors are amenable to quality management.

Chapter 16
Payroll: an Administrative Example

16.1 Introduction

This chapter describes in some detail how the payroll function operates in a typical organisation. One intention is to demonstrate that an apparently straight-forward administrative function, like paying employees, is much more complex than most people suppose. Its economic importance is huge because the payroll function is the channel by which most of the national income enters the economy, and it is also an important method of raising government revenues.

The other intention is to demonstrate, within the payroll context, the combined application of business and IT subjects. Thus subjects introduced in other chapters like organisation theory, cybernetics, and computer specification techniques, are illustrated in a tangible form through payroll administration. In addition payroll systems are a common IT application.

16.2 Payroll background

Payroll is important as the staff costs of running a business can easily exceed 50% of total costs. From the systems analyst's viewpoint it is also one of the most rigorous and demanding applications in business computing. Payroll systems are very sensitive to mistakes, and any failure may mean employees receive the wrong pay, or no pay at all. The Inland Revenue could penalise an employer whose software did not comply with tax legislation. Worse still, the law governing payroll changes frequently and it is often difficult to amend the payroll software within the short notice period given. This means that computer staff risk severe censure for any mistakes and often get little thanks if everything is working satisfactorily. All this makes payroll an unpopular application amongst computer staff generally.

16.3   Payroll statistics

The role of the payroll department in a business can be summarised as
the timely and accurate payment of all payees. A corollary of this is
strict compliance with the law and any contractual agreements.

To put this in perspective and demonstrate its importance, the UK
national statistics for payroll in 1990 were:

- Number of employees   − 22 million
  (excluding the self-employed
  and unemployed)
- Number of pensioners   − 9.8 million (paying pensions is
                                       a payroll function)
- Employed earnings   − £316 billion (about two-thirds
                                       of the national income)
- Income tax   − £49 billion
- National insurance   − £34 billion
  contributions

As an indication of how this applies to an individual, the national
average weekly wage for a male manual worker was £245 in 1990.

Given the above statistics it is hardly surprising that payroll is a
major 'industry' for IT companies who provide either payroll software
or payroll bureau services.

16.4   A stakeholder's view of payroll

The payroll function is controlled and operated by the employer.
However other parties have a stake in the proper operation of payroll
systems as well. Some of the main stakeholders are:

- *The employer*

On a crude level the primary purpose of the payroll function is meeting
the contractual obligation of paying the employee. It is similar to the
creditor accounting function in that the amount owed is calculated and
paid in a strictly regulated manner.

From a more sophisticated point of view the payroll is an essential part of the mechanism for motivating and controlling employees. For instance, a bonus scheme is there to motivate employees to produce or sell more. Clearly this aim would be frustrated by a payroll function which was unreliable in its calculations and slow in its payments. As another example some employers wish to provide services for their employees such as a savings scheme. This is part of an attempt to create the image of an enlightened sympathetic employer. Again confidence that the payroll function can deduct the right money and pass it on to a building society is essential.

- *The employee*

The employee is dependent on the payroll function for prompt and accurate payment. Sometimes the employees want to avail themselves of services provided by the employer through the payroll. For instance charitable donations can be deducted from an employee's earnings and transferred to charities by the employer.

- *The government*

The government has a mixed view of the payroll function. From one point of view it is part of the employment process, and it must be legally regulated to ensure minimum standards for employees. For instance the Employment Protection (Consolidation) Act 1978, Section 8 states that employees must have a payslip.

The government also views the payroll process as a convenient administrative machine which it can use for its own purposes. So the employer is asked to act, through the payroll system, as an unpaid tax collector and as an unpaid social security officer, for example when paying SMP (Statutory Maternity Pay).

- *Other parties*

There are many other parties who view the payroll function in similar manner to the government, i.e. as a convenient means of collecting money. These parties include, for instance, trade unions who use the payroll as means of collecting their subscriptions, or medical insurers who use the payroll as a means of collecting premiums for private health insurance. However unlike the government, which imposes legal obligations on the employer, all these other arrangements are freely negotiated.

16.5   Payroll administration

Payroll administration is complicated, although much of it is ideal for automation which has been applied for almost a century, e.g. with mechanical systems for recording the hours worked by employees. Payroll is suitable for automation because although complicated it operates according to strict rules, and there is often a large volume of work to be done quickly according to demanding timetables.

It is worth reviewing a typical payroll department in a medium-sized business to understand how the computer can automate some of its clerical functions. The basic job of such a department is as follows:

- *Prompt payment*

All payees must be paid promptly and accurately. Payees are not just employees, but also organisations like charities who are entitled to donations deducted from the employees' pay.

- *Operating Pay As You Earn (PAYE)*

PAYE is a complicated system of deducting income tax from the employee's pay and then passing the tax over to the Inland Revenue. PAYE involves using a whole series of official forms. The P60 form in Fig. 16.1 is a common example which is often printed by computer. The details on this form can also be sent to the DSS (Department of Social Security) on magnetic tape, although a hard copy version is always required for employees.

- *Providing management information*

Reports are produced such as the labour costs of running each department in a company.

Computers are used to perform most of the pay calculations which can be numerous and complicated. Computers also print the payslips and management reports. In many cases the employer's computer system links with bank computers for automatically transferring pay from the employer's bank account into the employee bank accounts. Where the employees are paid in cash, print-outs are produced showing the amount of money to put into each paypacket with the payslip.

Another aspect of payroll work is the way information flows on either paper or electronically. For example information can flow into the payroll department from:

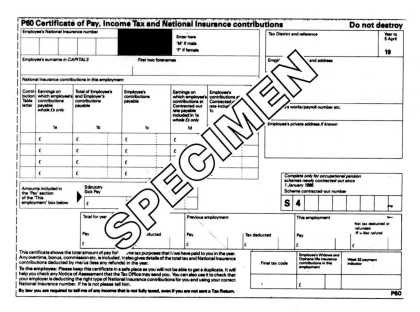

Fig. 16.1 A PAYE P60 form which must be produced for each employee at the tax year-end. A copy (called the P14) must also be sent to the Inland Revenue and DSS. These forms can be produced by a computer on pre-printed stationery.

- The personnel department, e.g. the details of pay rises.
- Ordinary departments, e.g. overtime hours worked by clerks in an accounts department at the end of the year.
- The Inland Revenue, e.g. new tax codes for employees.

Information also flows out of the payroll department, for example, to:

- The employees, e.g. a payslip.
- The pensions department, e.g. details of contributions to the pension scheme.
- Inland Revenue, e.g. a P46 tax form for a new employee.
- A building society, with details of employee savings deducted from wages.

Information flows such as these are illustrated on the data flow diagrams in Figs 16.3 and 16.4. These data flows are often on paper, but increasingly electronic methods are being used.

In a large local authority there could be 30 000 employees on the payroll and maybe 50 people involved in the payroll function. Large payrolls such as this are usually processed on a mainframe computer. Small payrolls, of say 100 employees for a small company, can either use a personal computer or a computer bureau. Payrolls are frequently placed with a bureau who, for a fee, perform all the necessary computer processing, and this provides substantial business for the computer services industry.

16.6 The organisation of payroll administration

Taking the example of a large organisation employing around 2000 people, then the payroll function might be organised as shown in Fig. 16.2. As can be seen, the payroll office is very much a finance function, though occasionally it is combined with the human resources function instead.

The organisation of a payroll department is a good example of Scott's pillars of classical organisation theory discussed in Section 6.7:

- *Division of labour*

In the organisation chart of Fig. 16.2, as is frequently the case, the payroll function is split between wages and salaries clerks. The division between wages and salaries is because of the different administrative burden each poses. Specialisation is also necessary as it can take

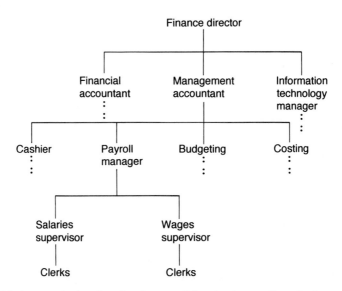

Fig. 16.2 An organisation chart for the payroll function in a medium-sized company.

several weeks for a new payroll clerk to learn the minutiae of paying, say, manual workers. These workers are often paid weekly in cash and their pay structures can be quite complicated with a large number of possible pay elements on top of basic pay, e.g. shift allowances, bonus, and overtime pay. Salaries are usually paid monthly and do not vary as much from one pay period to the next.

The payroll department is concerned with most aspects of paying employees with one major exception. The actual payment of cash wages is often done by the cashiers according to instructions given by the payroll administrators on print-outs. Other payees such as the Inland Revenue are paid by cheque, again according to instructions given by the payroll administrators. This is a security measure to avoid fraud and an example of segregation of duties.

● *Chain of command*

As shown in Fig. 16.2, the payroll chain of command reaches from the finance director through the management accountant to the payroll manager and then the supervisors in charge of the wages and salaries sections.

● *Span of control*

The organisation chart shows that the finance director is directly responsible for three managers, and the payroll manager is responsible for two supervisors.

● *Structure*

The whole of the finance function organisation chart in Fig. 16.2 demonstrates structure. The various related sub-functions such as paying wages and salaries are carefully grouped together to form the payroll department, which is itself grouped with the related departments like costing, under the management accountant. One reason for this association is that labour costs can be an important and complicated part of costing and budgeting.

16.7 Payroll procedures

Figure 16.3 summarises the payroll function as a context DFD (Data Flow Diagram). As discussed later DFDs are an essential specification technique used by systems analysts.

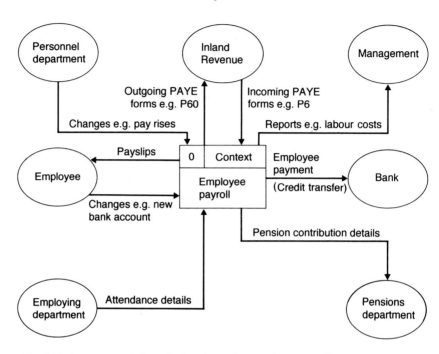

Fig. 16.3 A summary of the main functions of an employee payroll system as a context data flow diagram (DFD). In systems analysis DFDs are an important method of representing the relationship between data flows such as forms and clerical and computer processes. Lower-level DFDs are used to explain the detail of a system (see Fig. 16.4).

One of the payroll functions covered by Fig. 16.3 is the paying of employees by the payroll and cashier's department. The more detailed DFD in Fig. 16.4 shows pay calculations leading up to an employee payment. There are many other payroll processes such as producing data for the financial and management accounts. Some comments on the payment process implied by the DFDs of Figs 16.3 and 16.4 are:

- *The collection of data*
As Figs 16.3 and 16.4 show, payroll data must be collected from various sources. For example bank account details are required from salaried staff who are paid by credit transfer arrangements. Attendance data from the employee's department is required to calculate the gross pay for manual workers. Also the Inland Revenue inform the employer of any change in an employee's tax status, e.g. by sending a P6 form.

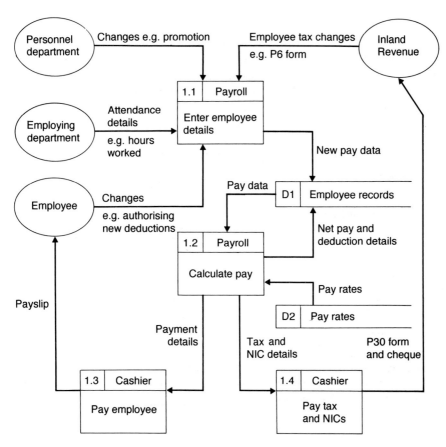

Fig. 16.4 A simplified data flow diagram (DFD) showing the process of paying manual workers and the Inland Revenue. In this case the payment process requires both a payroll office and a cashier's department.

In structured systems analysis, the boxes (processes) on a DFD can be defined in greater detail by another lower-level (more detailed) DFD or by text. Conversely a DFD can be summarised as one box on a higher-level DFD. So the payment DFD above would occur as one process box on a higher-level DFD (not shown) together with boxes representing processes like producing year-end tax forms. This higher-level DFD would in turn define the details of the context DFD of Fig. 16.3.

Note that the large DFD boxes represent processes, and the slender open boxes are data stores. Processes and data can be manual, computerised, or both. The lines on a ·DFD show the data flowing between processes, or from sources of data, or to the recipients of data. The data sources and recipients are represented by ellipses. The details of the data stores and data flows, e.g. the contents of forms, are defined elsewhere, for instance in a data dictionary.

● *Updating employee records*

This refers not only to the computer records which hold details such as basic pay and tax code but also to manual records. For instance, when an employee authorises the employer to deduct savings from his pay, then a form is used for this purpose and filed after the details have been entered into the computer.

● *Distributing reports and payments*

The computer payroll system produces a whole series of reports such as a list of current employees. The most important output is of course the payslips. Where manual workers are paid in cash, these are sent over to the cashiers to be placed in the paypackets with money. Once this is done the employees can be paid. In the case of monthly paid employees a magnetic tape may be sent through the BACS system (see later) to credit the employee bank accounts.

● *Control*

The whole payroll process is controlled from both a quality and cybernetic viewpoint. Quality is discussed in Chapters 15 and 26 and cybernetics, which is the science of control, is discussed in Chapter 19. At every stage of payroll processing there are checks to ensure that all the data has been correctly processed, and that the payroll system as a whole is meeting its objectives. For example computer systems provide various totals such as the number of employee records processed and the total tax deducted this month. These control totals can provide feedback. So if the number of employees joining this month is seventeen and the number leaving this month is twenty, then the number on the computer file should decrease by three. If this is not the case then something has probably gone wrong. See also Section 11.11. On a larger scale computer payroll reports provide management with feedback control over labour costs for a department or the whole organisation. When costs are excessive, they can then take action.

An indication of the work of a payroll department is given by the following timetable for the payment of weekly wages:

● *Monday*

The payroll data is collected and entered into the computer.

- *Tuesday*

The payroll data is again collected and entered into the computer.

- *Wednesday*

The payroll computer system is run and all print-outs and paypackets prepared.

- *Thursday*

Pay day and the paypackets are distributed.

- *Friday*

The payroll data is collected and entered for the next pay week.

As the above timetable implies weekly-paid employees are paid several days in arrears on a Thursday. This is because the data collected and processed during one week usually refers to the previous pay week. Besides the main payroll payment cycle, there is a yearly cycle where every tax year-end the payroll department prepare, via the computer system, various tax documents such as the P35. This is a schedule summarising the tax and national insurance contributions paid by each employee during the year.

16.8 Statutory procedures

The current legislation which imposes the Pay As You Earn (PAYE) system on employers is the Income and Corporation Taxes Act 1988. PAYE is a system which allows the government to collect tax from employees in relatively small amounts every pay period. By way of contrast, the self-employed pay their tax over a year in arrears as two lump sum payments six months apart. PAYE is a system for calculating, deducting, recording, and paying employee income tax. Though originally just a tax system it now effectively includes NICs (National Insurance Contributions), SSP (Statutory Sick Pay) and SMP (Statutory Maternity Pay). The Inland Revenue not only collects employee income tax from the employer, but also NICs on behalf of the DSS (Department of Social Security).

Basically under PAYE the employer must use the employee's tax code to calculate the tax deducted from pay every pay period. The tax code is provided on a PAYE form by the Inland Revenue. NICs must also be calculated. All these calculations, when done manually, use quite complicated tax and NIC tables. The total tax and NICs deducted is paid over to the Inland Revenue every month. Where SSP (Statutory Sick Pay) and SMP (Statutory Maternity Pay) apply, the employer pays the employee these social security benefits. The employer recovers the cost of these benefits from the tax and NIC deductions owed to the Inland Revenue. The money deducted from the employees is paid by the employer to the Inland Revenue every month.

An example of a PAYE standard form is given in Fig. 16.5 which shows the familiar P45. PAYE makes considerable use of standard forms and a list of the more common examples includes:

- P6 — notice of employee's tax code from the Inland Revenue.
- P9 — notice of an employee's changed tax code for the coming year.
- P11D — an annual return of expenses and benefits for a higher paid employee or director.
- P14 — an annual return of pay, tax, etc., for an employee sent to the Inland Revenue and DSS. It is identical to a P60 (see Fig. 16.1) which is the employee's copy.
- P30B(Z) — payslips to accompany the employer's payment of tax and NICs to the Inland Revenue every month.
- P35 — an annual schedule showing a summary of each employee's tax details.
- P45 — details of a person leaving or starting employment. (See Fig. 16.5)
- P46 — a form for employees who do not have a P45 from a previous employment, e.g. school leavers.
- P60 — employee's copy of the P14 above. (See Fig. 16.1)

PAYE must allow for numerous cases such as people starting work without tax documents, people dying in service, and leaving employment. This makes PAYE on its own a complicated system. When NICs, SSP, and SMP are included as extensions then the system is even more complicated. PAYE is a good example of a trans-organisational system, i.e. it involves several different organisations such as the Inland Revenue, the DSS, and employers. The PAYE forms are used to transfer information between organisations, and equivalent

P45

Details of EMPLOYEE LEAVING   **PART 1**

	District number	Reference number
1. PAYE reference		

2. National Insurance number

3. Surname *(Use BLOCK letters)* — Mr. Mrs. Miss

First two forenames *(Use BLOCK letters)*

4. Date of leaving *(in figures)* — Day M Year

5. Code at date of leaving
If Week 1 or Month 1 basis applies, please also write "X" in the box marked "Week 1 or Month 1" — Week 1 or Month 1

6. Last entries on Deductions Working Sheet
If Week 1 or Month 1 basis applies, complete item 7 instead

Week or Month number — Month

Total pay to date

Total tax to £ p

7 Week 1 or Month 1 basis applies £ p

...ployment £ p

8. Works number

9. Branch, Contract Department, etc.

10. Employee's private address ....
.... Postcode..................

11. I certify that the details entered at items 1 to 9 above are correct.

Employer

Address

Date   Postcode

INSTRUCTIONS TO EMPLOYER

● Complete this form according to the "Employee leaving" instructions on the P8 (BLUE CARD).

● Detach Part 1 and send it to your Tax Office **IMMEDIATELY.**

● Hand Parts 2 and 3 (unseparated) to your employee **WHEN HE LEAVES.**

● IF THE EMPLOYEE HAS DIED, please write "D" in this box and send ALL THREE PARTS of this form (unseparated) to your Tax Office **IMMEDIATELY.**

For Tax Office use

For Centre use

Amended	M/E	P

P45   HPB 1166 5/82

Fig. 16.5 On change of employment the common PAYE P45 form above is used to carry tax details to the Inland Revenue and the new employer.

data on magnetic tapes can optionally replace paper forms for the bulk transmission of data, e.g. for P60 forms.

16.9   Legislation

Much of the payroll process is governed by legislation. This legislation changes frequently, for instance in annual Finance Acts or occasional Social Security Acts. The payroll staff and computer systems designers usually find it difficult to keep up to date. The changes can affect virtually everything, e.g. software, office procedures, and stationery. In other words systems maintenance is a major problem with payrolls. See Section 13.4 for a wider view of employment law.

16.10   Business automation

Automation offers the advantages of labour-saving, quality, and speed. Most payroll automation involves the application of normal business computing, but there is some use of paper-handling machines, e.g. for trimming the sprocket holes of payslips. Cleverly designed pre-printed stationery is commonly used. As an example, payroll computer systems often print, for confidentiality reasons, a payslip inside a ready-sealed envelope using no-carbon-required paper. Microfiche are also used for storing historical records compactly in a human-readable form, though optical disks are currently being considered for this.

Payroll systems were amongst the first business systems to be computerised in the early 1950s. Payroll is an ideal computer application as it combines complexity with a high volume of transactions which must be processed according to a strict timetable. It also has a high degree of standardisation amongst different businesses because of PAYE and the like. This makes it a strong candidate for a software package. Even large organisations tend to use packages such as UNIPAY from Peterborough Software which is used to pay about 25% of the UK workforce.

As explained in Chapter 2, the essential role of a payroll computer system is to calculate pay, print payslips, and print year-end tax documents. Figure 16.6 shows a payroll mainframe computer configuration based on current technology. It is linked to a time-and-attendance (T&A) system which uses special terminals to collect automatically the

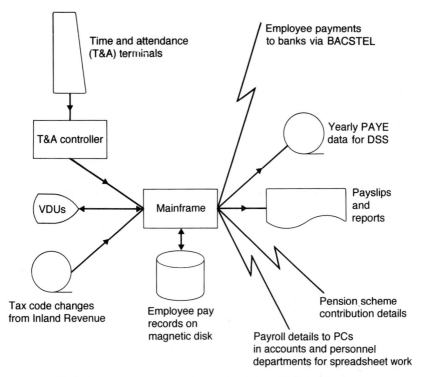

Fig. 16.6 An example of a mainframe computer configuration chart for a payroll system which includes employee time-and-attendance recording. Data is transferred by using magnetic tapes, permanent communication links, and occasional communication links (the lightning flashes).

details about employee time-keeping and passes these details over to payroll system. The BACS tape shown in the diagram allows the electronic transfer of pay credits to employee bank accounts. It is also possible to receive new tax codes on magnetic tape from the Inland Revenue.

Payrolls can be processed on a mainframe, mini-, or personal computer. The size of the computer merely influences such factors as the number of VDU terminals that access the system, and the maximum size of the magnetic disk files. The basic idea is to enter data via a VDU on which is displayed a form like the simplified example of Fig. 16.7. This is completed by entering data through the keyboard under program control. The data entered updates a magnetic disk file and can be further processed by other programs. For example records

```
┌────────────────────────────────────────────────────────────────────┐
│                    **** NEW EMPLOYEE SCREEN 1 ****                   │
│                                                                      │
│  SURNAME:      Babbage      FIRST          Charles    PAYROLL  A5423 │
│                             NAMES:                    NUMBER:        │
│                                                                      │
│  OCCUPATION:   Computer     DEPARTMENT:    Design                    │
│                Engineer                                              │
│                                                                      │
│  TITLE:        Mr           PAYROLL        01/01/1993 NIC      D     │
│                             START DATE:               LETTER:        │
│                                                                      │
│  TAX BASIS:    C            TAX SUFFIX/    P          TAX      500   │
│                             PREFIX:                   CODE:          │
└────────────────────────────────────────────────────────────────────┘
```

Fig. 16.7 A simplified example of a payroll data entry screen on a VDU. The display imitates a manual form. The cursor moves to each field in turn and awaits input. The computer highlights mistakes by techniques like displaying error messages, operating a buzzer, and flashing part of the screen. Other details such as monthly pay would be entered through succeeding screens. (Modern screens have extra features based on WIMPs (Windows, Icons, Mice, and Pull-down menus).

are updated by scanning the payroll disk file, calculating the tax for each employee, and changing the disk record for each employee using the new tax figure. The disk file can also be accessed by further programs, e.g. for printing the year-end P60 tax forms shown in Fig. 16.1. With modern systems like this the operator just selects the appropriate function such as 'Print P60s' by choosing from a menu of functions on the screen as shown in Fig. 16.8.

In outline, the computer payroll system performs the following functions which can illustrate the work of the computer systems designer:

- *Entering data*

Employee details such as pay, overtime hours, and national insurance

```
┌──────────────────────────────────────────────┐
│            **** TAX YEAR END ****             │
│                                               │
│   1. PRINT P35 SCHEDULE                       │
│   2. PRINT P60 FORMS                          │
│   3. WRITE P60s TO DSS MAGNETIC TAPE          │
│   4. PREPARE FOR NEW TAX YEAR                 │
└──────────────────────────────────────────────┘
```

Fig. 16.8 A simplified example of a payroll system menu display. Menus are an elementary but important design technique for giving clerical staff control over computer processing.

number are entered through the keyboard to complete a form on the screen as shown in Fig. 16.7. The computer software checks the data as it is entered, highlighting any input errors.

- *Storing data*

The employee details such as name or tax code are stored on the magnetic disk and can be retrieved and displayed at any time. The data is copied regularly onto magnetic tape for security.

- *Calculations*

Every pay period (for instance weekly or monthly) the payroll software is instructed to calculate the total pay of each employee and all their deductions such as income tax and national insurance contributions.

- *Outputs*

The computer prints payslips and reports such as the payroll summary which shows figures like the total pay and total income tax for all employees. Another simple example of a payroll output is shown in Fig. 16.9.

- *EFT (Electronic Funds Transfer)*

Payroll computers commonly create a magnetic tape for bank credit transfer payments. This is sent to BACS (Bankers Automated Clearing Services), a company owned by all the big banks. BACS sort together

*** CASH ANALYSIS ***		
	NOTES/COINS	VALUE £
20 POUND:	1676	33520.00
10 POUND:	72	720.00
5 POUND:	71	355.00
1 POUND:	861	861.00
50p:	63	31.50
TOTAL:		35487.50

Fig. 16.9 A simple example of a payroll report which is part of a control totals print-out. The cash analysis report provides an analysis of the number of notes and coins required to make up a set of wage packets when paying a group of manual workers in cash.

all the employee details for each bank and send the data to the bank on another magnetic tape. Each bank then credits the employee accounts. The employer's account receives a corresponding debit in a similar fashion.

As already mentioned, payroll computer systems present severe difficulties in terms of software maintenance and strict operational timetables. As a result many companies still prefer to avoid these problems and pay a bureau to do the computer processing of their payroll.

16.11   Linking with other business systems

Payroll systems need to be linked to other systems − for instance to pass details over to the main accounts system (the nominal or general ledger). These details can be printed on one system and entered manually into the other, but it is obviously more reliable to proceed automatically. The computer configuration chart of Fig. 16.6 shows several system links using both telecommunications and magnetic tapes.

The ultimate form of linking is to merge all the payroll details with those of other business areas onto a combined database. Human resource databases which combine payroll, personnel, and pensions data are one example. This can be difficult to achieve in practice, and so complete human resource databases are rarely found.

16.12   Compliance and quality

The problems of legal compliance and quality management with payrolls are severe. This means that the payroll software must meet all the requirements of legislation on tax, social security, and employment. It was once quite common for payroll software to contain design faults which meant that legal requirements were not correctly included in the system.

An example is payroll software performing calculations wrongly for one particular tax code due a mis-specification by the systems analyst. Furthermore, even where the computer specification is correct there are programming errors which mean the system is legally defective. More modern approaches to software quality control have tended to reduce these problems, e.g. the IDPM payroll scheme mentioned in Section 26.11.

Of course even high quality software can be wrongly installed or misused. The payroll staff must ensure that the whole payroll function operates with proper regard for the multitude of legal requirements. For instance, a computer payroll might correctly calculate the national insurance contributions of all employees. However, if a new payroll clerk, through lack of training, were to wrongly classify employees as contracted-in to SERPS (the State Earnings Related Pension Scheme) rather than contracted-out of SERPS then the national insurance calculations would be wrong. The required NIC rate is indicated by a Department of Social Security code letter which is usually an 'A' for contracted-in employees, and a 'D' for contracted-out employees. Simplifying a little, in 1991/1992 the code letter 'A' represents a combined employee and employer rate of 19.4% of pay and the 'D' a combined rate of 13.6%. Thus the difference is financially significant. Failure to apply payroll law, whether it is a computer fault or clerical error, can result in the employer being fined and, for instance, having to pay any tax undeducted from an employee's pay.

So far the emphasis has been on statutory obligations by the employer such as PAYE. However large employers have extensive contractual obligations to their employees. These are the numerous rules covering matters like rates of basic pay, sick pay, maternity leave, overtime, bonuses, and time-keeping. The payroll software and payroll staff must follow these rules as they are part of the employment contract. From the systems analyst's viewpoint these can be even more awkward than statutory obligations. The statutory rules are standard for all employers, but employment contracts vary considerably, particularly in the fine detail. Also the recording of contractual agreements can be very fragmented with lots of different documents recording different aspects, e.g. bonus agreements for one group of workers in one document, and sick pay in another.

Both the statutory and non-statutory rules change frequently and this creates a considerable amount of systems maintenance work for computer staff. The only way of having confidence in the development and maintenance of a payroll computer system is thorough quality assurance, mainly by systems analysts. As regards the operational quality of the system this is the responsibility of payroll administrators. As a final check financial auditors inspect both the IT and administrative aspects of payroll.

16.13   Security

Security and auditing are discussed in Sections 9.2, 9.4, and 11.12. They are particularly important considerations in payroll work. Traditionally payroll is a function that is vulnerable to armed robbery and fraud. As cash has declined as a payment medium in favour of cashless methods such as BACS, the scope for robbery has been diminished. Auditors are concerned with all aspects of security during their regular inspections of payroll systems.

Payroll is exposed to fraud by the payroll staff who ultimately control the payroll system. They can, for instance, place details of imaginary employees on the IT system and then fraudulently intercept payments to these imaginary employees without anyone noticing. Such imaginary employees are often called dummies, deadmen, or ghosts. One possible fraud is computer programmers changing the payroll software so that they receive extra pay. Another common problem is employee 'fiddles', like overstating the paid overtime hours worked, or the over-claiming of travelling expenses.

Confidentiality is also an important issue. A payroll system contains sensitive personal data such as an individual's pay, tax, and sickness details. Sometimes a payroll system is combined with a personnel system which may contain even more confidential data. The system of course includes not only computer files but also manual records. Computer systems concerned only with payment are exempt from the Data Protection Act, but in practice payroll systems are used for other purposes and therefore are subject to the Act. Also of course common-sense and good business practice require confidentiality.

16.14   Summary

- The payroll function can be used to illustrate many of the common requirements of business administration and business IT.
- Payroll payments are a very large proportion of the costs of running any business and represent about two thirds of the UK national income.
- There is considerable time-pressure in payroll work, particularly with weekly payments.

- Payroll office procedures such as PAYE and the supporting software are complex.
- Payroll is strictly controlled by statutory and contractual obligations.
- Because of the frequency of statutory and other changes, systems maintenance is a major problem with payroll systems.
- Quality management and financial auditing are important on-going issues with payroll systems.
- Security, and confidentiality are major concerns with payroll systems.

Part 3
Systems Development

Chapters 17 and 18 give an outline of the traditional and modern procedures which are used for developing IT systems. Chapter 19 gives an introduction to the underlying theory of business systems with an explanation of topics like cybernetics.

Chapter 17
Traditional Systems Development

17.1 Introduction

This chapter is concerned with traditional computer systems development which originated in the 1950s. The role of systems development methodologies and standards is also explained. Though the emphasis in this book is on analysis and design it should not forgotten that programming is usually a large part of systems development.

Modern versions of systems development started to come into use around 1980, although the traditional approach is still commonly met, and is relatively easy to understand. The next chapter discusses modern methods, particularly so-called 'structured' systems analysis and design, which may be considered an important refinement of the traditional approach. The study of systems development is a major subject with an extensive literature, and the discussion in this book is merely an introduction. Further reading can be found in Appendix V.

17.2 Systems development

Systems development is taken to mean the whole process of developing business systems. All the numerous types of business system are included such as health service systems for administering out-patient appointments, or insurance·systems which print policy renewal notices. The quality of business computer systems can be vital. If a computer invoicing system is defective customers can be under-billed, possibly costing good-will as well as sales revenue.

Crudely, the process of IT systems development is split between the programmer who writes the software, and the systems analyst who does everything else such as investigating the requirements for a new system. However analyst-programmers who undertake both analysis and programming activities are frequently met, particularly on small projects.

Systems development is supposed to consider all the elements that go into a business system and not just the information technology aspects, i.e. it *should* include not only hardware and software, but also factors like business forms, office procedures, documentation, and staff training. When a small business system is implemented the users often operate it themselves, e.g. by entering data through personal computers. With large mainframe systems a computer operations department may do much of the work for users, for instance batches of forms from users may be entered into the computer by data preparation staff. However the use of such staff is declining. Entirely manual clerical systems may also be included. There is, for instance, a Manual Business Systems Association which exists to promote manual systems for small organisations. These systems are based on special stationery such as multi-part sets of carbonless forms.

At the other end of the scale are highly-automatic systems which operate with only a small amount of human intervention. Technical systems such as the computerised control circuits of a washing machine often fall into this category. In this case it is only necessary to select the required washing sequence and the computer processor then controls the filling of the drum with water, heating the water, the churning action, the spin drying and so on. In practice, of course, most business IT systems involve both people and machines to a significant degree. However some computer staff and textbooks like to concentrate on the technical aspects, particularly software, to the exclusion of administrative and human factors. In this limited context software development and systems development become almost synonymous.

17.3   The range of traditional systems development

Traditional systems development addresses the problems of producing administrative IT systems. As already explained in Chapter 16, ordinary business systems such as payroll processing can be extensive and complicated in a large organisation such as a local authority. The computer software alone can take many person-years to develop and cost over a million pounds. It is because of these high costs that standard software packages were developed for common applications like payroll. Though packages reduce costs considerably for the user they still have to be developed by the software supplier. Also the work in selecting and

installing packages for a large business can still be considerable –
easily several person-months. By way of contrast there are small computer systems development jobs that only take an hour or so. A
common example would be changing a spreadsheet system to alter the
layout of a cash flow analysis. It should be noted that traditional
systems development is *not* readily applicable to some of the newer
areas of IT such as expert systems.

17.4   Methodologies

To ensure that systems are produced 'on time, on cost, and on quality'
it is essential that formal procedures are followed by systems development staff. These formal procedures are called methodologies. They
are especially important when several people are working on a computer
project over a period of years. They are basically concerned with the
correct and standardised application of proven techniques to systems
analysis, design, and programming. Methodologies also standardise
and improve the documentation and management of computer projects.
Methodologies are particularly associated with modern systems development and one important example SSADM (Structured Systems
Analysis and Design Method) is discussed in the next chapter.

The traditional approach to systems development has also been
standardised in some cases to form methodologies. For example in the
traditional NCC (National Computing Centre) systems development
methodology there is a standard form for listing the contents of clerical
documents such as purchase orders or stock requisitions. An analyst
would complete these forms during a systems investigation.

Readers are warned that the whole subject of systems development
techniques, approaches, and methodologies can generate much discussion and sometimes fierce controversy amongst both academics and
IT practitioners. Academics and computer consultants study 'compara-
tive methodology', i.e. the pros and cons of various methodologies. To
the layman all this may sometimes seem to be a futile discussion with
arguments over arcane trivia, rather like medieval monks disputing
how many angels can dance on the head of a pin. However it should be
remembered that the choice of a methodology is a fundamental strategic
decision in business IT. Methodologies govern the pattern of working
for systems development staff for many years. Also each methodology

has its own propagandists and money can be made from training courses, consultancy, and publications promoting a particular methodology.

A further point worth making is that 'methodologies' (systemised and standardised methods of working) are not just confined to IT. Thus auditors have methodologies for checking accounting activities.

17.5 Similarities with other technical work

The role of systems development staff can be compared to a tradesman, engineer, or architect. In some simple situations the systems developer has a role similar to a garage mechanic, or painter and decorator. A few words are exchanged between the customer and the tradesman explaining what is required. A car needs repairing or a room needs painting according to the brief verbal description. Sometimes a simple written quotation or a few brief notes describing the requirements are provided. Analysts and programmers often work in this informal fashion in smaller businesses, even though the informality is usually condemned as leading ultimately to chaos.

In a large business the systems development process is similar to that in engineering and architecture where formal specifications of new machines and buildings are very much the norm. The specifications take many forms such as engineering drawings and schedules of components and materials. In this analogy the analyst is equivalent to say an engineer or draftsman, and the programmer is equivalent to a welder cutting or joining metal according to the specification. In a factory there can be thousands of different drawings and material specifications concerned with, say, electronic components. Similarly the volume of documentation describing one business computer system can be hundreds of pages, and needless to say even a modest business might have thirty major computer systems.

The production of computer systems can be compared to the design of an engineered product such as a bicycle, radio, or aeroplane. The basic data has to be collected, designs prepared, and the final product specified. The scientific aspects of engineering design also occur in computing. These include IT design calculations and constructing prototypes to test out ideas. This comparison between engineering and computer systems has led to the idea of 'software engineering', i.e. the application of engineering ideas to the design and production of software systems. However the analogy cannot be taken too far as most engineering products are physical, whereas software is much more intangible.

17.6 The traditional systems development life-cycle (SDLC)

The conventional business system of the early 1970s was written in COBOL and ran on a mainframe. A typical small system developed in this era might print out summaries of company sales for a marketing department. One print-out for instance might show the totals of product sales by geographical area. The system might consist of ten programs and take twelve person-months of analysis and programming work. The bulk of the work, say eight person-months, would be programming. Such projects occur today and are frequently tackled in a similar fashion. The system would be developed according to the traditional SDLC (Systems Development Life-Cycle) which is shown in outline in Fig. 17.1. From its appearance this is sometimes known as the 'waterfall' model. As Fig. 17.1 illustrates, the basic idea in the analysis stage is to identify the requirements and collect any relevant facts. The system, particularly the software, can then be designed and programmed. It is then tested before being implemented for the user. The final output of the development process is software in a ready-to-use form and associated documentation such as a user manual for the system.

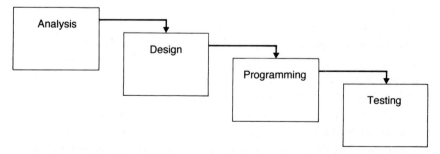

Fig. 17.1 A simplified view of the traditional SDLC (Systems Development Life Cycle). From its appearance this is sometimes known as the 'waterfall' model. This approach also underlies many modern methodologies as well. The basic idea is that output of one phase is the input to the next. For example, the output of the design phase is program specifications which are the input to the next phase which is programming.

It is essential to realise that there are outputs from each stage of the 'waterfall'. This is often documentation which is modestly formal, and at the same time natural to the business users and IT staff. Formality implies no more than the presentation of the documentation being similar to that of a business or technical textbook. The documentation from each stage is often many pages describing the current or proposed systems. Traditional systems documentation is supposedly over-wordy with a paucity of diagrams. However, diagrams are included and the documentation often contains copies of business forms, print-outs, and screen layouts similar to those shown in Figs 16.1, 16.5, 16.7, 16.8, and 16.9. The documentation involved in producing an entirely new system could run to several large volumes, much of it produced by the systems analyst.

The main stages of the traditional SDLC are illustrated in more detail in Fig. 17.2 and explained below.

- *Initiation*

There has to be a basis for selecting one project rather than another, and a means of authorising the analyst to do the work. The terms of reference of a project are a written authorisation which contains an outline of the expected work. The initiation of a project may come from several sources such as long-term business and IT planning, or ad hoc requests from users. In an ordinary business a departmental manager may find that manual procedures are too laborious and request extra computer assistance from the IT department. Software houses may systematically search for new software projects, products, and markets.

Any IT project should of course be compatible with the IT strategy of a business. The IT strategy or long-term IT plans determine matters like the general nature, priority, and timing of a project.

- *Feasibility*

A relatively quick investigation is done into a proposed computer application. The various options for new systems are examined, particularly their likely costs and benefits. As an example, an accounts department may want to know the likely costs and timescale required to produce a new costing system. It is usually possible to have cheap ('quick and dirty') versions of a system and expensive ('de luxe' or 'Rolls Royce') versions. Other options might involve comparing a mainframe version of a system against a local area network. Sometimes

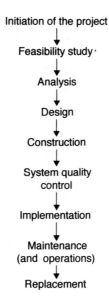

Initiation of the project

Feasibility study·

Analysis

Design

Construction

System quality
control

Implementation

Maintenance
(and operations)

Replacement

Fig. 17.2 A more detailed view of the traditional SDLC which assumes a conventional medium-sized business system written in a third-generation language like COBOL. The system might be implemented after two years. When the system comes into operation it is maintained for many years. The cycle from initiation to replacement might be over ten years. Over the whole life cycle there is usually more maintenance work than development work. The manpower requirements for analysts and programmers are shown in Fig. 17.3.

one option is not to proceed with a project, perhaps leaving an old system as it is. The scope of any work is a key factor that must be established early in a project usually at the feasibility stage. For instance, do the intended factory production control systems include raw materials purchasing or not? The main output of this stage is a feasibility report. This is used by both management and users to consider and approve one project option, perhaps with modifications.

The primary purpose of the feasibility study is to determine whether the project is worth continuing and what is the best way to proceed. However in some cases the job is so evidently essential or so straightforward that the feasibility study is skipped. For instance this is often done with simple maintenance where small changes to print-outs or screen displays are required for an existing system.

- *Analysis*

Assuming the project is considered feasible the systems analyst investigates in detail the current business system and future requirements. The investigation is typically conducted by interviewing clerical staff and collecting the forms and documents used. The investigation techniques used by an analyst are described in Chapter 21 and Chapter 22. The assumption is that many of the features of the current system are also required in a new improved future system. In some cases of courses there is no old system and the job of the analyst is then to identify the requirements for an entirely new system.

The main output is a specification of the current system and a list of future requirements. Users can check that the analysts have correctly understood and documented current procedures.

- *Design*

Based on the results of the analysis phase, the analyst designs a new system which incorporates the desired features where feasible.

As far as the management and users are concerned, the main output is a systems design which often includes pictures of the VDU screen layouts and print-outs similar to those shown in Figs 16.7 to 16.9. In theory, the design of office procedures and office jobs should be included, but there is a marked tendency to skim over such issues. The user then checks the proposed system. Any corrections are agreed and incorporated in a revised systems specification and the computer staff can continue to develop the system.

The analyst next designs and specifies the required software in more technical detail. The design of the hardware and software system requires a thorough technical understanding of subjects such as telecommunications and databases. As far as the IT staff are concerned, the main output is program or module specifications for the software.

- *Construction*

The programmers would use the analyst's software specifications to write ('construct') the required programs in a computer language, say COBOL, stipulated by the IT department standards.

Alternatively where a software package is used there may be little or no programming during construction. However some flexible packages, particularly payroll and pension packages, require an extensive number of parameters to define the user requirements to the software.

Parameters are options, or data that are fixed for a particular user, or fixed for a long period of time. An example of a parameter is the name of the user business which needs to be shown on every print-out. The VAT rate used in a sales invoicing system is another parameter. Where parameters are extensive, their entry into the system through a VDU must be considered a process akin to programming. Entering parameters is usually done by a systems analyst. The analysts also write any user manuals which explain how to operate the system.

● *System quality control*

The analysts prepare plans and data to test the system. This means setting up computer files containing, say, fictitious sales order data. These are used to prove that the programs can produce correct results, or that with a flexible package, the parameters have been correctly entered. In the early stages of testing there are usually many errors. These could include a spelling mistake in a print-out heading, a wrong total for a sales figure, or a program refusing to run and aborting. After any corrections are completed, the final tests should give perfect results. System quality control is more than testing. It also, for instance, includes checking the documentation for mistakes and omissions. See Chapter 26 for further details. At the end of this stage, or during implementation, the users should separately test and check the system. This is to ensure that it meets their requirements, and no errors remain.

● *Implementation*

The analysts supervise the installation of the hardware and software system and train the users in its use. In some cases this can be a massive task, for instance when a retail system is installed in many different branch shops. Implementation is often considered separately from development. See Chapter 24.

● *Operations*

Successful operational use is the main objective of the SDLC rather than part of it. Business IT systems can have an operational life of several years. However involvement by analysts and programmers is considered under headings like maintenance and support.

● *Post-implementation review*

This is a review of the project perhaps a few months after an IT system has been developed and implemented. The idea is to identify any outstanding problem areas and opportunities. Also a check should be made that the costs and benefits identified during the feasibility and design stages have materialised as estimated. It is also an opportunity to identify any lessons for future systems development work.

- *Maintenance*

The analysts ensure that any faults are corrected and that new requirements are incorporated into the system. Over the years, the amount of maintenance work can easily exceed the initial software development work. As mentioned elsewhere it is often stated that on average 80% of so-called systems development work is actually maintenance. Each maintenance job, such as amending computerised social security calculations, should also go through the main systems development stages such as analysis, design, construction, and quality control in their own right. The difference is that maintenance usually requires modifying pre-existing documentation and program code, and not producing these in their entirety.

Support is an important activity that is closely associated with maintenance and sometimes indistinguishable from it. An example of support is an analyst advising a user on how to use occasional facilities like year-end processing in a payroll system.

- *Replacement*

Due to factors like continual amendment, IT systems software becomes progressively more difficult to maintain and increasingly dated. Ultimately replacement is essential. Classic examples of this are 1960s systems written in 2nd generation languages (assemblers) which were replaced by 3rd generation language systems (written in, say, COBOL) in the 1970s. These may have been replaced by packages or 4th generation language systems in the 1980s. Thus replacement involves repeating the above steps every few years and systems have a life 'cycle'.

The manpower required for the traditional SDLC is illustrated in Fig. 17.3. The maintenance work persists for many years and in total usually exceeds the development work. The total life cycle work for analysts and programmers could be anything from a few person-months with a small IT sub-system to tens of person-years for a large adminis-

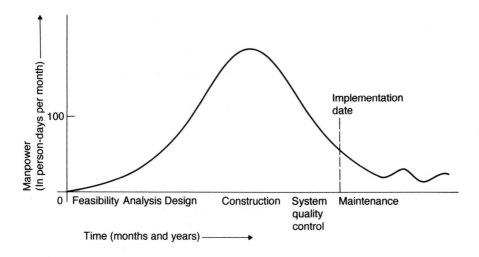

Fig. 17.3 A graph showing the typical use of manpower with the traditional SDLC. It assumes developing and maintaining a business IT system written in a third generation language. The maintenance costs look lower but persist for many years, and hence are greater in total. The manpower curve is similar for a system developed using third generation languages and some modern development methodologies. Note that implementation and operations are excluded from this graph as they are not development activities as such. Implementation is usually a separate project in its own right.

trative system. Further examples of the work done at each of the above stages are given in Section 2.7.

The description of the traditional systems life-cycle given above is merely an outline. There are innumerable variants, and sub-stages are often introduced. The terminology is also very variable. So the 'analysis' stage above is often called 'investigation', and the 'construction' stage is sometimes called 'build', or often just 'programming'. A 'systems design' may be roughly the same as a 'systems proposal' or 'systems specification'. Sometimes the systems design is split into two stages, namely 'business systems design' and 'technical systems design'. A business systems design is also called an 'external design' or a 'functional specification'. It is a set of designs for VDU screen displays and print-outs like those of Figs 16.7 to 16.9. A 'technical systems design' is sometimes called an 'internal design'. It describes how the hardware, software modules or programs, and computer files all link together to produce the screen displays and print-outs. Figure 16.6 is a high-level technical system design.

The general reasoning behind such life-cycle schemes is to ensure that each stage and sub-stage is correct and documented before proceeding to the next. That is, quality control checks are applied at the end of each stage, or sub-stage, or even to each piece of work such as a program specification. For instance, there is no point in doing any design work until the users agree that the requirements of the future system have been correctly identified.

Another advantage of splitting up the life-cycle work into fine detail is that it is possible to employ more specialist staff. So with one common arrangement a 'systems analyst' just produces the 'business systems design' or 'external design', i.e. the designs of screens and print-outs. A separate 'systems designer' produces the system technical design containing, say, a database design and program specifications.

Note that much of the documentation produced during the various life-cycle stages only has a temporary or historical value. Clearly, once the new system is implemented this is the case, for instance with the feasibility study and the specification of the current system (which has become the old system). Such documentation has a similar role to the scaffolding used to erect a building − it is a necessary part of the process, but not permanently required.

The above approach to the SDLC tends to assume the use of third generation languages like COBOL. However as indicated it can be modified to allow for other methods of developing systems like the use of packages which reduce the programming work significantly.

A more comprehensive and illustrated description of the traditional SDLC can be found in *Intermediate Systems Analysis* by D. Mason and L. Willcocks. This is another book in the Information Systems Series.

17.7 Standards

The traditional SDLC is often standardised, at least partially. This means that in any one computer department there are, for example, standard forms for listing the details of data to be stored on a computer file. The standards to be applied are rather bureaucratic and contained in manuals. Besides the forms to be used, the standards manual lays out such matters as the symbols to be used in diagrams, and a standard list of chapter headings for documents such as a specification of the current system and future requirements. In effect the standards manual tells the analyst or programmer how they are to do their job. If all systems are produced to the same standards then everything is consistent, whether it is the layout of a computer printed report, or the format of error messages on a screen, or the content of specifications. This makes it much easier for computer managers to monitor the progress of systems development.

The use of business systems is also easier if both clerks and analysts know that the run date of any computer report is always printed on the upper right-hand side irrespective of the person who designed or programmed it. Note that a systems development methodology is just one important example of a standard, but it must be used with other standards. A systems development methodology does not, for instance, define the standard format for numbering all the various screens and print-outs created by a system, e.g. SL03 for the third screen of a sales ledger system.

The NCC produced a manual which encapsulated many of the ideas on standards and systems documentation which were the current in the late 1960s. The NCC systems documentation manual became the basis for many individual company development standards. The investment in producing a modest methodology and standards manual is high — several months work perhaps, even when adapting other people's standards. Standards also refer to matters other than development, e.g. standardised procedures for setting and changing passwords for an on-line mainframe system. Smaller companies often avoid the issue by producing one system particularly carefully, and then use that as a model for designing and documenting other systems.

17.8 The limitations of traditional systems development

The traditional SDLC approach is often criticised, but variants are still used by IT staff for both business and technical systems. People with a business user rather than IT background also seem to like it. Furthermore quite a lot of old systems are still operational and their documentation is still traditional. Typical criticisms of the traditional SDLC are listed below.

- *Too simple*
The traditional SDLC is very limited. For instance it is an over-simplified version of how systems development does or should occur.

Reply:
The traditional SDLC as described above can work quite well provided it is applied sensibly to medium-sized computer projects up to a few person-years in size, and provided that the maintenance work is modest. Also it is an illusion to believe that there is one universal practical methodology that can cover all IT applications from a nation-wide social security system to a desktop expert system.

- *Too vague*

Even in its detailed form the traditional SDLC model is usually no more than a set of general guidelines on how to analyse, design and program business systems. This means that it needs considerable experience to apply it successfully.

Reply:
Some traditional SDLC standards manuals gave extremely detailed instructions on the procedures to be followed for the production and documentation of systems.

- *No rigour or structure*

Traditional specifications are not rigorous. Specifications are poorly structured, ambiguous, and incomplete. Many details were not included.

Reply:
This is probably true of much of traditional development. Though some would say that this was just due to the poor application of traditional methods and poor quality control rather than a defect of the techniques themselves.

- *Text-based*

Classical specifications tend to use text rather than diagrams for specifications. Text is often inappropriate for specifying complex administrative and computer processes. This leads to confusing voluminous documents which are never read.

Reply:
This is certainly true of many design specifications. However the criticism is probably invalid in general. Some business system designs from the 1950s to the 1970s made extensive use of diagrams, e.g. systems devel-

oped NCC style. Some business users are also quite happy to read and constructively criticise sensible text specifications. They also find modern specifications which make extensive use of diagrams voluminous, unnatural, and difficult to comprehend.

- *Lack of structured techniques*

The traditional methods of systems analysis and design lack structured techniques (as discussed in Chapters 18 and 20).

Reply:

This is broadly true as these techniques were only invented in the late 1970s. Some people however graft structured techniques into a traditional framework.

- *Inadequate emphasis on data*

As discussed later this contrasts with modern thinking. Modern views put considerable emphasis on the data used by an information system rather than the processes like calculations which use the data.

Reply:

It is probably true that people traditionally concentrated on processes at the expense of data. Attempts were sometimes made to correct this.

- *No standards*

Traditional development is only loosely standardised in practice. Different businesses have different detailed standards. Different standards are often found within the same organisation.

Reply:

This can be true with modern structured methodologies as well. Also, as explained in Section 17.7, standards embrace more than a development methodology.

- *Poor quality control*

Documentation and quality control (checking work) are often skimped.

Reply:

This can be true of modern structured methodologies as well. It is basically a matter of discipline.

- *Poor updating*

Traditional systems and programming documentation is often not updated properly when the system is changed. In this situation documentation can become misleading and useless in a few months.

Reply:

It was certainly true that amendments were separate documents and often not incorporated into an original specification because of the cost of redrawing diagrams and retyping text without modern software tools. The result could be an original specification with fifty separate documents amending the original specification. This reflects the lack of software tools in the 1960s and 1970s rather than any fault in the methodology. Structured analysis and design without software tools tends to suffer from the same problems.

- *No clear deliverables making management difficult*

Traditional development is poorly divided into project stages and tasks. Where the project is split into divisions they tend to be rather broad (like a 'feasibility study'), and poorly defined. Hence it is not possible to determine accurately how complete a project is at an intermediate stage. What traditional analysis and design lacks is a set of small 'deliverables', i.e. the division of the project into defined little packages of work which can be completed one by one. This lack of clear small deliverables makes it difficult to manage a project, and some say that traditional development is unmanageable!

Reply:

This is a partial truth. Methodologies based on traditional analysis and design probably did not have the deliverables as clearly defined in neat packages as their modern successors like SSADM.

- *Takes too long and is too expensive*

The traditional development approach can take years to develop large new systems. As a consequence development costs are very high.

Reply:

This is certainly true. However it also true of modern methodologies when tackled with inadequate software tools. COBOL programming can for instance be very tedious whether using modern structured techniques or oldstyle techniques. Modern software development tools can improve development times significantly with either old or new methodologies.

As can be seen most of the common criticisms of traditional systems development are exaggerations. However it is important to appreciate the above points if involved in a project using a version of the traditional approach. The three most serious objections mentioned above are the lack of rigorously-defined deliverables, the over-emphasis on processes at the expense of data, and the lack of structured techniques. As indicated, with care most of these objections can be overcome on smallish projects.

However there is no doubt that it is easier to be slipshod with the traditional life-cycle, and that there is less guidance on how to proceed. By way of contrast modern methodologies give extremely detailed procedures for developing systems. However discipline is necessary if these are to be followed. See also Section 30.10 which contains a more general discussion of the problems of systems development.

A personal observation by the author is that some staff using modern systems development tend to revert to traditional techniques. Conversely, other staff using traditional approaches drift towards modern methodologies by slowly adopting structured techniques. This means that the boundary between traditional and modern approaches is blurred in practice and continually changing.

The author's personal systems development experience using both traditional and modern techniques over twenty years has been moderately encouraging. Generally development procedures were followed, and extensive standardised documentation was produced at all stages. However, the author has visited many organisations where even rudimentary development procedures and documentation did not exist. Basically people were (and still are) writing complex software from verbal instructions and scrappy handwritten notes which were soon discarded. Furthermore, software quality control was skimpy. This has been confirmed by part-time and sandwich course students who spent long periods working in systems development, sometimes for major organisations. The usual excuse for this poor state of affairs is that methodologies, traditional or modern, are needlessly bureaucratic and there is no time for documentation. Suffice it to say that poor development procedures and lack of documentation can lead to poor quality systems which are difficult and expensive to maintain.

17.9 Summary

- IT systems development is analogous in some ways to the design of engineering, manufactured, and architectural products, e.g. cars and domestic houses. In particular extensive documentation such as specifications and drawings are required.
- Methodologies are standardised methods which define how to develop a computer system. Methodologies are a collection of working procedures, techniques, and documentation conventions.
- Both traditional and modern methodologies impose order and documentation on the systems development process.
- Informal approaches to systems development are common and lead to poor quality undocumented business IT systems which are expensive and difficult to maintain.
- The simple version of the traditional SDLC of Fig. 17.1 is sometimes called the waterfall model. It is a loose general framework, and many variants and refinements exist. The waterfall model requires a systems development project to progress through analysis, design, programming, and systems quality control prior to implementation, operation, and maintenance.
- Variants of traditional systems development are often met, particularly with smaller projects. However, traditional development does have weaknesses which modern methodologies attempt to correct.

Chapter 18
Modern Systems Development

18.1 Introduction

This chapter provides the background and an outline description of modern systems development methodologies. A more detailed discussion of modern methodologies can be found in other books in the Information Systems series, particularly *Information Systems Development* by D. E. Avison and G. Fitzgerald. Most modern methodologies address the weaknesses in the traditional systems development life cycle discussed in Section 17.8. The discussion below is mainly about the analysis and design aspects of the SDLC (Systems Development Life-Cycle) rather than programming which is a vast subject in its own right. The boundary between systems design and programming (construction) is unclear and depends very much on the methodologies adopted and the preferences of each organisation. Sometimes the boundary is determined by the nature of the IT project and the staff involved. Much of the following discussion does of course refer to TPSs (Transaction Processing Systems) and MISs (Management Information Systems).

As already mentioned in the previous chapter standardised versions of the traditional systems development life-cycle like that of the NCC were introduced in the 1970s. These were detailed and bureaucratic involving the analysts and programmers in working through the various stages such as analysis of the current system and producing copious documentation in a standardised way. However, a new approach arose in the late 1970s called structured analysis and design. It was inspired by the earlier and related ideas which made up structured programming, and it also incorporated ideas from database theory. Structured analysis and design is explained in outline below, and the techniques are described in greater detail in Chapter 20. However suffice it to say that structured analysis and design was an approach rather than a methodology, i.e. it was a series of concepts and techniques. In essence, structured analysis and design involves greater use of diagrams, and a greater

239

emphasis on the analysis of data. As the adjective 'structured' implies it also involves the systematic and rigorous specification of business operations and software in levels of increasing detail.

The next development was the combination of structured analysis and design ideas with standardised terminology, diagramming notations, and procedures. This has led to the rise of structured methodologies in the 1980s such as SSADM (Structured Systems Analysis and Design Method). As with their traditional predecessors, methodologies such as SSADM are contained in large manuals and prescribe a detailed way of analysing and designing systems. However they are more rigorous.

Modern structured methodologies are also amenable to automation in the form of an analyst's workbench. This means that the analyst can be guided and helped by a computer system in the preparation of specifications. With both traditional and modern development methodologies there is an overriding requirement to ensure that an IT project serves real business needs and complies with long-term business and IT plans. Modern methodologies are often theoretically superior in this respect.

18.2   The key features of structured analysis and design

Both structured programming and structured analysis and design are concerned about improving the quality and productivity of systems development work by using better techniques. Simplifying considerably, one of the main ways structured programming set out to improve the quality of software was by insisting that programmers rigorously break-down software into small and manageable self-contained pieces of computer code. Essentially it was the rigour that was new.

Structured analysis and design are not particularly concerned with the implementation of IT systems. Also, rather surprisingly, structured analysis often has little interest in the techniques used to collect facts and identify requirements. So the techniques of systems investigation such as interviewing users or observing office procedures remain much the same as they are in the traditional approach. Structured analysis is more concerned with the analysis of the facts collected during a systems investigation and the methods of specifying the findings.

The main concepts of structured analysis and design are:

- A pictorial approach.
- Restricted use of text.
- Levelling (also known as hierarchical decomposition).
- Logical and physical specification.
- An emphasis on data.
- 'Deliverables' or 'products'.
- Thoroughness.

The above concepts are explained in more detail below. Their application is explained further in Chapter 20.

18.3   A pictorial approach

It is a tenet of structured analysis and design that diagrams are an intrinsically better means of specification than text. This means that pictorial methods of specifying systems are used in preference to text. See Figs 16.3, 16.4, and 20.1 to 20.4 for examples. With a little training even business staff can use them. In general diagrams are supposed to be easier to comprehend, more precise, and less likely to contain inconsistencies.

18.4   Restricted use of text

As a corollary of the pictorial approach text has a reduced role, but it is not entirely eliminated. The view is that natural languages like English are inappropriate for specification. Also the excessive use of English, frequently hundreds of pages of text, made traditional analysis very unwieldy. By using diagrams as a major documenting tool it is possible to limit the use of English and reduce verbiage and imprecision. Where English is used it is often applied in a strictly controlled manner called structured English. Figure 20.4 shows an example of a business process documented using structured English.

18.5   Levelling

Levelling means that a process is specified systematically in levels of increasing detail, e.g. using a set of diagrams. Levelling can be applied to clerical or computer processes and is sometimes called 'hierarchical decomposition'. How this applies in systems development is illustrated in Figs 16.3, 16.4, and 20.4 where payroll administration is specified in progressively greater detail. The idea of using increasing levels of detail is very old. For instance a non-fiction book could be written progressively from a title, then a list of chapter headings, then a list of paragraph headings, and then the contents of the paragraphs. To some extent this method is also used with traditional systems development. However in structured analysis and design the process is used extensively and very rigorously.

The reason for adopting levelling is basically to break-down a large project into a series of manageable pieces of specification work. These pieces of work must be all compatible with each other, and the resulting specifications must fit together coherently. By dividing up analysis and design in a rigorous and progressive manner it is possible to split the work between several people, or for one person to do each part of the detailed work successively. Taking another example a sales order processing system might be diagrammed as three major processes namely: order intake, warehouse despatches, and sales accounting. A series of DFDs (Data Flow Diagrams) would represent each of these in progressively greater levels of detail.

18.6 Logical and physical specification

This concept often causes some difficulty for beginners and for that reason it is explained both below and again in a different context in Section 18.10 below. Structured analysis and design seeks to distinguish clearly between the logical (or abstract) rules for processing data and the various physical means of actually processing the data. Similarly it distinguishes between the logical or abstract requirement to transfer or store data, and the physical means of doing this. So logically a payroll system must calculate and handle tax data. The calculations may performed physically by humans using a calculator, or physically by computers. The data may be stored physically on paper, or physically on magnetic disks, or on magnetic tape. The result is that structure diagrams and specifications must refer either to the logical rules for processing or handling data (i.e. *what* is required), or the physical means for achieving this (i.e. *how* it is done). In their final expression, logical specifications are also reduced to their simplest form. For example any redundant processes or duplicate data stores are removed from the specification.

For clarity it should be mentioned that physical processing and physical storage refers to the physical means of dealing with data. It does not refer to the physical items that the data represents. Thus structured techniques can deal with the *data* about manufactured products and the *data* about machine tools in a factory. These techniques do not normally deal with the products or machine tools themselves.

18.7 An emphasis on data

It must be remembered that even ordinary systems can require dozens of different data items (also called data elements, attributes, or fields). For example some data items for a personnel system are name, address, occupation, and basic pay. Structured methods have imported a lot of the techniques developed for designing databases and used them for ordinary computer applications.

There are a whole series of techniques called 'data modelling' and 'data analysis' which are used to analyse, refine, and specify the data needed for a business system. See Section 20.7 for further details and Figs 20.1 and 20.2 for one technique used to specify data. The modern view is that, at the very least, data is as important as the processes which maintain and use it. Data is often viewed as more fundamental than processes which is the view of database proponents. Data is not only seen as more central but also as more stable than processes. Thus there have been frequent changes over the last few decades in the payroll calculations (processes) concerning NICs (National Insurance Contributions). In contrast with these changes to the calculations, the format of a National Insurance Number (data) has been the same for over 40 years, i.e. two alphabetic characters, six numeric characters, and then another alphabetic character as in BC753476A.

18.8 Deliverables and completeness

The division of a project into fine steps which each produce a 'deliverable' or 'product' is a feature of a methodology rather than a general approach such as structured analysis and design. In this context a deliverable or product is something self-contained and useful like a set of diagrams or a quality control plan. However structured analysis and design make it easier to divide up the work so that deliverables are produced which contribute progressively to the completion of an IT project.

Structured methodologies place an emphasis on including fine detail. The basic idea is to ensure that nothing is omitted from the final results. One method of ensuring this is partial duplication, i.e. to some extent work is duplicated on different occasions. For example the various types of diagram used to specify a system all give different but overlapping views as to how the system handles data (see Section 20.7). The different pieces of work are then cross-checked for consistency. This means that specifications of the current system and the design of a new system are all comprehensive and detailed. A system documented with SSADM can produce specifications consisting of many pages of diagrams and text. To ensure even greater thoroughness considerable emphasis is put on user involvement and quality control.

18.9   Similarities with traditional methodologies

As mentioned in Section 17.8 many, but not all, of the weaknesses of traditional systems development were due to indiscipline and limited skill. In a nutshell traditional systems development was often the victim of sloppiness, and modern methodologies can suffer the same fate. Most propagandists naturally tend to stress what is seen as different about modern structured analysis and design. To many older IT practitioners and some students these claimed differences seem small or exaggerated.

There are many traditional analysis and design approaches which have been absorbed by modern structured methodologies. An example is the insistence in SSADM on carefully checking of the results of each stage before progressing to the next. This is found with traditional approaches and is almost common-sense. Also as discussed above the modern approach incorporates older ideas from database theory and structured programming. It would be better then to see modern structured analysis and design as an extension and improvement of the traditional approach. Modern methodologies can then be regarded as the result of a series of continual on-going small improvements brought together within a more rigorous framework.

18.10   Logical and physical analysis and design

A key part of structured analysis and design is logical and physical specification. As already mentioned, in essence a physical analysis or design makes reference to the physical aspects of an information system such as magnetic disks, or the use of a pink purchase order form, or Mary Murphy the purchasing department manageress. The logical analysis or design of a system refers to the logical processes and logical data. This is irrespective of the actual physical method of carrying out the processes or storing or moving the data. So the logical algorithm for working out the cash-flow into or out of an organisation can be specified irrespective of whether the calculations are physically performed using a personal computer with spreadsheet software as illustrated in Fig. 25.2, or whether they are physically performed manually on pieces of paper.

Figure 18.1 gives a simple illustration of the relationship between analysis and design in terms of logical and physical specification. From this point of view analysis is determining the specification of a current system and the requirements of the future system. Usually of course many of the requirements met by the old system are also to be met by a future system. Design is producing the specifications of a new future system.

As Fig. 18.1 illustrates, the essence of systems analysis and design is to produce:

• *A physical specification of the current system*
This can be done for instance by using data flow diagrams (DFDs) like Fig. 16.4. These represent the flow and storage of physical data on paper to be processed by people. Alternatively the information may be physically in electronic form and processed by machines. Usually, of course, a system is a mixture of manual and machine methods of storage and processing.

• *A logical specification of the current system*
From an examination of the physical specification a logical specification is

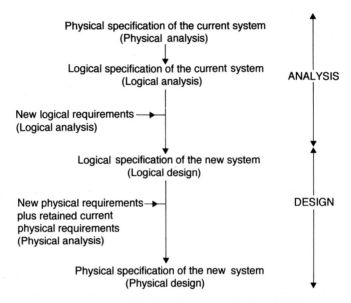

Fig. 18.1 An outline of the relationship between analysis and design incorporating logical and physical specification. The details depend on the methodology and are more complicated in SSADM.

prepared. This reduces the current system to its simplest abstract form removing all references to the physical methods which process and store data. It also removes any duplication of operations and data. In physical systems processing and data are often duplicated. For example, data is duplicated in manual and machine systems by producing copies of documents like invoices for convenience and efficiency of operation. Preparing a logical specification free of physical details and in its simplest possible form is supposed to make the essence of a system clearer.

- *A list of new logical requirements*

These are the new abstract requirements identified during the systems investigation. For instance, they could be new rules for accepting sales on credit, or amendments to a stock re-ordering calculation.

- *A specification of the new logical system*

This is the result of combining the current logical system with the new logical requirements. So all the retained current logical requirements are included together with any amendments and new logical requirements.

- *A list of new physical requirements*

These can be identified during both the analysis and design stages. They could for instance include the fact that a new system must be based on personal computers, or that the system must operate in Manchester rather than London.

- *The new physical specification*

This is a design for a future system which incorporates all the retained current system features and the new requirements. As it is a physical specification of a future system, i.e. a design, it must meet all the new logical and physical requirements. One logical design can usually be implemented in several physical ways. This is true even when some physical constraints are imposed such as requirement that the process must be operated by particular group of people. For example, sub-contracting payroll computing to a bureau may be prohibited, and as a result the system must be run 'in-house'. Even with physical restrictions such as this, the same logical system can often be implemented physically in several acceptable ways. For instance there may be some jobs which can be sensibly done either by people or by computer or some combination of both.

This approach of separating logical and physical requirements is supposed to make the design process easier by concentrating on one set of issues at a time. Logical design forces analysts and users to consider *what* a system is trying to achieve without the confusion of how it is to be done. Physical design decides *how* the system is to meet its logical requirements. Logical and physical specification are thus seen as separate exercises.

Section 6.9 mentions the idea that IT offers the opportunity to redesign business activities radically. By way of contrast it is not unknown for new IT systems merely to automate or semi-automate poor administration and do nothing to address the fundamental problems. The distinction between logical and physical aids the devising of new and innovative systems unencumbered by ideas from the past.

Needless to say not all analysts make a rigorous distinction between logical and physical specification, particularly those working in an ad hoc fashion or still using variants of old methodologies. Also there can be different approaches to producing logical and physical designs. For example SSADM is more complicated in this respect and requires the production and evaluation of 'options'. These options include alternative outline logical and physical designs for the new system. Once an option is agreed a new detailed logical design can be prepared which then leads to a detailed physical design. One reason for doing some outline physical designs before detailing the logical design is to avoid attempting something that is logically desirable but physically expensive or impossible.

18.11   Modern systems development methodologies

There are many methodologies theoretically available which incorporate the above ideas on structured analysis and design. In practice only a few standardised methodologies dominate the IT market. Some current UK and foreign analysis and design methodologies are:

- SSADM – the main UK systems analysis and design methodology outlined below.
- LSDM – Learmonth and Burchett Structured Development Method, a UK proprietary methodology similar to SSADM.
- JSD – Jackson System Design, a UK methodology.
- MERISE – a French commercially-marketed methodology.
- SADT – Structured Analysis and Design Technique, a proprietary American methodology.
- STRADIS – Structured Analysis, Design, and Implementation of Information Systems, a commercially-marketed American methodology.
- Yourdon – an influential American methodology.
- Information Engineering – an important methodology which expressly adopts a more strategic approach to analysis and design.

Technical IT systems have their own methodologies such as MASCOT (Modular Approach to Software Construction Operation and Test). Separate methodologies also exist for programming, e.g. JSP (Jackson Structured Programming).

Extensive manuals contain the full description of each of the above methodologies and outlines are published in books. A summary of SSADM is given below. Further details can be obtained from the bibliography in Appendix V.

18.12   Structured Systems Analysis and Design Method (SSADM)

SSADM was devised by the UK consultants Learmonth and Burchett Management Systems (LBMS) and the CCTA (Central Computing and Telecommunications Agency) which is responsible in the UK civil service for training and some procurement. SSADM now has its own Design Authority Board supported by the CCTA as well as other organisations such as the BCS (British Computer Society). The Board is responsible for future strategy. SSADM has been in use since 1981 and been the dominant methodology in the civil service since 1983. It is also extensively used by other public and private sector organisations. SSADM is most appropriate for large-scale projects though adaptations of it for small systems exist. It is designed to interface with software products such as 4GLs (Fourth Generation Languages). SSADM is also compatible with some other standardised approaches, e.g. PRINCE a project management methodology also supported by the CCTA.

SSADM is 'open', i.e. publicly available and can be used without licence or payment. It is currently available in two versions. Version 4 was introduced in 1990 and should eventually replace Version 3. The description below is based on SSADM Version 4. To give an illustration of how methodologies evolve a brief description of Version 3 is also given. A flavour of how SSADM documentation looks in its entirety is given by a case study in G. Cutts' book *Structured Systems Analysis and Design Methodology* which is in the Information System Series. The case study in Cutts' book is an analysis and logical design of a sales accounting system and consists of over 100 pages of SSADM-style forms and diagrams.

18.13   The main features of SSADM

SSADM is, as the name implies, primarily concerned with analysis and design. It uses its own terminology some of which is used below. Even standard terms like 'requirements specification' and 'data flow diagram' have their own special nuances within SSADM. Feasibility is an optional phase depending on circumstance. However compared to the traditional SDLC stages with similar names, SSADM is more detailed, more rigorous, and uses modern techniques. The output of SSADM is quality assured documents. The main final documents are effectively the technical design specifications for the new business computer system. The main final documents produced are:

- The physical data design of the system (computer file or database specifications)
- Software specifications, input/output formats, and computer dialogue designs

There are other intermediate documents produced of which the most important is the requirements specification of the future system for user management approval.

18.14   The Main Stages of SSADM Version 4

To produce the above documents the analyst must progress through the five core 'modules' of SSADM Version 4 as shown in Fig. 18.2. Modules are analysis and design procedures which produce documents. The outputs of one module are the input to the next. Modules gradually develop the system until the final physical design documents are produced. The core modules are explained in more detail below:

- *Module 1 − Feasibility*
The objective is to carry out an assessment of the proposed computer system and to determine whether it is worth proceeding with a full SSADM project. This involves an outline systems investigation and producing a list of business and technical options to meet the requirements. Each option is accompanied by a cost-benefit analysis to help identify the preferred option. Low-risk circumstances may justify skipping the feasibility module and proceeding straightaway onto Requirements Analysis.

- *Module 2 − Requirements Analysis*
This involves a detailed investigation and charting of the current

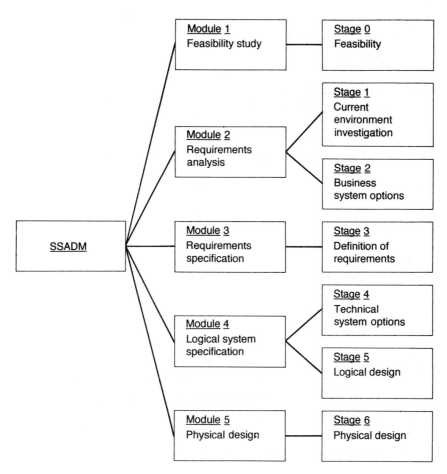

Fig. 18.2 The relationship between the modules, stages, and components of SSADM Version 4. The steps within each stage provide a definition of the module and stage names. The step names are listed in Section 18.15.

business system. The flows of data, for instance on forms like credit notes, are recorded. The data stored by the system, such as employee information in a payroll department, is also analysed. Problems with the current system are recorded, e.g. slow processing of sales orders. The requirements of the new systems are identified, e.g. in terms of security. A series of business options are outlined, for example a centralised system at head office or a decentralised system where branch offices are involved. One option is chosen.

● *Module 3 − Requirements Specification*
This Module develops the system in terms of the detailed processes and data required

● *Module 4 − Logical System Specification*
Various technical options are designed and examined, e.g. mini and micro-computer systems. The most suitable option is chosen for detailed logical design. The logical process and data requirements of the new system are designed in detail.

● *Module 5 − Physical Design*
The logical requirements for data storage are used to design physical disk files or a database. The logical processes are used to design software to process the data. Input/output formats are included, e.g. for EDI (Electronic Data Interchange). Computer dialogues are designed, for instance VDU menu screens.

18.15 The SSADM steps

Each 'module' is sometimes subdivided into 'stages' as illustrated in Fig. 18.2. A module or stage is also sub-divided into pre-numbered 'steps'. In all there are 33 steps which are each further subdivided into several tasks. Each of these tasks consists of basic jobs like preparing a particular diagram. A summary of the Version 4 modules is given below in terms of the main steps:

● *Module 1 − Feasibility*
  Stage 0 − Feasibility
    010: Prepare for feasibility study
    020: Define the problem
    030: Select feasibility option
    040: Assemble feasibility report

● *Module 2 − Requirements Analysis*
  Stage 1 − Investigation of Current Environment
    110: Establish analysis framework
    120: Investigate and define requirements
    130: Investigate current processing
    140: Investigate current data

150: Derive logical view of current services
160: Assemble investigation results
Stage 2 − Business System Options
210: Define business system options
220: Select business system options

- *Module 3 − Requirements Specification*
Stage 3 − Definition of Requirements
310: Define required system processing
320: Develop required data model
330: Derive system functions
340: Enhance required data model
350: Develop specification prototyping
360: Develop processing specification
370: Confirm system objectives
380: Assemble requirements specification

- *Module 4 − Logical System Specification*
Stage 4 Technical System Options
410: Define technical system options
420: Select technical system options
Stage 5 − Logical Design
510: Design user dialogues
520: Define update processes
530: Define enquiry processes
540: Assemble logical design

- *Module 5 − Physical Design*
Stage 6 − Physical Design
610: Prepare for physical design
620: Create physical data design
630: Create function component implementation map
640: Optimise physical data design
650: Complete function specification
660: Consolidate process data interface
670: Assemble physical design

For the exact meaning of the above steps which use SSADM terminology the reader should refer to publications on SSADM Version 4.
Some of the above steps within a particular module can be done in

parallel. As an example of the outputs of SSADM the objective of Step 130 is to investigate and define current processing in terms of DFDs (Data Flow Diagrams). One key aspect of SSADM is regular reviews of work often at the end of each step and also at the end of each stage which helps maintain quality. SSADM also encourages user participation.

18.16   Deliverables and tasks

Each step results in a set of 'products' (the SSADM term for 'deliverables'). These are created by the tasks within the step. For example Step 640 above is concerned with optimising the physical data design. This involves two SSADM tasks. So when using a database system the first task would be calculate the magnetic disk storage required. The second task would be to estimate the timings of critical parts of the new computer system in terms of disk accesses and computer processing. If the answers from either task are unsatisfactory, the design must be adjusted, e.g. by reducing the amount of historical data stored so as to use less disk space.

18.17   SSADM Version 3

Methodologies continuously evolve, both as the result of changing circumstances and improvements suggested by experience. A few details from Version 3 of SSADM can illustrate this. It was superseded in 1990 by Version 4 and should be progressively replaced. Just a few of the main differences between Version 4 and Version 3 are:

- A more flexible methodology using a core set of essential SSADM techniques and procedures with interfaces to different software development environments, e.g. using third generation languages like COBOL or fourth generation languages.
- Alterations in the structure of SSADM to emphasise decision points.
- Techniques like data modelling have been modified. (Data modelling includes techniques like the ER diagrams explained in Section 20.7.)
- The introduction of prototyping standards (see Section 18.22).

Though the conceptual changes in Version 4 are not major, the detailed changes are extensive and irritating to someone familiar with Version 3. Training courses are available to ease the 'migration' to Version 4.

As an illustration of the Version 4 changes the main stages of Version 3 are listed below:

- Stage 1 – Analysis of Current System Operations and Current Problems
- Stage 2 – Specification of Requirements
- Stage 3 – Selection of Technical Options
- Stage 4 – Data Design
- Stage 5 – Process Design
- Stage 6 – Physical Design

The above stages are also divided into steps, and the steps divided into tasks. There are 40 steps in Version 3 which are different in detail from those in Version 4.

18.18 Why use a methodology?

As already explained, ordinary business systems can be extensive and complicated in a large organisation such as an insurance company. The computer systems themselves can be of crucial importance to an organisation. Errors in the development or operation of administrative IT systems like invoicing can have serious consequences. Conversely good systems can considerably improve business performance, e.g. by cutting costs.

The typical advantages claimed for a modern methodology like SSADM or Information Engineering are:

- Provides a standard framework for all staff and projects.
- Training systems analysts is easier.
- Makes project control easier by providing a defined set of tasks and deliverables.
- Incorporates the best techniques in a standardised way, e.g. dataflow diagramming.
- Improves systems development productivity.
- Improves the quality of the final computer system.

- Improves communication between all parties, e.g. the analyst, the user, and the programmer.
- Improves communication between one generation of analysts and the next via high-quality specifications.
- Simplifies staff training and recruitment.
- Provides a series of documented steps, making it easier for a new analyst to replace a previous analyst part way through a project.
- Makes it easier to provide automated support with software tools.
- Flexible interfacing with other aspects of IT, e.g. project management and programming.

Methodologies often only cover part of the SDLC. For example as the name implies SSADM only covers feasibility, analysis, and design. Methodologies are often seen as reducing everything to form-filling and constant references to the manual. In fact some IT practitioners and business staff condemn major development methodologies as an exceedingly ponderous, bureaucratic, slow, and expensive way of producing IT systems. They are also seen as making the work of systems analysts tedious, boring, and uncreative. One partial response to this with SSADM has been to produce a cut-down version of the methodology which may be applied to smaller low risk projects. CASE can also take a lot of the 'slog' out of formal methodologies.

18.19   Systems maintenance

The bulk of systems analysis and programming work is actually maintenance. In a nutshell methodologies ease the maintenance by providing good documentation and minimising the number of errors that need correcting. See Sections 23.7 and 23.8 for further details.

18.20   Changes over the last two decades

The changes in the systems development life-cycle over the last two decades can be illustrated by contrasting how a sales invoicing system might have been developed in the early 1970s and in the early 1990s in a medium-sized company with a small computing department.

In the early 1970s the documentation for a system would have been typed and all diagrams hand-drawn. Programs and data would still often be prepared 'off-line', i.e. written by hand onto forms and punched onto cards or paper tape for entry into a mainframe computer. On-line work via terminals was expensive and rationed. The programs would have been written in COBOL.

By the early 1990s nearly all systems documentation is word processed and DTP (Desktop Publishing) is in frequent use. Diagramming software is used by a substantial minority of systems developers. The programming is often in fourth generation language like INGRES, although COBOL and its rivals are still popular. Networked micro-computer systems are often replacing small mainframes and mini-computers. Most work is now done via a terminal or a personal computer. Package software is more readily considered in the 1990s than in the 1970s.

In smaller computer departments the application of systems development methodologies in the 1990s tends to be much as it was in the 1970s. The ideas are understood, but only partially applied. In large computer departments, or on large computer projects, methodologies are taken much more seriously. The usual explanation offered for this discrepancy is that small computer departments do not have the time or resources for the 'bureaucratic' approach to systems development.

18.21 Comments on systems development methodologies

Methodologies usually apply within a limited range of system development activities. Thus Jackson Structured Programming (JSP) as the name implies can be used in the construction phase of the life cycle. A methodology like JSP is compatible with, say, SSADM as they both cover different parts of the SDLC.

The view of systems development and methodologies given so far is very much based on developing IT administrative systems. This view does not readily embrace other types of IT application, e.g. Decisions Support Systems (DSSs). Again methodologies are often incomplete in the sense that SSADM, for instance, is not too concerned with how systems are investigated, but more with how the findings are documented. The techniques, even the 'methodology', of investigation is considered a separate issue.

There are other methodologies which place less emphasis on formal specifications and which have a role in systems development. The most obvious example is prototyping which is discussed below. Other methodologies concentrate on the human factors in business IT as discussed in Chapter 14 and Section 19.16.

To both the practitioner and the outside observer the whole area of systems development methodology and standards is confusing. This is because no one methodology has been adopted as *the* standard, though SSADM and Information Engineering are commonly used in the UK for large business systems. Furthermore, even where SSADM or a rival is adopted, old systems documented in previous ways persist for years. Also other organisations such as customers and suppliers may use different methodologies. In practice, this can be resolved by remembering that the variety of methodologies and related matters in any one business is manageable. Also most methodologies have similar principles and objectives. It is usually not too difficult to overcome the frustration of using a different terminology and different symbols on diagrams when the underlying concepts are similar. A system documented using an alien methodology is much better than an undocumented system.

Another important point is that methodologies and techniques are still evolving. The obvious example is the replacement of Version 3 of SSADM by Version 4. More radical approaches are also being introduced. An example of this is 'object oriented' analysis, design, and programming. Object oriented approaches require a totally different method of thinking about software design. Simplifying considerably an 'object' is seen as a combination of data and program code. So a employee 'object' in a computer personnel system is a combination of the data about employees and the means of processing the data. Systems are designed and programmed out of (software and data) 'objects' which communicate with each other. Systems produced with object oriented techniques are supposed to be easier to build and maintain.

18.22 Prototyping

Prototyping involves constructing a preliminary version of a system using a quick-programming system such as a fourth generation language. In its basic form prototyping involves writing a program to produce a few screen displays and letting the user suggest modifications. In this case because the emphasis is on discovering the user's requirements via interactive displays, calculations and other processing can be omitted or simplified. Prototyping is also discussed in Sections 2.8 and 22.19. It can be simply an investigative technique or almost a development methodology.

- *Throw-away prototyping*

As mentioned above, the idea is to identify the users' requirements and once this is done the prototype can then be discarded. Development then proceeds in the normal fashion.

- *Evolutionary prototyping*

The idea is to refine the prototype successively with the user until a complete working system is produced. Rapid development can result, particularly with simple systems. However this type of prototyping is not favoured by those with a more formal approach to systems development.

- *Other types of prototyping*

Prototypes can be produced for several other purposes. One example is producing a prototype for user familiarisation and training prior to the arrival of the complete system. Prototypes can also be constructed for experimental purposes. For instance one can be constructed to decide on the best standard for the HCI (Human Computer Interface) in terms of the screen layout, the format of error messages, and the use of pull-down menus.

18.23 Automation of systems development

Most forms of engineering use techniques like CAD (Computer Aided Design). The comparable automation of systems development is discussed in Section 4.6. Primarily it means using the software tools which are listed there. Preparing the voluminous specifications and documentation of modern IT systems is tedious without computer assistance. For instance, structured systems analysis and design really requires some form of computer system for preparing, storing, and editing the extensive number of diagrams used. An analyst's workbench is more comprehensive as it can, for instance, also check that diagrams follow established rules.

18.24 Summary

- Traditional systems analysis and design has gradually given way to structured approaches. Structured analysis and design involves extensive diagramming, rigorous levelling, the use of logical and physical specification, a greater emphasis on data, and thoroughness.
- The distinction between logical and physical specification is important. The logical specification describes the 'what' and the physical specification describes the 'how'.
- Methodologies are standardised methods which define how to develop a computer system in great detail.
- SSADM is perhaps the most important analysis and design methodology in the UK.
- The use of rival methodologies does create some confusion. However the underlying principles such as structured techniques are often common.
- Prototyping is a popular approach − some see it as almost a development methodology, and others merely as a systems investigation technique.
- The use of software tools has considerably eased the problems of producing drawings and specifications with structured methodologies.

Chapter 19
Theory of Business and IT Systems

19.1 Introduction

Chapters 17 and 18 gave an introduction to traditional and modern business systems development. This chapter contains an elementary discussion of the theory underlying the systems met in administration and business. Many of the theoretical views below are incorporated in practical management and computer projects without much controversy. Indeed the concepts are sometimes used almost subconsciously. However a minority of these theoretical views are controversial, and some are perceived as 'academic' by practitioners.

19.2 Why automate?

The first common-sense question is to ask why bother with business information technology at all. This is an important issue because computer staff frequently have to justify new systems or amendments to old ones. In fact this is one of the key parts of a feasibility study.

Typical reasons for introducing new IT are:

- *Replacement*
For example an old system is reaching the end of its life and must be replaced by something. An updated version of the old system taking advantage of modern technology is an obvious solution. In some cases it is not the hardware which is reaching the end of its life, but the software. Some software is badly written and has been amended so many times that every small change is a major task. Bespoke payroll software is vulnerable to this problem. New software can then be worthwhile, especially if designed for ease of amendment which makes maintenance more economic and reliable.

● *Tangible benefits*

Sometimes an old system is satisfactory and has a reasonable life-expectancy. However a system based on new technology can offer significant improvements in operational efficiency, e.g. manpower savings. Early computer systems allowed significant reductions in the clerical labour necessary to operate an administrative system. Another possible tangible benefit is using new IT for greater speed in producing results.

● *Quality*

The quality of computer systems is usually better than the corresponding manual systems. For instance a computer-printed invoice has a better appearance and is more accurate than a handwritten one.

● *Security*

Computer systems can be more secure than manual systems. It is, for example, difficult to copy manual records frequently. But putting computer data onto magnetic tape is easy, and this can then be stored in a fireproof safe. Even unauthorised access to data can be more easily restricted with computer systems, e.g. by encrypting data. There is the assumption here that the scope for improved security is actually exploited, which is not always the case!

● *Better management information and decision making*

A common argument for many new systems is that they will improve management information, e.g. by producing summary reports on sales activities. Indeed EISs (Executive Information Systems) are sold on the idea that they can present information to senior management in an attractive graphical form. Good information systems alert managers promptly to opportunities and problems, e.g. a sudden unexpected drop in the sales of a major product. Besides providing better information to improve business decisions, computers can automate or assist in the decision-making process, for example DSSs.

● *Competitive advantage*

A company wants better IT systems than its competitors, e.g. to attract more customers by giving better service. Reservation systems for booking flights have been seen as crucial in this respect by airlines.

- *Transformation*

Sometimes IT provides such significant benefits that it allows a significant shift in the method of working. This is sometimes expressed as 'quantitative change becoming qualitative change'. As an example take a systems analyst preparing high-quality overhead projector transparencies and documentation for a presentation to IT users on implementing a new system. Prior to DTP (Desktop Publishing) rough hand-drawn transparencies were sometimes used to supplement typed notes. Occasionally, where time and cost permitted, a commercial artist was used to produce transparencies. Often for routine meetings they were just not prepared. The argument was that it should be done well, which was expensive and time-consuming, or it should not done at all. There are now no excuses. By using DTP the job can be done quickly, cheaply, and in a quality-fashion. The nature of routine presentations is thus transformed.

19.3   Cost-benefit analysis

The usual approach to justifying or selecting any new project or system is to conduct a cost-benefit analysis. This technique is of course used when designing new manufacturing processes or considering new public works such as airports or motorways. The basic idea is first to ensure that the benefits exceed the costs, and secondly to select the best of several proposals. In computer projects cost-benefit analysis is mainly found at the feasibility stage. This is where possible designs for new systems and possible plans for future projects are outlined, together with their costs and benefits.

The normal way of regarding costs and benefits is to consider them as either tangible or intangible. Tangible costs or benefits are things that can be measured or estimated. Often, but not always, a tangible benefit or cost can be translated into money. Thus common tangible benefits are manpower savings and a common tangible cost is new equipment. Both of these can be converted into cash by using the appropriate wage rates and prices. Tangibles may include other measurable things such as more rapid computing, but this is not always easy to value. Thus it can be difficult to put a cash value on the benefit of faster computer printing, even though it is easily quantified. Intangible costs or benefits are those subjective things that cannot be easily measured or estimated, e.g. a deterioration in staff morale, or better quality screen displays. Despite the difficulties of measurement some people try to quantify intangibles partially, e.g. by using a rating scale such as 0 = very bad to 10 = excellent.

Once the costs and benefits have been identified then the cash profit or loss on a proposal is the first thing to be calculated. The non-cash benefits and costs are then usually listed with, perhaps, some subjective comments as to their value. Thus for a new local area network system a simplified case might be:

(1) Tangible benefits:
- £20 000 (This is the net cash saving over five years. It is the result of subtracting the cash costs of the new system from the cash costs of an existing mainframe system.)
- Better response times with interactive work and faster processing with batch work such as printing.

(2) Tangible costs:
- These have been included in the net cash savings above.

(3) Intangible benefits:
- More flexible user control over the operation of the system.
- Superior interactive computer displays using windows and mice.
- Improved output quality.

(4) Intangible costs:
- Weaker security.
- Greater user responsibility for computer operations.

This simple cost-benefit analysis indicates the difficulty for the decision makers. Clearly on tangible cash grounds the case is good. However the intangible costs of weaker security and increased responsibility must be balanced against the financial and intangible benefits before accepting or rejecting the proposal. There are some situations where the intangible benefits justify heavy net cash costs, e.g. some companies are prepared to pay for good public relations where the benefits are almost entirely intangible.

There are many practical problems associated with cost-benefit analysis in practice. For instance it can be difficult to produce reliable estimates for staff and equipment savings. The timing of costs and benefits must also be taken into account. Many costs fall into the early stages of a project whilst benefits may grow slowly or be delayed for several years. Calculations become more complicated when interest charges are taken into account on the cash costs and cash benefits spread over the life-time of a project.

Another problem is determining the time span, usually several years, over which costs and benefits are examined. Furthermore there can be a 'ripple effect' when introducing a new system. The ripple-effect is all the changes which spread outside the boundary of the system and the time-span considered. The ripple effect may be good or bad. It is usually small as the name implies.

19.4 The value and quality of information

One common argument with computer systems is that they improve management information. Can a price be put on new information or better information? Clearly it can. So, taking an extreme example, certain knowledge of the winner of a future horse race is obviously worth a lot of money to a gambler. Even knowledge of the increased probability of a particular horse winning is valuable. Of course the assumption here is that the knowledge is confined to a few people. This needs to be translated into a management context. Good information from a computer system can increase the probability of improved management decisions and hence improved business operations such as sales or production. The information can then be said to have value.

Take a simplified sales example. With current forecasts a distribution business often loses 5% of sales because it is out of stock when retailers want to buy items. Suppose a new computerised forecasting system provides information which results in a reduction of lost sales from 5% to 3% of turnover. Then the computerised information is worth the profit on the extra 2% of sales which could be tens of thousands of pounds with high volumes. In practice, this is of course difficult to evaluate, but it is not impossible. This perspective can be summarised by saying that the value of information is the financial benefit of the reduction in uncertainty which the information offers. Before valuing information its quality must also be taken into account in terms of factors like accuracy, completeness, timeliness, relevance, and ease of use. Trade-offs are often accepted e.g., approximate information today may be of more value than accurate information next week.

19.5   Systems theory

There is a theoretical approach to systems called General Systems Theory (GST). It sees any system as a set of interacting components within a boundary which separates the system from the outside world. Most systems are not 'closed', but 'open', i.e. they interact with the outside world. Systems in this general context include chemical reactions, the weather on a planet like the Earth or Jupiter, the circulation of blood in an animal, an animal in its entirety, a social system such as a tribe of primitive people, an industrial system such as a factory, and so on. The more elementary systems such as chemical reactions or electric motors are amenable to school science, i.e. to experiments and simple mathematics. Weather systems are complex but can be modelled using advanced mathematics and high-speed computers. The question then arises as to whether systems such as a factory can be treated in a similar fashion. The answer is yes, and to some extent this is the area that OR (Operational Research) tackles by applying mathematics to problems like production planning. Social systems are more intractable but subjects like sociology attempt to deal with them.

Systems theory tries to deal with the underlying nature of all these different types of system in terms of concepts which include:

● *Components*
A system is a structured collection of components, e.g. machine tools in a factory.

● *A boundary*
There is a boundary between the outside world (the environment) and the system. For example, the glass screens of VDUs are part of the physical boundary between computer and manual office systems.

● *Interaction*
The components of a system interact with each other, and sometimes the outside world. For instance, the staff in an office pass work onto

each other. Interaction between the components of a system is sometimes known as 'coupling'. Tightly coupled components are linked closely together, i.e. one component can have an immediate and strong effect on another. Loosely coupled components have weaker links. For example a factory traditionally reduces the coupling between its production operations by having stocks of part-finished work between the operations. In this way, a failure of one operation does not immediately affect succeeding operations allowing time to fix the fault.

- *Processing*

Where a system interacts with the outside world the system usually processes or transforms inputs into outputs. This idea is shown in Figs. 19.2 to 19.4. A mill for instance has raw materials such as raw cotton as input. This is processed by spinning operations to produce cotton thread wound on bobbins as output.

- *Hierarchy*

Systems are often based on a hierarchy, i.e. they contain sub-systems which contain sub-systems and so on. So a computer hardware system contains a processor which contains circuit boards which contain integrated circuits.

- *Control*

Systems are controlled externally or control themselves. Thus as part of monitoring the selling process in a business the accountants monitor customer debts to ensure that they do not become excessive.

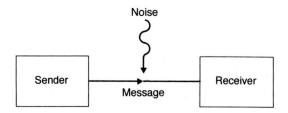

Fig. 19.1 A model of a communications channel which can represent not only electronic communications, but also, say, a customer mailing a typed order to a supplier. Noise is anything which interferes with accurate transmission, for instance, typing errors in the sales order.

● *Holism*

Systems are holistic and not just mere groupings of components. This means that the parts of a system must be considered together as part of a whole rather than separately. For example, it is no use planning holiday leave for one member of staff without considering when the others take their holidays. Holism also implies the rather obvious idea of emergent properties, i.e. when systems are created characteristics emerge which are not possessed by their individual components. Thus the emergent property of a factory might be the ability to assemble motor cars quickly. The people and machines inside it cannot do this individually. A related concept is 'synergy' which is the extra benefit from the components of a system acting together. So a systems development team can produce more together than the total of the team members working separately. All this is sometimes summarised by saying that the whole is greater than the sum of its parts.

● *Deterministic and stochastic properties*

Deterministic systems are predictable in their behaviour. Thus the solar system is deterministic because the position of the planets can be forecast decades ahead. By way of contrast many business systems are stochastic which means that their behaviour is only predictable in terms of probabilities and statistics. For example, in the personal computer market, forecasts of the extra sales demand, which might result from increased advertising, can only be approximate. In some cases the stochastic aspects, i.e. the errors and statistical fluctuations, may be small enough to be ignored.

Systems theory can also be considered to be a rather loose association of several related subjects such as cybernetics (the theory of control) and information theory (the theoretical principles behind the storage and transmission of information). Some of these ideas and subjects are discussed in more depth below. Systems theory has a rather abstruse image to most practising computer staff. It tends to be applied at a common-sense conceptual level rather than as detailed techniques.

19.6 Hierarchy and system boundaries

As already indicated, systems contain systems which contain systems and so on. Section 18.5 discussed 'levelling' or the hierarchical division of administrative systems into smaller and smaller sub-systems. A business is a system composed of sub-systems. Figures 6.1 to 6.6 and Figs 7.1 to 7.2 effectively show various sub-systems such as a marketing or finance department in a traditional hierarchical way. These however are rather static views of the organisational system. Figures 16.3 and 16.4 illustrate a more dynamic view of both the hierarchy and the interactions between sub-systems (processes). These diagrams show the interaction between the various system components by flows of data.

One of the important practical problems of IT systems analysis and design is deciding on the boundary of a system or sub-system. For example, during systems design an important practical decision is the dividing line between manual and computer processes. Thus some administrative calculations may only occur a few times per year and systems analysts and managers may be unsure as to whether or not they are worth computerising. In most cases of course the decision is reasonably clear.

19.7 Cybernetics

Cybernetics is that part of systems theory which is concerned with communication and control. Examples are:

- Communications, e.g. between electronic devices or between humans.
- Control, e.g. controlling the arm and gripper of a robot which is assembling electric motors in a factory; or controlling the staff on a computer project.

In a wider context, an animal, for instance, is a cybernetic organism consisting of a series of sub-systems for breathing, the ingestion of food, and the like. An animal's body needs to control factors like its temperature and heart rate. Similarly a business, like an animal, consists of a series of sub-systems, e.g. the stock and finance sub-systems. These sub-systems must be operating properly if the business is to be viable and thrive and prosper in a hostile environment.

19.8   Communication

The basic idea of communication theory is shown in Fig. 19.1. There is a channel connecting a sender and receiver with noise interfering with the transmission. This concept is important in electronics. But it not only applies to a telephone link between two people, or a telecommunication cable between a VDU and a mainframe. It also applies at the level of two organisational departments communicating with each other via paper forms and electronic messages, or a manager receiving a printed budget report from a computer system. Good communication obviously depends on factors like a common language (or agreed code with machine systems), an operative link, and the rate of transfer of data. In particular, the 'noise' should be low. 'Noise' may be cross-talk or crackles on an electronic link which interfere with the transmission of data. In a paper-based communication system 'noise' may be errors on a print-out. The designer of a communication system has to cater for all the factors mentioned if the link is to work satisfactorily.

19.9   Control

Control theory is applied in the design of many machine systems, e.g. in electronic amplifiers. Some variables in a process are controllable, e.g. the volume of goods purchased for sale by a retailer. Other variables are uncontrollable. For example a retailer cannot control the level of unemployment in a country which affects sales. However, a business can change a process to react to uncontrolled variables. For example a business, to survive when experiencing poor trading conditions, can cut costs by reducing the number of staff.

Control of a technical or business process can take place before, during, or after any events which disturb the process. This leads to one simple but useful three-fold division of control:

● *Pre-control*
The controlling action is pre-emptive and takes place before the disturbing events become serious. An example is preventive maintenance of computer equipment or vehicles which are checked and serviced regularly to minimise disruptive break-downs.

● *Concurrent control*

Monitoring and control are exercised concurrently with a process. Concurrently means that within the natural timescale of the system the timelags are small. So within sensible limits the data on a process needs to be up-to-date and any responses to problems must be reasonably swift. Depending on the situations reasonable timé-lags and reasonable response times might be anything from seconds to weeks. For instance, checks may be made on car components stamped out by a press tool every twenty minutes. This might prove that the components were drifting away from the specified size due to wear of the punch and die, and that these should be changed. Conversely controlling a sales campaign may involve delays and responses measured in weeks.

● *Post-control*

Control is exercised after the event, e.g. audit checks may reveal that fraud occurred months before. This is the least effective form of control.

Cybernetic thinking influences both management practice and computer systems design. Of special importance in cybernetics is the idea of control loops which are particularly important with concurrent control:

● *An open-loop system*

Figure 19.2 shows an 'open-loop' system. Here the device (or human organisation) just continues to produce output in a preset way. Any departures from the ideal standard of output are ignored. In effect this represents no control at all. A simple example is an electronic clock which is left to run without adjustment. In a business context open-loop systems occur when there is 'laissez-faire' management, i.e. people

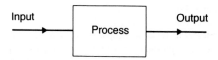

Fig. 19.2 An open-loop system where there is no means for the system to regulate itself. A simple example is a computer system automatically printing a stock analysis report every month.

are left to do their job with no supervision. Batch computer systems are another example. Some computer systems continue to produce printed reports in a fixed format whether they are wanted or not. So for instance sales analysis reports might be produced regularly every month-end with no check being made to discover if they are still what the user wants, or to see if any errors have occurred in the reports.

● *A feedback loop*

Figure 19.3 represents the feedback loop. Here the output, say factory production, is compared with a predetermined standard or target value. If there is a significant difference between the actual and target value corrective action is taken. For instance, if a factory is producing below its target extra shift working might be authorised to increase production. If production is over target then all current overtime working might be stopped. The information on the actual output of the system which is

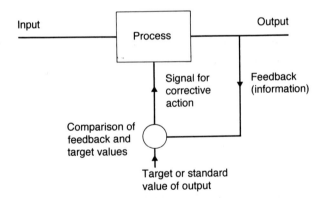

Fig. 19.3 A system controlled by a feedback loop. When the feedback information does not correspond to the standard value, then action is taken to adjust the input or process. An example is computer terminal display. Screen messages and bleeping provide feedback to the user about faulty input allowing immediate correction via the keyboard.

With engineering systems the feedback diagram can be more complicated. A sensor or detector is often shown. For a heating system this could be a thermometer sensing the temperature (the output). The sensor supplies the feedback signal from the output. The device which uses the signal to make a comparison with a standard value is known as a comparator. Another signal from the comparator is then fed into the actuator or effector for corrective action. A valve in a heating system can act as an effector by increasing or decreasing the gas to adjust the heating process to the pre-set target temperature. By analogy the terms detector, comparator, and effector are sometimes used with business systems and shown on diagrams.

compared with the target value is called feedback. The principle is also called error-actuated feedback. This name is used because it is the error, i.e. the difference between the actual output and the target output, that actuates the correcting action.

- *A feedforward loop*

Figure 19.4 represents feedforward control. Here the details of input to a system are 'fedforward' and the future output predicted. If the expected future output is different from the target value, action is taken. An example is training where details of new recruits are used to modify their training programme before they start. Suppose some IT recruits are discovered to have done COBOL at college. Then the information can be fedforward from the personnel department to the trainers. They could then omit basic COBOL programming from the training schedule, avoiding the predicted duplication and dissatisfaction.

Note that with control loops it is information that is fed back or forward. Control loops lead to the idea of 'management by exception', i.e. all minor departures from target values are filtered from a report and only major departures are accepted for corrective action. For instance a stock control computer system might only print out warnings if items were out-of-stock or significantly over-stocked. The numerous

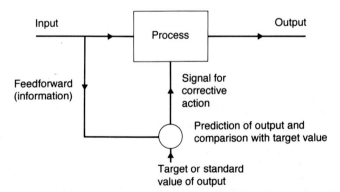

Fig. 19.4 A system controlled by feedforward. An example is a business which monitors raw material and labour cost trends to predict the future costs and profits of producing finished goods. This allows it to consider in advance such action as raising the price of finished goods so as to maintain profitability. As with Fig. 19.3 more complicated versions of the feedforward diagram can show sensors and actuators.

cases where there are small variations from the desired stock levels are ignored. Computer reporting by exception removes the need for human beings to examine a mass of trivial cases before finding the occasional important case.

Besides monitoring inputs and outputs information on the environment can also be used for control. So feedforward can also be used to predict and minimise the effect of adverse environmental changes. For example the negative effect on future sales from an impending VAT increase might be offset by more aggressive marketing.

Many forms of control action are continuous, e.g. advertising is increased a little to bring sales up to the target value. Other forms of control are discontinuous, e.g. switching on the lights if a room is too dark, and switching them off if there is enough daylight from the windows. This is called frequently called 'on-off' or 'stop-go' control.

Control loops can be hierarchical, i.e. there can be control loops within control loops. Thus a factory robot uses electronic feedback loops to control the position of its arm. However there are higher levels of feedback. For example, the robot and the machines it supplies are producing output which is monitored to ensure that scrap remains minimal. At a still higher level there are computerised costing reports for the whole manufacturing operation. These provide regular feedback to the factory management to check that the robot and all the other machines are being used in a cost-effective manner. With human systems in particular the recommendation is that control should be exercised at the lowest possible level of a hierarchy. So employees should be encouraged to make their own decisions and take action to control their own work rather than constantly asking their boss to do this for them.

As already implied a computerised MIS (Management Information Systems) is primarily concerned with providing feedback. A DSS (Decision Support Systems) is often predictive and therefore concerned with feedforward.

Where information is fedback or fedforward, time lags must be relatively insignificant. It can be shown that where people or machines use out-of-date information then unstable erratic results are probable from the controlled system. Thus feeding back information on low sales six weeks late could lead a production planner to cut manufacturing output just as sales were actually starting to increase again!

19.10 The law of requisite variety

This 'law' suggests that for full control the controlling system should have a variety which matches the thing controlled. This implies, for instance, that budgetary control on its own is an inadequate way of controlling a business. A business is subject to many varied events like staff losses and competition. Attempting to control costs or revenues alone is just not enough. Of course in practice businesses do usually monitor other factors like staff losses and competition and take action when they are severe. However the general point stands that the variety of controlling systems should be adequate for their task.

19.11 Stability

A stable system continues to operate in normal states indefinitely and resists any disturbing effects. Perhaps the ultimate example of stability is the solar system where the planets have continued to orbit the sun more or less as today for millions of years. This is despite the gravitational interference of the planets on each other, and other disturbing effects such as the influence of nearby stars. One of the great questions in astronomy is whether the solar system is truly stable over long periods of geological time and whether, say, the earth's orbit could change significantly with catastrophic consequences for living creatures. The comforting answer is that the solar system is probably stable in the long-term. A more practical business example of stability is the ability of most businesses to survive the adverse but temporary effects of an economic recession.

Managers and systems analysts are concerned to design stable business systems. For instance one objective is to ensure that the office and operating procedures in payroll administration are such that employees are paid on time despite sickness amongst payroll clerks, and despite computer failures. Stable performance of a payroll business system is of course ensured by simple measures like having ready access to temporary staff or having a standby computer in the event of hardware failure. This ability of systems to overcome or resist the effects of minor disasters is often called 'resilience' in computer circles.

So far the discussion has concentrated on the stability of a system in terms of its ability to resist a transition to undesirable states. However systems may be unstable in other ways such as major oscillations in behaviour triggered by small changes in their inputs or environment. Such systems are in engineering terms inadequately 'damped', i.e too sensitive to changes. An example is the large fluctuations in factory production discussed in Section 19.15 below.

19.12   Homeostasis

The environment in particular can contain many uncontrollable variables, e.g. the weather. The ability of a self-regulating organism or organisation to maintain a stable healthy state in a changeable world is called homeostasis. So the body temperature of a human being remains constant despite major changes in the temperature of the environment. Similarly a factory tries to maintain the required output. It does this in many ways such as constantly maintaining and repairing its equipment to keep producing. Homeostasis is usually the result of a whole series of control mechanisms working together.

19.13   Sub-optimisation

One of the problems with system design is that one part of a system or a sub-system can be improved at the expense of another, or at the expense of the whole system. At the very least the extra benefits of an integrated design embracing the whole system are lost. This is called sub-optimisation. An example from systems analysis is designing several distinct master files for a set of applications rather than one integrated database. Each file-based application might be efficient in itself. However one cost of designing systems and files separately is duplicated and inconsistent data. This can be significantly reduced with an integrated database system.

19.14   Decision making

An important aspect of management is often seen as decision-making. Many decisions in business administration can be automated, or at least provided with computer assistance. A classic example is stock control. In this case when the quantity in stock falls below a certain level (the re-order point) new goods are ordered. This is called 'structured' decision-making and can be readily automated using computers because it is based on clear rules. Other decisions are termed 'unstructured' because the rules are not clear and if they exist they are at best merely guidelines. Unstructured decisions can involve novel or occasional situations such as whether to take over another company or produce a new product. Some of the more difficult unstructured decision making involves human problems. Of course many business decisions fall into the immediate category of semi-structured decisions, e.g. deciding on the revised selling price of a software package. People making 'semi-structured' decisions can benefit from some computer assistance, e.g. DSSs.

19.15 System dynamics

System dynamics attempts to represent the behaviour of business and other systems by a set of equations, i.e. it is a form of modelling or simulation. It is reminiscent of the way an engineer might calculate the behaviour of an electronic circuit. Needless to say the calculations are usually performed on a computer with an emphasis on graphical output. System dynamics can be applied, for instance, with a production and distribution system. The components in the system model are then retail shops, warehouses, and a factory as shown in Fig. 19.5. Each of these holds stock and orders goods according to a set of rules. The purpose of the stock-holding is to 'decouple' each unit partially from fluctuations in the supply and demand of items. Replacement stock might then be ordered when the stock reaches a minimum level sufficient to cover the delays in receiving replenishments. In an equilibrium state, the amount of goods flowing to customers from shops is equal to the factory production which is distributed down the supply chain. However it can be shown that this kind of system can act as an amplifier and that small changes in customer demand on the shops become large fluctuations in demand on the factory. Also the stock levels at various points, such as the warehouses of distributors, tend to oscillate wildly. This is illustrated in Fig. 19.6. The oscillations are caused by the combined effect of the time lags, stocks, and re-ordering rules of the system.

Fig. 19.5 An application of system dynamics where a factory, producing say footwear, is feeding supplies into a distribution chain ultimately to supply consumers. There is stock in the factory's finished goods store, the warehouses of distributors, and in the shops.

19.16   Hard versus soft approaches

With both traditional and structured approaches to systems development there is the underlying assumption that there is a 'best' system. This best system represents the optimum that can be done with the human, technical, and financial resources available. It may be that in practice only an approximation to the best system can be identified, designed, and built. However the nearer a systems development team get to the ideal system the better the job they have done. This view is called the 'hard systems' approach. It stresses 'hard' identifiable factors like money,

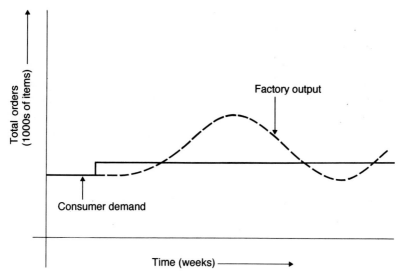

Fig. 19.6 The response of the supply chain in Fig. 19.5 to a small sharp change in consumer demand. The result is a major fluctuation in the output of the factory. The intermediate parts of the supply chain such as the distributors (not shown) also experience large fluctuations of both demand and stock levels. The amplification effect depends on timelags, stocks, and re-ordering rules.

time, and technology. It tends to treat business systems as machines. The alternative 'soft' systems approach considers the 'soft' factors in system design like human beliefs, personal preferences, and politics. These problems are ill-structured and fuzzy. Two examples illustrate the distinction between the two types of problem. An example of a hard systems problem is a flat tyre. The methods of dealing with the problem are fairly clear such as telephone the garage, or change the wheel. The contrasting problem is what should be done about the political and social problems of Northern Ireland? Clearly it is difficult to find a solution that satisfies all parties. These are of course perhaps unfair examples and compare two extremes. A reverse example makes the point. How do you a build a star ship for a modest price that has 1000 light-years range? Obviously this is a hard systems problem which is beyond current astronautical technology. An easy soft systems problem is how do you make squabbling and fighting children play together peacefully in a nursery?

The soft systems view is not just concerned with human issues, but also the goals of a system. Hard systems problems tend to assume that the goals are established and not controversial, e.g. the purpose of the new computer payroll system is prompt and accurate payment in an efficient and economical manner. This provides the software designer with an encouraging and philosophically secure framework. By way of contrast the soft systems view is prepared to face issues like what is the effect of a proposed new computer system on industrial relations and managerial policies. It tries to analyse these more political issues, and is seen as a way of developing understanding amongst the participants. There is a Soft Systems Methodology (SSM). This is covered in the Information Systems Series by the book *Multiview* written by D. E. Avison and A. T. Wood Harper. This book also explains how SSM can be used in conjunction with more conventional systems development approaches. See also Sections 14.9 and 21.5.

19.17 Is systems analysis and design necessary?

One of the first questions computer systems analysts should ask themselves is whether their jobs are necessary. Programmers and IT users can come up with rather hostile answers to this question! People new to business computing are sometimes puzzled about the role of the systems analyst. He or she is sometimes seen as a parasitic middleman between the user and the programmer. To some people the analyst is not only an unnecessary overhead, but can confuse the process of systems development. The answer is that the process of separating analysis from programming occurred very early in the history of computing in the 1950s. It was discovered then, with surprise, that business computing could be more difficult than technical and scientific computing. The study of business processes for computerisation was found to be time-consuming and difficult, often taking many months. The end product was the specification of a business system, including a specification of the software for the programmer.

It was also discovered that other aspects of systems analysis such as implementing systems were also demanding and time-consuming. All this led to the creation of systems analysis as a separate job. Basically what was true almost forty years ago is even more true today. The development and implementation of major systems requires person-months and often person-years. Any work of this scale demands a division of labour, and systems analysis and programming are a reasonable basis for the division. Also work on this scale demands formal documentation and proceduralised methods of working which is where methodologies make their contribution.

If anything the trend is against the programmer rather than the analyst. Developments like the extended use of packages and 4GLs tend to favour the analyst. In some cases systems analysis is split into more specialist jobs, e.g. systems design. However systems analysts may face legitimate competition in some areas from specialists like OR workers and industrial engineers.

It is possible for the user to replace both the analyst and programmer. The systems must of course be small both in terms of the work required and their impact within the organisation. This usually means basing the development on easy-programming systems and standard packages. The users have the advantage of understanding the application well. However users often have less appreciation and less skill in IT, and development and implementation work must interfere with their ordinary duties. It is likely that IT practitioners will face increasing competition from 'users' for systems development work. These issues are discussed further in Sections 28.16 to 28.18.

19.18   Views of systems analysis

Earlier chapters allude to different perceptions of the nature of systems development. For instance, Section 1.11 and Appendix II contain some comments on this issue. Most views on systems analysis stress one aspect of the subject as being of primary importance and a few common views are discussed below:

- *The specification view*
One view, often held by programmers, is that the primary job of a systems analyst is to produce precise and clear logical specifications for a new IT system. The systems designer and programmer then design and produce the software. The weakness in this view is obvious. For instance it includes the narrow assumption that the system is primarily software. It also ignores the importance of office procedures and the analyst's role in implementing IT systems.

- *The bureaucratic view*

In a large organisation IT systems are usually developed in line with a semi-formal or formal methodology. Methodologies such as SSADM impose a fixed method of developing a business system. For activities outside the development methodologies there are other standards and procedures. Together these can provide a comprehensive set of rules which the analyst and programmer can follow when developing a system.

- *The data-oriented view*

This view derives from database theory. The view is that data is central to business computer applications. This requires a comprehensive detailed analysis of the essential data used by an application such as stock control, or preferably by a large part of a business such as human resources administration. It can even be extended to the data used by a whole organisation. Once the analysis of the data is completed it is relatively easy to determine the inputs, processes, and outputs necessary to maintain and use the data. A computer database or master file can then be designed which contains and uses the essential data. This view is to some extent built into modern development methodologies, particularly Information Engineering.

- *The systems engineering view*

Administrative IT systems are similar to mechanical and electronic systems, so they can be analysed and designed in an analogous manner. Office systems generally can be treated in a manner similar to the production systems in a factory. According to this view clerks and managers are merely components in an office system along with computer programs and disk drives. This is an extreme version of the hard systems view mentioned above.

- *The human-oriented view*

This is a set of views which consider the human, social, and political aspects of organisations and systems as having overwhelming importance. These views stress subjects like ergonomics and socio-technical design, as well as the soft systems method considered above. See Chapter 14 for further details. The human-oriented view is sometimes criticised for taking an over-sensitive and over-elaborate view of common sense human problems. It is also criticised for downgrading the business and technical aspects of systems analysis.

- *The business analysis view*

The business analyst tends to have less involvement in computer technicalities and more involvement with IT users and management. For example there may be a requirement to raise the quality of administration. Computer systems may only be a small part of this project, which might concentrate primarily on analysing staff performance, office procedures, business forms, and the departmental organisation. This type of work is really a modern form of O&M (Organisation and Methods). Business analysis may also critically examine fundamentals like should a business have a pensions scheme or a pensions department. Ordinary systems analysts tend to accept such pension arrangements and merely seek to maintain or improve their computerisation.

19.19 Summary

- There are many reasons for automating business systems such as lower operating costs, improved quality, and better management information.
- Cost-benefit analysis is an essential technique for assessing computer systems in terms of tangible and intangible costs and benefits.
- Information can be valued in cash terms. This can be done by assessing the financial improvement which results from obtaining the information.
- Systems theory provides useful concepts for systems development staff, and its concepts are used to design business systems.
- Feedback and feedforward are important cybernetic concepts.
- The stability of systems is their ability to maintain a desired state even if there are disturbing factors. The performance of a system may also oscillate undesirably.
- Homeostasis is the ability of complex self-regulating organisms and organisations to maintain a steady state despite significant disturbance.
- The law of requisite variety demands that the variety in the process controlled should be matched by the variety of the controlling systems.
- Sub-optimisation can be a problem with business systems.
- Decision-making can range from structured to unstructured. IT can assist with business decision-making.

- Systems analysis is relatively easy to justify as a job separate from that of the IT user and the programmer.
- Both traditional systems analysis and its successor structured analysis are part of the 'hard' systems approach. The soft systems approach considers human issues.
- There are many views of systems analysis, e.g. the most important aspect of analysis is producing specifications; or human issues are the primary concern.

Part 4
Systems Analysis

Chapters 20 to 26 explain the basic principles and techniques applied by systems analysts to develop and implement computer systems in business.

Chapter 20
Specification and Documentation

20.1 Introduction

This chapter discusses the contents of the main documents, such as feasibility studies, which are produced during the SDLC (Systems Development Life Cycle). It also outlines the specification techniques such as DFDs (Data Flow Diagrams) that are an essential part of systems analysis. Software design and programming have a similar set of techniques which are not discussed here. Producing documentation is an essential part of IT systems development. It is often falsely seen as an expensive irksome chore, but as explained below it is difficult to develop and maintain a system without documentation. However poorly documented systems are frequent. Lack of documentation involves the inevitable penalty of making both development and maintenance work more difficult, more unreliable, more time-consuming, and more expensive.

Each systems development methodology lays down the procedures used to create and approve documentation in a standardised manner. These cover such matters as layout, terminology, and diagramming symbols. Development methodologies are often supplemented by standards unique to a particular business. Even where rigorous methodologies and standards are in force, old systems produced under a previous regime are frequently not re-documented for years. Old but adequate documentation is sometimes lost. Computer departments with different standards are sometimes merged. Systems are often acquired, for instance a system may be transferred from one organisation to another to save development costs. Professionally produced software packages are invariably documented in a different way from the internal standards of the buyer. Also, of course, organisations vary enormously in the discipline applied to producing and maintaining documentation. As a result people experience considerable variations in the quality, quantity, and approach to IT documentation. The general description below is based on what is commonly met in the way of both traditional

and modern systems documentation. The specific documentation techniques briefly described below are those of structured analysis and
broadly SSADM-compatible. Only an outline is provided here, and the
books in the Bibliography of Appendix V should be consulted for a
more detailed discussion of current methodologies, specification techniques, and diagramming methods.

20.2   Purpose and use of documentation

Why document? Bitter experience with undocumented or poorly
documented systems soon demonstrates the value of proper documentation. The fundamental reason for documentation is that business IT
systems are far too large and complex to rely on verbal communication
and memory. It is difficult to maintain an unfamiliar make of motor car
without the right manuals! So by analogy maintenance without documentation should be far worse with computer systems which are much
more abstract and variable than cars. Missing or poor documentation
can result in the following for both IT and user staff:

- *Mistakes and inconsistency*

During development it is easy to make mistakes where much of the
communication between user and analyst, and between analyst and
programmer, is verbal. Without documentation disputes can occur
because of misunderstandings. Mistakes may of course be rectified
when testing software, but this is costly. For example one of the minor
consequences of poor program specifications is the correction of inconsistent screen displays during systems testing. So one screen display
may have the screen identification number on the left and another may
have it on the right. This sort of situation occurs where each individual
analyst or programmer decides randomly where to display such data.
With proper standards, and written specifications checked in advance,
problems of this kind are minimised.

- *Unreliability*

Even the staff who established a system find their memories are unreliable. Because of lack of documentation they find it difficult to carry
out the less frequent tasks, for instance year-end procedures. In practice
the more organised people often compile personal files full of useful
titbits of information.

- *Difficulties for other staff*

New staff find it difficult to learn how to operate an undocumented system. They are dependent on their colleagues, and gradually learning from their own experience of the system. This takes time and is very wasteful of human effort. Established employees with no previous experience of an undocumented system have similar difficulties.

- *Maintenance problems*

The maintenance of an undocumented system is a nightmare for analysts and programmers, even those who have some knowledge of the system. Everything has to be deduced from the comments of users, inputs, outputs, and program source code, i.e. the situation requires an informal version of reverse engineering (see Section 22.20).

- *Unnecessary additional investigations*

Without good documentation analysts are forced into repeated systems investigations when the system is to have major amendments or extensions, or to be replaced. With a well-documented system, analysis is considerably reduced as most of the work has already been done.

- *Loss of expertise*

There is a major risk with undocumented systems that the expertise and knowledge carried in people's heads is lost through natural wastage before it can be conveyed to new staff. This means that in some situations there is no-one who understands a system and no documentation either.

One approach to undocumented systems, adopted with reluctance, is to try to document them as a form of preventive maintenance. This means that when a software bug occurs, or system changes are required, then at least some basic documentation is available. Documenting such a system requires the hard work of discussions with users, collecting copies of screen displays and print-outs, and reverse engineering of the software. See Section 22.20 for a discussion on reverse engineering.

To counterbalance the above discussion it is only fair to add that there has always been a school of thought opposed to documentation. This school stresses the problems of documentation, e.g. there is too much of it, it is inaccurate, it is rarely read, it is difficult to keep up-to-date, and so on. According to this view much of the effort spent in producing documentation can be more productively employed elsewhere. This view is often espoused by those who favour rapid and evolutionary development techniques such as prototyping.

20.3   Self-documenting systems

Some people have argued for self-documenting software, i.e. programs that are so well written that there is no need for documentation to understand them. Systems can be self-documenting in two senses. Firstly as far as the users of the system are concerned a well-designed system makes its own use obvious — it should all be apparent from the data screens, help screens, and print-outs. Secondly the software code can be either automatically documented as part of the development method, or the program code is so clear that it can be easily understood even by non-programmers. These are ideals for which some software developers have striven for a long time and which are difficult to achieve with large systems. This is not to say that software cannot be made easier to use and easier for maintenance programmers and the like to understand. There is just a severe limit to what can be done without formal documentation.

20.4   List of typical systems documentation

The discussion of the SDLC in Chapters 18 and 19 makes frequent reference to the production of documentation. As an example the typical documentation required for a sales order processing system can easily be hundreds of pages in total. The terminology used to describe documentation and the details documented can depend very much on the methodology adopted, local standards, and project requirements. Some typical documents produced by the traditional SDLC are listed below. These however occur in one form or another with most methodologies, particularly with large systems:

- Terms of reference.
- A feasibility study.
- A current systems specification.
- The new system requirements.
- The new system design.

- Program or module specifications.
- Program documentation.
- A quality control plan and test data.
- Operating specification.
- User manuals.
- Plans for systems development and implementation.
- Maintenance documentation, e.g. proposals to change a system.

Under most old and new methodologies these documents are regarded as 'products' or 'deliverables'. Real examples of each of the above could contain tens of pages.

20.5 Contents of main documentation

The outlines below give a more complete idea of the contents of the main SDLC documents listed above. The details depend on the methodology and local IT standards.

- *Terms of reference*

This provides formal approval from management for the analyst to proceed with a project. It specifies the scope of the project in terms of its objectives, resource constraints, and the business and technical areas to be tackled. For instance the terms of reference may specify that an analyst is to conduct a feasibility study into replacing a raw materials stock control system in a factory. This requires an investigation in the purchasing and production departments, and the study is to be completed within six weeks. In the writer's experience terms of reference are often verbal or omitted altogether.

- *Feasibility study*

This contains an outline study of the existing system, an appraisal of weaknesses and future opportunities. It concludes with a set of options for the future, e.g. amend the existing system, or replace it with a new bespoke system, or replace it with a system based on a software package. Associated with each course of action should be outline system designs, and project plans. As explained in Section 19.3 a cost-benefit analysis should accompany each of these options. Frequently of course there is only one main way of proceeding, or there is no feasible alternative to the current system. Needless to say the analyst is also expected to provide some personal comments on the various options and a personal recommendation as to which option should be adopted. Many projects stop at the feasibility stage, for instance because the net benefits look unattractive compared to other projects.

- *Current systems specification*

This is often a physical specification of the current system. If the analyst is fortunate much of this may already exist, but often there is little previous documentation. In which case this has to be prepared by investigation from the beginning. Sometimes the old documentation does not match the new methodology so it has to be translated into the new format.

The current systems specification contains a detailed description of the existing business system in words and diagrams. It should cover both existing computer systems and office procedures. Traditionally it would include copies of business forms, print-outs, and computer screen displays. The documentation should consist of a description of the system as a whole using the diagramming and other specification techniques described here or an equivalent. As discussed in Chapter 18 the modern approach is to provide both a physical and logical specification of the current system. It is always surprising how intimidating an apparently simple system can be in terms of tens of pages of data flow diagrams. Business and technical metrics are an important part of the description of a current system, e.g. the number of policy holders for an insurance system, and the amount of disk space used to store data on them.

- *New system requirements*

This is primarily a brief description of the logical and physical requirements of the new system. It is often presented as a simple list of features. A critical appraisal of the existing system is sometimes included, as well as a list of its problems. The overall goals and constraints of the future system should also be considered (see Section 23.5).

- *New systems design*

The design specifications are similar to the specification of an existing system except that they describe a future new system. Traditionally the new system is mainly described in physical business terms such as screen layouts and office procedures for users. Figures 16.1 to 16.9 give an idea of how a system can be specified pictorially. It must also be described in physical technical terms, e.g. magnetic disk files, telecommunication links, and programs.

With a structured approach there are separate logical and physical designs. In SSADM Version 4 the new system is mainly specified in logical terms at the end of Module 4. At the end of Module 5 a physical design is produced in terms of specifications for screen displays, software, and computer files or a database. The design specification for the new system should include performance estimates and targets for the proposed system, e.g. terminal response time calculations and detailed costings.

The design specification of a new system is perhaps the most important document as it is the core of the agreement with the users as to what will be produced. For this reason it is sometimes called a 'systems proposal'. In a software house it would be the basis of a formal contract. The project and implementation plans are sometimes presented with a new system design. The technical design of the system, which often primarily concerns the intricacies of the software, is frequently not presented to users in detail. This can be seen as an internal matter for systems development staff which would bore or baffle administrative users.

The reverse situation is where an organisation is putting a system out to tender with outside suppliers. Besides asking for commercial information as illustrated in Fig. 22.1 a 'requirements specification' is attached to the invitation to tender. In theory this should be a logical design with some essential physical requirements such as the need for a large payroll system to run on an ICL mainframe. The suppliers can then propose, say, a physical design based on a particular software package. In practice 'requirements specifications' attached to a tender often comprise a specification of the current physical system together with a list of desired new features.

● *Program or module specifications*
These are often regarded as part of the physical design and there could be dozens or even hundreds of specifications for all the modules or programs in a large software system.

- *Program documentation*

This is produced by programmers and describes for instance the detailed design of each program, e.g. structure diagrams such as those produced as part of JSP (Jackson Structured Programming).

- *A quality control plan and test data*

See Chapter 26.

- *Operating specification*

This describes such matters as the set up of the software, computer job control language statements, operating instructions, and operational requirements, e.g. in terms of magnetic disk storage and special stationery.

- *User manuals*

These describe how a computer system is used. For example with a computerised stock system the manual explains how a new item of stock would have details like its name and cost set up on the system. The method of preparing a stock valuation report would be explained. Other aspects such as notifying the IT staff of computer problems or apparent faults are often included. Modern systems often also have an on-line help system. This is a simple computerised manual and by pressing the right keys the user gets information on the screen describing how to use the system. As well as general information the user information is often specific to the context, e.g. when using a screen to enter the details of a new employee, help information can be selected which is only pertinent to that screen.

- *Plans for systems development and implementation.*

See Fig. 30.1, Fig. 30.2, and Section 24.8 for simple examples.

- *Change proposal*

This is similar in concept to a new system design specification except that it describes proposed changes to an existing system, i.e. it concerns maintenance.

20.6   Additional documents

In addition to all the above documents systems analysts may also have to prepare other documents such as:

- Invitations to tender − these request a quotation from a supplier for hardware, software, or services (see Fig. 22.1 for part of an example).
- Contracts with customers and suppliers, or service level agreements which are internal 'contracts' with other departments in the same organisation as explained in Sections 26.2 and 26.14.
- Correspondence with users and suppliers.
- Minutes of meetings.

Business documents such as those listed above are as important in their own way as the more mainstream systems development documents.

20.7   Documentation techniques

As explained in Section 18.3, modern structured systems analysis and design places considerable emphasis on pictorial techniques for specifying systems in preference to the use of text. The main diagramming techniques are outlined below. There are many variants of the symbols, and the approach here has been to use SSADM-compatible diagrams unless stated to the contrary.

- *Entity relationship (ER) diagrams*

The purpose of an ER diagram is to show the entities in a system and their relationships. An entity is something fundamental such as a customer or product about which a system needs to hold data. Taking a sales order processing system as an example it is fundamental that the system holds data such as the name and address of customers. Sales orders are also fundamental and the system needs to hold data on them such as the quantity of goods ordered and the agreed delivery date from the warehouse.

Other entities relevant to a sales order processing system are warehouses (there are often several from which goods are despatched); products (there are usually several products quoted on each order and invoice); deliveries (one order might refer to several future deliveries), and sales invoices. Another aspect is that the products sold are purchased from many different suppliers. Already the verbal description of the entities and their relationships is getting complicated and confusing. The situation can be represented and clarified pictorially by an ER diagram.

Figure 20.1 shows part of an ER diagram for the sales order processing system. Using the ER diagrams it is relatively easy to represent business situations that seem complex in words. ER diagrams can also be checked with user staff. In SSADM the term LDS (Logical Data Structure) is used to describe an ER diagrams. ER diagrams model the real-world and provide a high level logical view of the data a system must process. They specify the relationship between entities such as customers and orders, or employees and departments. For instance a

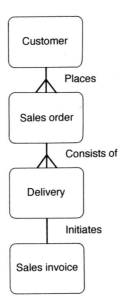

Fig. 20.1 This shows part of an ER (Entity Relationship) diagram for a sales order processing system. Entities are something of importance, like customers and orders, about which a system needs to hold data. One relationship between the entities above is that a customer 'places' sales orders.

  The diagram shows that one customer can place several orders and that each order can consist of several deliveries and that each delivery results in one sales invoice. A more complete ER diagram might contain entities like warehouses, products, and suppliers. The 'crowsfoot' notation is used to represent 'one or more' in a relationship. A plain line represents one of an entity.

department 'contains' employees, the relationship being 'contains'. ER diagrams also form the basis of the physical design of computer files and databases. As an example, take customer and order details stored on magnetic disk. A terminal enquiry requires a display of orders for a particular customer. Clearly the software must provide the link between the customer and order data on the magnetic disk and so emulate the logical relationship shown in the ER diagram.

● *Entity life histories (ELHs)*
ER diagrams represent a static view of the data of a system. However, this data changes over time. Entity life histories show how entities are changed over time by events. Figure 20.3 provides an example of how a bank account entity is affected by various events over its lifetime.

● *Data flow diagrams (DFDs)*
The use of DFDs is illustrated in Figs 16.3 and 16.4 for a payroll system. The purpose of the DFD is to show how data flows between processes and where data is stored. DFDs can only show a few boxes on one diagram. This introduces the idea of using further lower level DFDs to define each of the boxes on a higher level DFD. This is the structured analysis way of using hierarchical decomposition whereby a

```
┌─────────────────────────────────────────────┐
│                                              │
│   ENTITY DESCRIPTION                         │
│                                              │
│   Entity name: CUSTOMER                      │
│   Explanation: A business to whom Kangaroo   │
│                Electronics                    │
│                supply components, usually on  │
│                credit.                        │
│                                              │
│   ATTRIBUTES:                                │
│   Sales Account Number:                      │
│   Customer Name                              │
│   Address                                    │
│   Post code                                  │
│   Sales Area                                 │
│   Customer Classification Code               │
│   Credit Rating                              │
│                                              │
└─────────────────────────────────────────────┘
```

Fig. 20.2 A simplified entity description listing the attributes (data items) which describe the customer entity in Fig. 20.1. Sales Account Number is underlined because it is a key (a unique identifier) of a customer. Further details of attributes like the format, length, meaning, and content are sometimes included. However more often these details are in a separate data dictionary.

process is specified in greater and greater detail. So a set of DFDs can be prepared at several levels of detail − high, middle, and low. The lowest level of DFDs can use other methods to specify the process in each box, for instance as a paragraph of technical English. The specification of a process in a DFD at the lowest level is called by terms such as a 'mini-spec', or in SSADM an EPD (Elementary Process Description). An example is shown in Fig. 20.4.

● *Structured English*
Structured English is a restricted form of English which resembles a high-level programming language. However, the syntax is not as rigorous as that of a programming language. Structured English can be used in mini-spec or EPD to specify the lowest level processes in a set of DFDs. The idea is to eliminate some of the confusing complications of ordinary English. Figure 20.4 shows an example.

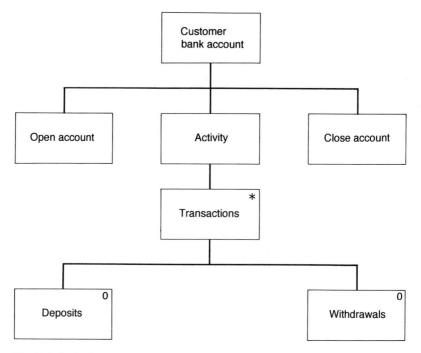

Fig. 20.3 A simple entity life history (ELH) diagram for a bank account. This shows all the actions which happen during the life-time of an entity like a bank account. An '*' indicates repetition, and a '0' indicates an option.

```
GROSS PAY CALCULATION ·

For each Employee do the following:
  Set BasicPay, OvertimePay, ExtraPay to Zero
  If HoursWorked are 40 or less then
     Calculate BasicPay = (HoursWorked × PayRate)
  End-If
  If HoursWorked are greater than 40 then
     Calculate BasicPay = (40 × PayRate)
     Calculate OvertimePay = (HoursWorked − 40) × PayRate
                                   × 1.5
  End-If
  If FirstAidWorker then
     Add FirstAidAllowance to ExtraPay
  End-If
  Calculate GrossPay = BasicPay + OvertimePay + ExtraPay
```

Fig. 20.4 A simplified example of structured English describing part of a pay calculation process like that of Fig. 16.4. The End-If statement is used to terminate the effect of a previous If condition. Structured English is one way of specifying the processes at the lowest-level of a set of DFDs. Real examples might break the pay calculations down to form a set of separate processes and include matters such as bonuses, shift allowances, and tax calculations.

● *Defining data*

There are many ways of defining data in detail. In SSADM, for instance, there are entity descriptions identifying all the data items (fields) associated with an entity. For example with stock data two data items are Product Number and Quantity In Stock. See Fig. 20.2 for another example. The details of the data flows in a DFD also need to be specified, e.g. the contents of documents moving between clerical operations. The term 'data dictionary' is a loose term often used in computing to describe any collection of data definitions. The data dictionary not only specifies the name of a data item, but also such matters as its valid range of values, say £0.01 to £100.00 for the sales price of an item. Computerised data dictionaries are common and provide a convenient method of storing data definitions for both analysts and programmers.

● *Defining hardware and software*

DFDs are a general purpose notation used to specify both logical and physical processes. They can be used to specify the physical processing and storage of data by clerical procedures, hardware, and software.

However other diagramming techniques are sometimes more appropriate. For example, the configuration chart of Fig. 16.6 specifies the major hardware components of an IT system. Similarly there are several other diagramming techniques used for software design.

The Information Systems Series describes other specification techniques elsewhere. For instance see *Software Engineering for Information Systems* by D. C. McDermid. Note that all the above techniques give overlapping descriptions of the data and processes in a system. For instance, with a sales system a customer entity would also appear as a customer data store on a DFD. This is a necessary and useful consistency check.

20.8   Methodologies and standards

A systems development methodology lays down the precise way in which a system is to be documented. As an illustration just take two steps in Stage 1 of SSADM Version 4 (Investigation of Current Environment):

- *Step 130 − Investigate Current Processing*
This involves preparing DFDs of the existing physical system.

- *Step 140 − Investigate Current Data*
This requires preparing an LDS (Logical Data Structure) which as already mentioned is the SSADM term for an ER diagram.

SSADM uses a series of standard forms on which to present analysis and design specifications. There are over 40 different forms for SSADM Version 4, for instance form S04 is used for DFDs. Local IT department standards could define the way operating specifications are prepared.

20.9   Software tools

The above documents are often produced on a good word processor supplemented by diagramming software. In some cases a higher standard of presentation is required and then DTP (Desktop Publishing) is used. As discussed in Section 4.6, an analyst's workbench can be used to considerable advantage. Documentation may be maintained inside a computer and be called up on-line via a VDU. This is done with both systems development and user documentation. As already discussed user manuals are frequently replaced at least partially by on-line help screens. In this situation, printed versions of the documentation take on a subsidiary role.

20.10   Ratification of specifications

In both traditional and modern systems analysis, the user is supposed to check analysis specifications and confirm that they describe the current system. Similarly with design specifications, the user is supposed to confirm that the design is what is required. If there are errors or misunderstandings the analyst must rectify them before the user agrees to the document. Asking the administrative user to check reams of documentation has difficulties such as:

- The documents are forbiddingly large and complex.
- The checking is only cursory and the user's approval has only superficial value.
- The user prevaricates or even refuses to sign the specification as being correct. This tends to be the case where the users realise that signing a specification as being correct makes them responsible if the system has design faults, or key facts have been omitted from the analysis.

There are several partial solutions to these problems. For instance users can be trained in analysis techniques' so that they are more comfortable with specifications and their implications. The specification process can also be broken down into small manageable amounts which is a built-in feature of SSADM. Prototyping can sometimes be used as a more natural way of working.

20.11   Quality control

Methodologies like SSADM include strict quality control procedures for the documentation created at all stages. For instance Version 4,

Step 160 (Assemble Investigation Results) is primarily quality checks of the DFDs and other documentation which represent the current system. Quality control of systems development documents is mainly by reviews and inspection of documents. Where CASE tools are used some simple checking is automatic. For example a CASE tool can check an ER diagram for omitted or duplicated entity names.

20.12 Summary

- An important requirement of systems development is to produce IT systems in a thoroughly documented fashion.
- There are severe penalties associated with developing, operating, and maintaining undocumented systems.
- Each stage in the SDLC has associated with it documents which are regarded as 'products' or 'deliverables'. The details and terminology used depend on the methodology.
- As far as the systems analyst is concerned the main documents produced in systems development are: a feasibility study, a current systems specification, a requirements specification, a new systems design or systems proposal, program or module specifications, quality control plans and test data, and a user manual. There are often numerous other documents such as project plans. The precise meaning of these terms is very variable.
- The primary specification techniques of structured analysis and design are: ER diagrams (LDSs in SSDAM), ELHs, DFDs, data descriptions of various kinds, and structured English. There are many other techniques.
- Quality control is a vital part of the documentation process.

Chapter 21
Background to Systems Investigation

21.1 Introduction

This chapter discusses the importance of investigation and its role in IT systems development. Terms like fact finding, fact gathering, and requirements analysis mean roughly the same as investigation. However the analysis stage of the traditional systems development life-cycle is more than just an investigation to collect facts and user requirements. It also implies that the findings arc processed, organised, and documented. Processing in this context might mean, for instance, a simple statistical analysis of an existing system. For example on average 2500 sales orders are entered into the computer each week and about 50 of these contain one or more clerical errors. Documenting could mean drawing diagrams like Fig. 20.1 to represent the results of investigating an order processing system.

The purpose of an investigation is usually to collect all the information needed to produce a new or amended IT system. This information includes the future requirements, factual data, constraints, goals, and the problems of the current system. See Section 23.5 for a further discussion. The most common techniques for investigating business systems are interviews with users, and collecting examples of documents like invoices. Techniques used for systems investigation are discussed in the next chapter. Section 30.11 also discusses the problems of systems investigation.

21.2 The range of systems investigations

Initially systems investigation seems like common sense. However it soon becomes apparent that this is a daunting task with large systems. It is difficult to identify exhaustively all the information needed to produce a new or changed administrative system within the hurly-burly of an operating business. The detailed requirements are often extensive and complex. For instance a modest payroll system has well-over a hundred forms, screens, and print-outs which are in regular use. Manual and computer processes, like the production planning procedures in a factory, can be complex and abstruse. Investigating the current system in such circumstances may require dozens of interviews. Then there is the common experience of business users appearing not to know, or perhaps not wanting to reveal, what all the requirements are.

Of course some system requirements are outside the scope of users. For example some detailed requirements may be derived from IT practices, e.g. security techniques for encrypting telecommunication messages in banking. Requirement details can also come from specialist sources such as business mathematicians or auditors. Figure 21.1 summarises the purpose, progress, and dangers of a systems investigation.

Investigation is perhaps the most crucial systems development activity, and varies according to circumstances. There is clearly an enormous difference between investigating the amendment of one data field on a personnel VDU screen, and investigating a whole new pensions administration system for an insurance company. The fact finding in the first case might involve a few minutes, and in the latter cases many months.

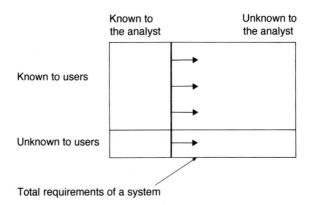

Fig. 21.1 The 'mullion' diagram divides up the knowledge of business system requirements into zones. At any point in time during an investigation there are zones known only to the user or only to the analyst, as well as a common zone. There is also a zone which is unknown to both. The arrows show how the analyst's knowledge expands during the investigation. The danger is that some requirements may still be unknown to the analyst at the end of the investigation. Any requirements that are unknown to the user and the analyst must be obtained from other sources such as consultants and official literature.

A minor amendment to a VDU screen could result in a page of documentation, and in many cases such simple changes are regrettably made without producing any documentation. In the case of a whole new system the investigation may result in a specification consisting of several volumes.

One important task is to establish early exactly what is the scope of an investigation. For example, does a proposed human resource database include only payroll and personnel data and does it exclude pensions data? It is obviously important not to omit anything of importance from an investigation and also avoid wasting time and money collecting irrelevant information. Clearly the design of a new system depends crucially on collecting the right information, and many failed computer systems can be attributed to poor systems analysis. Figures 26.2 and 26.3 show the consequences of poor investigations. All this makes project managers and systems analysts quite anxious when investigating a large and complex business system of which they have little prior experience. To complicate matters further there is usually pressure for quick results.

21.3   The reasons for systems investigation

Investigations can occur at most stages in the systems development life-cycle. In fact they occur whenever information is required in con-nection with IT work.

Perhaps the most common reasons for a business or technical systems investigation are:

- Determining the requirements of a new system.
- Determining the modifications needed to an existing system.
- Seeking improvements for a system.
- Documenting a system which has little existing documentation.
- Auditing a system.

Investigations may be cursory at the feasibility stage where the objective is to determine whether or not a project is viable. However, as already stated, a thorough investigation is necessary during the analysis stage as wrong or missing information can lead to expensive problems later in the life-cycle. Investigation can occur in connection with detailed design work. For instance a quick investigation can narrow the selection of software packages down to considering three suppliers whose products can then be investigated in depth. Another example is designing data collection systems. Here hardware such as optical mark readers must be investigated. Implementation work can also lead to special investigations, for instance determining the best way to convert data from an old computer system to a new one.

When a new system is being considered, the nature of the old system is usually investigated in depth. This is because any new system must usually meet most of the requirements met by the old system. Often in fact the main requirement is to transfer the system from old to new equipment merely to take advantage of technical improvements, or because the old equipment is at the end of its working life. However it is not uncommon to include some business changes and a few entirely new requirements as well. Where a system is being maintained it is possible to investigate just the nature of the changes and ignore the unaltered features. The majority of the system is then not examined. The danger with this approach is that limited understanding may lead to problems because of any unexpected side-effects resulting from changes.

Investigation can be viewed in terms of logical and physical specification as explained in Sections 18.6 and 18.10. Where the intention is to replace the old physical system then many of the physical details like forms and print-outs have limited relevance for the future as they are often replaced. What usually matters is the logical specification of the old system as much of this is usually incorporated in the new system. There is the argument that a deep understanding of the old system, particularly the old physical system, causes the analyst subconsciously to design new systems which resemble the old. This could lead to losing some of the benefits of new technology. However the risk of omitting major requirements seems to outweigh the theoretical benefits of ignorance. Furthermore there may be problems and weaknesses with the old system which provide lessons for future systems. In maintenance situations the old physical system is often of supreme importance as it is a prime requirement that it is retained with only minor changes. This happens, for example, where the maintenance exercise is to change payroll tax calculations, or speed up the processing of transactions by 'tuning' both clerical operations and computer processing.

Investigations may be conducted for reasons other than ordinary systems development. For example, a financial audit is really a special type of investigation to identify whether an accounting system is being operated correctly, and to identify any weaknesses which could lead to error, fraud, or failure.

21.4 Documentation

If a systems analyst is investigating existing computer systems they *should* already be documented, and the information should be up-to-date. In this case the analyst can collect the existing documentation, which may be more difficult than it at first appears with large systems. Then he or she should use techniques like interviewing and observation to help understand the existing documentation. This is an ideal, which is not often met. Sometimes the documentation has always been scanty, sometimes it has been lost, and often it is woefully out-of-date.

The analyst usually documents the results of his or her investigation, and then asks the IT user staff to check the work. After any amendments, the users can certify the documents are correct. These documents can range from typed interview notes to a voluminous specification of the current or proposed business system.

21.5 Hard and soft facts

Hard facts are objective and easy to verify, e.g. the life assurance system is written in the programming language COBOL and runs on an IBM 3090 mainframe. Soft facts encompass human affairs and matters of opinion. For example the management-style in the advertising department is democratic, and the working practices are informal.

Normal analysis investigations officially aim to collect hard facts. The soft facts are usually inferred as a by-product of the normal analysis work. Soft information is important to analysts and computer salesmen. This is particularly true in the early stages of a project, as it influences the approach and plans. For instance in an authoritarian environment the analyst or salesman can concentrate on persuading the boss or an authorised deputy to accept their proposals. In a democratic environment they must influence more people to get a decision in their favour.

Soft facts can be deliberately collected, occasionally as part of a formal methodology, or more commonly on an informal basis. One common informal technique is frequently used by computer salesmen and systems consultants. They deliberately collect information, particularly soft information, during relaxed social contact with IT customers in a restaurant or pub.

21.6   Qualitative and quantitative data

Qualitative information describes a system without any mention of numbers, e.g. the data flow diagram in Fig. 16.4 describes the flow and storage of data. A simple list of the types of form used in an office is another example of qualitative data. Quantitative data specifies timing or amounts, e.g. the number of different products made in a factory. Other examples of quantitative data are: weekly payslips are printed on Wednesdays; a sales clerk takes three minutes to check an incoming order; and the labour cost of running a research and development department is one million pounds per year. The term 'metric' is sometimes used in computer circles to describe quantitative data such as the number of sales invoices printed each day. In the author's experience, systems analysts collect and use quantitative facts less effectively than qualitative information. The use of quantitative techniques is discussed in Chapter 25.

21.7   The six questions

One simple view of investigation is that the results should be able to answer the six questions of what, where, when, who, how, and why. For example at the beginning of a project to computerise the employee share scheme of a major company, the following six questions could be answered after a little investigation:

● *What?*
It is an employee share scheme approved by the Inland Revenue under Section 186 of the Income and Corporation Taxes Act 1988. Such schemes work by purchasing the company's shares out of company profits for the employees. A formula is used to allocate shares to

individual employees. Potentially all 4000 full-time employees of the company can be members of this particular scheme.

- *Where?*

The share scheme is to be administered at head office in London.

- *When?*

The scheme and its administration must be operating in six months time.

- *Who?*

The pensions staff (five people) will administer the scheme under the company secretary.

- *How?*

A personal computer software package is seen as appropriate. However this is for the systems analyst to investigate and produce recommendations.

- *Why?*

The purpose of the share scheme is to increase employee motivation and commitment to the company, and effectively to increase their remuneration in a tax-efficient way. The scheme is managed from the company secretary's department because the staff are familiar with this type of legal administration. Computerisation is believed to be a cost-effective method of relieving the burden of administration.

Clearly the six questions can be used to check that all necessary information has been collected at any level, whether that of a whole system, a clerical job, or the use of a document. As already indicated, answers should include both quantitative and qualitative information.

21.8 The user's role

Most IT theorists and practitioners pay lip service to the idea of pro-active user involvement in systems analysis and design. As regards investigation, users are encouraged not only to give information passively when asked, but also to volunteer information and ideas that may be helpful. Another vital role for users is checking the findings of an analysis investigation or checking the design of a proposed new IT system. Approximations to this ideal are often achieved. However, departures from the ideal can be towards passive and active resistance, or in the opposite direction towards user dominance of IT projects. This is discussed further in Section 14.5.

The users of IT systems are often seen as the ultimate source of authority or information for confirming that investigation findings or the design of a system is correct. However, there can be many other sources of information and authority besides users, for example senior management, auditors, suppliers of IT equipment, and business consultants.

21.9 Investigation and methodologies

In general terms there is nothing special about the way systems investigations are conducted under modern methodologies such as SSADM or its rivals. Techniques such as interviewing are used by them all. Stage 1 of SSADM Version 4 is called Investigation of Current Environment. As discussed in Section 18.15 this analysis stage attempts to investigate and document in diagrammatic form the current system as a prelude to designing a new system.

Many IT development methodologies are not overtly interested in soft data. Though there is often considerable interest it is usually considered too subjective and controversial to document. It may be that an investigation reveals that an administrator is hostile towards IT staff. Perhaps this is because of previous unfortunate experiences with computer systems! However stating this baldly in a feasibility report may not be very diplomatic. As this sort of information is useful it is often passed on verbally. A few methodologies are specifically interested in human issues, and deliberately set out to collect and record soft data in a formal way.

Of course each methodology has its own unique way of dividing up the work and documenting the investigation results. The findings of an investigation are often represented as data flow diagrams, e.g. SSADM-style as in Fig. 16.4. In SSADM Version 4 the requirements for a new IT system are catalogued on an S42 form. The advantage of using forms is of course that they standardise the presentation of the investigation findings.

21.10   Infrastructure projects

The fundamental procedures used by IT departments for their own work, administration, and management are sometimes called the 'infrastructure'. The infra-structure includes the systems development methodology, IT budgetary control, and activities like security procedures in computer operations. The infra-structure underlies all the standard procedures of an IT department. Analysts and other development staff such as programmers may be required to analyse the existing infrastructure, usually with the objective of improving or extending it. So an analyst might be involved in a project to investigate the use of a new development methodology, or revise help desk procedures for user support. Another example would be developing formulae and the associated administration for charging the users of IT services.

21.11   The work of the analyst in computer services

The work in computer services is extremely diverse ranging from a computer bureau providing a commercial payroll processing service, to a software house providing military software for defence contracts. As regards investigation the job of an analyst in a software house can include the following:

- *Research and development*
New software products (packages) can be derived from several sources such as generalising bespoke systems for existing customers. Sometimes new software packages are produced from first principles with no precedents. A major problem, particularly with new software products, is analysing the future requirements for a range of customers. In this R&D environment the analyst often needs good conventional investigation skills, market research skills, and also a knowledge of commercial and technological forecasting.

- *Sales support*

Analysts provide the applications and technical backup for sales staff. In a small software house they may also act as sales people, particularly for minor projects, to modify software installed with existing customers. Part of their role is to investigate the customer's business and IT requirements and together with the sales personnel provide a competitive quotation.

- *Maintenance*

Analysis is an essential precursor to the changes required for standard software. Software house analysts usually treat any bespoke changes for individual customers as mini-projects and prepare a quotation to cover the work involved.

In software houses there is a considerable emphasis on accurately measuring the analyst's time and expenses spent on each job. To meet the pressures of cost, time, and commercial image, the software house analysts must change their approach from the more leisurely style adopted by analysts serving in-house users. There are many ways of doing this. For instance non-chargeable work may be minimised by carefully vetting every sales prospect before visiting them. Sometimes potential customers are asked to pay for investigation and quotation work. Another way of keeping down costs is to ask the customer to do an elementary systems investigation, e.g. by collecting forms and print-outs from an old IT system. Specialisation in particular fields like finance allows software houses to simplify and speed up systems investigations. This is because all their customers then have similar systems and similar requirements.

21.12 Summary

- Investigation is a crucial activity on which most stages of systems development depend. If key facts are not correctly identified a new system is bound to be defective.
- Existing systems should be documented already, and this considerably reduces the burden of investigation. However, some systems have never been documented properly and in other cases the specifications have been lost, or not kept up-to-date.

- Hard facts are objective and verifiable, e.g. a sales order form contains up to eight detail lines.
- Soft facts concern matters such as human affairs and opinions, e.g. the accounts staff are introverts.
- Soft facts are usually collected informally as a by-product of normal analysis and sales investigations. As they can markedly influence systems development plans it is important to collect this information at the beginning of a project.
- Quantitative data should be collected during a systems investigation as well as qualitative data. A common weakness is the inadequate collection and use of quantitative data.
- Six questions should be answered by the results of business systems investigation at most levels of detail. The six questions are what, where, when, who, how, and why?
- The user's role in investigations can be proactive as well as reactive. The user is often seen as the ultimate source of information and authority to confirm that investigation findings are correct. This may not always be the case.
- The infra-structure of an IT department can be a source of investigations and projects.
- The work of the analyst in computer services has differences from the analyst in an ordinary business, e.g. systems investigation may include IT market research.
- Software houses can exploit the commonality between customers and projects to reduce investigation problems.

Chapter 22
Investigative Techniques

22.1 Introduction

This chapter discusses the various techniques which are used when investigating the requirements of a business IT system. These investigation techniques include such methods as interviewing or automatically monitoring the operation of existing computer systems. As mentioned previously an investigation failure can destroy the value of the succeeding systems development work. This is because all other development work, like programming, assumes that the system requirements have been completely and correctly identified. Investigation errors can be expensive to correct when discovered during systems testing, or worse still during live use. For this reason it is useful to have a repertoire of investigation techniques which can reveal different information, or be used as a cross-check on each other.

Most systems development methodologies are concerned with the analysis and documentation of the information about a business system. They are not too interested in the means of collecting this information initially, and the investigation techniques below can be employed to support most methodologies.

22.2 Traditional systems investigation techniques

The following four techniques are the most commonly mentioned in textbooks:

- *Interviewing IT user staff*
People are asked about their work and their requirements for new systems. Interviewing is probably the main investigative technique.

- *Observation*
This involves watching office activities, e.g. an analyst can observe a clerk at work to see which forms are used and how they are processed.

- *Questionnaires*

Information on business systems is collected ·by asking people to complete questionnaires about their work.

- *Document collection*

When investigating a sales invoicing system, for example, samples of business documents such as sales invoices and credit notes need to be collected.

22.3 Interviewing

Given the intention to replace or modify a business system, the idea of interviewing is straightforward, i.e. systems analysts should ask all the staff concerned for the necessary information. The information gathered from all the participants should then represent most of what is known about the existing system, and also many of the requirements for a new future system. In most cases a reasonably broad view is taken of whom to include. So besides the departmental managers and their staff, other personnel such as senior managers, auditors, and mainframe computer operations staff are included where appropriate. Interviewing is a natural technique. It appeals to those who like human contact, and conversely rather frightens those who are shy.

22.4 The purpose of interviews

Interviews can have several purposes and these include:

- *Collecting 'hard' data*

When studying procedures in an industrial buying office, for example, for it is necessary to discover the number of suppliers and how purchases are authorised. The collection of hard data is the official reason for many investigations.

- *Collecting 'soft' data*

Opinions and attitudes are examples of 'soft' data. They are difficult to verify, but nevertheless important. For instance, an analyst often wants to know whether the users are likely to respond positively to a new system. Users who express an interest in IT, and who like challenges, provide an encouraging sign.

- *Verification*

This includes confirming and checking with the interviewee information which has come from various sources.

- *User participation*

Systems analysts and managers usually express the view that active user participation is essential for good analysis and design. Interviews can be used, for instance, to solicit opinions on the requirements for a new system. So a clerk can be asked for ideas on improvements to the design of computer-printed stationery.

Interviews can also be used for purposes other than collecting information. For instance an analyst can use interviews as a means of persuading staff to accept new systems.

22.5   Types of interview

There are various types of interview. These include:

- *Informal interviews*

The analyst usually knows the person concerned and arrives for a quick 'chat' on a few points. Though conducted informally, even casually, the analyst is still trying to collect hard or soft data.

- *Conventional interviews*

These are usually conducted formally on a one-to-one basis by appointment.

- *Remote interviews*

The most usual method is interviewing over the telephone, though teleconferencing can be used.

- *Structured interviews*

This where the analyst asks a fixed set of questions according to a checklist. The advantage is that everything is planned beforehand and cannot be forgotten.

- *Group interviews*

Where several people are assembled for the purpose of eliciting information. There might, for instance, be three users and two analysts.

22.6 Interviewing problems

Interviewing may seem an elementary technique, but it is difficult to conduct well and effectively. Each interview should be planned, and the time limit is effectively one hour for a person-to-person interview. Obviously care has been taken with both social protocol and questioning technique. Notes must be made and confirmed.

Interviews can have several disadvantages:

- Interviewing is expensive, e.g. both analyst and user might be costed at over £30 per hour each.
- Good interviewing is difficult, e.g. the analyst can fail to ask important questions.
- Poor conditions, e.g. constant interruption from telephone calls.
- Poor for detail, e.g. complex calculations are difficult to describe verbally.
- Vulnerable to factors like misunderstanding, social difficulties, and deception.

Despite the above objections, in practice interviewing remains by far the most popular investigative technique. In the author's experience small group interviews are usually the most effective despite the apparently greater expense.

22.7 Observation

As a formal technique the main modern use of observation is 'time-and-motion' studies on manual workers, for purposes such as setting bonus rates. One application with business systems is investigating the physical rather than logical aspects, e.g. observing the use of office machines such as shredders and copiers.

Observational techniques useful to the systems analyst include:

- *Direct observation*

This usually involves the analyst in carefully watching the work of personnel and machines.

- *Instrumented observation*

The use of cameras, tape recorders, and stop-watches is a common technique when studying manual work.

- *Automatic observation*

Computer and human work can be investigated further by using statistics compiled automatically by computer software, e.g. the number of sales invoices printed per day. Where the statistics produced by a computer system are inadequate, software 'probes' (special monitoring routines) can be inserted into the applications programs, for example to count the number of different transaction types from each terminal on an hourly basis. Cameras can also be used to record workplace activities automatically.

22.8   Activity sampling

A series of random observations are made on a process until a statistically significant number have been collected. For instance, a series of random observations in the offices of a large bank can give an idea of how much clerical work involves employee enquiries, form filling, use of a computer terminal, telephone work and so on. The principle is simple enough. Suppose a VDU has been observed in use during 10 out of 100 random observations over a week. Then it is reasonable to conclude that the VDU is always in use 10% of the time.

To provide accurate results, activity sampling requires a large number of random observations of office work over a reasonable period of time. The number of observations required can be hundreds for a valid conclusion. Special statistical formulae are used to determine the number of observations required. The observations are made by walking through the office at times listed in advance on a timetable. The result of each observation is recorded, e.g. a VDU was, or was not, in use. The time of each observation in the timetable is determined in advance using random numbers.

22.9   Systems analysis by walking about

One conclusion from the statistics of activity sampling concerns 'systems analysis by walking about'. Systems analysts often build up impressions about office activities by walking about an office on other business. Unfortunately these impressions are often regarded as firm knowledge based on reliable personal experience. However this is mistaken and even if the analyst has a perfect memory the number of observations is likely to be small and statistically insufficient.

Informal observations have their use. They can suggest that more formal fact-finding techniques should be used. For example casual observations may reveal that a personal computer is apparently not used. It may then be worth investigating whether this is indeed the case, and if so, why.

22.10   Limitations of observation

Formal observation is perhaps more contentious than any other technique in systems investigation, and it is disliked by many systems analysts. They often consider it irksome, embarrassing for themselves, and demeaning for the staff observed. User staff can have even stronger hostile feelings about being 'spied on'.

Many people feel uncomfortable when being explicitly and systematically observed. Sometimes they are hostile, and occasionally they are pleased at the interest in their work. A common consequence is an artificial modification of their normal working pattern whilst being watched. Frequently performance is worse than usual, and occasionally better. This is the 'uncertainty principle' (a concept taken from physics) where the effect of observing is to disturb the thing or person observed. When observation results in improved performance it is sometimes called a 'Hawthorne' effect (named after an American factory where an early work study project was conducted).

Detached observation is at its strongest where the facts speak for themselves. This is why it remains a major technique for studying manual work where the systems being operated are physical. The work of a dustman collecting rubbish bins or a factory worker operating a machine is often easy to observe and interpret. However office work is often intrinsically difficult to observe in a detached manner, and it is also fairly abstract. For example, observing clerks checking purchase invoice forms or completing VDU displays involves being physically close to them and requesting an explanation of the procedure. In other words observing office work frequently requires a simple interview as well.

22.11 Questionnaires

Questionnaires are useful in a minority of systems analysis situations. One classic example of the use of a questionnaire is where the analyst is trying to select a software package supplier. In this situation it is essential to collect a lot of basic data on the packages and their suppliers, and to collect it all in the same format. To make a comparison the analyst might prepare a questionnaire which all suppliers have to complete before their package is considered. An example of such a questionnaire is shown in Fig. 22.1. Questionnaires could also be used, for example, when conducting a census of the personal computer hardware and software used in the various departments throughout a company.

Designing good questionnaires is difficult. It is, for example, all too easy to ask confusing or misleading questions. Questionnaires often annoy people, and it is difficult to get everyone to respond. Normally they need to be kept brief and simple, which unfortunately means that not much information is collected. The analyst must also be prepared to chase people to complete them. However if there is an incentive, like making a sale as in Fig. 22.1, then people grudgingly tolerate quite extensive questionnaires.

22.12 The study of documents

The word document is often interpreted as a business form and examples are shown in Fig. 5.2 and Fig. 16.1. The detailed examination and

---

PALLADIUM INTERNATIONAL MINES PLC
INVITATION TO TENDER: ACCOUNTS PACKAGES
SUPPLIER DETAILS

(Please attach supplementary information where necessary.)

* Name of company:	Minerva Software Ltd
* Address:	123 Owl Boulevard Birmingham
* Telephone No:	021-123-4567
* Contact for queries:	Diana Jones Sales consultant
* Who owns the company?	The current directors
* When was the company founded?	1975
* How many staff does the company employ?	60
* Please provide a copy of company's latest accounts.	1993 accounts attached
* Please give details of customers who are willing to provide a reference for the company and the accounts software.	Details attached

---

Fig. 22.1 A page from a completed questionnaire sent out to potential software package suppliers. The questionnaire in this case is part of an ITT (Invitation to Tender) which invites suppliers to provide the background details to support a sales quotation. This has the advantage of ensuring that every supplier is asked the same questions and that the replies are in the same sequence and format.

charting of clerical document flows in manual systems is a major part of O&M (Organisation and Methods). It is also an important part of traditional and structured systems analysis. In practice this has to be done by simple interviews, studying the forms themselves (which often contain instructions), and observing the movement of forms around and between offices.

It is usually essential to collect samples of forms and other documents when studying a business computer system. The view of what constitutes a 'document' has to be extended with modern business IT systems. So sample print-outs of computer screen displays are also necessary, as well as samples of bar-codes, magnetic cards, and the like. Where the communication medium is automatic, then technical specifications become essential. For instance with EDI (Electronic Data Interchange) there is little visible sign of the transfer of data as there is with a paper-based system. In this case the technical specifications tell the analyst about the data being transferred.

22.13   Documentation

A broad distinction can be made between a document, e.g. a payslip or a business letter, and documentation, e.g. a set of accounts or a management report. Documentation is usually text ('literature'), and sometimes pictorial or diagrammatic. Its origin may be from inside or outside the organisation. For instance useful internal literature could be an audit report on financial systems. Examples of external documentation might be a government brochure, or information from an on-line database. In the author's experience valuable sources of information like these are under-used by most systems analysts.

22.14   Internal documentation

In most large organisations there is a consistent attempt to record business and technical activities. The resulting documentation is, in fact, one of the most important formal means of communicating detail.

The documentation available in a business comes in many guises. For instance an analyst working on production planning in a factory can examine engineering drawings, business forms, office procedure manuals, company magazines and so on. All these could provide some insight into the way the company and production planning process is currently operating. Some companies have formal archives and libraries. This wealth of documentation is often hidden away in filing cabinets, or stored in a computer in some cases. Company documentation can represent hundreds of hours of somebody else's work. Though in most cases this internal literature is not designed for systems analysis purposes it can save the analyst the hard work of trying to collect and process the same data again. Even apparently out-of-date documentation can give an insight into an organisation.

Some examples of commonly available internal documentation are:

- General − corporate plans, office procedure manuals, building and office layout plans, and management reports.

- Personnel — organisation charts, job descriptions, trade union agreements, and health and safety requirements.
- Accounts — audit reports and departmental management accounts.
- Marketing — sales catalogues.
- Production — engineering drawings, bills of material, and lists of manufacturing operations.
- IT and management services — IT strategy plans, previous studies of systems, software specifications, and computer operating instructions.

As just one example take job descriptions. Many large organisations have reasonably complete but rather brief descriptions of the work done by their employees. These job descriptions exist for most jobs, and Fig. 22.2 is a simplified example. As mentioned in Section 13.3 they are used for several personnel purposes such as preparing job adverts and job evaluation. Job descriptions can be compiled by a job analyst working in a similar fashion to a systems analyst, e.g. using interviews and observation. The emphasis is of course different as the job analyst is interested in what people do rather than how they process information. From a systems analyst's viewpoint job descriptions are not detailed enough. However they are a useful beginning, and can help provide the 'big picture' of what happens in an office. They are also useful for planning an investigation.

22.15 External documentation

There is an extensive amount of external information which may be useful to systems analysts. Reference books can be very useful, for instance most IT staff use the Computer Users' Yearbook. Legislation provides two important examples of useful external documentation:

- *Acts of Parliament*
As regards computing itself there are the Data Protection Act 1984, and the Computer Misuse Act 1990. However Acts of Parliament affect many business functions and hence the supporting IT. Statutory instruments (regulations) made under an Act may be more useful as they are more detailed. See Section 10.4 for further details.

```
┌─────────────────────────────────────────────────────────────┐
│                     JOB DESCRIPTION                          │
│                                                             │
│  Job title:        Works Manager                            │
│                                                             │
│  Responsible to:   Manufacturing Director                   │
│                                                             │
│  Staff controlled: Production Manager                       │
│                    Production Controller                    │
│                    Quality Control Manager                  │
│                    Buildings and Equipment Manager          │
│                    Industrial Engineering Manager           │
│                                                             │
│  Main role:        To meet agreed plans, budgets, quality   │
│                    standards, and delivery requirements by  │
│                    efficient control of manufacturing       │
│                    operations and ensuring teamwork         │
│                    amongst all staff.                       │
│                                                             │
│  Main activities:                                           │
│                                                             │
│  1. Planning       Develops manufacturing plans and budgets.│
│                                                             │
│  2. Development    Continually seeks to improve production  │
│                    methods.                                 │
│                                                             │
│  3. Control        Ensures that all production activities   │
│                    are controlled to meet agreed delivery   │
│                    dates. Meets financial, quality, and     │
│                    other targets.                           │
│                                                             │
│  4. Premises       Is responsible for all works premises    │
│     and Equipment  and equipment, and their maintenance.    │
│                                                             │
│  5. Security       Maintains the security of all premises,  │
│                    fixed assets, and stock.                 │
│                                                             │
│  6. Organisation   Ensures that the works organisation      │
│                    meets company objectives.                │
│                                                             │
│  7. Personnel      Controls all works personnel. Maintains  │
│                    sound labour relations and implements    │
│                    company personnel policies. Develops     │
│                    personnel to meet present and future     │
│                    needs.                                   │
└─────────────────────────────────────────────────────────────┘
```

Fig. 22.2 A simplified job description. These can save systems analysts a considerable amount of investigation work.

- *Government booklets*

An example is NI269, the Employer's Guide to National Insurance Contributions, which is available from the Department of Social Security. It is used by systems analysts working on payroll systems. The Customs and Excise produce guides such as booklet VAT 700 which is a general guide to VAT. There is a vast amount of such reference literature which is essential to business practice and the design of administrative systems. Besides mainstream government departments there are bodies founded by the government for specific purposes such as the Health and Safety Executive, and Equal Opportunities Commission. They also produce extensive literature.

Keeping up to date with legislative developments is a problem. This is usually done through specialist journals. For instance the fortnightly publication 'Company Secretary's Review' is probably the best comprehensive source of up-to-date practical information on legal matters such as copyright and financial law.

22.16 Databases

On-line databases can be very useful for the latest information as books are at least a year out-of-date. One example of a database service is Lexis, which is an on-line legal database. Sometimes analysts want to track down the latest Acts of Parliament and regulations relevant to their application area. It is then merely a matter of typing the right query into the terminal to receive the necessary details on, say, collecting local authority taxes. Obviously a modicum of familiarity with the chosen database system is required, and such systems can be expensive (several pounds for a brief session lasting a few minutes). Some databases may be distributed on floppy disks or compact disk. The advantage over a book is then the more compact form and the automatic searching facilities.

22.17 Office automation

These days much of the ordinary data used in a business is held and circulated by office automation systems such as ALL-IN-1 from DEC and OFFICEPOWER from ICL. These systems control the electronic equivalent of paper documents such as forms, circulars, memoranda, reports, and information on notice boards. The documents are prepared or retrieved by ordinary staff using networked VDUs spread throughout the organisation.

22.18 Other investigation techniques

The most common non-classical technique is prototyping which is very popular. There are a series of other investigation techniques whose use is occasional. However they can all form part of the analyst's repertoire and be used when circumstances are appropriate.

22.19 Prototyping

With modern prototyping the analyst typically uses fourth generation software to create a mock-up of the screens and print-outs of the new system. The users are then invited progressively to modify the prototype until they have the screens and print-outs they want. The prototype can then have further essential facilities added to make it fully functional. Alternatively the screens and print-outs can be used as part of the specification of a new system which is re-programmed with full facilities in a different language. Prototyping is popular and also discussed further in Section 18.22. It is sometimes regarded as a methodology, and sometimes as a design technique rather than an investigation technique. For instance the analyst must conduct a preliminary investigation using other methods to produce the first version of the prototype. Prototyping is basically restricted to the interactive aspects of systems.

22.20 Less common investigation techniques

Some less used techniques are briefly described below.

- *Seeking precedents*
It is sometimes worth seeking a precedent. Precedents provide the benefit of other people's experience when facing similar problems or opportunities. Precedents are particularly useful for identifying a general approach to using new technology like automated warehousing, or complying with new complex legislation. They can also provide insights on how to improve mundane IT applications like sales invoicing systems. Examples of how other people have tackled IT and related projects can be found in articles, conference presentations, and case studies

provided by IT suppliers. Precedents can also be observed and discussed on visits to other organisations. (See also Section 22.21 below.)

- *Statistics*

Statistics is an important branch of applied mathematics which is discussed in Section 25.6. For instance the automatic monitoring of computer systems generates a considerable volume of detailed data. This can be processed using statistical techniques. As another example it is often necessary to make conclusions about matters such as computer input errors on the basis of a sample. For this to be statistically valid the sampling method needs to be carefully designed. In practice the systematic and rigorous application of statistics is unfortunately not popular.

- *Shadowing*

The analyst follows the user throughout the day with the user explaining his or her work as it is done.

- *Self-recording*

Clerical and managerial staff observe and document their own activities chronologically on work activity sheets.

- *Reverse engineering*

In general reverse engineering means preparing a specification by a careful study of a product. It is the reverse of normal (forward) engineering which involves proceeding from the specification to the product. It may however be necessary to reverse engineer some IT systems because of missing documentation. This is certainly an unpleasant process which involves reading through old program code to discover what old software actually does, and then redocumenting it. Software tools can help reverse engineer programs.

- *Modelling*

This technique is more used by business planners and engineers, and it is discussed in Sections 25.6 and 25.8. Mathematical models represent existing or proposed systems and allow the investigation of the behaviour of systems under varying circumstances. These models are often computerised and can be applied at any level, for instance from a whole factory down to one machine. So the behaviour of a production robot may be modelled on a computer to ensure that the moving arm does not smash into other equipment. Capacity planning provides plenty of examples of IT modelling, e.g. what would happen to the VDU response time if the mainframe work-load were doubled?

- *Business decision analysis and knowledge elicitation*

Semi-conscious mental processes are often used to make complicated decisions, e.g. in medical diagnosis. A less dramatic commercial example is selecting a supplier in a purchasing department. Such decisions are usually based on training and experience. Analysts designing expert systems and decision support systems must investigate these mental processes by a procedure called knowledge elicitation. One simple technique is to persuade the user to talk through a few real cases explaining his or her reasoning.

22.21   Business intelligence and espionage

The collection of data about other businesses is important to most commercial companies. Companies have to survive in a rapidly changing and ruthlessly competitive market, and this makes information a vital commodity. As IT can give a major competitive advantage, a shoe retailer or an insurance company, for example, need to learn about the IT systems of their competitors. In the computer services industry the collection of business intelligence is vital, and classed under various headings such as commercial information, market research, technical research, or product development.

There are many ways of collecting business intelligence but at its simplest level it could be articles in a trade journal like 'Computing' about a business competitor, a customer, or an IT supplier. Such articles include reports on a named business and discuss staff redundancies, complaints from customers, new software products, recent sales, or an IT strategy. Another source of information is the sales literature, technical manuals, and published accounts of a competitor. This kind of information is useful to managers, IT sales staff, and systems analysts. The author knows of several situations where business intelligence improved the design of IT systems, and improved commercial performance in areas like the pricing and marketing of computer services.

So called 'industrial' espionage is usually considered to be collecting intelligence information in an unethical or illegal manner. But some practices are merely 'shady' or just slightly disreputable. Industrial espionage itself is often legal, but the means used can be illegal, e.g. burglary to photograph documents, or hacking into a computer to extract data. From the reverse point of view it is also important to prevent sensitive data from leaking outside an organisation, particularly to competitors. The kind of information that is especially prized includes technical designs, sales plans, price lists, and customer lists.

22.22 Comments on investigation techniques

If the above fact finding techniques sound elementary it should be borne in mind that they are sometimes used on a large scale, e.g. investigating a large business system may require hundreds of interviews and hundreds of documents. Circumstances, such as poor industrial relations and short deadlines, may make the work very difficult. In the author's experience most individuals are not very competent at business systems investigations, and it is easy to become confused, make serious mistakes, and suffer demoralisation. Small analysis teams employing multiple techniques appear to do disproportionately better than individuals or large teams. The selection and application of investigation techniques needs to be planned and this is discussed in Chapter 30.

22.23 Summary

- The four traditional methods of collecting systems analysis data are interviews, observation, questionnaires, and document collection.
- Traditional systems analysis places considerable emphasis on interviewing users with minor alternatives like using questionnaires. The limitations of these techniques means that analysts must be prepared to use other approaches.
- Collecting and using documentation from both internal and external

sources is a key part of both systems analysis and business administration.

- There are many specialist publications, like government brochures, which can contain important information for the design and maintenance of systems.
- Many sources of information are now electronic, e.g. VDU screen displays which replace forms. On-line databases can be particularly useful for searching through large amounts of information, or when seeking the most up-to-date information.
- Prototyping is a popular investigative technique useful for interactive systems.
- There are a whole variety of techniques used to supplement and complement the traditional techniques of systems analysis such as interviewing. These additional techniques include automatic monitoring and reverse engineering.
- Where human knowledge is only partly conscious then knowledge elicitation techniques must be used for investigation.
- Gathering business intelligence can be an important part of a systems analyst's job, particularly in an IT company.

Chapter 23
Systems Design and Maintenance

23.1 Introduction

This chapter briefly considers the design and maintenance of business systems. Though design is usually considered a creative process, the final result is a specification for producing a future system. Maintenance essentially involves changing a system to correct, update, or improve it. When discussing design and maintenance many books tend to concentrate on software, omitting other areas. As usual in this book a business system includes everything, i.e. matters like office procedures and stationery as well as hardware and software.

Design work is frequently done by systems analysts and analyst-programmers. Sometimes specialist designers are used for the IT part of a system and programmers are often involved in software design. Data administrators or database administrators may be used for database design. The discussion below concentrates on TPSs (Transaction Processing Systems) such as the student record systems used in educational administration. Other types of system, for example DSSs (Decision Support Systems), require a modified or different approach.

23.2 Design background

When designing computer systems the range of possibilities is enormous. For example a very small system might be required in a computer department to log matters like complaints and change requests from IT users. The design could be based on a PC system which replaces written details in filing cabinets. Conversely a large design might be for an airline system which reserves seats on flights, and which is based on an international telecommunication network with a central mainframe.

Design means specifying a new system to meet the business and other requirements which have been identified during the analysis stage of the life-cycle. As Section 18.6 explains, logical design means designing the processes, data flows, and data storage in an abstract sense. For example, with logical design sales invoicing is seen as a set of pricing and VAT algorithms relying on abstract flows of input and stored data. The output results are seen as disembodied fields of data which make up an invoice. For any one logical design there are innumerable physical designs, e.g. the sales invoicing calculations can be done physically by hand, or with computers. The designer's job is to determine the best physical system given the circumstances.

Quantitative issues are important in design. For instance how many customer statements and debt reminder letters does the sales ledger system have to print each day. A major quantitative consideration is the cost of each system component and more importantly the total expected capital cost of a system. Operating costs are also a major consideration. Chapter 25 discusses the quantitative aspects of design.

The simplest method of designing an IT system is called output-driven design where the idea is to work backwards. The outputs are designed first, then the processes and data stores, and finally the inputs. So typically print-outs like Fig. 16.9 are designed, then the computer programs and disk files, and finally VDU inputs. However most methodologies adopt a more sophisticated approach.

As illustrated in Section 23.6 below, the exact details of the design process depend on the methodology adopted. Both traditional and modern methodologies often recommend outlining the design of several possible systems all of which meet the requirements. This often done at the feasibility stage. The intention is to identify the most promising for further work. In SSADM the alternative designs are called business and technical options. Clearly the development of outline design options and then a final design is a creative process. However with both traditional and modern methodologies there is an emphasis on a formal specification as the final product of the design process. The user is then expected to authorise the design specification as correct. Chapter 20 discusses the logical and physical specification techniques used by analysts and designers.

23.3 Physical design components

There is a large set of physical design components which can be used for most IT applications. Figure 26.1 illustrates the main components of a business system which are described below from a systems design viewpoint. The components include disks, VDUs, and preprinted stationery, all of which can be used for innumerable IT applications, e.g. for accounting, educational administration, taxation, and library management. Other crucial system 'components' are the human operators. Some design components are special purpose. For example, time-and-attendance terminals record the working time of employees who 'clock' in and out of work. These terminals cannot be used for much else. However time-and-attendance terminals often use general-purpose PCs as system controllers. Where special or general-purpose components are not available 'off-the-shelf' from suppliers then designers create their own. Usually this means designing 'bespoke' software or bespoke stationery. Bespoke hardware is occasionally produced as well. Bespoke means made for one particular purpose or customer. Using bespoke components increases the cost and time required to produce a system.

The systems designer must select, adapt, and combine standard, special-purpose, and bespoke components into a cooperative whole that meets the logical and physical requirements established by analysis. As an example Fig. 16.6 shows a configuration chart. This illustrates the main hardware components for a computer payroll system. As Section 19.6 explains one important decision is the boundary between computer and manual processes. Some processes may be either automatic or clerical and the choice between them is based on factors like cost, quality, speed, and convenience. A good design is not only technically sound with regard to the division between manual and automatic features but satisfies other criteria such as satisfactory costs and ease of development.

The following general comments on physical design apply to both traditional and modern methods of developing systems. There is no sharp division between design components like hardware, software, and interfaces as of course each of these must be designed to work with the other. The design activities associated with the main components of a business system design are described below:

- *Hardware*

This includes selecting a set of devices to work together such as optical character readers or factory data collection terminals.

● *Software*

This includes designing and specifying a bespoke software system as an integrated set of programs and modules. Alternatively a software package can be selected from a supplier. Systems which use modifiable packages or combine standard packages with bespoke software are common. Another approach is for an organisation to create a library of reusable software modules. These modules can then be used for different applications, sometimes after modification. An example is a software routine that checks calendar dates for errors as they are entered at a VDU.

With a bespoke system the design of software can be the major part of the total design and specification work. With packaged software of course the bulk of the work should already have been done by the supplier.

● *Interfaces*

These are often considered as part of hardware and software design. They include the physical design (layout) of VDU screens and print-outs as illustrated in Figs 12.4 and 11.2. They are sometimes called the user interface or HCI (Human Computer Interface). Interfaces (links) with other computer systems need to be designed to transfer data via magnetic media or telecommunication links.

● *Data*

Data storage requires the detailed design of files and databases for a particular IT environment. For instance how is the data to be organised on a magnetic disk and how is it to be accessed using the available system software.

● *Miscware*

This is rather neglected in most books. It includes designing miscellaneous items like pre-printed stationery such as sales ledger statements, or bar-coded identification cards for library book borrowers.

● *External services*

A systems design often makes use of services provided by other organisations, e.g. public telecommunications services like Kilostream which is used to transmit data over long distances. Another example is where payroll work is contracted out to a bureau, but part of the bureau service is to provide an interface magnetic tape containing payroll costs for in-house accounting systems. Such services require careful investigation, selection, and sometimes tailoring.

- *Procedures and work practices*

The design of clerical procedures is an important but often neglected part of systems design. This requires laying down, for instance, exactly how the system is to be used. So when materials are issued from a factory store, for example, then the details must be immediately entered into the VDU of the stock control system. If this is not done promptly the computer stock records are not up-to-date and the transaction may be forgotten and never entered.

The term work practices is less specific than procedures and refers to the general way in which work is tackled. So a common essential work practice is to test amended computer programs before releasing them for operational use. It is also common for detailed procedures to lay down exactly how this is to be done. For example as part of a software release procedure the systems analyst may have to sign a form which certifies that a program is ready for use. Often systems analysts outline the necessary work practices for operating an administrative system and leave the design of detailed procedures to managers and supervisors.

Both work practices and procedures can be improved. For instance suppose the practice of briefing sales staff is adopted prior to any visits to new customers. The sales staff may then be able to use this knowledge about the customers to increase their chance of making a sale. Changing the detail of procedures usually offers minor benefits. Re-engineering work practices and work flows may lead to major improvements, especially if supported by the appropriate IT.

- *Documentation*

The structure and content of the user and operational documentation needs to be carefully designed before the analysts write them. This documentation includes training courseware, user manuals, and on-line help screens.

- *People*

The systems designer inevitably produces tasks for the human operators of a system. These tasks are part of the office procedures for operating an IT-based system. Grouping tasks into jobs however is also part of systems design. This leads onto areas like specifying the type of staff required and considerations like training. The principles of job design are covered in Section 14.9. Some design methodologies place great emphasis on staff considerations, e.g. the methodology called ETHICS (Effective Technical and Human Implementation of Computer-based Systems).

23.4   Location, timing and environment

In addition to the above list of design components other factors have to be included. One important factor in systems design is the spatial location or distribution of the components of a systems. Thus the staff may be in one building and the mainframe hardware in another. An airline reservation system may have terminals all over the world. The timing of business system operations needs to be planned, see for instance the payroll timetable in Section 16.7. As another example mainframe systems often provide an on-line service during the day and a batch processing service at night.

The environmental aspects of systems are important. In terms of human factors a sensible office layout is essential. This means taking care over factors like lighting and work space. The environment also influences hardware factors, e.g. is a terminal robust enough to work in the hot dusty atmosphere of a foundry?

Usually of course, the location, timing and environment, are imposed on the systems designer. For example the systems designer is told that the new system is to be operational during the working day, and it is to be used by the staff in the Manchester accounts office. In this case the designer can only suggest minor changes in the time-tabling of the IT service and the accommodation arrangements. On a few rare occasions everything is designed from the beginning with, for instance, new office arrangements being planned in conjunction with new computer systems. One effect of IT on modern organisational planning is that offices and staff can be distributed geographically. Staff can then be linked together via computer and telecommunication systems.

23.5   Design data

The analysis stage of the life-cycle should provide much of the data needed to produce a systems design. More data, particularly technical data, can be collected during the design stage. The following gives a broad break-down of the kind of information that is collected for design purposes:

- *Requirements*

These are the needs which can be specified clearly by the user or analyst. For example a computer pensions package in the UK must allow the printing of a standard RD550 form for the Department of Social Security.

- *Facts*

A large collection of factual data is required to design a system. An obvious example is the technical details of hardware such as the capacity of a magnetic disk drive. Statistics must be available on the application area such as the number of different products whose details are to be stored by a stock system.

- *Constraints*

These are restrictions imposed on designers. For instance company policy may insist that mainframe systems are designed to use the IBM database software DB2. Statutory requirements may mean that payroll maintenance changes must be implemented by 6th April. Some constraints are often implied, e.g. that the response time of a VDU is within three seconds, but it is always better to make constraints explicit.

- *Goals*

These are targets for the designer, e.g. the system must be developed as quickly as possible. In the case of a goal like this the designer has various strategies such as reducing the number of non-essential features in a design to ease the programming.

- *Problems*

For example the existing processing of sales orders is considered too slow and error prone. Processing must be more accurate and faster in future. The designer's job is to identify and agree a method of improving matters. Effectively problems must be translated into requirements, constraints, and goals.

23.6   Design and methodology

As mentioned in Section 23.2 above output-driven design is the simplest systematic approach to designing systems. With software it works backwards from the outputs like payslips to the software modules, magnetic disk files, and computer inputs. It works well for simple systems designed by experienced staff. However output-driven design is little more than one guiding principle and says nothing, for instance, about how to design computer data files. The principles for designing them must come from elsewhere. By way of contrast, development methodologies often address both practical and theoretical design issues in reasonable depth as discussed in Chapter 18. The following discussion uses SSADM to explain further the relationship between systems design and a development methodology. See Sections 18.14 and 18.15 for the SSADM Version 4 background.

Most of the steps up to Module 5 in SSADM Version 4 are concerned with producing a logical specification of the system requirements. There are exceptions to this, as for instance Module 4 is concerned with creating technical options. As mentioned in Section 18.10 these options are alternative outline physical designs created before the logical design is completed in detail. This is done because the physical design can affect the logical design. For example a logical design may not be capable of physical implementation with the resources available like time, money, and existing computer hardware. In this case it is usual to prune the logical design by eliminating some inessential features so that it becomes economically feasible.

The steps in Module 5 Stage 6 are concerned with translating the logical design work of earlier stages into a physical design. Steps 620 and 640 of SSADM concern designing computer files. Of course the same logical design can be embodied in different physical designs, e.g. the physical data design depends on the type of hardware and system software available. There are rules-of-thumb associated with SSADM which help this translation to a particular physical environment. For example if a database management system like ORACLE is used there are simple rules which guide the conversion during Step 620 from a logical to a physical data store design. With modern database software this is a high-level design and the software handles the low-level details automatically.

Sometimes, however, lower-level file-handling software is used instead of a database management system. Physical design might then involve records within files. The design of the files may also require consideration of blocks of records and the use of an index to find the records on the tracks and cylinders of a magnetic disk. Thus an entity like a customer in Figs 20.1 and 20.2 might become a disk file of customer records. With Steps 630, 650, and 660 of SSADM there are guidelines to help convert logical process specifications into computer software designs, e.g. 3GL program specifications.

23.7   Maintenance background

At the simplest level systems maintenance means that, say, a systems analyst writes a memo to a sales accountant. This confirms a request for small changes in computer-printed invoices. Over the years there can be dozens of such memos referring to the invoicing system alone and they provide a record of how and why the invoicing system has changed. The analyst might have to organise software changes and order new pre-printed stationery. Written instructions must be given to both the programmers and the stationery suppliers. The analyst has to treat each change as a little systems development project which must be managed to meet the accountant's requirements and deadlines. It should be noted that maintenance includes the standard life cycle stages, i.e. feasibility, analysis, design, construction, and system quality control. The only difference is that an existing system is being modified, often in small ways, rather than an entire new system being produced.

The IT management problem is that in a modest computer department there could fifty similar jobs in progress at the same time. The change in the computer-printed sales invoice is an example of apparently petty systems maintenance, i.e. modifying an existing system. Needless to say it is easy to make mistakes so the quality control must be good. Of course maintenance usually occupies more of the day-to-day work of a computer department than developing new systems. This is because developing an entirely new replacement invoicing system would be infrequent, say once every five to ten years.

23.8   Systems maintenance

Maintenance work can be classified as follows:

- *Corrective maintenance*

This involves removing errors from the original system, e.g. fixing a software bug, or redesigning an input form when a data field has been omitted.

- *Perfective maintenance*

This is where systems performance is improved, but the function remains the same, e.g. speeding up the printing of customer statements, or streamlining office procedures for greater efficiency.

- *Adaptive maintenance*

Systems need to be adapted to cope with new requirements, e.g. changing a sales system to cope with a new method of classifying and grouping products for sales analysis reports.

- *'Replacive' maintenance*

A system can become almost unmaintainable due to lack of documentation, poorly written software, and years of 'patching' (amendment). When a system approaches this state a realistic solution might be to replace the system entirely just to ease future maintenance.

- *Preventive maintenance*

This involves anticipating maintenance problems. For instance important programs that are known to be difficult to maintain because they are badly-coded can be rewritten for ease of maintenance. Alternatively the existing coding can be 'cleaned up'. Missing or out-of-date documentation can also be made good.

In practice systems maintenance also involves user support for operational systems. For example a user query may be caused by a genuine fault, or due to a misunderstanding based on lack of experience of the operational system. Whichever is the true situation the query must be addressed. Needless to say a systems development methodology must allow for maintenance activities. Furthermore, because development methodologies promote good designs they reduce the amount of corrective, perfective, and preventive maintenance. Also a good design should make adaptive maintenance easier.

23.9 CASE

Design and maintenance work by analysts and programmers can be considerably eased with software tools. In its ideal form CASE eliminates the need for physical design and programming. In this ideal situation the CASE software generates applications software from a set of requirements entered into the computer. Software maintenance can then be achieved by amending the requirements that have been entered and regenerating the applications software. This ideal can be achieved in some favourable situations. For example ICL QuickBuild Pathway can generate application code from diagrams like entity models and DFDs.

CASE tools help enormously with the production and editing of logical and physical design diagrams. Software tools can also allow the design of a hardware and software system to be simulated and its performance predicted. For an analyst-programmer, CASE tools such as VIASOFT ESW (Existing Systems Workbench) assist with activities like perfective and preventive maintenance as well as providing advanced approaches to testing. As a simple example, part of ESW can take undocumented source code, say in COBOL, and generate software documentation and design diagrams.

23.10 Configuration management

IT systems are changed during both development and maintenance. Keeping track of amended versions of system components like computer programs can become an important job called configuration management. See Section 24.3 for a discussion of this important subject.

23.11 Summary

- The details of the design process depends on the methodology.
- Systems design can be split into logical design and physical design.

- Logical design is the abstract design of data and processes. Physical systems design involves combining components like programs, disk files, and stationery.
- Part of physical design requires selecting special-purpose or general-purpose system components like laser printers, or designing bespoke components like computer programs.
- Besides hardware and software, systems design must embrace office practices and procedures (human tasks). The timing of system activities, their location, and the operating environment are also important parts of design.
- Quantitative issues such as performance and cost are a major consideration in design.
- Before design work can commence information on the following should be collected: system requirements, constraints, goals, and the problems with the current system. Extensive factual data such as the details of the current system and the price of new hardware is also necessary.
- Systems maintenance can be classified into corrective, perfective, adaptive, replacive, and preventive maintenance. Supportive work is also important.
- Software tools can make a significant contribution to design and maintenance.
- Configuration management involves controlling the various versions of the components of a system.

Chapter 24
Implementing IT Systems

24.1 Introduction

This chapter discusses the implementation of business IT systems which is a major part of the systems analyst's work. The word 'implementation' is used here in the sense of installing hardware and software, training the user staff, and generally setting up a working IT system. Implementation of major new or changed systems can be a stressful experience, and it can be the most time-consuming, expensive, and frustrating part of an IT project. It is where any failures, including development failures, are very visible, and analysts often carry a large proportion of any responsibility. This chapter also outlines 'configuration management', a subject which could have been included just as validly under systems design and maintenance. Configuration management is concerned with keeping track of the changes to a system. In particular it is concerned with issuing the correct new versions of software for operational use. As a word of warning the term 'implementation' can also mean implementing a design as a piece of software, i.e. programming or 'constructing' a system. This use of the word implementation to mean programming is usually found on technical IT projects rather than business ones, and the word is *not* used in that sense in this book.

The implementation of an IT system can easily become a major project in its own right. For instance it can involve the installation of a local area network in an office with all the attendant practical problems of organising the cabling. The software must than be installed and tested to the satisfaction of systems analysts and business users. Data must be transferred from the old system onto the new system, and the users must eventually abandon the old system in favour of the new. Most of the following discussion assumes that the business system is developed and implemented by professional systems development staff. Section 28.9 mentions the alternative scenario where the users develop and implement their own IT systems with only a little help from professional IT staff, e.g. via an information centre. However the general principles remain the same whoever is doing the work.

343

Implementation like development can embrace small and large jobs. For example it could range from the installation of a program amended to include an extra column of data on a print-out, to implementing new hardware and software for a 100 terminal network. Needless to say the implementation of amendments to a system is more common than implementing a whole new system. Thorough quality control is probably even more important during the implementation phase of an IT project than during development. This is simply because it is the last phase before the business system becomes operational, and it is the last chance to prevent the expensive consequences of serious errors. Of course all aspects of the work, both that of users and analysts, needs to be quality controlled. Quality management is discussed in more depth in Chapters 15 and 26.

24.2 Implementation activities

An implementation project can require anything from a few hours of work to many months. Suppose however a new business system has been developed, say for a business department concerned with pensions or accounting. Then, by definition, at the end of the systems development stage everything should be ready for implementing the system. Typically the following should be have been completed at the end of development:

- *Implementation plans*

Plans for implementing a system are usually agreed in draft form early in the systems development life-cycle. They may, for instance, be agreed in outline at the feasibility stage.

- *Hardware*

Quotations should have been received not only for new equipment but also for its installation.

- *Software*

Systems analysts must quality control software, particularly by testing, prior to delivery. Sometimes it is also tested and accepted by the user prior to delivery.

- *Miscware*

Quotations for special stationery, such as computer-printed cheques, should have been received. Supplies of miscellaneous ancillary items like diskettes and printer ribbons should have been identified.

- *Services*

All preparatory work should have been done to establish any services, e.g. hardware maintenance and telecommunication links.

- *Documentation*

User manuals and technical documents should be complete. On-line help information should be included with the software.

The implementation work could embrace the following activities:

- *Configuration management*

The control of the various versions of new and amended systems is called configuration management and this is discussed in Section 24.3 below. For example, with an amended payroll system the users or computer operators must be issued with correct versions of the modified software as well as modified versions of pre-printed stationery such as the P60 form illustrated in Fig. 16.1.

- *Hardware installation*

This includes such matters as providing power and signal cabling as well as installing computer hardware.

- *Software installation*

This requires setting up the programs in magnetic disk libraries. Often included with this is the task of setting parameters. Parameters are basically general data which is fixed for long periods. For instance parameters can define which types of printer the software is to use, security passwords, or the tax rates for payroll software. The parameters are merely values stored on a computer file. In some cases such as payroll software packages, preparing parameters can be a large job.

- *User staff training*

Details on staff training are discussed below.

- *User acceptance tests of the system*

The user must confirm that the analyst has not only delivered correct software, but also that it is correctly installed.

- *Data conversion*

Converting the main data from the old systems to the new is often quite difficult. For instance on changing a sales ledger system all the customer records must be converted from the old to the new system. Once set up the data must be checked, corrected, and if incomplete, extended.

- *Parallel running*

As discussed below, parallel running the old and new systems is just one common implementation technique. Comparing the results of the two systems running in parallel is a good quality control check.

- *De-commissioning*

The old computer equipment has eventually to be removed.

- *Post-implementation review*

Section 17.6 mentions that this is a review of the whole project by users and analysts. It covers both development and implementation. The review seeks to identify outstanding problems, whether expected benefits have materialised, lessons for future work, and further requirements. Terms with a similar meaning are 'follow-up study' and 're-evaluation'.

Naturally each of the above broad headings can be subdivided into a plethora of different tasks.

Sometimes the system is introduced incrementally, i.e. only a small part of the system is introduced at any one time. In this case development, implementation, and maintenance overlap. Parts of the system initially implemented may be amended before the later parts have been installed. In this case the new system facilities and their use gradually expands over months and years.

24.3 Configuration management

A configuration in this context is a set of compatible components (hardware, software, documentation, and miscware). Other items such as test data are also often included. In both development and implementation it is important that modifications to software, say, are strictly controlled. The term 'baseline' is often used and this represents a configuration, or part of a configuration, which is in a specified known state. For example a baseline could be a set of approved program specifications or approved test data. The baseline can only be changed by formal procedures from one approved state to another.

A set of software components and associated documentation authorised for use is often called a 'release'. Typically business IT systems have hundreds of components, mainly individual programs, but also preprinted stationery and manuals.

Configurations change over time due to systems maintenance, e.g. changing a sales invoicing system so that it uses new VAT rates. This means that there must be a means of identifying each component of an IT system and ensuring that the system as used consists of only the currently valid versions of each component. An important part of implementation (for a new or amended system) is careful control of the system configuration. For instance a common mistake is inadvertently releasing a version of a program which is still under development and untested.

Configuration management basically involves keeping track of the various versions of a system, or parts of a system such as its specifications. Related terms are 'change-control' and 'version control'. Configuration management requires formal procedures. For example with software these cover:

- Authorising changes to a software baseline.
- Modifying the baseline.
- Maintaining separate libraries containing the old and new official baselines.
- Keeping separate from the baseline libraries any intermediate versions of the software and documentation which are in the process of being changed.
- Authorising the new baseline, e.g. after quality control checks like testing.

- Releasing the baseline as new operational versions of the software and documentation.

Normally each component of a system such as a program, software module, or document has a unique identifier called a version number. For instance a current version of PC-DOS (the operating system on personal computers) is 5.0. In this case the old versions such as 3.1 can still be used, as the purpose of the new versions is primarily to offer extra facilities. However a 1989 version of a payroll system would not be valid in 1993 because of the intervening legal changes. Typically with version numbering schemes the significant part of the number, the 3 and 5 with PC-DOS above, indicates a major change, and the decimal part a minor change (.0 and .1 with PC-DOS above). The version number must be visible, preferably in several places, e.g. embedded in the program source code and automatically shown on any output such as screen displays, or as part of the footing of any documentation.

A further complication is compatibility − not all versions of software and hardware can operate together. For instance the documentation for word processing packages specifies compatible hardware requirements such as the amount of memory, the amount of disk space, the type of graphics interface, and the range of printers that are acceptable. It is common to find that a new version of a word processing package does not operate on an old personal computer because of such factors as inadequate memory. However in general with business systems the hardware is less strictly controlled than the other system components, and it is sometimes excluded from configuration management. This is because a software system is usually designed to be compatible with a range of hardware options, and because significant changes in hardware occur less frequently. As suggested already it is essential that documentation is updated in line with system changes. It can be very frustrating to use documentation which does not match the current version of the software.

All this means that the analyst must apply careful configuration management and ensure that only the correct version of the system components are released for use. The problem is worse for a systems analyst working for a software house who may be controlling configurations for dozens of customers. In this situation it is not uncommon for customers to have similar but different systems, e.g. standard software packages which have been modified for each customer. Special software packages are available to help with configuration management. One task, for instance, where these packages can help, is that of ensuring that the hundreds of components in a system are correctly identified and catalogued. Another task of these packages is managing the storage of all the software components and documents on magnetic media.

24.4 Converting data

The main records of a business system can be numerous. Typical examples are:

- Payrolls — thousands of records.
- Stock systems — tens of thousands of records.
- Share registers in public companies — hundreds of thousands of records.
- Bank accounts or Inland Revenue tax details — millions of records.

Converting the data from one business system to another requires considerable planning and effort. It is often done automatically and the system data is read from the old computer files and converted to the new computer files. This requires not only special software but also hardware which is compatible with both the new and old system, e.g. data can be transferred by telecommunications link from an old mainframe system to a large personal computer, and reformatted for use by a networked personal computer system. An alternative is to use manual records or print-outs of the old data and manually re-enter it into the new system.

The data conversion process may introduce errors, e.g. if done manually. Even if done automatically the old data may itself contain omissions and errors. Sometimes data needs to be converted from several sources, e.g. from both old computer files and manual records. There is also a timing problem in that the data is usually converted at a particular date. Any transactions between the date of conversion and date of live use also need to be included. Careful quality control is essential during data conversion.

24.5   Change-over

As already implied there are several methods of changing over from the old to the new systems in a typical business environment. The various implementation methods used include the following:

● *Direct change-over (sometimes called the 'big-bang' approach)*
For instance the old system is stopped on a Friday evening and the new system is available in a fully operational state on the following Monday morning.

● *Parallel (or dual) running*
The old system and the new are run together. The two systems should produce the same results except where differences are expected. The two systems are run together until there is complete confidence that the new system is operating satisfactorily. This is really a form of system testing using live data and live operating conditions.

● *Phased implementation*
The new system or systems are slowly introduced phase by phase as in the case of the pensions department in Section 24.8 below. Each phase may represent a sub-system. The old systems are gradually phased out as the new are phased in.

● *Incremental implementation*
The system facilities are implemented in small steps once the basic minimum system has been installed. This eases the burden of learning and conversion work for the users. It also confines any problems to one small part of the overall project. The distinction between a phase and an increment is basically one of size. In phased implementation each step is large, whereas in incremental implementation each step is small. Perhaps only one extra facility like a new print-out is added with each step. Evolutionary prototyping can be regarded as an extreme form of incremental development and implementation. With this approach the system is progressively changed and extended to meet the user requirements.

● *Distributed implementation*
This is used where there are several implementations of the same

system such as installing retail systems in a chain of shops. Typically the implementation plan aims to install the system on one site after another.

- *Pilot systems*

This approach is used where it is particularly important to gain operational experience of how a system is used. For instance a software house which devised pensions software would initially need to gain operational experience of their software packages prior to selling them openly. A pilot version of the system would have been installed with one particularly friendly and cooperative user on attractive terms for the user, e.g. free software and free support. The operational experience gained is used to modify the system design and above all to modify the procedures for installing and using the system.

A large central computer department installing similar versions of systems in lots of different retail branches or depots tends to work the same way. A pilot version of the system is first installed on a 'guinea-pig' site. The system is adjusted and user manual modified on the basis of the operational experience gained.

Once a system has been field-tested in this way there is considerable confidence about installing it repeatedly elsewhere.

24.6 Selecting a change-over method

Once a new system is installed, accepted by the user management, and the staff trained, then there is the job of actually changing from the old to the new system. There are several problems with this.

- *Time required*

The new system may take several weeks or months to implement as indicated for pension systems in Section 24.8 below. The delays can come from several sources. For instance not all the bespoke software may be ready at once, or the data alone may take weeks to convert from the old to the new system.

- *Limited human capacity*

The user staff cannot absorb too many changes at once. They have their ordinary jobs to do outside the computer project, and this is often one of the main reasons for slow progress. There can be periods in which they are struggling and depressed by the extra work and problems of implementation. To keep the project on time it is important that the systems analyst helps maintain the morale of the users otherwise the capacity to progress is reduced even further.

- *Risk*

The staff may not be very competent in operating the new system, and the system itself may have faults and deficiencies. This could be true even though the staff have been trained, and the system has been subject to strict user quality control checks like systems testing. In either case operating the new system could lead to serious problems. A most dangerous situation is where the old IT system has been abandoned, and the new one is not satisfactorily operational.

All the above arguments lead to the view that a phased or incremental implementation of new systems is best. This means that at any one time the work is manageable and the risks are small. Also as each part of the project is implemented it should yield benefits. However there may be situations where the direct change-over is essential. For instance English and Welsh local authorities in 1989 had no choice but to switch quickly from the old domestic rates system of local taxation to the new community charge arrangements. It was a legal requirement under the Local Government Finance Act 1988.

24.7   Maintenance

The bulk of the work of systems analysts and programmers is actually maintaining old systems. This means that when software is changed it has to be re-implemented, and small changes can happen frequently, say every few months. This may involve changing some or all of the installed software, and training users in the use of the new features. For instance in 1983 payroll systems had to incorporate radically new legal requirements called SSP (Statutory Sick Pay). The changed payroll software had to be installed and users trained to use the new features necessary to operate SSP. Some changes are of course actually alterations to the software and some amendments to office procedures.

24.8 Project management during implementation

Implementing a system is sometimes regarded as a separate project, or at least a separate phase, from development. This is because development and implementation are fundamentally dissimilar activities which require different skills. However they both require careful project management. The techniques of project management are discussed generally in Chapter 30. Project management is often more critical and visible during implementation than during development. This is because user staff are extensively involved and also because the work is more sensitive to mistakes. Because of this the very essence of implementation is planning and controlling. All the jobs that need to be done to install a successful working system must be carefully planned and monitored. Despite each separate implementation job appearing to be relatively straight-forward, the analysts can feel very vulnerable and exposed during implementation. If the system or the implementation plan fails it is the systems analysts who receive much of the blame.

Formal IT project management requires breaking the work down into phases, stages, and tasks. As an example, take the implementation of a set of business systems in a company pensions department by a software house. A typical company pension scheme might have 4000 employees in the pension scheme, with 1000 pensioners. There might be four staff in the pensions department. The implementation plan based on networked micro-computers might have the following phases:

- Phase 1 − Install the hardware and word-processing system.
- Phase 2 − Install the pensions accounting system.
- Phase 3 − Install the pensioner payroll.
- Phase 4 − Install the pensions record-keeping system.
- Phase 5 − Install the pensions calculation system.

This plan is based on the idea that the easier jobs should be done first to build up experience and confidence in the new computer systems gradually. However, business priorities could dictate a different sequence. For instance Phases 4 and 5 (record-keeping and calculations) are usually the most important and difficult in a pensions environment. These phases might be selected for installation first simply because the problems with the old computer system have become intolerable in these areas.

Phase 2 of the project, establishing the pensions accounting system, can used to illustrate the break down of the work into stages and tasks.

- Stage 1 – Install the accounting software.
- Stage 2 – Train the user staff.
- Stage 3 – User acceptance testing of the accounts software.
- Stage 4 – Convert the data from the old system to the new.
- Stage 5 – Parallel running.
- Stage 6 – Live running of the new accounts system.

Each stage can be broken down into tasks as follows. So for Stage 2 above, user training, this could be:

- Task 1 – Review with the user manager the system requirements, the implementation plan, and the training objectives.
- Task 2 – Formal classroom training for the pensions staff by the systems analyst.
- Task 3 – Hands-on training exercises with the accounts system for the user staff, supervised by the systems analyst.
- Task 4 – Further hands-on training exercises by the user staff without the systems analyst.
- Task 5 – A review with the pensions staff of the training and the remainder of the accounts system implementation plan.

An analyst working for a software house would normally use an overhead projector for the classroom training. A special training version of the accounts system would be installed on the computer for the exercises. This would contain perhaps only a few accounts, with, say, fifty typical transactions, all specially set up for training purposes. For more common systems CBT (Computer Based Training) exercises could be used.

Phasing and staging implementation projects spreads the work over a sensible time-span and aims to produce useful results regularly. User managers and analysts try to minimise implementation activities at awkward times, e.g. the holiday season, or during a peak workload period such as the accounts year-end. In practice, as discussed in Chapter 30, the above phase, stage, and task lists would also contain details of the timescale and the staff involved. For example for Stage 4 above, convert accounts data, the tasks might be:

Task	**Staff**	**Completion Date (Week Number)**
(1) Identify and prepare old accounts data for manual data entry.	Charles Dickens	20
(2) Enter old accounts data into the new system manually at the keyboard.	Jane Austen	22
(3) Check data entry details.	Charles Kingsley	24
(4) Final quality control check.	Emily Bronte and Mark Twain	25

These implementation plans can be converted into barcharts for greater clarity as illustrated by Fig. 30.2. Where a specialist software house is implementing systems, considerable experience is acquired. The implementation plans for any one customer are then a modified version of a standard and comprehensive model plan, which contains most of the tasks likely to be met in practice.

One of the most significant improvements in recent times is the introduction of project management software. Examples are Computer Associates' 'SuperProject Expert' and Hoskyn's 'Project Manager Workbench'. This software can automate much of the tedious detailed planning and charting. Above all, revisions of project plans and 'what if' analyses are easily done to take into account new circumstances and predict the consequences of proposed actions. For example 'what if' another pensions administrator were freed from normal duties for an extra day per week so that he or she could work part-time on finishing the pensions systems implementation – what are the consequences in terms of cost and timescale? One golden rule with the implementation of all computer systems is to plan for the worst, and always have a fall-back option should the new system be delayed. For instance, where possible the old system must not be removed at a fixed date, in case the new system is not ready in time.

24.9   Problem areas

Implementation is often a worrying and stressful time for administrative users. It is then the job of the systems analyst to be positive, confident, sympathetic and helpful, and to endeavour to keep an implementation project on course. Some common problem areas are listed below.

- *Estimating*

Systems analysts may be reasonable at estimating the number of person-days of their own time required to implement a system. However the bulk of the effort is often required from user staff for activities like parallel running. There is a tendency for systems analysts to leave the users to 'get on with it', without serious estimating or planning. The result can be that the users, lacking the experience of computer staff in these matters, grossly underestimate the work-load and time-scale required to implement their IT system. At the feasibility stage systems analysts may deliberately avoid estimating the amount of user effort required. If estimates were prepared they could make the project look unattractive. Note that implementation estimating is probably intrinsically more difficult than development estimating. Implementation planning involves estimating the work required for many different activities by both user and IT staff.

- *Timescale*

Implementation tasks are often completed late causing the whole project to suffer from protracted delays. One reason already mentioned is under-estimating the work required. Furthermore there is always the effect of the unexpected such as the resignation of key user or computer personnel. Another major problem is the interference caused by both IT and user personnel working on other tasks outside the implementation project. For example an analyst may be implementing one project and at the same time involved in a feasibility study for an entirely new and different system elsewhere. Similarly users must often carry out their normal duties and help implement the new system.

- *Equipment*

Though many users experience reliable equipment, frustrating faults in hardware and related areas are not unknown. Particularly daunting is the possible failure of turnkey systems (computer equipment like PC networks installed entirely in the users' own office). The quality of the engineering maintenance and the software supplier's help-line service can be crucial in these situations.

- *Capacity problems*

Some users also experience capacity problems as magnetic disks fill up faster than expected. This can occur where other systems are run on the same networked personal computer system, e.g. an executive payroll and an employee share scheme running on the same equipment as a pensions system. The answer is proper capacity management and planning.

- *Security and control*

The security and control issues of computer use are usually well-understood, but never-the-less precautions are often less than perfect. For instance in one case employee pension record cards were being used to set up a new computer system and were lost in transit. Turnkey systems demand a more rigorous approach to security — everything from measures against software viruses to contingency plans if the system becomes inoperative for any reason. Occasionally users can forget to security copy essential data.

- *Software and data quality*

Again, no matter how carefully the supplier's staff determine the requirements and tailor the software, only the business users can declare that it is correct. Most traditional and modern methodologies place considerable emphasis on users checking the systems documentation and software at various stages. However errors and misunderstandings are not always obvious, e.g. with complex calculations. This makes meticulous user acceptance testing absolutely vital and time-consuming. Painstaking quality control of the data transferred from old systems to new is also imperative. Even with these quality controls experience suggests that the system may still not be what is actually required.

- *Overlooked work*

New computer systems often involve lots of small jobs that are easily over-looked. For instance one of these is checking out the Data Protection Act implications of a new system, and taking appropriate action, e.g. registering the system with the Data Protection Registrar.

● *Support*

Good support services from a software supplier or in-house computer department are usually essential. For instance a telephone help-line, is frequently invaluable when implementing new software.

● *Human factors*

These are discussed in Chapters 13 and 14. One issue that is often only partially addressed at the analysis and design stage of the new system is its effect on administrative and clerical jobs. In theory systems analysts and user managers are supposed to think through these issues as part of the systems design long before the actual implementation.

Often, in a small office, the manager and staff slowly and quietly re-organise their duties on a practical ad hoc basis as systems are progressively implemented and changed. However switching systems can be a traumatic time for staff. Section 13.5 discusses the 'new technology agreements' between trade unions and management. These are found in larger organisations and lay down procedures for the introduction of computer systems generally and cover such staff matters as health-and-safety and re-training. There are model new technology agreements which can be adapted for different circumstances. However new technology agreements tend to be a first step concerned with the development and installation of a system. Other union agreements with management covering, say, job security and job evaluation may be invoked when a new system takes effect and its use expands.

24.10 Summary

● Implementation of new business systems can involve an extensive amount of work not only for systems analysts, but also users.
● Implementation needs to be planned carefully. It often includes tasks like hardware installation, user training, user systems testing, and converting data from the old to the new system.
● Configuration management is about controlling the changes to a system and the release of new versions of software. It means that the versions of the components that comprise a system must be strictly controlled. These components include software programs and modules, documentation, test data, preprinted stationery, and sometimes the hardware. A 'baseline' is a set of system components

in defined state which can only be changed by formal procedures.
- The methods of system conversion include: direct, parallel running, phased, distributed, and incremental transition. Pilot working is a way of acquiring operational experience of a new system. Each has their place according to circumstances.
- Implementation can be stressful for users, both because of the extra work and the apparent confusion of the transition process. Good support by systems analysts is invaluable during this period.
- Systems maintenance implies that software must be amended and re-implemented frequently.

Chapter 25
Quantitative Techniques

25.1 Introduction

This chapter discusses in simple terms the role of mathematics in business and IT. This can be an area of some importance for systems analysts as modern business computing offers considerable scope for exploiting mathematical techniques cheaply and effectively. Some IT users such as engineers and accountants are numerate and expect systems development staff to be familiar with quantitative applications of IT, for instance discounted cash flow calculations which are used for investment appraisal. Just as mathematics can be applied when designing engineering artifacts such as aeroplanes, so it can also be applied when analysing and designing IT applications, e.g. for predicting computer system performance. As discussed later, even the management of IT is amenable to mathematical techniques in areas like project control.

25.2 Elementary mathematics in business and IT

Much of business is concerned with things of a numerical nature such as this year's profit, or the total number of motor cars sold in the UK. Some numerical data is produced as an inherent requirement of business administration. For example the Inland Revenue requires the calculation and deduction of income tax from wages. Other numerical data is ultimately used for planning and control purposes, e.g. sales are too low and need to be increased. Obviously such figures are essential for proper management, and they are produced by both manual and computer systems as part of normal business operations.

Though mathematics is necessary in business, much of it is elementary and hardly worthy of the name 'mathematics'. For example, consider the sale of brake linings by a motor components supplier. In essence determining the yearly sales value is arithmetically trivial. It is merely a matter of adding up the figures on each sales invoice. In practice the administration is inevitably complicated because the sheer volume of transactions − say 5000 per week with all sorts of clerical errors and complications such as returned goods. It is of course the purpose of good administration and the supporting computing systems to handle all this in a satisfactory way. It is an old observation that the administration which guarantees quality figures is much more complicated than the mathematics involved.

IT capacity planning can provide another example of simple mathematics. Systems analysts often need to plan the amount of magnetic disk space needed for a computer application. This is often done in a straightforward way. For instance, with a personnel system if the data for each employee requires, say, 5000 characters of disk space, then for 5000 employees the personnel system requires:

$5000 \times 5000 = 25$ million characters of disk space

There is no doubt that a substantial number of managers and systems analysts see applied mathematics as straightforward. They regard applied mathematics as being little more than the adaptation of junior school arithmetic to cater for the needs of business. Some managers and systems analysts skimp even simple calculations like the disk space calculation above, and they rely totally on intuition or luck. Needless to say this approach is dangerous in that it risks significant under or over estimating. It could lead, say, to buying inadequate printers for a mainframe system, or discovering that the printers are under-utilised.

The sensible application of school mathematics has its limitations. It ignores the considerable business potential of more sophisticated mathematical and statistical techniques, especially when combined with modern computing. There is a historical trend to adopt a more mathematical approach, both to business and technical problems. Also advanced mathematical techniques are part of the training of many business professionals such as accountants, who expect to see these techniques applied. Another instance is the marketing manager who speaks of 'exponential smoothing' or 'regression analysis' (mathematical techniques sometimes used for sales forecasting). If systems analysts are to understand their users they must be willing to appreciate and sometimes apply the relevant parts of mathematics in the investigation and design of computer systems.

25.3   Historical origins

Historically only a small minority of people were numerate until the late 19th century. Simple arithmetic was of course adopted by ancient civilisations for elementary business accounting and government taxes. But even by the 18th century advanced mathematics was only used for the more exotic technical applications such as astronomy and navigation. One major 18th century innovation was actuarial science which is the application of advanced mathematics to the financial aspects of life assurance and pensions. Actuarial work involves complicated compound interest and probability calculations. This is because money is taken as premiums and invested over long periods. With simple life assurance for example there is only a pay-out if the policy holder dies. The probability of death in any one year depends of factors like age, and can be calculated from mortality statistics.

Throughout the 19th century advanced mathematics was applied more and more to technical problems such as the design of steam engines and telegraph systems, although business continued to apply elementary techniques. Statistics was also applied to data on crime and economics. In the early 20th century large clerical systems produced considerable quantities of data. There was then a recognition of the use of statistics in business as a method of extracting and presenting information from a mass of figures. Statistics was also applied to quality control in manufacturing.

Just prior to the Second World War it was realised that mathematical approaches could be applied to military problems. This military application of mathematics was called OR (Operational Research in the UK, Operations Research in the USA). For example one OR problem involved predicting quantitatively the effects of a bombing raid on a city in terms of human casualties and damaged property. Another problem was determining the optimum use of planes to search the ocean and destroy submarines. After the Second World War OR was applied to business as well as military problems, for example scheduling factory production. OR claims to be concerned with the application of scientific methods and problem-solving to military and business operations. However this is true of other disciplines such as industrial engineering and what distinguishes OR is its mathematical nature.

25.4 Modern developments

In the 1950s and 1960s the combination of mathematical techniques and computing was seen as an important business opportunity. In the 1990s this is even more true given that computers are much cheaper and easier to use. Computers simplify some of the big practical problems of business mathematics such as the collection of data and the regular application of mathematical techniques by ordinary staff. Manually both the data collection and mathematical processing can be prohibitively expensive. With business computing data is produced automatically as a by-product of ordinary administrative functions. Also, for applications like sales forecasting, computer programs can be written which analyse the history of invoiced sales. These programs contain all the necessary mathematics, and do not demand that the business user understands them in detail.

25.5 Use of mathematics

The main uses of mathematics are:

- Extracting and presenting information.
- Forming administrative rules.
- Estimating and prediction.
- Evaluation.
- Optimisation.
- Understanding technical and business processes.

The extraction and presentation of numerical information is a major business function of mathematics. This is often automated with IT systems, e.g. to prepare sales reports. In most cases it only requires elementary mathematics such as averaging, totalling, and drawing graphs. More advanced techniques are sometimes used, particularly statistics.

Mathematics is commonly employed to form administrative rules, e.g. in taxation and social security. These rules are often complicated and are perhaps better described as algorithms. There is a distinctive feature about using mathematical rules, in say taxation. Such rules have at best only a partial objective justification. Much of the justification for tax schemes and the like comes from subjective social and political views, whereas other applications of mathematics are justified by reference to logic and the real world. An alternative way of looking at this is to say that political and social views are given a mathematical expression.

The application of mathematics to estimation and prediction has a simple idea: it is cheaper to solve problems by theoretical calculations than to learn by expensive experience. This is the same principle as estimating the amount of paint and wallpaper required to decorate a room. An informed guess will usually result in either too much wallpaper and paint being bought, or too little. Mathematics is regularly applied in most branches of technology such as aerospace engineering to predict the behaviour of proposed designs. It can also be applied in both business and systems development, e.g. for estimating project costs.

Evaluation means assessing and comparing alternatives. Is a mainframe, for example, less cost effective than a mini-computer for a new IT application? Optimisation is identifying the conditions for best performance. Taking stock control as an illustration, what is the replenishment order size which optimises (minimises) the total of the administration and stock-holding costs? Clearly it is somewhere between a small order every day and one huge order every year, and it can be determined mathematically.

Perhaps more fundamentally, mathematics aids the understanding of both the technological and business world. This is done through modelling in particular which is discussed in Section 25.8 below. For instance mathematical and statistical studies of failure provide insight into the design and production of reliable electronic machines.

All the above uses of mathematics can be simple and done on paper, or complex using computers. In either case the principles and objectives are much the same. As far as the systems analyst is concerned the most important example of applied mathematics occurs during the feasibility stage of a system. The cost-benefit and related calculations done at this stage basically decide whether a project is worth tackling, and which is the best option for proceeding. As discussed in Chapter 29 it is not unknown for poor feasibility calculations to result in wrong decisions, e.g. a project is undertaken because the cost-benefit calculations have under-estimated the costs and over-estimated the benefits. It must be said, however, that in some cases there is a wilful desire to be over-optimistic.

The professional application of mathematics in business is mainly the province of OR workers and statisticians. However as already implied there are many business situations which require mathematical skills intermediate between an elementary and professional level.

25.6 Business mathematics

The mathematical techniques used depend on the nature of the problems and business. So statistics is important to a motor insurance company for analysing road accidents. Some techniques are used frequently, and a few common examples include:

- *Compound interest*

Many practical financial problems involve flows of cash over a period of time and the interest that can be earned or paid is important. One technique is discounted cash flow (DCF) which uses compound interest theory to determine the equivalent rate of interest generated by the cash flow returns on an investment or project. DCF or related techniques are used for appraising computer projects.

- *Statistics*

This is basically the mathematics of drawing conclusions from numerical data. It is one of the most fundamental and useful parts of business mathematics. For instance a statistical marketing problem is determining the correlation between the sales of sports footwear and the weather, measured in terms of rainfall per month. Another common application of statistics is quality control. Small samples of mass-produced goods are examined for faults. Statistical theory can then establish whether departures from standard are significant, or due to random fluctuations. Statistical sampling techniques can also be used by systems analysts as part of their work. One example is activity sampling which is mentioned in Section 22.8.

- *Modelling*

The use of mathematical models is very important and discussed in Section 25.8 below.

● *Queueing theory*
This is used for instance to calculate the computer delays in responding
to VDU input. Figure 25.1 shows a typical queueing theory prediction
of VDU response times. As the workload on the central computer
grows the VDU transactions are delayed in a queue in the computer's
memory before the central processor services them.

● *Linear programming*
This is *not* connected with computer programming, but is a mathematical
optimisation technique. With animal foodstuffs like cattle cake for
example it is desired to make the food as cheaply as possible. Linear
programming can determine the cheapest mix of raw materials like
cereals which meet the strict nutritional requirements. By using software
the linear programming can be repeated as the price of raw materials
change.

● *Decision theory*
This is a mathematical approach to making rational business decisions
especially when the outcomes are uncertain. For example it can take

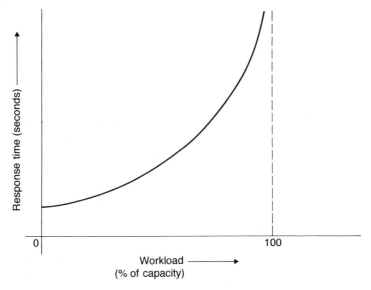

Fig. 25.1 A queueing theory prediction of deteriorating VDU response times as the
workload on a central computer approaches saturation.

into account the probability that projects might succeed, break-even, or fail.

Of course the techniques regularly used in business are a small subset of mathematics as a whole.

25.7 Metrics

A metric is computer jargon for a 'measure'. Some typical metrics are:

- Business — For instance measuring the size of a sales ledger by the number of customers.
- Hardware — e.g. a disk drive stores a maximum of 300 million characters.
- Software — for example the number of lines of executable COBOL code in a program is 1000 lines

    or

    the number of 'function points' in a computer system is 500.

    (A function point is a composite numerical score of the size of a piece of software. Mark 1 Function points are calculated from the number of inputs, outputs, files, complexity, etc. Each function point is crudely equivalent to 100 lines of COBOL.)

Before most mathematics can be usefully employed it is essential to have data, and metrics are actual data or estimates about things of interest such as the number of words produced per day by a systems analyst when writing a manual. Sometimes a metric is a proxy or substitute for some more subtle concept. So the quality of a computer program can be represented by the number of defects in the program — the fewer defects the higher the quality. This also raises the problem of precisely defining a metric — for example when is a defect a defect? An arithmetical error in stock control software which results in calculating the wrong stock level is clearly a defect. However take an unnecessary 'dead' software routine which is never executed as the computer always skips round it — is this a defect or merely inelegant coding? Also the concept of defining metrics can be taken too far. This is sometimes done for amusement in popular magazines and the like by asking readers to score their answers to questionnaires. These are supposed to measure such things as their honesty or their qualities as a wife or husband.

Underlying the use of metrics is a belief dating back to the ancient Greek mathematician Pythagoras that everything can be represented as numbers. More recently a similar philosophy was expressed by the Victorian scientist Lord Kelvin in the following influential quotation:

> 'When you can measure what you are speaking of and express it in numbers you know that on which you are discoursing. But when you cannot measure it and express it in numbers, your knowledge is of a very meagre and unsatisfactory kind.'

The simple reality of business and technical life means that it is important to define metrics of interest and then collect data about them. There is an old business saying: 'If you can't measure it, you can't manage it.' As an example it is difficult to control the abuse of a sick pay schemes without attendance metrics. One attendance metric is the number of days of sickness for each employee per month. The interest in metrics creates a considerable amount of work for systems development staff. This is because executives expect computer systems to produce many of their business metrics. Moreover analysts also need metrics for their own work, so clearly, an estimate of the number of different VDU screen lay-outs in an insurance system is one measure of the size of the system.

25.8 Modelling and simulation

Any scheme for representing something in the real world can be called a model. For instance the diagram of Maslow's hierarchy of needs in Fig. 14.1 can be regarded as a model of human work motivation. Another example of modelling is using small replicas or cardboard cut-outs of desks and machines to plan the layout of an office or computer room.

More importantly the behaviour of things in the real world can be represented approximately by algorithms or equations. As a simple example the equation below models the effect of the price of an item and any advertising expenditure on the sales revenue:

$$Q = a - b.P + c.A$$

where Q is the quantity sold per quarter year, P is the price of the item, and A is the advertising expenditure per quarter. a, b, and c are constants for the particular product concerned.

A special form of mathematical modelling is simulation. Simulation models usually include the effects of time, and attempt to imitate reality rather than merely representing it. So new stock control rules (algorithms) can be tested out by simulating their performance with the historical daily demand for goods. This means working out, either manually or by computer, for each day, what the replenishment orders and stock levels would have been using the new rules and historical demand. Hopefully the new rules show an improvement in average stock levels over the old rules with the same demand pattern. Notice that the calculations must simulate the despatch of goods and arrival of replenishments to determine what the stock levels would have been for each day in the past.

By way of contrast the sales revenue model above does not explicitly include time, and does not directly imitate or simulate the behaviour of customers buying goods in response to prices and advertising. Frequently a simulation model imitates natural variability and the effects of chance in the real world. Thus due to random factors deliveries of goods can sometimes occur before or after the supplier's estimated date. This variability can be included in simulation models by using probabilities and random numbers. Such techniques are jokingly called Monte Carlo methods.

Modelling is one of the fundamental parts of business mathematics. The use of mathematical or algorithmic models to simulate real-world process is also very important in science and technology. With all models the first question is whether they can represent the real-world situation reasonably well, and if so what are their limitations? Secondly, even if the model is accurate in principle, is it possible to determine the constants and variables? Take for example the sales model above which predicts sales on the basis of advertising expenditure and price. Can the constants a, b, and c be determined in a practical and economic fashion? Also the model assumes that the market can always be supplied with goods.

Another common model (which is also a simulation) is the cash flow analysis used to predict when a business is going to be short of funds, or more rarely when it has an excess of money. Figure 25.2 shows a

CASHFLOW ANALYSIS – £K						
Month >	Jan	Feb	Mar	Apr	May	Jun
* Sales	100	105	110	115	120	120
* Expenditure	90	90	95	100	110	110
* Cash inflow	0	0	100	105	110	115
* Cash outflow	90	90	95	100	110	110
* Cumulative net cashflow	(90)	(180)	(175)	(170)	(170)	(165)
* Bank balance (starts with £150 000)	60	(30)	(25)	(20)	(20)	(15)

Fig. 25.2 A simple cashflow model for a new business which starts trading in January. Customers actually pay for their goods two months in arrears. This means that the cash inflow lags the sales by two months. Expenditure items such as wages are paid in the month shown, so the cash outflow is the same as the expenditure with no time lag. Because there is a projected maximum deficit of £30 000 some way must be found of dealing with this, e.g. a loan or overdraft. The brackets () are an accounting convention for a negative quantity.

simple example. This cashflow model shows the difficulty of many small businesses – customers paying slowly in arrears. The consequence here, according to the model, is that the business must find up to £180 000 to finance the time gap between the cash outflow and the cash inflow. This is again an approximate model and the most dubious assumption is probably the sales line – how reliable is the forecast that the sales revenue will rise to £120 000 per month? The cash-flow model also illustrates the value of 'what-if' analysis. The model can make predictions showing the effect on the bank balance of pessimistic and optimistic sales assumptions – what if sales fell to £90 000 per month or what if they rose to £140 000 per month? Models are often built into computer systems, e.g. the DSSs (Decision Support Systems) mentioned in Section 3.4.

25.9 Computational aspects

Mathematical techniques provided by OR workers are sometimes incorporated by systems analysts into business systems. Areas such as sales forecasting and production control have already been mentioned as fruitful areas for applying this approach. However calculations have to be computationally feasible. That is, the execution of the mathematical algorithms should be completed by using a sensible amount of computer time. One example of a computationally infeasible approach which is simple to illustrate is provided by the famous 'travelling salesman' problem. A number of customers are based in different towns such as Preston, Manchester, Chester, Wigan, Stafford, and so on. The salesman based in Liverpool wishes to visit them on a round trip taking several days, staying overnight when necessary. However he needs to know the route which minimises the total distance he must travel. The simplest way to solve the problem on a computer is to evaluate the distance of each possible route. So part of one route could be from Liverpool to Wigan, then to Manchester, and next to Stafford. Once all possible routes have been calculated by the computer it can select the shortest. However it is easy to demonstrate that number of possible distinct routes, for 50 towns say, is enormous − about 3×10^{62} (algebraically the number of routes is $\dfrac{(N - 1)!}{2}$ where N is the number of towns, and N is greater than two). It is just not possible to perform this huge number of calculations. It would take billions of years, even with the a supercomputer completing a hundred million arithmetical operations per second!

Obviously infeasible calculations must be avoided, and it is often possible to find acceptable and computationally feasible alternatives. It may be necessary to sacrifice theoretical, or even practical, perfection.

25.10 Capacity planning

For the systems analyst one of the most important areas for applying simple or advanced mathematics is capacity planning. Basically this involves ensuring that there is enough capacity, e.g. sufficient printing speed for a computer system. The nightmare of every analyst is designing a system with a daily print job that takes longer than 24 hours! Once a system is operational there may be the need to plan increases (or decreases) in capacity, for example by adding more central processing power to cope with extra terminals.

Capacity planning needs to be part of the feasibility study for a system, though at this stage the calculations are obviously very approximate. More precise calculations can be done during the design stage. Typically the calculations can determine the type of equipment and the number of units like VDUs. Typical factors that need to be determined with a new system are:

- Processor power and memory needed.
- Disk space.
- Printing capacity.
- The number of terminals or work-stations.
- The speed of telecommunication facilities.
- Cost.
- The response time for terminal messages under various loads.
- The time to complete batch jobs like printing.

Without experience of the equipment the analyst is very dependent on the literature and advice of the supplier. Where there is experience of using the equipment for other applications then the calculations and system design can be completed with confidence.

Large scale computer operations on mainframes and telecommunication networks are easy to monitor automatically with software. In fact there is often an embarrassingly large amount of data available on such matters as processor and disk drive utilisation. Statistical software can reduce this data to meaningful information, often in a graphical form. This makes the capacity planning of the future use of existing systems much easier.

25.11   Software tools

Most mathematical techniques are not new, but what is new is the ease with which they can now be applied using computers. Software packages incorporating mathematical techniques are readily available. What is even better is the ability of most software to convert numerical results automatically into convenient graphs and charts. Some common examples are:

- *Spreadsheet systems*

Software products like Lotus $1-2-3$ are frequently used in business to handle the cash flow problems as illustrated by Fig. 25.2. They can also be used for numerous other applications such as estimating the price of the equipment configuration for a new computer system.

- *Statistics packages*

These allow the easy application of statistical techniques which often require tedious calculations. In essence it is only necessary to enter the numerical data and the required results are produced. Minitab is one popular example.

- *Special packages*

Special software is available for such purposes as capacity planning and project control. An example is SuperProject Expert which employs clever algorithms to plan the use of resources like the analysts and programmers needed to complete a systems development project.

25.12 Quantitative techniques applied to systems development

Quantitative techniques may be applied to managing systems development. For example how long is a computer project likely to take and how many systems analysts and programmers are required? One well-known simple mathematical model used for this kind of estimating is Putnam's 'software equation':

$$L = C.K^{\frac{1}{3}} .t^{\frac{4}{3}}$$

where:

L = the number of lines of program code in the system.

C = a constant, the 'environment factor', which depends on a series of parameters such as the development methodology, the technology used, and the management techniques. C might have a value of 2000 in a primitive environment and 10000 in a good one.

K = is the person-years required to develop and maintain the system over its lifetime.

t = the calendar time to develop the system in years.

Putnam's software equation can be used to calculate the effect of various changes. For example it can show quantitatively the known effect that small reductions in the delivery time have a major effect on the *total* amount of work to develop and subsequently maintain software.

Sections 30.4 to 30.6 discuss further some of the simple quantitative and graphical techniques that can be used in planning the development of IT systems.

25.13   Summary

- Mathematical techniques are increasingly incorporated into business systems.
- Computers make it easy to use mathematics because the software can hide many complications from the user, and the collection of much of the data can be automatic.
- OR and statistics are disciplines which can be important to systems analysts.
- Business professionals such as accountants and marketing staff are trained to appreciate standard mathematical techniques and may expect analysts to understand and apply them.
- Mathematics can be used for extracting and presenting information, administrative rules, estimation, prediction, evaluation, and optimisation. It is also used to provide an understanding of business and technical processes.
- Measurement is important in systems development. Metrics are business and technical measures such as the number of lines of program code in a system, or the number of people employed in an office.
- Software tools aid the application of mathematics and statistics.
- Capacity planning is an essential task at the feasibility and design stages of a system. It can also be used to plan the future usage of existing systems.
- Mathematics can be applied to the analysis and design of IT systems as well as their development and operation.

Chapter 26
Quality Management in IT

26.1   Introduction

This chapter discusses the management of quality as applied to both systems development and IT. Chapter 15 discusses quality in business generally and Chapter 24 mentions the user and systems implementation aspects. Ensuring the quality of IT systems is a major concern for systems analysts, programmers, and computer operations staff. An illustration of the importance of IT quality is given by the American telephone system which is of course computerised. Large scale disruption was caused for about half-a-day in 1990 when a software bug prevented completion of 44% of long distance calls.

26.2   Business systems quality

The general ideas of quality management discussed in Chapter 15 can be applied to business and technical IT systems. The main components of a business system such as software and pre-printed stationery are discussed in Section 23.3, and are illustrated in Fig. 26.1. This diagram can be used to consider quality from both a systems development and computer operations perspective. As the figure shows software is only a part of a computer system, but a vital part. It is probably unfair to

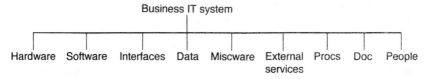

Procs – Procedures
Doc   – Documentation

Fig. 26.1 One common way of subdividing business systems to identify the components for design and quality purposes.

suggest that it is necessarily more error prone than other components of a business system such as the people or operating procedures, but bespoke software has that reputation. Software quality has become a subject of much interest, probably to the detriment of the other components of systems quality. As a result there is a tendency to regard system quality and software quality as more or less the same thing.

Failures in any of the components of Fig. 26.1, either singly or in combination, lowers the quality of the whole system. Each of the main components presents its own quality problems for the developer. Some examples of poor quality in system components are:

- Hardware   – wrong, missing, or defective equipment on delivery.
                 – poor installation work with cables trailing across work areas.
                 – electronic failures such as burnt-out power packs.

- Software   – bugs, e.g. program errors which lead to wrong figures on a print-out showing the product costs of a business.
                 – inadequate design such as help screens not being provided with an interactive system.

- Interface   – terminal screen displays for entering telephone sales orders which are inconvenient and have poor response times.
                 – wrong formatting of a magnetic disk file which transfers data between different systems.

- Data   – incomplete or erroneous data on computerised stock records.

- Miscware   – images on microfilm fading.

- External   – noisy communications over a public telephone
  services   network leading to loss of data and slow trans- missions.

- Procedures   – signatories do not examine or query cheque
  and work   payments prepared by some one else.
  practices   – documents rejected on computer input are not resubmitted.

                             − poor set up when using printers or paper hand-ling machines resulting in damaged and wasted computer stationery.

- Documentation   − no program specifications.
                             − an unintelligible user manual.
                             − no help screens.
- People   − no training in clerical and computer systems.

Each one of the above categories can also be subdivided. So even the performance of an individual person as a 'component' in the system can be subdivided into significant factors, for instance by considering the quality of the various skills the individual needs to operate his or her part of the system. Software quality can be considered in terms of factors like correctness, reliability, efficiency, usability, maintainability, testability, and so on. Metrics can be devised to represent these quality factors, e.g. software reliability can be defined in terms of the mean time between serious failures.

Another way of examining a system for quality purposes is chronologically through the SDLC (Systems Development Life-Cycle), e.g. in terms of the analysis, design, construction, testing, and operation of a system. For operational IT systems the supply chain can be followed from sources of input data to recipients of processed information.

Which of the above methods of examining system quality is adopted depends on circumstances. They can also be used together. So computer operations managers are likely to be interested in the supply chain and the system components view as a way of improving the quality of service. The chronological approach via the SDLC is not of particular interest to them, though it is very relevant to systems development managers.

A business system fundamentally provides a service based on hardware and software. So a computerised management accounting system primarily provides a budgetary control information service. In mainframe operations it is usual to have a service level agreement with users which specifies the details of the IT processing including quality metrics. So providing accurate budgetary reports to managers within five days of the month-end may be part of the agreement. Another example is where a service level agreement specifies the availability ('up-time') of a mainframe service and the VDU response time.

Managers are also interested in the more intangible aspects of quality such as customer satisfaction with the service offered by an information centre help-desk.

26.3 Range of faults

In business systems there is a range of quality failings from the trivial to the catastrophic. Some faults may be tolerable either because they are:

- Aesthetic, e.g. a garish use of colours on forms or terminal screens.
- A nuisance, e.g. a sluggish VDU response time.
- Circumventable, e.g. spooling (writing print-outs temporarily to a disk file) is defective, but direct printing is satisfactory.
- Easily corrected, e.g. VDU input errors are detected and rejected on a batch processing run rather than at the input stage.

Middling faults can sometimes be tolerated if they are few in number and known. For instance one *known* wrong total on a monthly sales print-out can be handled by manual totalling whilst correction of the software is inaugurated for the next run.

Faults may be fatal, e.g. the software system sometimes 'crashes' when asked to perform an occasional but vital function such as preparing the final accounts from a nominal ledger. Other faults may be unacceptable, e.g. sporadically miscalculating VAT on sales invoices.

Quality gurus tend to suggest that none of the above should ever occur as zero-defects is the quality objective. In most businesses there is an explicit or implicit AQL (Acceptable Quality Level) − more correctly it is often an acceptable defect level. If defects actually do occur preventive action demands not only correction in the widest sense but also an investigation to track down the reason for the error to make sure that it does not re-occur.

As the above sections illustrate business systems can have their quality specified in terms of a large number of variables and attributes with quality failings from the trivial to the disastrous. This contrasts with engineering components such as ball bearings where quality tends to be a question of meeting the specification in terms of a few variables and attributes such as diameter, hardness, and polish. In engineering terms a business system compares roughly to, say, an ocean-going ship where the faults can range from a loose door handle to a major leak in the hull below the waterline, i.e. there are numerous variables and attributes to control. Basically this implies that the specification, assurance, and control of quality is much more extensive and complex with business systems than is usually believed.

26.4   Defect creation, propagation and amplification

The exact nature of each step in an IT project depends on the methodologies and standards adopted, as well as the circumstances. However each step in the project can introduce errors (creation), or fail to detect errors from previous stages and pass them on to the next step (propagation or transmission), or even make the bugs worse (amplification or compounding). Thus errors in a design specification may be programmed into a system. The specification errors may also be included in any user documentation. This may lead to further errors as the consequent faults in the office procedures result in erroneous data stored in the files or database. Naturally considerable efforts are made to stop this expensive proliferation of errors. If possible the errors from one step are detected and corrected or blocked from spreading into the following steps as shown in Fig. 26.4.

To illustrate the problem in more detail take the example of designing and programming a payroll package. Using Fig. 26.4 Step N involves preparing a program specification from the payroll system design (Step N−1). Step N+1 is writing a payroll program. Then errors could be generated and propagated as follows:

- 5 errors from Step N−1, e.g. a data item (field) omitted from a screen design. (Transmission)

  Net errors   = 5.0
- 3 errors from Step N−1 detected (or blocked) by QC.

  Net errors   = 2.0
- 2 remaining errors multiplied by 3.
  For example there are several similar fields on a payroll record such as overtime pay, basic pay,

gross pay, taxable pay, and net pay. Due to the
confusion of similar names the wrong name is used
repeatedly. (Amplification)

Net errors	= 6.0

- 15 new errors introduced e.g. a greater-than sign
  (>) is inadvertently used instead of a less-than sign
  (<). (Creation)

Net errors	= 21.0

- QC is 70% efficient and 30% of the errors are
  passed on to Step N+1 (programming).
  (Propagation)

Net errors	= 6.3
- Total increase in the number of errors.	= 1.3 (or 26%)
(Net amplification)	

Continuing this example the programming step would probably
further increase the errors. One approach to this problem as discussed
below is increased systems testing to detect and eliminate errors. Another
approach is trying to prevent the occurrence of the errors in the first
place. In practice both approaches are used.

26.5   Systems development quality

Many modern approaches to systems development are really just more
rigorous versions of traditional methods. One important feature of
modern views is that more effort ought to go into the analysis and
design stages of the SDLC (Systems Development Life-Cycle) to reduce
problems at the later stages, i.e. a preventive approach to quality. The
net effect of good and bad systems analysis is illustrated by Figs 26.2
and 26.3. Basically these graphs illustrate that a good job by the
analyst is essential to prevent serious and expensive problems later in
the SDLC. The defect propagation example in Section 26.4 above
makes the same point. Another feature of modern approaches is a
greater emphasis on QC at all stages of the SDLC. More rigorous
analysis, design, and documentation, combined with extensive QC
should make programming more straight-forward. It should also reduce

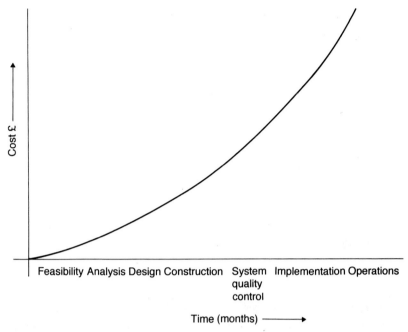

Feasibility Analysis Design Construction System Implementation Operations
                                          quality
                                          control

Time (months) ⟶

Fig. 26.2 An illustration of the (possible) rising cost of fixing an error made at the feasibility stage of systems development. The cost of fixing the error at the later stages can become increasingly higher. Similar curves can be produced for errors made at the analysis, design, or construction stage.

Basically the later an error is detected the more expensive it is to correct the error itself and any knock-on consequences. Thus if a feasibility error is corrected at the operational stage then there are probably design, programming, and user documentation changes. Worse still much of the data on computer files may need amending.

the corrective and perfective work during the system quality control and maintenance stages of the SDLC.

An important part of modern quality thinking is not merely defect elimination but the continuous improvement of products, services, and business activities. In a systems development context this requires a constant striving for the improved use of current techniques and innovation such as new CASE tools.

The approaches to maintaining quality during the development process are listed below.

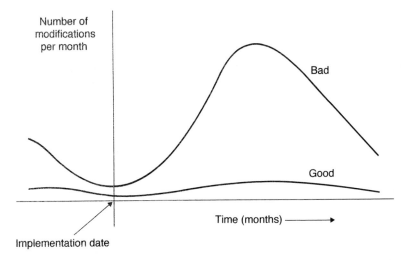

Fig. 26.3 The contrast between good and bad requirements analysis. The graph shows the number of corrective and perfective modifications in a live system due to faulty analysis. The graph shows that it takes the users some time to realise the deficiencies in their system. This is partly because it takes time to learn to use a system, and partly because the analysis deficiencies tend to occur with the more infrequent and subtle requirements. Similar curves can be drawn for system design errors.

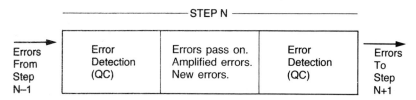

Fig. 26.4 An error propagation and generation model showing how faults can be transmitted, created, or magnified during a systems development process. The error detection includes correction, but it is not usually 100% effective.

● *Standards and methodologies*

For example JSP (Jackson Structured Programming) is an important programming methodology which can improve the quality of software.

● *Inspection methods*

This includes techniques like reviewing documents and program code.

- *Testing*

Running extensive controlled tests on computer systems before use is vital. Once analysts and programmers have completed their tests, it is normally imperative that users conduct their own separate acceptance testing.

- *Debugging*

This is not a separate technique but the process of identifying and removing bugs (faults) from systems, particularly the software. The term is used more by programmers than analysts and involves activities like inspection and testing to identify bugs and then correct them.

- *Certification*

This is where an independent body certifies that software matches a specification.

- *Tuning*

The adjustment of a system so that its performance is improved.

- *Software tools*

General purpose software tools often raise quality. There are also software tools concerned specifically with software quality.

- *Formal proving*

A rather theoretical technique which involves proving 'mathematically' that a program is correct. Formal proofs are awkward to apply, to anything other than small programs, even under academic conditions. The technique is only at the research stage and it is difficult to see how it can be applied sensibly to business software.

- *Configuration management*

This involves ensuring that the right versions of software and other system components are used together at the right time. See Section 24.3 for further details.

Most of the above approaches are discussed later in the chapter. Because of the pervasive nature of quality it is sometimes difficult to separate out quality control issues from topics like systems analysis and systems maintenance, i.e. each activity in the SDLC involves quality considerations and vice versa.

There is a view that producing software is radically different from, say, the production of manufactured goods. Producing software on-time, on-cost, on-quality certainly seems to be more difficult in practice. A typical reply is that this is only true because of the amateur craft approach often adopted to producing software. The solution lies in adopting the practices of 'software engineering' with a commitment to quality. Clearly however there are some unique aspects to both business systems and software, e.g. the abstract nature of the work. These unique features must be respected and allowance made for them in the quality management.

26.6   Methodologies and quality

Traditional systems development methodologies emphasise quality control at the various life-cycle stages, e.g. user validation of system specifications, desk checking programs, inspection of program code by a senior programmer, and so on. This is to minimise the problems illustrated by Fig. 26.2. The practice is often less than ideal, i.e. the QC is skimped because of reasons like pressure to meet deadlines. Modern methodologies and practices are theoretically more thorough than traditional methodologies, i.e. there is even more in-built QC. However in practice they are vulnerable to the same problem, i.e. skimping QC. QA procedures are designed to prevent this short-sighted thinking.

SSADM Version 4 is described in Section 18.15 and the PRINCE project control method is discussed in Section 30.5. Modern approaches such as these try to incorporate quality management (mainly via QA and QC) into the whole systems development and project management process. Some examples of the details are:

- Creating a quality environment, e.g. a quality policy and an organisation structure for managing quality.
- Regular user involvement.
- Formal quality reviews − see Section 26.7 below.
- Assembly steps at the end of each step where all the documentation is brought together and checked.
- Constant cross-checking of one piece of work against another, e.g. DFDs are checked against entity diagrams − see Section 20.7.

Also of course the in-built standardisation and structured techniques of any modern methodology should contribute significantly to quality. The effect of poor quality analysis and design is illustrated in Fig. 26.3.

26.7   Inspection

Inspection is a surprisingly good and effective quality control technique with software. This is especially true when it is formalised and involves several people as well as the author of the document or program code. Various terms are used each with their own nuances − for instance walk-throughs, reviews, and audits. The basic idea is to check the documentation or code carefully, preferably with others. Inspection can often mean laborious checking, e.g. word-by-word with text and symbol-by-symbol with diagrams. Where the process is formalised, documentation is produced such as error logs, change requests, and follow-up action lists.

26.8   Testing

Testing business software is often straightforward in principle. The basic idea is to feed data into the system and see if produces the right results according to the specifications. For instance with a sales order system the details of customer requirements are fed into the computer. The output of the system is checked to see if the processing is correct, e.g. has the computer printed the correct picking lists for selecting warehouse items for despatch. Test cases are designed to check all the common and uncommon conditions which occur in practice. For example, one test case can contain deliberate errors, e.g. a delivery date in the past. Another can contain unusual but valid conditions, e.g. one order being split into ten deliveries on different future dates. Thorough testing requires an extensive number of test cases and it can never, in theory, be exhaustive.

Not only must good test cases be prepared but also the expected output must be documented. There is a somewhat sloppy tendency to feed the test data into the computer and check the results after the software has been test run. It is much more preferable to work out the expected results in advance and then make a simple comparison with the test results. The production of good systems test data contains the same amount of work as writing several programs, requiring maybe several man-weeks of effort. This amount of work, and it is vital work, requires careful planning. The production of a test plan (or more generally a quality control plan) is a step in many systems development methodologies or project control methods.

One important aspect of testing arises particularly during systems maintenance and was mentioned in Section 2.7. Normally during maintenance the amended features are checked by a change test. Clearly however when amending a system, changes can be inadvertently introduced into supposedly unchanged parts of the system by both the analyst and programmer. This might be due to a programmer accidentally altering code which should remain the same. Also the design changes introduced by an analyst could have unexpected side-effects. This means that for safety all the unchanged features of a system must be re-tested. Testing the unchanged features of an amended system is called regression testing.

The author has seen many situations where regression testing was regarded as a bureaucratic, fussy, and needlessly time-consuming chore, but when performed it revealed unexpected faults. In one unfortunate case a systems analyst under pressure decided that he had no time or need for regression testing a payroll system. The change testing was satisfactory and the analyst released the system for live use. Several thousand people were wrongly paid because the programmer had accidently altered some standard payroll calculations which were required to remain the same.

26.9   Exhaustive testing

Dijkstra, a software engineering authority, is often quoted as saying that software testing reveals the presence of bugs and not their absence. A corollary of this is that exhaustive testing is rarely feasible. Take as an example the testing of a simple program for a stock system. There are billions of possible combinations of all the different values of data fields such as stock quantity, cost per item, depreciation factor, re-order level, and re-order quantity. Any one combination of the values may be wrongly processed due to an error in the application code (in BASIC, C, or COBOL say), or worse still due to an error in the computer language software (an interpreter or compiler). The computer processing time alone to generate and test all the combinations would be infeasibly long, and it would be impossible for a human being to check the billions of cases even if they were printed. This may seem extreme but experience suggests that some combinations of values do unexpectedly produce erroneous results. Fortunately the 'at-risk' combinations of values can often be predicted in advance and deliberately tested. For example suppose software is to print out a 'high stock' warning containing the details of an item where the value of its stock exceeds £5000, then it is a good idea to put in test data that gives stock values just under and just over £5000.

26.10   Testing techniques

Despite arguments about the theoretical incompleteness of testing it is a fact of systems development that properly designed software tests can be very effective. The reason for this is that good test data is designed to expose problems that experience shows to be common. The areas that are unlikely to contain bugs are only lightly tested. Thus with the previous stock valuation warning message a few well-chosen values are enough in practice, if not in theory, for adequate testing. However if there were only a few test cases for every few lines of software code then a real system consisting of tens of thousands of lines of code requires a vast amount of test data. Fortunately test data can often serve several purposes simultaneously which means that the number of test cases required is usually large but manageable. As a minimum dozens of test cases are required to test a simple business system.

The point needs to be made again that the planning of tests and the preparation of the large number of test cases required is a major task for a typical business IT system. One important method of preparing tests is to produce data systematically which 'exercises' the features in a functional specification of a system or software module. Functional specifications for programs and software modules are common. In theory they are only concerned with the physical inputs, outputs, and data stores, and the logical rules connecting them. The physical design of a software in terms of the structure of the code should not be mentioned. For instance functional specifications describe outputs like the P60 form in Fig. 16.1. In this case the payroll test data needs to be stored on a computer file. When the payroll software is run the expected printed data is specified by the P60 stationery design. Errors such as over-printing the pre-printed text of the P60 form can then be easily detected and corrected.

There are many testing concepts, techniques, and terms. They often overlap in meaning and are often used in combination. Common examples include:

• *Black box tests*

In computing black box testing means testing what the system is supposed to do with *no* knowledge of how it works. This means that the inputs to the software should produce outputs according to a functional specification. The above example of checking the printing of a P60 form is a black box test. No assumptions are made about the details of the software design or the program code. This is the most important technique for testing business software and it is used by IT users and systems analysts as well as programmers. The term 'black box' comes from electronics. It refers to a device whose function is known but whose design and components are unknown, hidden, or irrelevant.

• *White box tests*

This is testing what the software does with a reasonable knowledge of how it is designed and programmed. For example in the last stages of writing a new COBOL program the test input to the software can be planned so that it exercises the sections of the program that have been particularly difficult to code. Sometimes selected lines of code are tested. Software tools such as a trace facility are often used with white box testing. Trace software displays on the screen the sections or lines of software that are executed when the program is running. This can show for instance that execution path through a BASIC program is erroneous. By their very nature white box techniques are used mainly by analyst-programmers and programmers.

• *Grey box tests*

This is a cross between black box and white box testing. It involves basing tests on knowledge of both the functional specification and the software design or program code. For instance a standard black box test could be extended to test thoroughly a few heavily-modified sections of code. The knowledge of the software design or program code is often partial, particularly when testing during software maintenance.

- *Interactive testing*

Interactive testing is a form of white-box testing. The software is executed line by line under the control of a programmer at a VDU using a special software tool. The software can usually be stopped and its state examined at any time. The software can also be amended and the execution path through the code changed at will.

- *Module and integration testing*

The 'modules' of a system may be programs or parts of programs. With module testing the software components are separately tested. Basically integration testing involves testing the modules of a system when they are brought together. This is done by systematically adding a few modules together and then testing. The process is repeated until the whole system has been assembled out of the modules and tested as a whole. Needless to say modules can sometimes work individually but not together, e.g. because of interfacing problems.

- *Mutation tests*

This attempts to test the efficiency of the tester and the test data rather than test the software itself. The program code is corrupted (mutated) to see if the deliberately introduced code errors can be caught by testing. It can also give an indication of the fault tolerance of a system.

- *Error seeding*

This is a variant of mutation testing. Known errors are introduced ('seeded') into the software to give a measure of the tester's efficiency. Suppose a tester detects 60% of seeded bugs as well as some unseeded and previously unknown bugs. Broadly the assumption is that 60% of the unseeded unknown bugs have also been found, and 40% of the unseeded bugs remain undetected.

- *Static analysis*

This is really a form of automatic inspection of code for factors like inconsistencies, uninitialised program variables, and code metrics (statistics). It can be done manually but software tools automate the work and are more thorough. Static analysis is really an extension of the checking function of a language compiler.

- *Alpha / beta tests*

Alpha tests are final tests by the user in the developer's environment. Beta tests are run by the users in their own environment.

- *Other*

There are many other types of testing which are often named according to their purpose or technique. Some testing may not be explicitly called 'testing' but actually is, e.g. parallel running. Performance and capacity tests are important because the system must be demonstrated as performing adequately with a normal work-load. For instance this means demonstrating that it can run with tens of terminals not just the few used in ordinary testing. Another important example is human factors testing where a system is examined not so much in terms of its business and technical logic, but more for the human problem areas, e.g. glare from reflected light on VDU screens, or confusing error messages.

26.11   Certification

Certification and related schemes are an important part of quality generally. Perhaps the most important example is certification of quality management systems under BS 5750 as discussed in Chapter 15. Software is sometimes validated as complying with the appropriate standard by an organisation such as a professional body. A commercial example is the IDPM (Institute of Data Processing Management) schemes for certifying financial software. These schemes are, for example, particularly useful as a quality indicator for people selling or purchasing accounting packages. The certification process involves subjecting the software to a set of standard tests which cover the normal and legal business requirements. The limitation of the technique is that it can only apply to standard features.

Changing the emphasis from software to the whole system then auditing is a major certification process. Financial and other forms of auditing are really a method of certifying that systems meet their objectives satisfactorily. To pass an audit a system must be of reasonable quality and comply with recognised standards. Auditing tends to consider the whole of a system including staff and procedures from a particular perspective, e.g. the quality of book-keeping with a financial audit.

26.12 System tuning

'Tuning' refers to the adjustments necessary to improve the performance of a system. It can refer to any aspect of a business system such as the hardware, data, software, or office procedures. An example of hardware tuning is adjusting the position of files on magnetic disks to reduce the time spent accessing data. The speed of telecommunication lines can also be increased for faster VDU responses. Software can be tuned by identifying critical program code which is inefficient, and rewriting it. For instance this can be important where there are a large number of mathematical calculations, or where there are large data files with hundreds of thousands of records to be processed. In either case inefficient coding can make a big difference to the processing time. Office procedures can be tuned by simplifying or eliminating human work where possible.

26.13 Software tools

Most software development tools such as analyst workbenches improve quality, even if they just make the development process less laborious and improve presentation. Software tools like language compilers and analyst workbenches also include specific facilities which detect simpler errors such as DFDs where the boxes are isolated with no data flows in or out.

There are many software tools, or facilities within tools, which are used specifically for QA and QC purposes. These include:

- Static analysers which analyse program code for weaknesses and dangerous practices.
- Code auditors which check the program code for standards.
- Test harnesses − these are used for testing code modules which are intended to be run with supporting software.
- Test file or data generators − these generate an extensive number

of test cases by accepting a computer-readable description of the
test data required.

- Path or data flow analysers – these trace the execution path through
  the program code. Even spreadsheet software often includes facilities
  for stepping slowly through instructions to aid the identification of
  coding errors.
- Coverage analysers – these analyse the code covered by a set of
  tests. This is useful for identifying untested or lightly tested areas
  of code.
- Comparators – the output from a set of tests can be stored on
  magnetic disk and automatically compared with a set of expected
  test results also stored on disk. The software prints or displays any
  differences between the actual and expected results, and considerably reduces the checking required.
- Software 'instrumentation' – program code inserted in the software
  to monitor factors like usage.
- Performance monitors – these measure the use of machine
  resources.

26.14   Computer operations

Computer operations departments provide a set of services and the
routine of the work makes some aspects of QC more straight-forward.
Some quality metrics can be collected and analysed automatically. For
instance the use of hardware resources by an accounts system can be
analysed by a mainframe operating system. Many of the QC procedures
are merely standard accounting and administrative disciplines, e.g. the
segregation of duties described below. As mentioned in Section 26.2
above, computer operations departments can have formal service level
agreements with their users. These define such matters as the deadlines
for batch runs like printing payslips.

Just some of the approaches to maintaining quality of an operating
computer system include:

- *Inspection*
For instance checks on printed output to ensure there are no defects
such as faint printing.

- *Sampling*

Samples of input or output can be checked to ensure that errors remain minimal.

- *Testing*

Limited tests can be conducted with operational systems to ensure all is well. For instance the disaster procedures for a fire can be partially emulated to check that everything is satisfactory. The partial emulation consists, say, of asking the staff to imagine that there is a serious fire and requesting them to follow the emergency procedures. Such testing is often called a 'rehearsal' or 'drill' and is partly a form of refresher training for the staff concerned. Weaknesses are often exposed by disaster emulations − for example emergency exits cannot be opened, the fire proof safe containing security copies of data is left open, and the recovery instructions for setting up the systems at another computer site are inadequate.

- *Data validation*

Software should be designed so that data is rigorously checked as it entered. For instance, with a personnel system M or F might be acceptable as codes indicating male or female, and any other values would be rejected with a request for correct re-entry into the terminal.

- *Controls*

A good systems design ensures that significant totals are regularly checked to ensure that both the computer system and human users are doing the right thing. Segregation of duties is also important. See Section 11.11.

- *Security procedures*

For instance computer system passwords should be regularly changed to prevent unauthorised access. See Section 9.2.

- *Financial auditing*

Regular visits from an auditor ensure that weaknesses in the operational control of a system are detected. Such weaknesses may be either in the design or because staff have become lax. See Section 11.12.

- *User surveys*

Users can for instance be surveyed by questionnaire on how they perceive the quality of an IT service. Deficiencies or suggestions for improvement from the users' perspective can then be detected, and action taken.

As with all business activities computer operations should seek continuous improvement.

26.15 Summary

- IT systems development and operations can benefit considerably from quality management. Besides eliminating faults both can be continuously improved, e.g. by using new technology.
- An IT system is a mixture of hardware, software, interfaces, data, miscware, documentation, procedures, and people. Each of these components has its own quality considerations.
- Defect propagation is where a defect is passed through a series of processes without being eliminated. In some cases defects may be amplified.
- The main techniques for software quality control are inspection and testing. User acceptance testing is normally vital. Certification is important in some cases.
- Inspection, particularly on a group basis, is surprisingly efficient at detecting errors in documentation and software code.
- Completely rigorous testing is theoretically impossible. However careful test planning, design, and execution are essential quality assurance and control activities.
- Changes to systems should always be tested. Regression tests are also essential. This means testing the supposedly unaltered parts of an amended system.
- There are many different types of testing, e.g. white and black box testing, performance testing, and integration testing.
- There are many ways of ensuring the operational quality of computer systems, e.g. proper data control procedures and service level agreements.

Part 5
IT Management

Chapters 27 to 30 give the background to the computer industry and describe the management of business information technology. The general problems of technical projects and systems analysis are also discussed.

Chapter 27
An Outline of the Computer Industry

27.1 Introduction

This chapter outlines the structure of the computer 'industry'. In the context of this book the computer 'industry' covers organisations such as computer manufacturers and software houses. The wider IT industry, which in particular includes telecommunications, is *not* considered here.

Estimates of the world-wide computer industry are for sales of about $650 billion in 1992. For further details of the computer industry see Section 5.6. Most of the discussion below focuses on the UK, but as mentioned in Section 5.15 the European Community is now an important consideration. The West European software and computer services market alone has been estimated at $100 billion for 1993. Most UK businesses of any size, including IT companies, must now expect to operate in Europe, and European companies already operate in the UK. A good IT example of this is the Sema Group which is the result of a merger in 1988 between British and French companies. IT has always been a world-wide industry and dominated in the past by American multinational companies. This is likely to continue, but with European and Japanese companies having a more prominent role.

Systems analysts often work for organisations like software houses, though other titles such as systems consultant or systems engineer are used. Furthermore systems analysts who work for ordinary businesses are often involved in buying IT products and services. This has become even more important as there is a current business trend, mentioned in Section 5.16, which favours 'out sourcing' or 'contracting-out'. Facilities management, which is discussed below, is one example of out sourcing, and another example is contracting out software maintenance.

IT offers considerable opportunities for enterprise either in the form of off-shoots of existing businesses or entirely new companies. There have been spectacular successes like the emergence of Dell and Amstrad as personal computer suppliers in the 1980s. Of course the risks are high in IT and there have been numerous failures such as UK mini-computer supplier Digico which went into receivership in 1984.

27.2   Businesses selling IT systems and services

There are several types of business which exist primarily to provide IT-based products and services. Some examples include:

● *Freelance work*
Individual contractors hire out their systems development skills to other businesses. The most common form is contract programming where a person works alongside a client's own staff, writing say COBOL software. The contract with a client is for the duration of a project, often for a few months.

● *Employment agencies*
Agencies find employment for both ordinary employees and contract staff. Though in principle many types of staff can be handled, in practice it is often necessary to specialise in a field like IT.

● *Bureaus*
Computer bureaus (more correctly spelt bureaux) were originally formed to provide IT services for smaller companies which could not afford the expensive mainframe equipment of the 1960s and 1970s. Typically bureaus handled computer processing for accounting and payroll. Basically the input data was entered on forms and sent to the bureau who returned the input together with computer outputs such as sales invoices and print-outs. The charges for the bureau service were related to the amount of work done or computer time used.
Though bureau work has generally declined with the availability of small cheap computers it is still popular for payroll work. This is because payroll is such an awkward application with tight deadlines and frequent legal changes affecting software. Bureau work overlaps to some extent with facilities management which is explained below.

● *Facilities management (FM)*
This service is provided by specialist companies and involves taking over a substantial amount of a client's computing − both development

and operations can be considered. It can be seen as an extension of traditional bureau activities. There is a fear that the client might lose control of vital systems and be at the mercy of the FM supplier.

- *Software and systems houses*

Software houses basically produce package or bespoke software for their clients. Most software houses are small with say 10 to 200 employees. Figure 6.3 illustrates the organisation of a small software house. A few software houses are very large with several thousand employees. However large software houses tend to be amalgamations of smallish groups of employees sharing common facilities such as accounting and marketing. A software house sometimes provides hardware by recommending a particular equipment supplier. A systems house can provide hardware and maintenance services on its own account as well as software. Usually systems houses are bringing together equipment and software from various sources.

Many software houses tend to specialise in particular application areas called 'vertical markets', e.g. Peterborough Software with about 400 employees specialise in human resource systems and are probably the largest UK supplier in this field. Large general software and systems houses are usually divided into subsidiaries, divisions, departments, or teams specialising in particular areas. For example, Logica, as a large systems and software house, employed over 3700 people world-wide in 1991. It has separate subsidiaries covering IT application areas such as telecommunications, defence, finance, and industry.

- *Hardware suppliers*

Manufacturing IT equipment is quite an old industry in the UK. ICL, for example, traces its ancestry back to 1904. Although much manufacturing is international there is still a significant amount which is UK-based. Needless to say manufacturers often provide plenty of software with their equipment, particularly system software, e.g. operating systems and COBOL compilers. Many smaller suppliers exist both for peripherals and complete computers, e.g. Amstrad. There are also organisations which sell second hand hardware.

- *Consultancies*

Pure consultancies exist to advise organisations on computing as well as other business and technical matters. In theory they are objective.

Large consultancies are often associated with firms of accountants or software houses. Hardware and software suppliers often employ sales or systems consultants who have a good knowledge of how their products should be used, but they are obviously not impartial.

- *Miscellaneous*

Because information technology is so wide-spread it has led to a whole range of new businesses covering activities like on-line database operations, electronic publishing, IT training, and high-street equipment dealers. VANS (Value Added Network Services) are another important activity. An example is 'Telecom Gold' which is a public electronic mail service. IT is also supported by traditional but vigorous publishing of books and journals. For instance the trade journal 'Computing' has a weekly circulation of about 120 000.

As already implied there is often no clear distinction between the various types of IT business. So a software house may offer consultancy and commercial training.

27.3   The systems analyst in computer services

In the UK tens of thousands of systems development staff work in computer services, and the range of activities can be very large, from conventional business systems like accounting to defence work. As previously indicated computer service organisations like software houses vary enormously in size. At one end of the size spectrum is the one-person company used by contract systems analysts to sell their skills. At the other end of the size spectrum are companies like EDS (Electronic Data Systems) with 50 000 employees world-wide.

Systems analysis in computer services can differ from systems analysis in the internal IT department of a large business. The primary difference is that the computer services analyst usually works with paying customers, who are scattered across the country. By way of contrast the in-house analyst works with users who are frequently not charged for IT services. These users are fellow employees who are often located on the same factory or office site as the IT department. Though computer services are perhaps the most important example, there are other areas where systems analysts have a similar role, e.g. in sales support for computer manufacturers, or in consultancy. Some of the development-oriented work done by systems analysts in computer services is described in Section 21.11. But there are also after-sales and support activities such as working on help-desks and providing training courses.

27.4   IT departments acting as computer services companies

IT departments are discussed in depth in Chapter 28. Traditionally the IT users in an ordinary organisation cannot choose their IT supplier. They are forced to use their internal IT department. The economic advantages of a free customer-supplier relationship appeals to some organisations and it is an old and fairly popular strategy to at least partially simulate free market conditions internally. An IT department in this sort of situation is in effect forced to act more like a bureau and systems house and has to sell its services to user departments in the same organisation. In this environment IT services, such as the use of a systems analyst, are charged to the user at something approaching commercial software house rates (say £50 per hour). Where the user department also has the right to obtain IT services from outside the organisation, the internal IT department almost becomes a computer services company, and in some cases may take on commercial work from outside the organisation. In the public sector there is 'competitive tendering' where internal departments (not just IT departments) must bid for the work they do against outside suppliers. This happens for instance with street cleaning.

27.5   Business associations

For most major types of business there are various trade, professional, and other business associations. Crudely a trade association represents employers, and a professional association represents employees or the self-employed. However in both cases employment issues are just one concern amongst many, because as the names imply it is usually the whole of a trade such as computer services or the whole of a profession like accountancy that is of interest. Perhaps the major UK business association is the CBI (Confederation of British Industry). The following is a list of the more important computer associations in the UK:

- *The CSA (Computer Services Association)*

The CSA has a membership of about 300 software houses and computer bureaus. The CSA is a trade association which exists to promote computer services and maintain high standards of service and expertise amongst its members. It has specialist groups concerned with matters such as quality assurance, office automation, data protection, and defence work.

- *The British Computer Society and Institute of Data Processing Management*

These are both professional bodies setting their own IT examinations. They also promote many activities of interest to IT practitioners and their employers. Other professional bodies such as those for accountants also have IT-related activities. A sample of professional examination questions, many of which are IT-related, is included in Appendix III.

- *The NCC (National Computing Centre)*

The NCC is an important non-profit making organisation originally founded by the government in 1966 to promote the use of IT. It provides software services, training, information on IT, consultancy, and publications, often on a commercial basis.

- *User groups*

These are business associations for the users of particular types of hardware or software, for instance the IBM CUA (Computer User Association). Another example is DECUS, for users of Digital equipment, which has about 8000 UK members. Software houses often have user groups for their products. User groups provide a forum for discussions on the use of hardware and software, and a means of coordinating the communication of requirements to the hardware and software supplier. User groups may be administered by part-time volunteers from amongst the members, or by full-time staff.

The main value of all these organisations is that they provide excellent sources of business and technical information to the practising systems analyst and programmer. So the BCS has specialist groups covering a diverse set of IT subjects like expert systems, payrolls, databases, and software engineering. These specialist groups allow systems developers access to the latest thinking in a particular subject. This is done through meetings and publications. Trade and professional organisations also represent the interests of their members in political circles by influencing the government, particularly where legal and economic developments are concerned. The government often invites comments from such associations over proposed legislation. The proposals are included in official documents like 'green papers'.

One feature of trade and professional associations is that they impose minimum standards of behaviour on their members. These are enshrined in codes of conduct or practice. They are designed to guarantee that businesses and the public can have confidence in organisations or individuals who effectively claim membership of these associations as a symbol of quality. Breach of these codes, e.g. by unethical or incompetent conduct, can lead to the association taking disciplinary action against the member. As an example the CSA code of conduct imposes several commitments on members, some of which are listed below:

- To provide clear agreements which should be followed in good faith.
- To provide proper security for client's confidential information, records, documents, and programs.
- To provide good and safe working conditions for employees.
- To work continuously to improve employee skills.
- To refrain from recruiting other members' employees for the purpose of obtaining trade secrets and contracts.

27.6 Government support for IT

Governments have traditionally encouraged the IT industry for reasons like its importance in defence, and its perceived economic importance as an industry of the future. There are many ways in which governments can promote IT, e.g. offering military and civil service contracts or devising schemes which provide financial assistance to promote research.

Some examples are provided from history. The first punched card machines were developed for the US Census Bureau and used for the American census of 1890. During the Second World War the UK government designed and built Colossus. This was a wartime electronic computing machine for deciphering enemy coded messages. ENIAC, the first electronic computer, was constructed in 1945 in the USA for ballistics calculations. In the 1980s the aim of the American Defence Department with its Strategic Computing Initiative was to develop advanced military systems which included massive parallel processing, expert systems, and speech recognition. In the UK the Alvey scheme was set up in 1983 to provide funds for research and development into advanced IT in areas like software engineering and integrated circuits. Currently there is a European Community funding scheme called ESPRIT (European Strategic Programme for Research in IT).

On a more commercial level ICL received considerable financial support from the UK government during the 1970s. Also small computer businesses have been founded using the UK government Enterprise Allowance Scheme. This provides an entrepreneur with a small income for a year whilst he or she establishes their business. A further way in which governments affect IT is through legislation and this is discussed in Chapter 10.

27.7 Summary

- The computer industry is based on manufacturers, software houses, and a whole series of miscellaneous businesses such as those providing on-line database services.
- The work of the systems analyst in computer services has differences from the analyst in an ordinary business. Primarily an analyst in computer services is dealing with customers or potential customers rather than users.
- Ordinary IT departments can adopt the style of an independent computer company when dealing with their own internal users. This can mean that the user pays for IT services and is treated like a customer.
- Computer and related associations such as the BCS and CSA are an important source of information for systems developers.
- Government has an important influence on the IT industry, e.g. through defence work and funding schemes.

Chapter 28
IT Organisation

28.1 Introduction

This chapter describes how IT staff and their work is organised in an ordinary business, rather than an IT company. It gives a high-level view. A more detailed presentation of IT management is given in Chapter 30. Expenditure on all aspects of IT can range from a few hundred pounds a year in a small business to over £200 million per annum in a major bank. Clearly where the annual IT expenditure is measured in millions of pounds then the organisation of IT is a crucial issue.

Systems development staff rarely work alone, and most business computer projects involve several people. A list of the people inside an organisation associated with an IT project could include the user department manager, the administrative and clerical staff, auditors, the analysts, the programmers, and computer operations staff. External personnel could also be involved such as consultants and IT suppliers. Of course most of these people, including the analysts, work within a formal organisational structure. Typically this consists of several sections making up a department under the control of a manager. In addition to the permanent departmental organisation there is often an additional transient organisation which exists for the duration of an IT project. This is usually a set of temporary committees to control the project, and sometimes temporary teams to do the work.

28.2 Main functions

In the discussion below it is important to remember the fundamentals of IT employment. These fundamentals persist over decades and throughout most types of organisation. The two main areas of IT work, are 'development' (designing and producing systems), and 'operations' (using the IT equipment and associated systems).

Crudely, development is systems analysis and programming. Maintenance, that is the continual modification of existing systems, is usually classed as part of development for organisational purposes. Maintenance is the bulk of the work for analysts and programmers, and work on the development of new systems is less frequent.

A high street bank could process 20 million transactions per day, and handle over 10 million customer accounts, and this requires large-scale computer operations. Modern IT operations include activities like data entry, operating mainframes, controlling magnetic tape libraries (there can be thousands of tapes for a large mainframe installation), and supervising large telecommunication networks. Data control is an important operations function which, as the name implies, involves clerical control of the input and output of data with IT systems. There is a tendency for most books on IT, including this one, to concentrate on systems development and give a skimpy discussion on operations. However, operations, though undoubtedly humdrum, is more important on a day-to-day basis, and provides considerable IT employment. Where mainframes are necessary there is an increasing trend to automate computer operations which reduces the requirement for staff. Automatic operations are approached, for instance, by using software which requires little manual intervention, discouraging printing, and by restricting the use of magnetic tapes.

As discussed below there is always a debate as to the role of the IT users both in the development and operation of systems. For instance entering data in bulk from paper forms into computer systems can be part of the clerical job in a user department. Alternatively a specialist data preparation section can do the work as part of a computer operations department. Large specialist data preparation sections with tens of staff still exist, although they are declining.

28.3   Pre-classical IT organisation

Most early data processing equipment in, say, the period between 1920 and 1960, was controlled under an accountant, company secretary, or senior administrator. To some extent this survives in some businesses today where the finance director is in charge of the computer department. The accounting machine was one common electro-mechanical computing device which was, as its name implies, usually employed in an accounts office. Modern personal computer systems have encouraged a reversion to something similar to this early method of organisation. The punched card installations of the past had an accountant managing a supervisor in charge of operators and data preparation staff, i.e. something similar to the organisation for a small mainframe.

28.4   Classical IT organisation

Mainframe computers suitable for business were introduced in the 1950s and became popular in the 1960s. They were very expensive and difficult to use, needing specialists such as the systems analyst, programmer, and computer operator. The mainframe also demanded an expensive air-conditioned environment because the hardware produced considerable amounts of heat and was sensitive to dust and humidity. Data preparation staff were also required to transfer data from forms onto punched cards or punched tape for entry into the mainframe.

The inputing of large quantities of data and the distribution of the printed output required the supervision of specialist data control clerks. Most of the software was bespoke, i.e. specially-written for each organisation. This software was often written in second generation languages (also known as assemblers) or later using third generation languages like COBOL. Mainframe environments still retain some of these features in an updated form.

Mainframe technology was too expensive and too cumbersome to be used any other way. If a company was too small to afford a mainframe then a bureau service was the answer. Effectively this meant sharing mainframe facilities with other businesses.

Given this relatively primitive and expensive technology producing software was time-consuming and costly. Software packages were not popular until the 1970s. All these factors encouraged a central department under a data processing or computer manager. The organisational structure adopted is illustrated in Fig. 28.1.

Although criticised, the classical DP department of Fig. 28.1 is capable of considerable refinement. Its structure is still found in many organisations, though perhaps in a disguised form such as Fig. 28.4. In large modern versions various specialist functions such as telecommunications and quality assurance are included as separate sections.

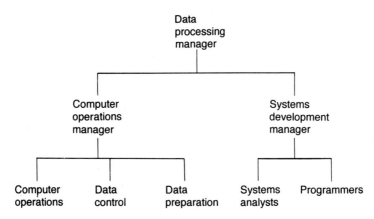

Fig. 28.1 The organisation of a classical data processing department in a medium-sized company using a mainframe.

28.5   Post-classical IT organisation

The main criticism of the classical data processing department was that it had a monopoly. Business systems were produced or amended slowly and IT staff were accused of not understanding or responding to the needs of their users. Also, of course, the systems used were inevitably ponderous and inconvenient by today's standards. The cheap easy-to-use technology of the late 1970s and 1980s allowed a more responsive approach to user needs, and several methods were adopted to provide this. The simplest approach was merely to call the computer department something more modern like an information services department, but otherwise retain a fairly classical organisation to support modern hardware and software systems. Some systems were based on mini- and personal computers in addition to those using mainframes. So an extra team of analysts and programmers was then specifically set up devoted to small business systems. This arrangement is still common.

Another popular idea is to set up an Information Centre or PC Centre, alongside the traditional DP structure. Such centres are discussed below and provide support to a user department which is interested in at least partially developing and operating its own systems. The users can develop and operate their systems on personal computers, mini-computers, or even mainframes by taking advantage of software packages and fourth generation languages. Figure 28.3 shows how the information centre is included alongside other more traditional functions.

28.6 Decentralisation

Instead of having one central IT department for a large organisation the alternative is several small IT departments. For instance each subsidiary in a group can have its own IT department. These IT departments can be autonomous, or part of a federation with a small central IT department setting the IT strategy for the group. There is a view that decentralised IT provides a more responsive service for user departments.

28.7 The IT subsidiary

Section 27.4 mentions that both public and private sector IT departments may have to compete to provide services to user departments. The user departments are often under no obligation to accept these services and can sometimes choose alternatives from outside the organisation. Some large businesses formalise this position by establishing a subsidiary company to provide IT services to the parent organisation and its other subsidiaries. The IT subsidiary is also encouraged to trade in information services in its own right as a profit-making organisation on the open market. One central government approach is to set up an IT 'agency'. An agency in this context is a civil service department with considerable independence (see also Section 5.16).

28.8 Parallel professions

There are several occupations related to systems analysis within a modern business. These include O&M (Organisation and Methods) which is an approach to improving office systems, OR (Operational Research) which is basically business mathematics, and work study which is the scientific approach to examining both manual and clerical work. Appendix II contains some details on these related occupations. In a large company there may also be internal management consultants and some personnel department staff who act as job analysts. They produce job descriptions and evaluate jobs for grading purposes.

In a manufacturing company there may be specialist engineers continually seeking improvements to manufacturing processes and helping to install new processes. Their work could include the administrative and staffing aspects. Various hybrid jobs exist with titles like 'industrial engineer'. This can involve both work study, production engineering (with some IT), and possibly OR. Professional statisticians are another related group of staff.

All these jobs can and do overlap. As their primary purpose is to help management operate and change a business there is a view that most of these occupations can be brought together in one department called a management services department. In practice this is often, but not always, a department predominately staffed by IT people with a some O&M officers and a few OR staff. An outline organisation chart for a management services department is shown in Fig. 28.2.

28.9   End user computing

IT in the early twentieth century office was controlled by administrators, particularly accountants. As regards computers, the technical end-users of computing service have often done their own programming. So engineers in the early 1970s would write their own programs, say in FORTRAN or BASIC, on-line via a teletype to a mainframe. Alternatively they might have a primitive mini-computer under their own control.

During the 1960s and 1970s business mainframe technology required

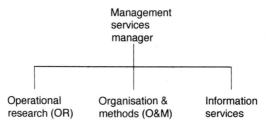

Fig. 28.2 The outline organisation chart of a management services department. The OR and O&M sections are often quite small. The information services department might be organised as in Fig. 28.1 or 28.3.

centralised control of the computer facilities under a DP manager. However the modern small mini-computer and the personal computer make it perfectly possible to resort back to office staff controlling their own data processing. The move away from mainframe-based systems towards smaller hardware configurations is sometimes called 'down-sizing'. End-user computing can mean that these staff are only responsible for computer operations such as changing the print ribbons or ink cartridges on printers and the regular security copying of essential data. It can also mean that staff are responsible for the software, even to the extent of writing their own programs. Often however there are some core software packages, say for accounting. The user staff then only 'program' the production of special reports using a report-generator or spreadsheets.

When the hardware or software is upgraded or otherwise changed, a user specialist takes a leading role with help from any external IT staff, say from a software house. To some extent this is the only way of working in a small business, although even in some large businesses users have been able to 'liberate' themselves from the control of a central computer department. Where the IT work becomes significant, full-time specialist IT staff may be employed in the user department with titles like systems administrator or user analyst.

However when every user department declares independence and installs its own systems, the consequence is anarchy. The practical results are inconsistent hardware and software, an unnecessary duplication of facilities, and the loss of purchasing discounts. One view is that these problems are small compared to the benefits. However there is the other difficulty of a lot of amateur systems. To meet these problems IT departments usually propose user control combined with some form of central regulation. One common approach, as already mentioned, is to establish an Information Centre which advises user staff and helps them install their own systems within a common IT strategy. This is sometimes called 'managed freedom' or 'regulated freedom'. The cynics refer to it as 'controlled chaos'.

28.10 Information centres

An information centre is essentially a section of an information services department which provides advice to users who wish to do their own computing. Its functions include:

- Elementary computer education.
- Training on the use of software products.
- Personal computer support including the installation of hardware and software and the provision of a 'hotline' enquiry service.
- Hardware and software product evaluation.
- Support for standard software products. A standard in this context is the local standard of the information centre. For example one standard might be to impose the exclusive use of the Lotus 1–2–3 spreadsheet.
- Security.
- Networking.
- Maintenance of hardware and software.
- The provision of assistance to users developing their own software, e.g. programming advice.

The information centre may cover just personal computers when it tends to be known as a PC centre. Often it covers central computing as well as the use of PCs.

28.11   Modern IS functions

A large modern IS (Information Services) department, in say an insurance company or government department, can employ several hundred staff, and there are various ways of organising them. Figures 28.3 and 28.4 give some idea of how a large centralised IS department is organised. The contrasting decentralised approach of several small IS departments is discussed in Section 28.6 above.

A large IT department can include numerous highly specialist jobs which are perhaps only part of the job of an analyst, programmer, or computer operator in a small company. Some of the more important jobs include:

- *Systems programmer*
The person who maintains the operating system and other systems software.

- *Network support officer*
This job involves monitoring and maintaining telecommunications networks.

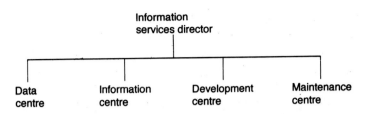

Fig. 28.3 One possible way of organising computing today. A 'centre' is just modern jargon for a department. The data centre is concerned with mainframe computer operations, and the information centre with helping users with their own computing either on PCs or on the mainframe. The development centre concentrates on producing new major software systems, and the maintenance centre on maintaining old ones.

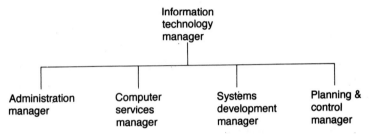

Fig. 28.4 The first level of managers for an insurance company with over 500 IT staff. The administration manager controls such matters as personnel management of IT staff and security. Computer services includes the data centre (computer operations) and telecommunications. Systems development is analysis and programming. Planning and control involves matters like IT strategy and quality assurance.

Some other jobs which effectively are specialised forms of systems analysis include:

- Database administrator

The person who controls and develops the use of large databases.

- *Quality or standards analyst*

This job is concerned with the quality management of systems analysis, programming, and operations. It also involves monitoring work to ensure standards and quality control procedures are actually employed in a proper fashion.

- *Capacity planner*

The planner ensures that the capacity of the hardware is adequate for current and future systems, e.g. ensuring that there is enough magnetic disk space. This job often comes under the computer operations manager.

● *Technical writer*

This job involves writing user manuals and help screens. It is an important occupation for a supplier like a computer manufacturer or a large software house.

The BCS (British Computer Society) publishes the ISM (Industry Structure Model) which defines most IT jobs, and factors such as their organisational level and the qualifications needed. It can be used for purposes like career planning and job design within IT.

It is common to group together some of the above jobs like systems programmer or database administrator into a 'technical support' section. This section provides technical assistance to both development and operations staff.

28.12   Project organisation

In addition to the permanent departmental organisation of a business there is often an additional temporary organisation to manage systems development projects. This temporary organisation exists for the duration of the project, say several months and possibly years. The temporary organisation often includes the systems development project team itself which is sometimes built up during a project and then dissolved at its end. The staff are then re-allocated to other work. The temporary project organisation almost invariably includes some kind of management committee or board staffed by both senior user and IT staff with perhaps somebody from general management. The purpose of the project board or committee is to direct and control the project.

28.13   Pools and teams

With regard to systems analysts and programmers there are two main methods of organising them. Firstly there can be a pool of analysts and a pool of programmers. Analysts and programmers are allocated work on the basis of availability and capability. This means that if an analyst has just finished a stock control assignment, his or her next task might be on accounting. In a small IT department ordinary managers can control this, but in a larger organisation some kind of matrix or account management are required (see Sections 6.9 and 28.14).

In the team approach there is a mixed team of analysts and programmers with perhaps six staff. They work on nothing else but one project. Alternatively they work for a fixed set of users in one application area, e.g. accounting systems. To allow flexibility these teams often have analyst-programmers who can switch between analysis and programming according to project requirements. As discussed above, a project team may be dissolved when its work is completed. A team supporting an applications area like accounting or manufacturing is sometimes misleadingly called a project team as well. Such teams can continue indefinitely with a mixture of development and maintenance work.

28.14 Account management

Some organisations with large IT departments imitate computer companies and use 'account' managers. The term comes from sales management where, for financial reasons, a customer is referred to as an 'account'. The idea is that each account manager looks after a particular set of users, e.g. the factory production department. The account manager's main responsibility is customer or user relations, and this can include acting as a:

- Salesperson − persuading users to take IT services.
- Project manager − organising and ensuring development work for a user is completed satisfactorily.
- Service manager − ensuring that the installed systems and services of a user continue to function well.

An account manager obtains whatever a user or project needs from other parts of the IT department, e.g. analysis skills, programming skills, or mainframe services. This sort of matrix management arrangement is discussed in Section 6.9 and used by large organisations, software houses, and computer suppliers.

28.15   Outsourcing

Outsourcing is letting outside businesses provide services. Facilities management (FM) is one form that was introduced in Section 27.2. Broadly FM is where an IT company agrees to take over all or part of the computer operations of an ordinary organisation. FM can also include the systems development activities. In theory the FM organisation has the extra skills and efficiency to offer the client business a good deal in terms of price and quality of service, and still make a profit. The client's computer staff are sometimes transferred to the FM company and are supposed to benefit by having better IT career prospects. Needless to say these benefits may or may not materialise. There is a fear that the client may surrender control of IT systems to the FM provider. However a good contract with a reputable provider is a reasonable defence against this.

Other forms of outsourcing include employing computer consultants and contract programmers, or contracting out some software maintenance work. Often consultants and contractors are fitted temporarily into a conventional section of systems analysts or programmers. See also Sections 9.7 and 9.8.

28.16   Computeracy

A substantial minority of office staff have always been familiar with information technology in its broadest sense for over 50 years. The personal computer and photocopier are, after all, merely the successors of the accounting machine and duplicator of the past. Surprisingly office 'labour saving appliances' were on the examination syllabuses of business professional institutes in the 1930s. However, as discussed, there was a period between 1950 and 1980 when IT facilities were often centralised in printing departments and mainframe computer rooms. This made IT more remote and mysterious to ordinary staff.

Much of the technological advance of the 1980s and 1990s has placed IT back in the office under the control of ordinary staff. In fact the use of office machines is now so widespread and so important that office workers find them difficult to avoid.

Modern professional and academic courses in business studies have also increased the amount of computing on the syllabus, and many business professionals have both substantial training and experience in IT. At a junior level most college clerical training includes a significant amount of practical IT such as the use of word processors and spreadsheet systems. IT training providers have also targeted user staff at all levels. The net result of this process has been a substantial increase in user IT expertise, sometimes referred to as computer literacy or 'computeracy'. Needless to say the level of user expertise is not consistent and ranges from poor to excellent. Systems analysts must of course accommodate these developments, and as discussed above, the information centre is one response.

One suspect conclusion from all this is that users can develop and operate their own computer systems. This leads to press articles with titles like: 'Does the IT Department Have a Future?'. The argument is justified by modern easy-to-use office technology and improved user IT training at all levels. However there are several fallacies here. One obvious objection is that if, say, personnel administrators are developing their own systems they cannot be carrying out their main duties thoroughly. A second objection is that different users inevitably develop systems in an inconsistent manner, and an organisation soon acquires incompatible hardware and software in various departments. A third objection is that integration or linking of systems between departments becomes much more difficult.

28.17 Hybrids and duals

One standard objection to computer staff is that they are over-technical and not interested either in their employing business or business in general. One inevitable consequence of this perceived perspective is poor systems that do not meet business and user needs. This rather slanderous view is often emphasised in a mildly abusive way by describing computer people as 'techies' or 'electronic plumbers', or more politely as 'technicians'. This is probably an unfair exaggeration, but combined with other trends it has been very influential as regards the organisation of IT. One defence by computer staff has been to use the word 'business' liberally at every conceivable opportunity, e.g. with phrases like business computing, business analysis, business-oriented, and business solution. Related words like 'commercial' are used to avoid monotony. This response is often summarised by the commandment 'IT must serve the business'. Doubtless it is a rather unconvincing slogan to both the business executive and clerk.

One superficially-attractive solution, much promulgated recently, is to provide extensive business education and training for systems analysts and computer managers. This view has the support of professional bodies and has for instance been promoted by the Institute of Data Processing Management (IDPM) for a long time. Some of the modern proponents tend to recommend a masters degree combining business and IT. Also in the UK there are many degree and sub-degree qualifications such as HNCs (Higher National Certificates) which make some concessions to this combined approach. They consist of either a little IT with business studies, or a little business studies with IT. All this leads to the concept of the 'hybrid' person who combines both business and technical expertise, particularly at a senior level.

An alternative concept is the 'dual', i.e. the person who is doubly qualified in business and IT. This again is quite an old idea and both colleges and professional bodies have always managed to persuade some technical staff (not just computing staff) to accept their business training. As just one example amongst many there is the financial diploma offered by the Certified Accountants.

A more alarming prospect for the traditional data processing person is the idea that technical personnel are not suitable for managing business computing. Furthermore they can be regarded as unsuitable for many aspects of business systems analysis. This leads to the idea that the managers of IT and systems analysts should be experienced in general business administration as well as holding formal business qualifications. Alternatively, as discussed above, users should have more control of IT. According to this view much of modern computing work only requires relatively low-level skills thanks to current technology such as application software packages and fourth generation languages. Any more advanced work, say on telecommunications, requires good technicians, firmly managed by people who are predominately business practitioners.

Professional bodies in the UK such as ICSA (Institute of Chartered Company Secretaries and Administrators), or those representing accountants such as CIMA (Chartered Institute of Management Accountants), have, for a long time, provided their members with IT management training as part of their main business education. A sample of the IT examination questions from these professional bodies is shown in Appendix III. As discussed before, academic institutions have more recently adopted this approach too, and are attempting to produce fully hybrid qualifications.

In software houses specialising in particular business areas such as pensions or accountancy, the use of fully-qualified or part-qualified business practitioners as systems analysts is quite common. With the internal financial systems of a large business, it is common to appoint a systems accountant to perform much of the analysis and design work associated with IT systems. The systems analyst liaising with a systems accountant inevitably has a more technical role.

28.18   User IT specialists

One old method of improving systems development and operations is to recruit users for IT work. This can be done in several ways. One way is to appoint a user IT officer who supports all the IT activities within, say, a personnel office. This person is sometimes called a user analyst and their job can include installing new equipment, developing systems, and liaising with an IT department or information centre for more advanced support. Another way is to recruit user liaison officers into IT systems development teams. This improves the understanding of the business and user requirements in systems design and implementation.

28.19   IT strategic planning

Sections 5.11, 8.9, and 8.10 introduced corporate and IT planning which leads to long-term strategies that guide the development of a business. Long-term in this context means over five or more years. Corporate plans cover such matters as developing new products and markets. Though the terminology is often confused, a strategy can be seen as a mixture of policies and outline plans. IT plans should aim to produce new systems, or adapt old systems, to support the future activities of the business. In practical terms IT strategic plans need to be aligned with overall business objectives and business plans.

Section 4.2 explains how an IT strategy can also lay down policy decisions. Such strategic policy decisions significantly affect the systems development work and its organisation. Some examples of IT policies or standards are:

- Wherever possible hardware is to come from one particular supplier such as Compaq for personal computers. Only ICL is to provide mainframes.
- All systems development is to be based on a specific 4GL like ORACLE.
- Software packages are to be used in preference to bespoke systems wherever possible.
- Systems are to be developed using a particular systems development methodology like IE (Information Engineering).
- The IT organisation is centralised.
- All recruits to systems analysis must have a relevant college degree or professional qualification.

An essential product of IT strategic planning, or information systems planning, or whatever term is used, is a long-term development plan. This in essence lays down the timetable for several years, and specifies which systems are to be developed and when.

A whole series of rival management techniques and methodologies are available to help prepare strategic IT plans. For example Information Engineering as a systems development methodology explicitly covers strategic IT issues. Another well-known planning methodology is BSP (Business Systems Planning) from IBM. A primary feature of this methodology is interviewing senior executives, and defining an information 'architecture' for the business. The architecture shows the relationship between business data, organisational processes such as purchasing, and the information systems. The priorities for developing the systems are based on what is useful to executives and criteria such as cost. There are software tools to help prepare strategic plans.

28.20 Summary

- IT work is divided into development and operations and this is capable of being organised in many ways. Operations is more important on a day-to-day basis.
- Classical IT departments provide a centralised development and

operations service to users. In a modified form this type of organisation is still popular for mainframe applications.

- Modern computing with its cheap reliable hardware and software has encouraged end-user computing.
- End user computing requires both regulation and support. The information centre and PC centre provide an important way of achieving this.
- Systems analysts may work in a separate group from programmers. Alternatively they may work in a combined team with programmers.
- Analyst-programmers are used for flexibility. Also more specialist types of analysis work exist, e.g. capacity planning.
- Account management is one way of co-ordinating the IT services provided to users.
- The level of user computeracy has increased considerably over the last few years. Users often have considerable experience and training in IT. Computer staff need to take this increased sophistication into account.
- Modern thinking about IT places considerable emphasis on business training for IT managers and systems analysts to the extent of recommending 'hybrids' or 'duals' who are trained in both business and technology.
- IT strategic plans need to be aligned with business plans.

Chapter 29
Project Failure

29.1 Introduction

Much of business systems development is concerned with project management. As a means of learning from the past this chapter outlines some well known examples of engineering and computer projects, several of which were dramatic failures.

Systems development mainly involves projects rather than routine work. These projects vary in size from, say, a few person-days, to a person-century. The project may be a simple piece of systems maintenance such as changing the layout of a mainframe print-out, or conducting a feasibility study for a new hospital computer system, or developing a nation-wide system for government administration. All projects from the smallest to the largest have an element of risk, and they can fail at all stages. To some extent there is perhaps a perverse tendency to concentrate on what goes wrong rather than what goes right. However computer projects are notorious for failure, and the computer press carries stories every week with headlines like:

- IT Project Spreads Alarm Through Whitehall
- Local Government Axes Software Project Because of Mounting Costs and Delays
- Financial System Fiasco Continues
- Payroll System Chaos

The more dramatic things that can go wrong on technical projects are illustrated by cases like the R101 airship. This airship came to grief as a blazing wreck on a French hillside. Engineering projects failures are instructive and contain important warnings for IT staff. Any IT manager or systems analyst wishes to minimise risks and it is a good idea to learn from other people's mistakes. Whilst the examples discussed below mainly concern development failures it is worth remembering that systems also fail in use because of poor operations practice.

Dramatic examples of this can occur, for instance an aircraft collision. Sometimes a development or design fault is compounded by operational errors. This was the situation in 1979 with the nuclear reactor accident at the Three Mile Island power station in the USA.

29.2 Some major non-computing failures

Engineering has lot in common with IT systems development, which indeed some people see as a form of engineering. In particular the aviation industry is a rich source of dramatic examples for IT projects. Aviation, like IT, is based on a continually advancing technology. It is commercially important, and constantly offering new opportunities and the threat of obsolescence. A common fear, frequently mentioned by computer project managers, is a project like the Concorde airliner, i.e. a project which is technically successful, but costs too much, takes too long to develop, and is no longer relevant commercially when it is eventually completed.

The failed engineering projects below illustrate a multitude of problems. These include trying to implement a half-proven concept, over-optimistic planning, poor estimating, design weaknesses, poor management, pressure to achieve results making a bad situation worse, and poor quality control. Similar problems occur in abundance on computer projects.

- *The Panama Canal*

The French engineer de Lesseps successfully completed the Suez Canal in 1869. In the 1880s he organised a company to dig a canal across the isthmus of Panama. The estimating of the engineering work was over-optimistic, there was financial mismanagement, and tropical diseases badly affected the work force. Ultimately the company was forced into liquidation and de Lesseps was sentenced to imprisonment for fraud. Needless to say, little useful work was done. Later the Americans successfully constructed a similar canal in Panama.

- *The R101 airship*

In the early part of the 20th century airships seemed to have better transport potential than aeroplanes. The R101 was a commercial airship designed in the UK in late 1920s. It crashed in flames in France in 1930 on its maiden flight to India. It had experienced design problems such as inadequate lifting capacity, and delays in the building programme. The authorities were under pressure to demonstrate successful results. This led to the flight despite inadequate testing and known problems with the airship.

- *The Comet airliner*

The Comet airliner was designed in the UK in the late 1940s and was flying in the early 1950s. The first few models all crashed in mysterious circumstances killing the passengers and crew. Careful examination of the wreckage, and tests, demonstrated a design weakness which caused the metal around cabin windows to fail. This had not shown up in tests before the aircraft had been flown, because of subtle differences between the conditions during testing and the conditions during operational flights. Even with hindsight this appears to be one of the almost unavoidable risks associated with new technology.

- *TSR2 and the Concorde*

The TSR2 was a 1960s military aircraft project originally budgeted at £90 million. Costs continued to rise and the project had a likely completion cost of £750 million when it was eventually cancelled.

The design of Concorde, the Anglo-French supersonic airliner, in the 1960s is a classic example of commercial failure being combined with technical success. The plane flies well and carries passengers super-sonically. However its development costs were grossly over budget, it had environmental problems, and it could not compete economically with jumbo jets. The project could not be cancelled because of the contractual agreement with the French who were partners in the project.

- *The collapse of Rolls Royce*

In the late 1960s and 1970s Rolls Royce tried to develop a new aero-engine the RB 211. The excessive costs and delays in developing the new engine caused the whole company to become insolvent. There were many factors in the Rolls Royce 'crash', amongst which were competitive pressure, poor estimating, mismanagement, and over-confidence derived from a successful history in developing aero engines.

- *The Flixborough explosion*

In 1974 the Flixborough chemical works of Nypro exploded killing 28 people and injuring almost 100 more. Two thousand buildings in the vicinity were damaged. The accident was caused by the failure of some temporary pipework which was inadequately designed, and there was no safety testing.

● *The Hubble telescope*
In 1990 the Americans launched the Hubble astronomical telescope into earth orbit. The telescope focusing was discovered to be seriously faulty due to errors in the main mirror. Correcting the fault whilst the telescope is in orbit is going to be difficult and very expensive. Simple mistakes in quality control procedures during manufacturing were the cause. Budget and political pressures are also seen as contributory factors.

29.3 Engineering successes

As illustrated above the history of engineering is full of disasters. It is similarly full of successes, and to preserve some sort of balance it is important to mention a few. Some well known examples are:

● *The Wright brothers*
The Wright brothers are an inspiration to any individual inventor or pioneer. They were bicycle mechanics who invented and built the first modern aeroplane entirely by their own efforts in 1903.

● *The Panama Canal*
As mentioned above the Panama Canal was eventually opened successfully by the Americans in 1916. This was the result of careful planning and management.

● *Rocketry*
During the period 1932 to 1944 to Germans overcame all the severe engineering problems associated with liquid fuel rockets and developed the V2 missile.

● *The Manhattan project*
The successful development of the atomic bomb by the Americans during the Second World War was based on fundamental research in

physics. However the real achievement was the enormous engineering and industrial project required to produce the nuclear explosive and weapons.

29.4 Some major computer failures

• *Victorian calculating machines*

Charles Babbage was a mid-19th century professor of mathematics who attempted to build large mechanical calculating machines called difference engines which could weigh several tons. They were intended to calculate tables of figures for purposes such as navigation and life assurance. Babbage later designed a mechanical computer (called an analytical engine). Babbage received considerable financial support from the UK government. However he failed to construct more than a small working demonstration model of his difference engine. He is believed to have failed primarily because of project management problems. The design of his machines has been demonstrated to be sound. His tendency to continuously revise his ideas and to be over-ambitious certainly did not help. Two Swedes, a father and son, called Scheutz, used Babbage's ideas to construct working difference engines, but there was very little interest in using them, and their achievement fell into obscurity. Basically the Scheutz family had marketing problems.

• *DVLC*

A famous problem project in central government was the computerisation of DVLC (Driver Vehicle Licencing Centre) in the 1970s. By 1975 the project was late and its cost doubled from the original estimates to £350 million. The number of staff required to run the system increased from 4000 to 8000. The new centralised system cost more to run than the old manual system operated manually from local offices. DVLC is also quoted as an example of inadequate attention to human factors in job design in the 1980s. Clerical jobs were very narrowly designed, tedious, and closely monitored. It was difficult for an individual to get a clear view of the whole system, and motivation and output were low. For example there was one job for opening mail, and another for examining its contents. Staff were also not trained to handle telephone queries or errors. Delays of months could result in processing applications for licences which gave the Centre a bad reputation. To improve matters jobs were redesigned and small teams of staff created.

- *Nimrod*

The Nimrod project of the mid 1980s was an airborne defence early warning system. The airborne computer hardware was found to be inadequate and it was difficult to make the software identify radar images. After spending £800 million the project was scrapped and a competing American system purchased.

- *Social security*

American social security systems are large and complicated, as are their UK equivalents. The American Social Security Administration (SSA) needs to hold details on 260 million people. It administers major income support and social service programmes, and is strictly controlled by complex legislation. From its beginning in the 1930s until the 1960s it had been a leader in applying IT. By 1982 the computer systems contained over 12 million lines of COBOL and other program code which had been developed over many years. The systems were also technologically out-of-date, and mainly undocumented. Systems maintenance was made more difficult by continual legislative change. There were problems with the computer operations, e.g. old mainframes. Also the 500 000 magnetic tapes used to store social security data were disintegrating and this caused errors and reruns. In 1982 a full systems modernisation plan was adopted which involved projects like improving equipment and the use of software engineering disciplines to upgrade existing software. The modernisation was expected cost one billion dollars by 1992. The SSA management claimed a 25% improvement in productivity due to the plan. As a simple example, IT improvements reduced the time to receive a social security card from six weeks to ten working days.

There is much more to this complicated case such as the managerial problems and pressure from the American government for premature staff savings. Also, unlike most of the other cases above, this one continues into the future. However one IT lesson is that a huge organisation like the SSA can go from being a leader in IT to being endangered by old undocumented systems.

● *The £105 million mistake*

One job of the UK Department of Employment is calculating the retail price index. There was a miscalculation of the index for 18 months from 1986 due to a simple error in computer software. This meant that index-linked state social security benefits were under-paid by £105 million, which eventually had to be repaid.

29.5 Major computing successes

Again to preserve some sort of balance it is only fair to mention some of the successes in computing:

● *Harvard Mark I*

One of the first computers was completed in 1944 and called the Harvard Mark I Automatic Sequence-Controlled Calculator. It was built by Howard Aiken of Harvard University with help from IBM. The Mark I was used for about 15 years (far longer than any modern computer). Aiken had the benefit of studying the ideas of Babbage and others. He also used the proven electro-mechanical technology of the era, and had good management and financial backing.

● *Apple computers*

Steve Jobs and Stephen Wozniak built their first personal computer in a garage. In the late 1970s they founded the hugely successful Apple computer corporation – see Section 5.6 for the business metrics.

● *COP (Computerisation of PAYE)*

This was a very successful Inland Revenue project in the 1980s. The purpose of COP is to computerise the administration of employee income tax. The project was estimated to cost £180 million at 1980 prices and it was planned to eliminate several thousand jobs. In 1991 the networked computer system had about 40000 terminals nation-wide and held the records of around 30 million taxpayers.

29.6 Minor horror stories from business computing

The problems of the R101 or the Rolls Royce collapse were fundamental managerial flaws rooted in excessive optimism early in a project, and then a failure to act on this when the problems become only too apparent later. In such situations there are often early warnings which are ignored.

The following examples describe failures connected with various stages in computer projects over the period 1960 to 1990. The scale is far less grand than the famous engineering disasters above, but the problems are similar. Some of the details have been changed to conceal the identity of the organisations concerned.

- *IT product names*

As discussed in Section 10.10 and 10.11 trade names are important forms of intangible property which have commercial value because of the 'goodwill' associated with them. For any product or service the main objective is clearly to find a convenient and distinctive identifier with attractive associations. The problem is that the attractive names are over-used, e.g. names from Greek and Roman mythology. For instance Pegasus, the mythological flying horse, is currently used as the name of a company producing accounts software. The name has also been used for a 1950s computer, an aero-engine, and a despatch service.

One particular software house adopted the name SEXTANT for its new financial software package, despite warnings that this was likely to have been used by other companies. No search was conducted to refute or confirm the doubts. A rival company then wrote saying that they had the 'rights' to this name, which they had been using for years. The original software house was forced to change the product name to COLMAN. Having learnt the lesson from the first name the software house conducted a search which confirmed that COLMAN was not used in their field. The necessary changes to all the sales and other literature were expensive and time-consuming. As an ironic touch a Mr Colman wrote to the software house protesting that his name was being used. Although he had no legal right, he suggested that the software house change the product name.

- *Under pricing*

Several software houses bid for a fixed price contract to write programs to clear specifications for a factory production system. The directors of the customer company chose the lowest bid, which was only 30% of the next lowest bid. The factory computer staff warned that according to their internal estimates the lowest bid would lead to big losses for the software house concerned. They doubted that the cheapest software house would complete the job satisfactorily. The directors however stuck to their 'bargain'. The cheapest software house had soon spent more on wages than the bid price and was nowhere near completing the work. Eventually it defaulted on the contract and withdrew its staff without receiving any payment. The software was not completed, and legal action was not worthwhile.

The customer had to go back to the other software houses who had originally bid for the work. They all refused to bid for fixed price contracts again. The only terms on which they would accept the work were by payment according to the amount of programmer time used – at say £45 per hour. A well-established software house was chosen and the project was completed at a cost 20% higher than the highest original fixed-price bid. The project was also late because the original software house had defaulted. However the final quality of the software was good. There are lessons here on the difficulty of estimating even for a fixed well-defined piece of work. Also, of course, trying to drive too hard a bargain or to exploit a major weakness is often counter-productive.

- *Over-commitment*

A software house was concerned about lack of business and was tendering simultaneously for work to deliver bespoke systems to several large customers. The possibility of winning orders from several customers simultaneously was dismissed as remote. Unfortunately the software house did receive several large orders nearly simultaneously from customers who all wanted the work doing during the same period. The only way out of the situation was to offend one very large customer by declining to do the work in the originally quoted period, or indeed within any sensible timescale. As a result the software house lost a large attractive contract. Also a prestigious customer was lost for ever to the competition. The software house then put a moratorium on all sales activities for several months and did successfully retain all its other customers, ultimately completing their projects successfully. Clearly this is a common problem for software houses and to a lesser extent for internal IT departments. Next to the fear of too little work is the fear of too much. The usual attitude, as here, is that the latter situation is by far the better of the two evils. Though the problem in this case was perhaps unavoidable, the initial attitude was too cavalier, and a proper response to over-commitment was not thought through in advance.

- *New equipment*

A manufacturing and wholesaling company wished to install a new model of computer and new on-line systems. The mainframe computer supplier was given a full specification of the business and technical requirements of the proposed new systems. The supplier then put in a sales proposal based on its mainframe system and the customer's requirements specification. The proposal was accepted and the mainframe installed. Firstly the high-speed printer was discovered not to take multipart pre-printed stationery without jamming. Fortunately the customer's staff had included all the stationery requirements in their system specification. As a result the supplier had to provide another more expensive printer for the original price. Later the telecommunications software was discovered to be defective and would not work. It required numerous and lengthy tests to demonstrate that the supplier's communications software was at fault and not the customer's application software or the hardware. Relationships between the customer's staff and the supplier's staff became acrimonious. Eventually everything was put right. However, this cost the supplier the price of the extra equipment supplied free-of-charge, and both customer and supplier lost the staff time spent in investigating and rectifying the problems.

- *A complete failure*

A company decided to completely revamp its distribution systems by establishing new administrative IT systems for sales orders processing and sales accounting in new offices. The installation of the IT systems was a complete disaster. For example the company, for a while, lost track of what goods had been despatched or which customer had received them. The cause was grossly incompetent systems development and bad implementation.

- *Defective software*

A sales invoicing and sales ledger system was amended by a major manufacturing company. The system was supposedly fully tested by a systems analyst. A couple of weeks later customers complained about wrong invoices. On investigation the software proved to be defective, and it was estimated that about one in ten invoices had been wrong over the previous fortnight. Several thousand invoices had been sent out to customers over the period, and they all had to be carefully examined to see if they were affected by the fault. If they were affected the customer had to be contacted with some embarrassment, and manual corrections made to the invoices. This required considerable overtime working by the computer and sales accounting staff. The cause was incompetent testing. On examining the systems analyst's documentation several examples of the fault were found in the computer test results, but they had not been recognised.

29.7   Some conclusions

As the above examples suggest there is a spectrum of project results ranging from a catastrophe to a brilliant success. There are of course many projects, computer or otherwise, that are mediocre or combine good and bad features. There are numerous detailed explanations of why individual projects fail. The main reasons suggested by textbooks and practitioners for the failure of administrative IT projects include:

- Lack of user participation.
- Lack of planning and control.
- Poor management.

In the author's experience, whilst these are often not perfect, they are not the main reasons for failure. User participation, planning and control, and adequate management, are necessary, but not sufficient conditions. Good design and good quality assurance are essential. Risk, particularly with innovative systems and large projects, is also a major factor. However project risks can sometimes be quantified. Mathematical techniques and software tools are available to examine the risks and potential benefits in a project. Needless to say all techniques and tools have limitations and require reasonable data. For instance even with hindsight could any sensible assessment be made of the probability of success for the Wright brothers? Fortunately most IT projects are not novel and there is usually some data and experience to guide IT managers and their staff. Whilst there is no *guaranteed* method of ensuring a successful project there are approaches that minimise the risk of significant failure. Chapter 30 discusses some of the more routine problems in IT systems development and their solutions, as well as methods for managing IT projects.

As some of the examples above suggest, human folly and wishful thinking often have a major role in most project disasters. Realistic thinking at least means that major failures can be identified early and hard decisions taken like terminating the project rather than continuing to throw good money after bad. In practice, as the R101 and Rolls Royce collapse show, this may be politically and emotionally difficult.

29.8 Summary

- Computer projects have a reputation of being subject to failure.
- Well-known failures such as the R101 airship or Comet airliner contain lessons for IT staff.
- Major failures on both computer and non-computer projects can often ultimately be attributed to collective folly.
- Poor initial estimating and planning at the feasibility stage often lead to cost and time over-runs as the original estimates and plans are invariably over-optimistic. This was a major factor in the insolvency disaster of Rolls Royce, and the Concorde and TSR2 projects.
- Other project errors include bad design, e.g. the R101; inadequate quality control, e.g. the Comet airliner and R101; and poor maintenance, e.g. Flixborough.
- Further difficulties can be caused by: legal problems such as difficulties with intellectual property rights; poor contracts; and inadequate consideration of human factors when designing clerical procedures to support IT systems.
- Project management attempts to manage and contain risk. Quantitative techniques and software tools can be used to assess the risks in a project.
- Realistic thinking and making hard decisions about projects may be difficult to achieve in practice, but it is often necessary.

Chapter 30
Management of Systems Development

30.1 Introduction

This chapter provides an elementary view of the management of business systems development with the emphasis on the conventional systems analysis aspects. As described in earlier chapters systems analysis and programming can be expensive and important activities. They must therefore be managed to ensure as far as possible a business and technical success and minimise the consequences of any failure.

As Chapter 29 explains there are various ways of organising the systems analysis and programming functions. These functions can also be combined with related disciplines such as operational research. Often, but not always, a manager is in charge of both analysis and programming. Sometimes a computer operations role is also combined with analysis or programming, particularly in a small business. Systems analysts themselves often act as project managers, and they often have other staff under them. For instance, a senior systems analyst may supervise a couple of systems analysts, a consultant or contractor, and a trainee.

30.2 POSDCIR and IT management

POSDCIR is a useful acronym for summarising the nature of management. POSDCIR stands for Planning, Organising, Staffing, Directing, Controlling, Innovating, and Representing. It was discussed in Section 8.4 from a general point of view and is illustrated below in an IT context:

- *Planning*
A fair amount of IT management is devoted to producing plans. There should be a hierarchy of compatible plans ranging from a long-term strategy for IT covering the whole organisation, to a schedule of next

month's work for the analysts and programmers in the marketing systems team. Good plans are an essential ingredient in successful IT management.

- *Organising*

The organising role of a systems development manager is greater than that of most other managers of equivalent status such as accountants. The reason is that much of the work of the systems development manager is governed by projects, and to some extent each project needs its own special organisation. By way of contrast the work controlled by many user managers is of a more settled nature. Still, even for a systems development manager the general organisational framework is fixed in the short term. However new projects may require the assembly of new teams, which is often done by taking staff from old teams as well as recruiting new staff. In addition to assembling a team to develop new systems, the manager must also ensure that there are project boards or committees to supervise the progress of the project until it is complete.

- *Staffing*

The staffing (human resources) required for systems development is by no means under the exclusive control of the systems development manager. When appointed the manager usually inherits any previous staff. Furthermore he or she must follow the human resource policies of the organisation as a whole. Staff issues are discussed in Chapters 13 and 14.

- *Directing*

Direction in IT is to a large extent provided by corporate plans, IT plans, and IT policies. It is, of course, the role of IT managers to interpret these in a practical way for their staff.

- *Controlling*

As already implied, the hard part of IT management is actually complying with plans. Control implies a system for monitoring progress and taking corrective action if there are any significant departures from the plan. It could also mean, for instance, disciplining an analyst for persistently producing unsatisfactory specifications.

- *Innovating*

In an era of ceaseless change and technical progress every manager must innovate to some degree. This is particularly true in business systems where the underlying technology can change significantly over a three year period. In practice innovation often means small improvements like introducing new software tools.

- *Representing*

Both managers and systems analysts often have a representative role. They must represent the IT function at internal business meetings. They must also represent the business to salesmen, and if they work for an IT business they must represent it to customers.

30.3 Principles of project control

The essence of project control is to ensure that sensible plans are prepared and met. The plans may be the basis of legally binding contracts for a software house. Even with in-house users they form part of a kind of quasi-contract. Sections 19.7 to 19.9 explains how cybernetics provides a model for controlling all sorts of managerial and administrative activities. Basically the project plan represents a standard that must be achieved, and a simple example is shown in Fig. 30.1. Actual progress on the project is fed back and compared to the plan and any departures require correction. So if a project is running a few days late the action required may be overtime working to make up the lost time.

The plan itself is based on the work that must be done and the resources available. So the plan in Fig. 30.1 is based on the work necessary to investigate a purchase ledger system and prepare a feasibility study using two analysts as the main resource.

Budgets are really resource plans. Budgetary control involves comparing the actual use of resources to that allowed or estimated as reasonable to achieve objectives. Many budgets are financial, e.g. human resources are costed using wage rates, and an example of this type of budget is shown in Fig. 11.2. Some resource plans may be expressed in other terms such as person-days. In terms of control theory, budgetary control attempts to plan the use of resources, particularly finance, and to take corrective action if the use of these resources is excessive.

Task	Analysts	Task Completion Date
* 1. Collect all existing documentation on purchase ledger IT system	Robin	26/3/93
* 2. Interview accounts and purchasing management	Robin	2/4/93
* 3. Interview accounts staff and collect forms	Marion	2/4/93
* 4. Interview purchasing staff and collect forms	Robin	16/4/93
* 5. Interview internal audit	Marion	23/4/93
* 6. Interview computer operations staff	Marion	23/4/93
* 7. Investigate options for new system	Robin/Marion/ John	21/5/93
* 8. Prepare feasibility study	Robin/Marion	18/6/93
* 9. Check feasibility study	John	25/6/93

Fig. 30.1 A simple timetable or task-list (with dates) used for project control. The project in this example is to prepare a feasibility study for improvements to a purchase ledger system. The staff concerned may well have other work during the same period. The timetable can be refined to include extra data such as start-dates and the number of person-days per task.

All plans make assumptions and often contain explicit allowances for problems or 'contingencies', for instance the sickness of key members of the project staff. Sometimes excessive contingency allowances are covertly built into a plan. This practice, sometimes known as 'padding', involves techniques like deliberately over-estimating the amount of work required in person-days and deliberately under-estimating the productivity of staff. This practice makes it relatively easy to achieve targets like the delivery date or budgeted salary bill, because the padded estimates cover most contingencies. The objection is not so much to the practice itself but using it in a manner that is deceptive.

30.4 Simple project control

One of the most elementary forms of project control is a timetable or task list showing the tasks to be completed, the staff names, and the completion dates. These task-lists as shown in Fig. 30.1 are simple to understand and easy to prepare. They are useful and frequently used. They allow management and users to keep track of a project by comparing actual completion dates against expected dates and to take appropriate action where there are delays or other problems. As explained in Section 19.8 this is normal feedback control. However feedforward control can also be used, but this involves prediction. As an example Robin in Fig. 30.1 is taken ill after commencing work on the project. The forecast is that he will not return to work within twelve weeks. This will clearly delay the project by many weeks if no special action is taken. However if his colleague Alan can be allocated to the project in his place then the disturbance could be minimal.

On a simple project like the feasibility study of Fig. 30.1 the project manager would have a quick review with the staff every week, followed by a brief verbal report to user and IT management. There might be a formal project committee meeting once a month when this, and probably other projects would be considered. The project committee would consist of representatives of general management, the users, and IT staff. Its purpose would be to review progress on projects, and authorise any major corrective action or any major changes in the design or implementation of IT systems.

The use of simple timetables has several problems. For instance there is no explicit allowance for the fact that staff might be working on another project, nor is the work content of each job shown in person-days. However as hinted there is often an implied and rough-and-ready allowance made for such problems when setting the completion date of a task. Barcharts, called Gantt charts, show similar information to a simple timetable but in a more graphic manner. An example of a Gantt chart is shown in Fig. 30.2. A more complicated example of project planning is illustrated in Section 24.8 where the implementation of pension systems is used as an example.

30.5   Advanced project control

These days only the simplest projects are tackled by drawing up simple timetables. More sophisticated approaches, which are often used together, include:

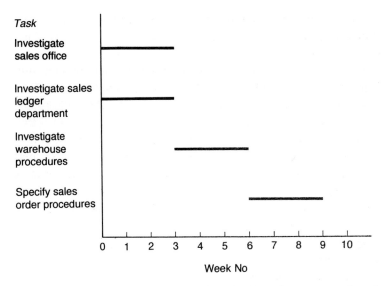

Fig. 30.2 An illustration of a Gantt chart. Project planning software can produce these charts very easily.

- *Advanced planning techniques*

One example is the use of planning networks where a project is seen, and diagrammed, as a network of interlinked tasks to be completed in a particular sequence. Such techniques are frequently supported by software tools.

- *The use of a formal project control methodology*

One example is PRINCE (PRojects IN Controlled Environments) which is used for large projects. The PRINCE procedures are extensive and require several volumes of documentation to explain them in detail.

- *The use of software tools*

Project management software is in common use and assists in the preparation of plans such as timetables and charts. More sophisticated is an IPSE (Integrated Project Support Environment) which attempts to integrate all the software tools used on a project into a harmonious whole. For example computerised project status reports can use data collected from the individual CASE tools used by each person on a project. In this instance the project status would automatically be updated as each data flow diagram is completed with a CASE tool.

The project control methodology should be compatible with the development methodology, e.g. PRINCE is compatible with SSADM. As illustrated in Section 18.15 a methodology such as SSADM provides a complete breakdown of an analysis and design project into dozens of pre-defined steps each of which are further sub-divided into small tasks. This makes project management easier. Project control methodologies include an arrangement of controlling boards or committees, incorporate quality assurance, and use standardised planning and reporting documents.

30.6   Quantitative techniques

The preparation of timetables and Gantt charts implies some form of estimating. Thus for programming work the number of lines of code, written in COBOL say, is often estimated for each module and program to be produced. The number of lines of program code can be converted into the number of programmer-days required. A productivity rate is assumed, e.g. 20 documented and tested lines per day. Estimating programming work is not too difficult when it is based on experience and a good system design specification.

The general application of quantitative techniques is discussed in Chapter 25. In the context of project control they also have considerable application as the example in Section 25.12 illustrates. At a more mundane level the following example shows how the duration of a task is determined:

- Investigating warehouse procedures is estimated to require 6 person-days.
- The analyst concerned is available for only half of each working day because of involvement in other projects.
- The initial estimate of working-days required is:

$$\frac{6}{0.5} = 12 \text{ working days}$$

- The analyst is on holiday for a week during the period of the

investigation. Therefore the *estimated* elapsed time is: 12 + 5 = 17 working-days.
- The agreed start-date is Monday 14th June 1993 therefore from the calendar the completion date is Tuesday 6th July 1993.

Clearly there are a several assumptions here. Firstly the job is assumed to be 6 person-days. Secondly a person-day refers to some kind of average person and the actual analyst might be better or worse than average. This can be crudely taken into account by scaling the original estimate up or down to allow for the weakness or strength of the individual actually assigned to the job. Thirdly of course there is no allowance for factors like sickness or overtime working.

30.7 Project data collection

Formal control of an IT project requires considerable documentation. For example:

- The original project plan.
- Timesheets need to be completed by analysts and programmers each week recording the amount of time spent on each of their tasks during the week, and the status of each task at the end of the week.
- The timesheet data needs to be fed into a project planning computer system and various reports produced showing the current and predicted situation.
- Progress reports need to be prepared giving the status of projects and recommending any special action by managers or committees.

30.8 Project infrastructure

The successful systems development manager and successful analyst devote considerable time to ensuring that the 'infrastructure' of a project is right. The infrastructure is all the factors that help a project reach a successful conclusion. Some infrastructure matters, like the development methodology and the software tools to be used, are often pre-ordained, e.g. by IT policies. However IT managers and their analysts can adopt various approaches prior to a project to improve its infrastructure. Some examples are:

● *Senior management commitment*
In particular the senior management must provide active support and some degree of personal involvement.

● *Access to all relevant data*
This could include computer department standards manuals, planning data such as staff performance rates, and the IT and business plans.

● *Management framework*
Establishing a proper project control framework like PRINCE is essential.

● *Establishing good relations*
There must be good relationships and good communications with the user management and other interested parties such as auditors.

● *Promoting cooperation and participation from user staff*
This can be done through presentations on the purpose of the project and explaining the roles of users and analysts. Some techniques like prototyping are good for demonstrating a genuine commitment by IT staff to user participation.

● *Informal resolution of minor problems*
For example suppose the user management have complaints about the quality of an analyst's systems implementation work. It is better that these issues are raised informally with the project manager by pre-arranged agreement. This allows the problem to be solved before coming to the attention of the formal project committee.

● *Ensuring that answers are ready in advance*
Standard answers are needed for potential problem areas. For example questions on possible staff redundancies resulting from new IT systems could be answered by reference to new technology agreements as discussed in Section 13.5.

- *Specialist training*

Some elementary general computer training can also be arranged for users. Systems analysts may need prior training as well, for instance a course on accounting for analysts who have no prior knowledge of the field.

- *Quality assurance*

For instance the means of certifying the correctness of specifications and software need to be established with users early in a project.

- *Organising the analysis team*

All relevant skills need to be available to the project team, e.g. by using user liaison officers, business consultants, and operational research analysts.

30.9 Special features of systems development

Are there any special aspects of systems analysis and programming which make them different from any other business and technical activities? A common management answer is that all the differences are minor and that the principles of good management apply to systems development much as they do for any other business and technical work. It is sometimes difficult to persuade people that systems development is significantly different from project work in building or engineering. In fact any attempt to claim systems development as different is seen as preparing excuses for poor performance.

However some people argue that the abstract nature of systems analysis and programming means that systems development is not the same as other jobs. Progress whilst constructing a ship or a building is visible in a very tangible way. Software and office procedures are intangible and progress is more difficult to assess when producing them.

Another important consideration is that performance is governed by human factors rather than machines. It is well-known that where work output is primarily due to human effort then the difference between the best and worst performance can be enormous. In systems analysis and programming a factor of ten is often quoted, i.e. the best person can produce ten times as much as the worst. In the past many staff have been new to systems development work and relatively untrained. Also much of systems analysis by its very nature cannot be routine. For instance it is difficult to predict how much effort is required for a systems investigation as the very purpose of the process is to discover unknowns. Also the work of the analyst depends to a large extent on the cooperation of other people.

30.10   The problems of systems development

As demonstrated in Chapter 29 systems development can present many problems. Some of these like cost over-runs are common to all types of project work. The main problem areas facing a systems development manager can be classified as follows:

- The business environment, e.g. a financially weak business which cannot easily afford good equipment and sufficient staff.
- Management, e.g. lack of understanding about IT development leading to demands for unrealistic delivery dates.
- Human factors, for example distrustful and uncooperative user staff.
- The IT environment, e.g. only rudimentary software tools in use.
- Project planning and control, for example seriously under-estimating the work required to complete a project stage.
- The systems development life-cycle, e.g. inadequate investigation of business requirements leading to defective system designs.
- Quality assurance, for instance poor software testing leading to systems being implemented with serious bugs.
- Implementation, e.g. inadequate training of user staff leading to numerous calls for assistance when a business system is first implemented.
- Maintenance, for example lack of documentation makes it difficult for analysts and programmers to correct faults and change systems.

Clearly the fundamental factors like proper feasibility studies are important determinants of the success or failure of a project. If an IT system is the equivalent of the R101 airship a well or badly-written user manual is not going to make much difference. Sometimes a set of smaller factors can make a significant cumulative difference. Thus the productivity of each person in a team of analysts and programmers can help make the difference between profit and loss for a software house with a fixed-price contract.

The compounding of all the numerous potential problems that can affect a project makes systems development generally, a risky activity. The probability of some kind of failure is high on most computer projects. Usually however the 'failure' is not dramatic. For instance, an IT system can be delivered late with some initial quality problems and complaints from the users, but eventually it works in a lack-lustre and pedestrian fashion.

The sort of difficulties discussed above are real, but it should be remembered that the job of IT staff is to provide business and IT solutions. A major role of systems development managers is to direct their staff to the solution of such real world problems. Also systems analysts have to respond positively and retain the confidence of user staff, even when the prospects look bleak!

30.11   Systems analysis problems

Programming is a more defined activity than systems analysis and its problems are, at least in principle, easier to solve. Systems analysis however can present some special problems which an IT manager may have to resolve. Some are listed below as questions with a brief answer.

- Whom does the analyst serve − the business as a whole, several different user departments, or the IT department? Each of these can have conflicting requirements.
  Answer:
  The facile answer is that this sort of problem is resolved through a corporate plan and a derivative IT systems plan. These should reconcile potential conflicts at higher levels. Also the resolution of conflicts between the various groups in an organisation is the job of senior management. If people are playing politics then there is no easy answer.

- How can the requirements for a new system be established when there are difficulties in identifying or communicating with users?

Answer:

This problem can occur in varying degrees. For example there is often no convenient user when producing an entirely new software package. Another illustration is where systems analysts are opposed by users and cannot conduct proper investigations. There are several ways round these difficulties, and it is possible to at least partially adopt a user-less approach to systems analysis. As mentioned in Chapter 22, there are several techniques which do not depend on the co-operation of the users. For instance system requirements can be established through formal documents such as government regulations, or by observing the use of an existing system by automatic methods such as software probes to log the activity. Another example is developing a new general purpose software package. A business consultant who knows the application area well can be used as a substitute for a user.

- What are the problems of large analysis projects?

  Answer:

  Big administrative systems and big software systems usually offer disproportionately more problems than small systems. Obviously an analyst who is responsible for replacing a major mainframe sales order processing system run by tens of clerks faces more severe problems than an information centre analyst who is installing word processing software for one user on a personal computer. Not only are the general business and technical problems disproportionately greater on big systems, but so are the human and management problems. Large systems are legendary amongst computer staff for their 'black-hole' effect. That is, large projects appear to absorb extra staff continually. The staff find it difficult to escape other work. The project takes so long and requires so much special knowledge for systems maintenance that managers tend to keep the same staff on the project for years.

- Where do systems begin and end?

  Answer:

  The scope of a system needs to be determined early in a project, e.g. at the feasibility stage. It is determined by both investigation, and negotiation with management and users. Clearly the scope of a project, or the boundary of a system, is a major determinant of matters like development costs and timescale. For example when revamping accounts systems are some or all of the following systems included: the sales ledger, the purchase ledger, the general ledger, and management accounts? It is also important to establish the boundary between the manual and computer systems, i.e. how much of the total system is to be automated?

- How do you estimate the amount of analysis work in a project?
  Answer:
  Project plans are based on estimates, and poor estimates can lead to major problems. For instance optimistic estimates frequently lead to systems being delivered late and over their budgeted cost. Estimating analysis work is more difficult than estimating programming work because programming estimates can be based on a firm software design specification. With analysis work, a pilot investigation can establish approximately factors like the number of people to be interviewed, the number of entities in the system, and the number of business documents. With experience this can be related to the number of person-days of analysis and design required after allowing for all the various circumstances such as the methodology being used.

- How can a manager deal with 'analysis paralysis'?
  Answer:
  Analysis paralysis usually occurs when IT projects become stuck at the feasibility, analysis, or design stages. Usually the analyst is confused. For instance he or she may be unable to document or analyse investigation data. The analyst may be unable to produce reports such as a feasibility study. Any work the analyst does produce is vague, superficial, inconclusive, and lacks good recommendations. In extreme cases the analyst just halts, or continues with minor or irrelevant work.
  Analysis paralysis tends to affect individuals rather than groups. Sometimes it is an inability to 'see the wood for the trees'. It can be caused by factors like inadequate skills, lack of experience, lack of confidence, fear of the consequences of producing wrong work, and poor morale. A typical way of solving analysis paralysis is for a more capable and experienced analyst to provide assistance until the blocked work is satisfactorily completed.

- If users continue making frequent changes to their requirements how can the IT staff cope?

Answer:
The usual way of dealing with this is to insist that the users 'freeze' their requirements after a particular date until the system is developed. Changes can then be accepted as part of systems maintenance.

- How can users be persuaded to certify as correct an analyst's specification of a current system or design of a future system?
  Answer:
  Users can be just dilatory, or more likely they are afraid of certifying in writing that a large specification is correct. They realise that if they have failed to detect errors this could lead to expensive mistakes. There are several ways of dealing with this. One approach is for the users to certify one small part of a specification at a time. SSADM lends itself to this approach with its large number of steps and tasks. Another approach is for the analyst to 'walk-through' the specification page by page with the user. See also Section 20.10.

- How is it possible to cope with the fact that the analysis and design of most IT systems demands a good knowledge of the application area such as manufacturing?
  Answer:
  General systems analysts can, given enough time and support, cope with a totally unknown business area. If general systems analysts are used it is essential to allow for the extra time required and also provide other help such as special training in the application area. Of course there is often insufficient time, patience, and other resources. Then the only sensible alternative is to use analysts who have a prior knowledge and experience of the application area. Even more preferable is using analysts with relevant formal training and qualifications.

- How can a manager or systems analyst deal with ethical problems?
  Answer:
  Poor professionalism and poor workmanship are shown by activities like corner-cutting, short-sightedness, and carelessness. However some IT activities are deliberately unethical, or even criminal. A typical example of shady practice is where a software house delivers fixed-price bespoke software full of bugs to a customer at a busy time. The customer, because of other commitments, cannot then

perform acceptance tests before the contractual deadline, of say one month ahead. The bugs are found when the customer eventually tests or uses the system. However the customer then has to pay extra to have the bugs removed. The BCS (British Computer Society) and other professional bodies produce codes of conduct and practice to deal with such situations. The weaknesses of these codes is that they can be seen as merely moral exhortations for competent professionalism and upright dealings with everyone.

The problem for the individual is how to handle the situation where the organisation or department as a whole adopt unethical or incompetent practices. The easy answer is to resign and find a job with an honest, responsible, and competent employer.

30.12 Improving systems development

Systems analysis and programming can be continually improved just like any other business function. For example, methodologies need updating like transferring from SSADM Version 3 to Version 4. Concentrating on systems analysis some suggestions for the key factors which can be examined and improved include:

● *Organisation*
The organisation of system development work may be capable of improvement.

● *Management*
Superior techniques and project management software can all contribute to better performance.

● *The analysis process*
This can sometimes be improved by enlarging the range of techniques employed. The performance of analysts using standard techniques such as interviewing can be improved through training. Using a superior methodology can give long-term benefits.

● *Automation*
The use of software tools can bring significant productivity and quality benefits to analysts. See Sections 4.6 and 26.13.

- *Human resources*

The quality of the analysts and programmers in a business can be improved over time by more careful recruitment and by professional development. It is also important to prevent a loss of skilled capable staff to other businesses. Similar strategies can be applied to user staff to make them more capable of absorbing and even developing IT systems.

30.13 Summary

- The acronym POSDCIR is a useful way to summarise systems development management.
- The management of systems development is characterised by the importance of planning and ensuring the adherence to plans.
- Committees or boards are often used to control systems development and implementation projects. These committees consist of general management, users, and IT management, and meet regularly, say every month.
- There is a whole series of project control approaches from simple task-lists to formal project control methods like PRINCE.
- Software tools such as project planning packages can be very useful.
- By its very nature planning depends on quantitative techniques.
- Project administration requires regular data collection and reporting.
- Managers and systems analysts need to establish a good infrastructure to support the successful completion of a IT project.
- Many of the problems of systems development can ultimately be traced to human and management problems.
- Systems development does appear to have some characteristics which make it difficult to predict and control. This is more true of systems analysis than programming.
- Systems development is by its nature a somewhat confusing and uncertain process. Part of the role of a systems analyst is to provide clarity for others like clerks, programmers, and managers.
- Analysis is more uncertain and presents a wider range of problems than programming. Typical problems include estimating analysis work, analysis paralysis, user reluctance about certifying specifications, and frequent changes in user requirements. Most of these difficulties can be overcome.

- Ethical problems do occur in IT work and, professional codes such as those of the BCS provide guidelines. However enforcing adherence to such codes is difficult in practice.
- Better performance in systems development usually comes from improving the various factors like staff training and software tools.

Part 6
Appendices

Appendix I
Abbreviations

(Some trade names are not included.)

3GL	=	Third Generation Language
4GL	=	Fourth Generation Language
AQL	=	Acceptable Quality Level
ATM	=	Automated Teller Machine
AT&T	=	American Telephone and Telegraph (Company)
BACS	=	Bankers Automated Clearing Services
BACSTEL	=	BACS Telecommunication Service
BASIC	=	Beginner's All-purpose Symbolic Instruction Code
BCS	=	British Computer Society
BS	=	British Standard
BSI	=	British Standards Institute
BSP	=	Business Systems Planning
CAD	=	Computer Aided Design
CAM	=	Computer Aided Management
CASE	=	Computer Aided Software Engineering
CBI	=	Confederation of British Industry
CBT	=	Computer Based Training
CCTA	=	Central Computer and Communications Agency
CIMA	=	Chartered Institute of Management Accountants
COBOL	=	Common Business Oriented Language
COM	=	Computer Output on Microfilm
COP	=	Computerisation of PAYE
CPIS	=	Computerised Personnel Information System
CPU	=	Central Processing Unit (in computing)
Cr	=	Credit
CSA	=	Computer Services Association
CUA	=	Computer User Association
DBMS	=	Data Base Management System
DCF	=	Discounted Cash Flow
DEC	=	Digital Equipment Corporation
DFD	=	Data Flow Diagram
DP	=	Data Processing

DOS	=	Disk Operating System
Dr	=	Debit
DSS	=	Department of Social Security/Decision Support System
DTI	=	Department of Trade and Industry
DTP	=	Desktop Publishing
DVLC	=	Driver Vehicle Licensing Centre
EC	=	European Communities/European Community
EDI	=	Electronic Data Interchange
EDS	=	Electronic Data Systems
EEC	=	European Economic Community
EFT	=	Electronic Funds Transfer
EFTPOS	=	Electronic Funds Transfer Point of Sale
EIS	=	Executive Information System
ELH	=	Entity Life History
EM	=	Entity Model
ENIAC	=	Electronic Numerical Integrator and Calculator
EPD	=	Elementary Process Definition
ER	=	Entity Relationship
ES	=	Expert System
ESW	=	Existing Systems Workbench
ESPRIT	=	European Strategic Programme for Research in IT
ESS	=	Expert System
FAST	=	Federation Against Software Theft
FM	=	Facilities Management
FORTRAN	=	Formula Translation (computer language)
GEC	=	General Electric Company (two large companies in the same business with the same name)
GST	=	General Systems Theory
GUI	=	Graphical User Interface
HCI	=	Human Computer Interface
HMSO	=	Her Majesty's Stationery Office
HNC	=	Higher National Certificate
HND	=	Higher National Diploma
HRM	=	Human Resources Management
IBM	=	International Business Machines
ICL	=	International Computers Limited
ICSA	=	Institute of Chartered Secretaries and Administrators
IDPM	=	Institute of Data Processing Management
IE	=	Information Engineering
IKBS	=	Intelligent Knowledge Based System
IMS	=	Institute of Management Services

IMT	=	International Money Transfer
IPR	=	Intellectual Property Rights
IPS	=	Institute of Purchasing and Supply
IPSE	=	Integrated Project Support Environment
IRS	=	Information Retrieval System
IS	=	Information System(s)/Services
ISM	=	Industry Structure Model
ISO	=	International Standards Organisation
IT	=	Information Technology
JCL	=	Job Control Language
JSP	=	Jackson Structured Programming
LAN	=	Local Area Network
LBMS	=	Learmonth Burchett Management Systems
LDS	=	Logical Data Structure
LIM	=	Lotus Intel Microsoft (interface)
LSDM	=	LBMS Structured Development Methodology
MICR	=	Magnetic Ink Character Recognition
MIS	=	Management Information System
MMI	=	Man Machine Interface
NATO	=	North Atlantic Treaty Organisation
NCC	=	National Computing Centre
NCR	=	National Cash Register/No Carbon Required (for multi-part stationery)
NI	=	National Insurance
NIC(s)	=	National Insurance Contribution(s)
NINO	=	National Insurance Number
O&M	=	Organisation & Methods
OA	=	Office Automation
OCR	=	Optical Character Recognition
OR	=	Operational Research
P&L	=	Profit and Loss Account
p.a.	=	Per Annum (Per Year)
PAYE	=	Pay As You Earn
PC	=	Personal Computer
PC-DOS	=	Personal Computer Disk Operating System
PDET	=	Programmable Data Entry Terminal
PIN	=	Personal Identity Number
PLC	=	Public Limited Company
PONC	=	Price of Non Conformance
POS	=	Point of Sale
POSDCIR	=	Planning, Organising, Staffing, Directing, Innovating, Representing

PRINCE	=	Projects In Controlled Environments
QA	=	Quality Assurance
QC	=	Quality Control
R&D	=	Research and Development
SADT	=	Structured Analysis and Design Techniques
SDI	=	Strategic Defence Initiative
SDLC	=	Systems Development Life Cycle
SERPS	=	State Earnings Related Pension Scheme
SMP	=	Statutory Maternity Pay
SPC	=	Statistical Process Control
STRADIS	=	Structured Analysis Design and Implementation of Information Systems
SSA	=	Social Security Administration
SSM	=	Soft Systems Methodology
SSADM	=	Structured Systems and Design Method
SSP	=	Statutory Sick Pay
SWOT	=	Strengths, Weaknesses, Opportunities, and Threats
SWIFT	=	Society for Worldwide Interbank Financial Telecommunication
T&A	=	Time and Attendance
TQM	=	Total Quality Management
TPS	=	Transaction Processing System
UK	=	United Kingdom
UPS	=	Uninterruptable Power Supply
US(A)	=	United States (of America)
VAT	=	Value Added Tax
VANS	=	Value Added Network Services
VDU	=	Visual Display Unit
WIMPs	=	Windows, Icons, Mice, and Pull-down menus

Appendix II
General Terms Related to Business IT
and Systems Analysis

II.1 IT and related jargon

IT and related fields are full of specialised jargon, and the haphazard use of terminology is wide-spread, leading to considerable confusion. Worse still IT vocabulary is changing and expanding. There are also several terms which are used to describe business IT technology in a general way, all of which have different nuances. The following sections contain a list of common generic terms related to business IT, and a list of terms related to systems analysis. They may be used as part of a job title or departmental title, e.g. management services officer, IT department, or DP department. Needless to say each organisation has its own terminology, or its own interpretation of common words.

II.2 Terms related to business information technology

- *Business automation*

Any method of automating administration is implied. It includes electronic information technology and mechanical office equipment such as franking machines which automatically stamp envelopes for posting.

- *Data processing (DP)*

An old but common term which implies the use of computer systems to process business data, e.g. a computerised invoicing system. Such a system not only stores and outputs data, but also processes it, for example by calculating the value of a sales invoice. Variants which mean almost the same thing are EDP (Electronic Data Processing) and ADP (Automatic Data Processing).

- *Information systems*

Any computer and telecommunication system which handles data is an information system. Data processing systems are included, but so also are on-line database systems such as Prestel. Here data is basically called up on a screen for reference without any processing. For instance an on-line database system can show a list of films showing at a local cinema.

- *Information services*

This term implies any service based on IT, e.g. data processing, electronic mail, on-line databases, and internal telephones.

- *Information technology (IT)*

This is perhaps the most modern term listed here. In general information technology implies computers and electronic telecommunications, but it can also include such things as microfilm. An extreme definition includes not only radio and computers, but also a printing press, filing cabinets, and paperclips! However in business an IT department is responsible for applying information technology through systems analysis, programming, and computer operations. It may also be responsible for other 'management services' (see below).

- *Management information systems (MIS)*

Strictly this term implies a category of system which provides management information like the total annual purchases from a particular supplier. The term MIS department in practice is just another term for a DP or IT department.

- *Management services*

See next section.

- *Office automation*

This includes such topics as word processing and electronic mail, but not data processing.

- *User computing*

This is sometimes called end-user computing. It implies office IT users developing and operating their own computer systems.

II.3 Terms related to systems analysis

- *Business analysis*

This has several distinct meanings. In computing circles it usually means computer systems analysis with a business rather than technical bias. Sometimes more literally it has little to do with computers and is the analysis of businesses, or business projects, often from a financial viewpoint. Under another interpretation, sometimes favoured by academics, it means a more philosophical and sociological approach to solving business problems.

- *Computer or IT systems analysis*

This is often abbreviated to systems analysis, or just analysis. The words usually imply not only analysis for computer or other electronic systems in business, but also their design and implementation. This book is primarily concerned with IT systems analysis. The term came into use into the late 1950s with the introduction of early mainframe computers into business administration.

- *Data analysis*

A specialist part of systems analysis concerned with analysing the data to be stored and used by a computer system, particularly in a mainframe environment. The term is also used outside computing to imply the statistical analysis of numerical data.

- *Industrial engineering*

The combination of management services techniques like work study and OR with engineering, often, but not exclusively, in a factory environment. It is sometimes used as a more modern term for work study.

- *Information engineering*

Sometimes this term is used to imply a more technical approach to systems analysis particularly with large IT systems. Similarly software engineering implies a more technical version of computer programming. Confusingly Information Engineering is also the name of a particular systems development methodology.

- *Information systems engineering*

A term sometimes used to imply a more technical and professional approach to all aspects of IT systems.

- *Management services*

A concept which involves the integration of business computing (including systems analysis) with related disciplines. Some major examples of related disciplines are O&M (Organisation and Methods), OR (Operational Research, basically mathematics applied to business), and work study (basically the study of human and machine work to improve efficiency). The idea is to offer a multi-disciplinary approach to the management problems of running a business. In practice management services tends to be mostly business computing including IT operations with only a small contribution from other disciplines.

- *Organisation and Methods (O&M)*

O&M is very similar to computer systems analysis except that traditionally it concentrates on designing and improving clerical systems without using computers as such. It used to concentrate on office equipment such as photocopiers leaving mainframe computer systems to the systems analysts. However the spread of cheap office mini- and personal computers made the distinction less clear, as they are often considered to belong to both O&M and systems analysis. However O&M still tends to concentrate on clerical procedures, and non-computer office machinery. The term O&M pre-dates systems analysis, and originated in the early 1940s. The Americans use the term Systems and Procedures for O&M. Unfortunately the importance of O&M has significantly declined over the years.

- *Operational Research (OR)*

It is called Operations Research in America. In theory it is the study of the operations of an organisation to seek improvement. Another view would be that it involves the application of scientific methods to solve the problems of organisations. In practice it is distinguished from other management services occupations by its application of advanced mathematical techniques.

- *Operations*

In general the term refers to the core routine activities in a business, e.g. producing goods in a factory, running a warehouse in a distribution company, or clearing cheques in a bank.

Computer operations refers to all the regular activities required to make a computer system function, e.g. entering data, loading magnetic tapes, distributing large volumes of print-out, and scheduling work on mainframes. There is a historical trend away from specialist computer operations staff. The operations work is then given to the ordinary administrative staff using modern IT systems. However specialist computer operations staff are still essential in large organisations using central computing. Computer operations is often contrasted with systems development.

- *Productivity services*

Those aspects of management services which are concerned with human and machine productivity, e.g. work study.

- *Systems analysis*

Usually this implies computer systems analysis (see above). Sometimes the words systems analysis are interpreted more literally as meaning the study of systems in general. This rather academic approach involves studying the common features of say the solar system, the ecological system of planet Earth, the circulation of blood in an animal, the UK economy, a shipyard, and electronic circuits.

- *Systems development*

Basically the combination of systems analysis and programming which is necessary to produce business and technical IT systems. Frequently the amendment of existing systems (maintenance) is also implied.

- *Systems maintenance*

Correcting and improving existing business systems, or adapting them for new circumstances. Maintaining old systems constitutes a major part of the work of systems analysts and programmers in both business and technical fields.

- *User analysis*

This is systems analysis by IT users. Sometimes it is done on a part-time basis by ordinary office staff. Sometimes it implies a specialist systems analyst who works permanently in a user department as one of the normal staff. In practice user analysis often involves minor programming jobs and hence it is more realistically described as user development.

- *Work study*

The scientific study of human and machine work to determine the best methods of working and set performance levels.

Appendix III
Examples of Examination Questions

III.1 Background to the examination questions

This appendix contains IT and business examination questions. It provides some advice on how to tackle them. There is also a full solution to one question which should give students an idea of the quality, quantity, and presentation required in higher-education and professional examinations. Most of the questions used are from the examinations of the British Computer Society (BCS), the Chartered Institute of Management Accountants (CIMA), and the Institute of Chartered Secretaries and Administrators (ICSA). These were selected because all are professional institutes operating under a Royal Charter, and the author has some familiarity with their syllabuses and students. Also full collections of examination papers and the examiners' comments are readily available from these institutes. Similar questions are available from other professional institutes. Occasional academic examination questions have been included where no suitable professional questions could be found.

Examination questions assume a syllabus which is not obvious to a person reading a question in isolation. For instance some questions can be answered in either a simple or advanced manner. It should be remembered that only questions which are broadly compatible with the theme of this book have been selected. The questions are *not* usually representative of the institute or examination paper from which they were taken. ICSA has numerous examinations covering topics like Scots Business Law, Irish Business Law, Financial Accounting, Company Law, and Taxation. The BCS also has papers in subjects such as Computer Technology, Programming, and Computational Methods, all of which have little coverage in this book. To give a good answer some of the questions below require more information than is given in this book. However the questions listed should give IT and business students an insight into what is expected from them in academic and professional examinations. They should also be useful when revising for examinations. Students should read Sections IV.5 and IV.6 in Appendix IV for a discussion on examination technique.

III.2 Example of a solution

The examination question below is accompanied by an answer (a 'solution') produced under simulated examination conditions. It is *not* presented as a perfect answer, just a reasonable one that could be produced in the time available. The question should be answered in about 35 minutes.

● *Question:*
What is the "project team" approach to organising data processing staff.
Compare this approach with an alternative, identifying the advantages and disadvantages of each.
(BCS Part I, Data Processing, *1985)*

● *Suggested answer:*

PART 1 PROJECT TEAMS

Project teams in information technology or data processing departments often consist of mixed groups of systems analysts and programmers. Hybrid analyst-programmers are also often found in such teams. Additional staff such as librarian/secretary might also be included. The term can be a slight misnomer. In a typical company project teams are responsible for a related set of computer applications, e.g. those concerning accounting or manufacturing. The team is usually headed by a project manager or project leader. The basic idea is that the team contains all or most of the skills and resources necessary to fulfil its role of developing and maintaining systems in a particular application area. The basic organisation is illustrated in Fig. III.1.

The team size might range from 2 to 20 people. Large teams are often subdivided into sections. Project teams are also used for large one-off projects which may take a few years. Again a mixture of analysts and programmers is used.

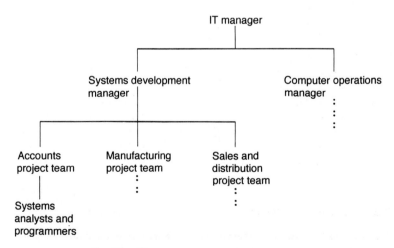

Fig. III.1 IT project team organisation.

PART 2 ALTERNATIVE WITH ADVANTAGES AND DISADVANTAGES

Alternative

One important alternative is the 'pool' or 'functional' approach. Here there is a separate pool of systems analysts and a separate pool of programmers. Work is given to any person in a pool who is free, e.g. an analyst might receive accounts work one month and stock control work the next. The idea is illustrated in Fig. III.2. Other organisational ideas also exist such as placing IT staff permanently out with user departments.

Advantages and disadvantages

Some advantages of a project team:

(1) Team members specialise in application areas and become proficient in them. They get to understand user staff well.
(2) Motivation can be good because of team spirit.
(3) Improves relationships with IT users.

Some disadvantages of a project team:

(1) It is more difficult to cope with a fluctuating workload. Project teams can become over- or under-loaded. Disruptive transfers of staff in or out of the team may be necessary with large fluctuations in workload.
(2) There may be difficulties with integrated applications which span several teams, e.g. setting up a database.

Some advantages of the pool approach:

(1) Good staff utilisation is easier to achieve.
(2) Integrated applications can be easier.
(3) Consistent standards are easier to maintain.

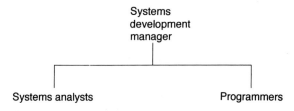

Fig. III.2 The 'pool' method of organising systems analysts and programmers.

Some disadvantages of the pool approach due to the fragmentation of the work are:

(1)   User relationships are more difficult.
(2)   Project management is more difficult.
(3)   Motivation can be weaker.

● *Comments*

The BCS examiners' comments on answers to this question were fairly typical, and they found it difficult to award marks in many cases. However like everyone examiners tend to note the bad rather than the good. Their comments on candidates' answers noted: accepting project teams uncritically as a way of life, failure to understand the question, no detail on team structures, few examples of organisation charts, the alternative approach sometimes omitted, and extremely vague comments on the advantages/disadvantages of project teams.

   This type of question is quite common, but can be difficult to answer even if a candidate is familiar with the subject. There is some uncertainty about the examiner's meaning of the phrase 'project team'. The solution sensibly addresses this and uses both interpretations. With such questions there is no easy way of knowing when enough detail has been given. The only response to this is to ensure that the main points are given under each heading, and to add further comments later if time permits. Much more could have been written in the above answer. But for many people this would be at the expense of using the time required for other questions.

   As regards the presentation the following points should be noted:

(1)   The solution is 'structured', i.e. it uses headings and lists, and the paragraphs are short.
(2)   Simple diagrams are used.
(3)   Examples are used, e.g. a manufacturing project team.
(4)   The words of the question are repeated in the headings in particular. This helps a candidate answer the question as asked, and helps the examiner identify the appropriate parts of the answer.

III.3   Examination questions with comments on solutions

(The following questions are meant to be answered in about 30 minutes depending on the paper. Often an examination paper consists of, say, nine questions of which five or six must be answered in three hours.)

(1)   *Explain the work and responsibilities of the following:*

   (a)   analysts;
   (b)   programmers; and
   (c)   operators.

(ICSA, Information Systems, *June 1987)*

Comment:

This a very a common type of question testing essential practical knowledge. It is a reasonably easy question provided the student has a modest combination of book learning and practical experience. Students on academic courses tend to do badly on this type of question. For them the only way to acquire the necessary knowledge is book learning backed by discussion in tutorials, plus practical activities like visits to IT departments.

As examples should always be given to support abstract comments it is suggested that a student states at the beginning that their answer is based on a scenario like a small manufacturing company, or a branch of the civil service. The main part of the answer for the analyst and programmer could be structured by considering the traditional systems development life-cycle and asking what is their role at each stage. For an operator the main events during a week would probably suffice, e.g. daily security copying and re-ordering stationery.

Questions of this type are usually found on introductory business and technical courses. A straightforward answer is usually expected, with a brief mention of the complications and refinements for top marks. However such questions can be a danger to candidates who have first-rate practical experience and good theoretical knowledge. Because they know so much they find it difficult to concentrate on the basics of the answer, which they consider trivial. Instead they can produce an unbalanced answer concentrating on, say, the more complex or unusual issues related to each job.

(2)   *Discuss the nature of incorporation. How can incorporation be achieved?*
   (ICSA, Introduction to English Law, *December 1990)*

Comment:

These brief questions are often known as 'one liners', and most people find them difficult. This is also what lecturers would consider a good question because it is succinct and makes them think deeply, as well as stretching the examination candidates!

Even though this is on an introductory paper ICSA would demand a sophisticated answer as it is very central to the occupations at which they are aiming such as company secretary. However for IT students thinking of setting up their own business as a contractor or software house it is also a very relevant question. For this reason similar questions sometimes occur on business-oriented academic computing courses.

A brief discussion is required of 'corporate personality', e.g. a company has a separate legal identity from its members (the shareholders). An IT student would then briefly discuss the registration and issuing of shares in a private or public company. Only a passing mention of other types of corporation would be necessary, e.g. local authorities and chartered bodies like ICSA or the BCS.

A more sophisticated business-oriented answer would also discuss the legal aspects of incorporation, e.g. when companies commit criminal acts. Statutory and case law references would be cited. Practical complications such as foreign companies could be mentioned. The main legal procedures leading to incorporation and the documents required would also be expected, usually with a trading company as an example. An answer at this level is considerably beyond this book.

(3) *Discuss the extent to which an organisation may protect itself against unauthorised copying of computer software.*
     (ICSA, Information Systems, December 1989)

Comment:

This is a difficult but contemporary practical question. It is first important to establish the context. For example, major public companies often use large amounts of bought-in software such as popular PC packages. Inadvertent copying of software, infringing copyright, can then be a problem, particularly with personal computers. A software house is also concerned to prevent software theft through deliberate illicit copying and this presents an entirely different scenario.

The answer could refer to strict security procedures to control the use of software. For example a legitimate copy of the software might only be kept and used on a central mini-computer. The managerial or administrative aspects of the answer could refer to staff instructions, e.g. staff should not make illegal copies of personal computer software for business use. Unapproved domestic use, or the resale of software would also be specifically prohibited. Recruiting reliable and honest staff is important as in all such matters. In addition it would be sensible to mention rights and penalties under software contracts and the Copyright Designs and Patents

Act 1988. The use of hardware and software control devices such as dongles could also be included.

(4) *Evaluate three methods of fact-finding.*
Discuss the relevance of the three methods of fact-finding with respect to a stock control system to be developed in an organisation with a central administrative section but geographically distributed warehouses.
(BCS Part I, Analysis and Design, *1985)*

Comment:

This is a typical systems analysis question which could occur on either a business-oriented or technical course. The first part initially requires a brief description of fact-finding techniques such as interviewing, observation, and reverse engineering. The more awkward part is evaluating them, i.e. identifying their strengths and weaknesses. A common mistake is merely to provide a description of the techniques and no evaluation. Again brief examples are useful, e.g. an example of reverse engineering is producing a business or technical specification by studying the COBOL programs of an old undocumented accounts system.

The second part gives a stock control scenario. This a common practice for both business and technical examinations. It is a very searching method of examining because in this case not only does it require a knowledge of the techniques but also a knowledge of the standard features of stock control and associated administration.

It is essential that students refer to the scenario as instructed. A common mistake is abstract answers which make little or no reference to the data given. If further background detail is introduced by a student from experience or reading then its origin should be clearly identified. For instance a student might state that he or she had worked on a similar warehousing system for consumer goods and give a simplified warehouse organisation chart to illustrate the people to be interviewed.

This type of question is often popular with candidates, because it appears superficially easy, and is the sort of practical problem that is rightly often presented in tutorials. However students for professional examinations should always remember that some candidates will have extensive practical experience of similar scenarios and these candidates are in a position to give very good answers.

A way of relating the answer to the question can be illustrated with interviewing. Because the warehouses are geographically scattered then some managerial and clerical staff could be interviewed over the telephone. This could be efficient and effective if used carefully.

(5)   *A business has decided to computerise its Information Systems activities.*

   (a)   Discuss the personnel and social considerations involved.
   (b)   Compare and contrast two methods of changeover to the new system.
   (BCS Part I, General Paper 1, *1989)*

Comment:

This is a question which illustrates a common examiners' trick. Examiners are often concerned that students might learn part of the syllabus and rely on being able to choose sufficient questions to pass. One simple way of discouraging this is by combining two or more different parts of the syllabus in one question, which is what the BCS has done here.

   No scenario has been given so the students are free to introduce their own examples. With part (a) this could be informal resistance from clerical staff to an analysis investigation. Reference to the theory of human factors is desirable, such as the importance of ergonomics when designing systems based on personal computers or VDUs. Some practical personnel aspects such as trade union new technology agreements could be mentioned.

   With part (b) an example like implementing a new local authority payroll system could be chosen. The question wants a comparison of two systems implementation methods only, e.g. parallel running or immediate change-over to the new system. A common mistake is to consider more than two methods, which wastes time as marks can only be given for two. The difficulty with this type of question is covering all the main points in the time allowed.

III.4   List of examination questions

(The following questions are meant to be answered in about 30 minutes depending on the paper. The questions quoted above have been repeated for completeness. The questions below are roughly classified to correspond with the main sections of the book.)

● *PART I: INTRODUCTION*
   (1)   Discuss the recent impact of computers on office practice.
         Describe the facilities provided by typical equipment in a modern 'electronic' office.
         (BCS Part 1, *General Paper I*, 1985)

(2) Much of the past effort in developing management information systems has focused on the operational levels of the organisation. Examine what you feel are the opportunities and problems in developing information systems which provide support to the highest management levels of the organisation.
(ICSA, *Management of Systems*, December 1987)

(3) What are local area networks, and why have they become so successful?
(ICSA, *Information Systems*, June 1987)

(4) A software development company is to replace its current computing facilities.
   (a) Suggest software development tools that could be obtained and describe the advantages they would bring.
   (b) How would the acquisition of a Data Base Management System be of advantage to this company?
(BCS Part 1, *General Paper II*, 1988)

- *PART II: BUSINESS MANAGEMENT*
(5) Discuss the nature of incorporation. How can incorporation be achieved?
(ICSA, *Introduction to English Law*, December 1990)

(6) Assume that in 1992 all the barriers to trade in the EEC will be dismantled. As the assistant to the managing director of a company producing consumer goods for which there is competition from many firms within the EEC, *you are required* to write a report setting out the implications of this development for the company and each of the elements of management, i.e. planning, organising, direction (motivation, etc.) and control.
(CIMA, *Management*, November 1989)

(7) A company owns and operates 50 small hotels in its home country, 30 more in five other countries of the EEC, and six in Africa. The hotels are purpose-built to the company's design. Each one has about 25 rooms, a lounge area, and a restaurant in which simple standard food is served. The hotel manager has about ten staff.
   You are required to draw an organisation chart (or charts) suitable for this company with notes as appropriate, showing clearly at which levels the important functions of the business are managed.
(CIMA, *Management*, November 1989)

(8) Define and explain the principal elements of a Corporate Plan.
State the contributions to the plan expected from:
   (a) a senior functional manager,
   (b) a Chief Executive.

(Answers should include examples from an organisation with which you are familiar.)
(ICSA, *Management: Principles and Policy*, December 1990)

(9) State the role of a first line manager, for example a supervisor, in any organisation with which you are familiar.
Explain his/her duties and responsibilities.
(CIMA, *Management*, May 1991)

(10) A major principle of management concerns the span of control.
   (a) Explain this principle.
   (b) An office manager may have a broad or narrow span of control. Discuss the advantages and disadvantages associated with both these approaches to organisational structure and supervision in an office.
(ICSA, *Office Administration and Management*, December 1987)

(11) Examine the factors management must consider when evaluating the security of information systems. Your answer should cover both physical security and security from unauthorised human intervention.
(ICSA, *Management of Systems*, June 1987)

(12) Discuss the extent to which an organisation may protect itself against unauthorised copying of computer software.
(ICSA, *Information Systems*, December 1989)

(13) (a) Briefly explain how business and IT planning interact.
   (b) With regard to intellectual property rights, trade secrets, and related matters outline the following:
      (1) Their importance to a software house producing business systems.
      (2) The legal background and practical methods of protecting such assets.
(Derived from an internal IT examination, Liverpool Polytechnic, 1990)

(14) (a) Illustrate how the final accounts of a company are prepared under the double-entry system. You could for instance trace how a couple of transactions become incorporated in the balance sheet.
   (b) Discuss briefly the role of spreadsheet and related systems for business modelling. Concentrate on using examples from financial planning.
(Derived from an internal IT examination, Liverpool Polytechnic, 1990)

(15) (a) Describe the basic components of an industrial organisation and the flows of information between them. Discuss the corresponding managerial functions.

(b)   Explain the concept of depreciation and discuss its importance in the financial assessment of computer systems.

Describe briefly a method of calculating depreciation.

(BCS Part I, *General Paper 1*, 1988)

(16) Your company produces four major products which are sold through salesman on a national basis. Discuss the information needs of management in relation to the establishment of standards, types of variances and profitability reports you would recommend should be produced.

(ICSA, *Management Accounting*, December 1989)

(17) As in all areas of organisations, budgeting and budgetary control are necessary in the office.

(a)   Define the terms budgeting and budgetary control.

(b)   Explain in simple terms, the operation of a system of budgetary control in the office.

(ICSA, *Office Administration and Management*, December 1986)

(18) A business has decided to computerise its Information Systems activities

(a)   Discuss the personnel and social considerations involved.

(b)   Compare and contrast two methods of change-over to the new system.

(BCS Part I, *General Paper 1*, 1989)

(19) *You are required* to explain *four* strategies for managing change, giving the advantages and disadvantages of *each*.

(CIMA, *Management*, November 1989)

(20) A feature of the work of the Systems Analyst could be described as the management of change. Outline ways in which a systems development group could minimise the negative aspects and maximise the positive aspects of organisational change.

(ICSA, *Management of Systems*, December 1987)

(21) What do you understand by the terms 'quality control' and 'quality assurance'? How can these concepts be applied by a local authority in preparing one of its services for compulsory competitive tendering?

(ICSA, *Services Administration by Local Authorities*, 1989)

(22) What personnel records are needed in a typical organisation? What are the relative advantages and disadvantages of clerical versus computerised record-keeping systems?

(ICSA, *Personnel Administration*, December 1989)

- *PART III: SYSTEMS DEVELOPMENT*

(23) A car spares distributor's current strategy for information processing is

based upon the use of on-line terminals to a central processor. Customer order processing has been established for some time: inventory management is to be the next major application to be linked into that existing system. Subsequently a stock purchasing system will be developed with inventory management.

Describe the system life cycle for the inventory management application, showing the stages involved in that cycle and their deliverable outputs. Comment on the impact on those whose normal activity will be influenced by this application.

(BCS Part 1, *Analysis and Design*, 1987)

(24) How would you organise and action an appraisal of the value and cost of an organisation's information systems?

(ICSA, *Management of Systems*, December 1990)

(25) Illustrate the main features of a management control system, clearly indicating the location and role of detectors, comparators, activators and feedback.

(ICSA, *Management of Systems*, December 1986)

(26) Referring to an organisation with which you are familiar, explain how an Information Technology system might be used to improve specific clerical and administrative operations.

(ICSA, *Public Administration*, December 1989)

(27) The management of EM Ltd is keen to adopt Structured Systems Analysis and Design Method (SSADM) as the standard framework for information systems development within the company as an alternative to the unstructured development which has taken place in the past.

You are required:
(a) To discuss the advantages which are claimed for a structured systems development method like SSADM.
(b) To describe the way in which data flow diagrams (DFDs) are used in a structured analysis and design method.

(EM Ltd is a fictitious company manufacturing motor components described at the beginning of the examination paper.)

(CIMA, *Information Technology Management*, May 1991)

(28) (a) Discuss the factors in systems development which could justify the use of CASE software.
(b) Describe the major stages in systems development where CASE software is likely to be applied.

(BCS Part 1, *Analysis and Design*, 1991)

- *PART IV: SYSTEMS ANALYSIS*

(29) Assume an organisation known to you is to replace an existing computer system with a new in-house development.

Describe the activities involved in the study of the present system and the identification of new requirements. Identify the contents of the resulting specification of requirements.

(BCS Part I, *Analysis and Design*, 1988)

(30) (a) Outline the typical contents of a requirements specification and an invitation to tender.

(b) Explain the role each would play in negotiations with a computer supplier for the provision of a system compromising both hardware and software elements.

(ICSA, *Management of Systems*, June 1987)

(31) A small company is considering the computerisation of its warehouse system. As a systems analyst you are required to perform a fact finding exercise.

(i) Describe in general interviewing as a fact finding technique.

(ii) What would be the aims in interviewing the Managing Director of the Company?

(iii) What would be the aims in interviewing a clerical member of staff?

(BCS Part I, *General Paper I*, 1990)

(32) Evaluate three methods of fact-finding.

Discuss the relevance of the three methods of fact-finding with respect to a stock control system to be developed in an organisation with a central administrative section but geographically distributed warehouses.

(BCS Part I, *Analysis and Design*, 1985)

(33) Consider, with examples, the range of methods and procedures an organisation might use to conduct the implementation phase in systems development.

(ICSA, *Management of Systems*, December 1987)

(34) Write short notes about FOUR of the following:

(a) Context diagrams;

(b) Dataflow diagrams;

(c) Structured Walkthroughs;

(d) Integrated Project Support Environments (IPSE);

(e) Computer Aided Software Engineering (CASE).

(BCS Part 1, *Analysis and Design*, 1990)

(35) Explain the role of debugging in the software development process and

discuss the software tools for debugging which are currently available.
(BCS Part II, *Paper 2 System Architecture and System Programming*, 1991)

(36) With reference to a practical example describe the testing and review activities involved at each stage of an application's development and installation – from planning to post-implementation.
(BCS Part 1, *Analysis and Design*, 1988)

(37) Discuss the problems of evaluating the performance of a computer system.

   Explain why the Millions of Instructions Per Second (MIPS) measurement is not usually a reliable guide to computer system performance.

   Illustrate your answer by considering:

   (a) a microprocessor based workstation; and

   (b) a mainframe computer running typical commercial applications.

   (BCS Part II, *Digital Computer Organisation Paper 2*, 1990)

(38) Explain how you would estimate the effort and minimum elapsed time required to develop a software system expected to contain about 50 000 lines of delivered code.

   Suppose your estimate was 20 man-years spread over two years of elapsed time but that your manager is proposing to agree to deliver the system after 18 months at cost which still only allows for 20 man-years of effort.

   Explain why this is likely to be unwise.

   (BCS Part II, *Data Processing Paper 1*, 1990)

● *PART V: IT MANAGEMENT*

(39) Explain the work and responsibilities of the following:

   (a) analysts;

   (b) programmers; and

   (c) operators.

   (ICSA, *Information Systems*, June 1987)

(40) What is the "project team" approach to organising data processing staff?

   Compare this approach with an alternative, identifying the advantages and disadvantages of each.

   (BCS Part I, *Data Processing*, 1985)

(41) Your district council, a medium sized authority in a semi-rural area, has developed its use and application of computer technology in an ad hoc manner over the past ten years.

   The Director of Administration has persuaded his colleagues that in order to progress the effective use of information technology, the

authority should develop a comprehensive information strategy.
(a)   Briefly outline how you might assess the information needs of the authority.
(b)   Draft the criteria and method you would use to identify the:
   (i)   current state of information technology and support within the authority;
         and
   (ii) an outline information technology strategy which identifies the key issues that the authority must focus on in order to develop a clear policy for the future which makes full use of the convergence of developments in computing and tele-communications.
(ICSA, *Local Authority Administration 1*, December 1990)

(42)   End users are often represented in the project group responsible for developing a new system.
   Describe what form this representation may take and explain how users can contribute to the development of the system.
   (BCS Part I, *Analysis and Design*, 1991)

(43)   The term 'Facilities Management' has several different meanings within the computer industry. Discuss the ways in which partial Facilities Management and full Facilities Management could be adopted in a company. Discuss the impact their introduction would have on the company and on its Information Technology services.
   (BCS Part II, *Management in Computing*, 1990)

(44)   As the Data Processing Manager in a large organisation how would you organise a study to determine staff development needs in your unit, given constant up-rating of hardware and software facilities?
   (ICSA, *Information Systems*, June 1987)

(45)   Outline the main techniques which a company might use in order to deal with risk and uncertainty in its project appraisal procedures.
   (ICSA, *Business Finance*, December 1990)

(46)   Evidence from user's initial experiences in introducing office automation suggests that success is by no means guaranteed. Consider what you feel are the main factors contributing to successful implementation.
   (ICSA, *Management of Systems*, December 1986)

(47)   Examine the techniques which are available to assist in the planning and control of the implementation phase of a large computer-based system.
   (ICSA, *Management of Systems*, December 1986)

Appendix IV
Examination Advice for IT Students

(The following comments and advice to some extent reflect the personal experience of the author. He has been a computer practitioner, a lecturer, an examiner, and has recently sat further examinations in IT and business himself. The comments apply to the UK, and the situation may be different in other countries.)

IV.1 The prejudice against IT examinations

Managers in the IT and personnel fraternity are generally not well-disposed towards computing examinations, or IT education in general. Therefore it is worth clarifying both their value and limitations. This is an emotive subject, but it is only fair that students understand the position. To some extent IT students must be prepared to defend their qualifications both at a job interview and with colleagues. Students of business studies, particularly for recognised professional bodies, are in a more encouraging position.

As indicated in Chapter 28 the student of IT faces various prejudices with regard to computer employment. For instance these prejudices may favour narrow practical IT experience, college degrees in any subject, or a semi-mythical reverence about 'business'. There is also some fair competition from people qualified in, say, engineering or the business professions. These prejudices are not universal, just very common, and most students meet them sooner or later.

There has been a tendency for employers to tolerate the idea that *relevant assessed* business and technical education is unnecessary. The worst example of this evil is the practice of recruiting university graduates with non-relevant qualifications preferentially into computing. This demotivates those without degrees and those with relevant qualifications (including relevant degrees). It has also reduced commitment to accredited learning in IT. The propaganda in favour of the 'varsity' man or woman, or the 'school of hard knocks' has served to protect staff with weak educational and weak professional backgrounds from criticism, and it has generally lowered standards.

Even where qualifications matter it is probably better on the technical side of computing to have a degree in a mathematical subject or engineering, combined with a little computing. On the systems analysis and management

479

side a business degree is traditionally less favoured than a professional qualification, probably because a professional qualification usually implies several years practical experience as well as examination training. Sometimes even being 'part-qualified' in a professional business field such as accounting or insurance is seen as adequate grounding for a systems analyst! However even in sympathetic environments a pure computing qualification seems to carry relatively little extra kudos over any other technical or scientific degree.

IV.2 Vindicating IT examinations

Summarised in a few words the common view is that computer examinations are not about the 'real world'. The general arguments against this prejudiced attitude usually vindicate a whole academic or professional course rather than just the examinations:

- *Occupational objectives incorporated*
Most business and technical examination courses are specifically designed to serve particular 'real' world needs. This has been true for at least a century in the UK whether considering mining engineering, banking, or law. Such courses are intended to advance the student's knowledge and skills in specific occupations. Examination courses undoubtedly achieve this. IT courses are much the same in this respect.

- *Examinations are 'bookish'*
This is partly true but so what! Books on subjects like gardening or car mechanics contain lots of useful knowledge, and the same is true of books on IT. Many skills can be learned or improved using books. Examinations are good at testing knowledge and certain skills, e.g. diagramming, calculations, and evaluative reasoning.

- *Practical assessment*
It is certainly true that it is difficult to assess some skills entirely by examination. Computer programming is an example. Such skills however are normally assessed by coursework or projects which are often part of examination schemes.

- *Experience often vital*
Professional examinations expect students to use their practical experience as well as their studies. Many questions begin with phrases like 'Using a computer system known to you...', or 'From your own experience...'. Indeed it is very difficult to pass some IT examinations without both good practical experience

and good theoretical training. Academic sandwich degrees insist on a year's practical experience. Professional qualifications insist on, say, three years practical experience on top of examination success. Indeed students for professional examinations, particularly in computing, often complain that it is unfair to ask students to acquire the high level of practical expertise expected.

- *Mismatch often due to a narrow perspective*

There is sometimes a mismatch between examination learning and what students see at work. So a COBOL programmer might meet undocumented accounting systems when at work, but not expert systems. Usually this is just a way of saying the workplace is conceptually narrow, behind the times, and tolerates poor practices such as developing undocumented unstructured systems. Examiners work hard to ensure that their papers have a contemporary but realistic flavour, and reflect good practice.

Often examination topics do match the workplace requirements in total. This can then lead to the narrow complaint that the syllabus contains material which is superfluous to the work of a particular employee. What is forgotten is the attempt of the syllabus designers to provide a general basis for a career in IT.

- *Objective assessment*

Examinations are probably the most objective and equitable form of assessment that ordinary people meet in their lives. An examination is a target with a clear syllabus. Students, particularly for professional examinations, are allowed to develop the necessary knowledge and skills in their own way. Cheating is almost impossible. Appraisal at work, or in any other area of life, is unlikely to be as objective.

- *Intellectual stamina*

Passing an examination course of any kind indicates qualities of intellectual stamina. This is particularly true for part-time or distance-learning students who often demonstrate immense strength of character by succeeding in their examinations under difficult conditions. For instance students are sometimes known to be working overtime in their job with no time off work for distance learning, but they still succeed in passing difficult examinations.

IV.3 Limitations of examination schemes

Examinations and related means of assessment such as project work have clear limitations. There are desirable employee attributes such as honesty which examinations do not purport to test. A more serious consideration is the uncertainty of application. Just because a person has certified knowledge and skills is no guarantee that he or she will apply these constructively in the way the employer wants. This leads into the whole area of employee motivation.

A major practical limitation of IT examinations is caused by lack of standardisation. IT in practice has many features that are unique to a particular technical and business environment. For example one environment may be the civil service using ICL mainframes systems developed using SSADM with ORACLE as the programming language. Another may be a bank using IBM mainframes systems written in COBOL using Information Engineering as a methodology. Usually IT education can only address the general features of both environments, e.g. compilers, databases, structured analysis, accounting systems, and management. The practical aspects of educational courses use varied but common IT environments, e.g. C programming and Unix.

IV.4 Conclusions concerning IT examinations

What is the net result of the common belittling attitude to IT examinations? Well in practice many computing students are studying out of interest in the subject, for the useful things they can learn, and to demonstrate intellectual stamina. This is all extremely laudable given the discouragement. However to some extent it is up to the student and qualified IT practitioner to promote the rational view that a person who succeeds on a reputable IT course has demonstrated both commitment, stamina, and competence well-above those unqualified in IT.

There are ways of overcoming the prejudices against IT examinations – one being a business qualification with IT, which when combined with good experience does carry some recognition. Secondly Chartered Engineer status for technical IT professionals is certain to be important in the future. Thirdly there is a move towards insisting that practitioners are certified by taking highly specific qualifications, e.g. in project management or SSADM. However, dispiriting though it may be, those qualified via a conventional academic computer studies course are unlikely to be accorded the recognised status of the banker or lawyer. This is perhaps part of the traditional British contempt for technical education.

IV.5 Preparing for examinations

If you are taking an academic or professional examination course in business information technology or related subjects the work is not intended to be easy.

To achieve success you must be prepared to work hard and be sensible about priorities. Commonsense advice about professional and academic examinations has been given for over a century. It is only an extension of the advice that is given about school examinations. However it is frequently not followed with the result being predictable failures. The general advice includes:

- *Rules and syllabus*

Above all understand the philosophy of the assessment scheme, and follow the rules and syllabus of your course. This is not always as easy as it sounds. For instance many textbooks are not designed to support a particular syllabus and the relevant parts have to be carefully selected for study. Clearly credit can only be given for work done according to the published rules and syllabus. Work done outside this framework cannot be given credit no matter how worthy.

- *Personal prerequisites*

Students need basic prerequisites to start any course, otherwise failure is almost certain. This includes such factors as good motivation, diligence, ability, adequate foundation knowledge, elementary skills like written English, good health, and sufficient resources, e.g. finance. But it is a frequent and sad experience to find students regularly trying to tackle advanced courses for which they do not possess the necessary personal prerequisites. The commonsense approach is to correct any deficiency before starting a course. If there is any serious and persistent difficulty then it is wise to consider abandoning or postponing a course. For instance if a student discovers that he or she is on a course which they loathe then it is probably better to resign early and do something more constructive. Remember that some students have just managed to survive miserably for years on a course for which they are unsuited. Such people often withdraw in the end or fail their final examinations disastrously. There are usually obvious signs like repeated resittings of intermediate examinations.

- *Personal organisation*

It is an old belief that an orderly approach to study is essential for examination success. This covers such matters as keeping notes in an organised fashion, setting aside specific times for study, planning, and self-discipline. Discipline means attending lectures on time, and saying 'no' to social events or leisure activities which disrupt study periods.

- *Discussion*

Regularly talk over the course rules and syllabus with lecturers and fellow students. Make sure that you understand what is required in assessment terms from each topic as it is learned. This is particularly important for distance-learning students as they are less likely to pick up the details informally.

● *Past examination papers*
Study past examination questions, examiners' comments, and model answers. Understand the problems imposed by a particular examination format, e.g. answering six questions out of nine in three hours. Try to find some information on the marking schemes. These are normally confidential, but lecturers can usually give an unofficial view.

● *Textbooks*
Students do not buy enough textbooks which are often excellent value. Some students buy books merely to feel comfortable but do not work through them. A set of good books used properly can considerably boost examination performance. Lecture notes are usually only intended to be a guide or supplement, and not a substitute for a book. As mentioned above it is important to identify those parts of a book that are relevant. Apparent duplication of subject matter in different books is often a good thing. Two or more descriptions of the same subject, like IT methodologies, can often be complementary. Reading them together can make understanding easier, provide different examples, and give extra insight.

● *Regular work*
Work regularly and use time productively. As has been said so often of examination courses: continuity of work is essential for progress, and procrastination is the thief of time.

One big problem can be courseworks and projects which on academic IT courses have to be submitted regularly and are part of the final assessment. Working on courseworks and projects can create an illusion that everything is progressing well. However this is often at the expense of studying examination material on a regular basis.

It is essential to work regularly towards an examination success. For instance study systematically a section of the recommended books every week, be attentive and ask questions in lectures, and do the work set in tutorials or distance-learning exercises. Making and building up notes is an important way of being involved with the subject matter as well as being essential for revision. The cumulative effect means that revision at the end of the course is true revision and not new learning. Trying to learn new material during the revision period leads to a mental overload and there is little time to find help with the queries.

● *Active learning*
Make sure that much of your learning is active in the sense that the subject

matter is used and applied. Passive learning has an important place, e.g. reading a textbook. But if you learn actively then skills and knowledge develop quickly and are retained. Active learning means asking questions in lectures, doing exercises in tutorials, and discussing the subject with lecturers and fellow students. Wherever possible apply examination material in courseworks, projects, and real-life work. Fluency in writing good English, drawing diagrams, and doing mathematics can only come with continual practice. Feedback is very helpful, e.g. from exercises marked by the lecturer.

- *Exploiting employment*

If you are working in suitable employment you can systematically boost examination performance. Try to get placed where you can use examination knowledge and skills as part of your job. Mix with different types of IT and user staff, e.g. systems programmers and accountants. Ask questions and collect data on the computer arrangements where you are work. This is particularly important if you want to give convincing examination answers based on experience. In the weeks prior to an examination try as part of your job to make sure that you are writing frequently, e.g. letters and reports. This will allow you to practice speedy written communication for the examination. It is important that a certain amount of your practice is handwritten. Too much word processing means that hand writing performance deteriorates. Unfortunately it is currently impractical to allow students to word process examination answers!

- *Miscellaneous sources*

Try to make each subject tangible, e.g. by visits to see relevant computer applications and watching TV documentaries. Use journals, magazines, sales brochures, and video tapes as sources of contemporary examples. Copies of relevant journal articles and the like should be filed in your notes. This is particularly important for professional examinations where there is often an emphasis on contemporary IT issues.

- *Assignments*

Many terms are used like practicals, exercises, courseworks, and projects. The basic idea is that you learn by doing. Again it is essential to understand the rules and expectations of a piece of work. For instance students often do excessive amounts of work which gain little in the way of extra marks. Even where the work is open-ended, which is usually the case with project work, there are guidelines as to the quantity of work, e.g. 100 pages of typing and diagrams for a project report. With projects, because each one is different, it is usually possible with the permission of a lecturer to examine a previous marked example.

- *Revision*

Revision prior to an examination needs to be planned. Just reading notes and books repeatedly is tedious and ineffective as it is not active learning. In an examination, writing, diagrams, and calculations have to be done quickly with a fluency that can only come from practice. Answer past examination questions at least in outline from notes and books as part of the revision process. Practise drawing common diagrams and performing typical calculations. Learn all the syllabus material. Learning part of the syllabus and relying on being able to pick suitable questions is dangerous. Examiners often ask questions that require an answer combining several different parts of the syllabus. The choice of questions is sometimes restricted as well.

- *Professional examinations*

Professional examinations present special problems and can undoubtedly be more difficult than equivalent academic examinations. There are several key differences. Firstly they are usually national, or even international, external examinations set by a remote institution. Secondly they refer frequently to employment situations and practical experience. Thirdly students can and often do take them on their own, via the rather lonely route of a distance-learning course. Fourthly they are often part-time, frequently with little time for study or instruction being given by the employer.

All these factors can make learning more difficult and students should do everything possible to overcome the problems, e.g. by attending special week-end revision courses sponsored by professional bodies. Contact with an experienced lecturer or tutor and other students is invaluable for professional students. A sympathetic employer can provide real help, for instance with day release. However when all is said and done it is feasible to pass professional examinations alone, by evening and week-end work, without any outside support like a correspondence course. This requires a combination of good practical experience, disciplined study of relevant books, and in particular working through plenty of sample examination questions. Needless to say this is an arduous, unpleasant, and risky route to a qualification.

Obtaining the requisite practical experience can be frustratingly difficult for a few students. If a suitable trainee job cannot be found then the only realistic alternative is to consider academic courses in IT where experience is not usually required, and some attempt is made to provide practical exercises.

IV.6   The examination itself

(The following assumes conventional written examinations with questions similar to those in Appendix III.)

- *Venue*

Even for full-time students examinations are often held in unexpected or inconvenient places. Candidates for professional examinations often have to travel tens of miles to a neighbouring town. It is imperative that students know exactly where to go in advance, and give a generous allowance for travelling delays.

- *Planning*

Having studied previous examples the format of the examination paper should present no surprises. The examination rubric should be read and followed. Having read the paper and planned the sequence of answers a sensible amount of time must be allocated for each question. It is a good idea to do the easiest question first as a confidence booster.

- *Answering questions*

Students must read each question carefully. Marks can only be given for answering the question given. The big common danger is answering a similar but imaginary question simply because of careless reading. Underlining key words on the question paper is one defence against this problem. It forces students to consider the question wording carefully. Another trick is to echo the words of the question as part of the answer which again help to keep the student on the right track.

A minute or two spent planning in terms of headings, rough diagrams, etc is very beneficial in terms of producing a coherent answer. It has the psychological effect of bringing all the relevant learning to the top of the student's mind.

- *Presentation*

A structured answer is generally superior to an essay type answer. An example is given in Appendix III, Section III.2. A structured answer uses a heading for each paragraph, lists of items, diagrams, and so on. These are easier for a student to write and easier for an examiner to mark.

Answers should be spaced out not cramped. Start each new question on a separate page. Rough work and planning work should be crossed through. Some people put the rough work in a separate examination booklet which makes the work both easier and neater.

Whilst neat writing and careful diagrams are to be encouraged it is clarity that is expected rather than calligraphic illuminated manuscripts. Extensive use of colour and over-elaborate diagrams are just a waste of precious time. Minor problems with English such as the occasional misspelling are often not penalised, but there is a limit to what examiners can tolerate.

Appendix V
Bibliography

The following publications develop subjects introduced in the various parts of this book. The classification is only approximate. American books have a different perspective and terminology from UK books.

PART I
INTRODUCTION

Schultheis, R., Sumner, M. & Bock, D. (1992) *Management Information Systems*, Irwin, Homewood, USA.

Blissmer, R. H. (1991) *Introducing Computers*, Wiley, New York, USA.

PART II
BUSINESS MANAGEMENT

Cole, G. A. (1990) *Management Theory and Practice*, 3rd edn. DPP, London.

Needham, D. & Dransfield, R. (1990) *Business Studies*, McGraw-Hill, Maidenhead.

Clutterbuck, D. & Crainer, S. (1988) *The Decline and Rise of British Industry*, Mercury, London.

Drucker, P. F. (1989) *The New Realities*, Heinemann, Oxford. (An American view.)

Lobley, D. (1990) *Commerce*, John Murray, London.

Woodcock, C. (1988) *The Guardian Guide to Running a Small Business*, 7th edn. Kogan Page, London.

Winfield, I. (1991) *Organisations and Information Technology*, Alfred Waller, Henley-on-Thames.

Keenan, D. & Riches, S. (1990) *Business Law*, 2nd edn. Pitman, London.

Reed, C. (1990) *Computer Law*, Blackstone, London.

Bull, R. J. (1990) *Accounting in Business*, 6th edn. Butterworths, London.

Hackett, P. (1989) *Management:Personnel*, 3rd edn. John Murray, London.

1992, Payroll Handbook, 6th edn. Tolley, Croydon.

PART III
SYSTEMS DEVELOPMENT
Avison, D. E. & Fitzgerald, G. (1988) *Information Systems Development*, Alfred Waller, Henley-on-Thames.

Cutts, G. (1991) *Structured Systems Analysis and Design Methodology*, 2nd edn. Alfred Waller, Henley-on-Thames.

Eva, M. (1992) *SSADM Version 4: A Users Guide*, McGraw-Hill, Maidenhead.

Avison, D. E. & Wood-Harper, A. T. (1990) *Multiview*, Alfred Waller, Henley-on-Thames.

Lucey, T. (1991) *Management Information Systems*, 6th edn. DPP London.

PART IV
SYSTEMS ANALYSIS AND DESIGN
McDermid, D. C. (1990) *Software Engineering for Information Systems*, Alfred Waller, Henley-on-Thames.

Mason, D. & Wilcocks, L. (1987) *Intermediate Systems Analysis*, Alfred Waller, Henley-on-Thames.

Parkin, A. (1987) *Systems Analysis*, 2nd edn. Edward Arnold, London.

Pressman, R. S. (1992) *Software Engineering*, 3rd edn. McGraw-Hill, New York, USA.

Smith, D. J. & Wood, K. B. (1987) *Engineering Quality Software*, Elsevier, Barking.

Burn, J. & O'Niel, M. (1987) *Information Analysis*, (Paradigm) Alfred Waller, Henley-on-Thames.

PART V
SYSTEMS MANAGEMENT
McNurlin, B. C. & Sprague, R. H. (1989) *Information Systems in Management*, 2nd edn. Prentice-Hall, Englewood Cliffs, USA.

Yeates, D. (1991) *Systems Project Management*, Pitman, London.
(Books now published by Alfred Waller were previously published by Blackwell Scientific Publications, Oxford.)

Index

(Items are followed by section number or figure references.)

490